D1155972

The Gift
of Immortality

The Gift
of Immortality

Myths of Power
and Humanist Poetics

Stephen Murphy

Madison ● Teaneck
Fairleigh Dickinson University Press
London: Associated University Presses

Associated University Presses
440 Forsgate Drive
Cranbury, NJ 08512

Associated University Presses
16 Barter Street
London WC1A 2AH, England

Associated University Presses
P.O. Box 338, Port Credit
Mississauga, Ontario
Canada L5G 4L8

The paper used in this publication meets the requirements of the American National Standard for Permanence of Paper for Printed Library Materials Z39.48–1984.

Library of Congress Cataloging-in-Publication Data

Murphy, Stephen, 1957–
    The gift of immortality : myths of power and humanist poetics / Stephen Murphy.
        p.   cm.
    Includes bibliographical references and index.
    ISBN 0-8386-3685-3 (alk. paper)
    1. Literature—History and criticism.   I. Title.
PN86.M87   1997
809.1—dc20   96-33207
                                                                              CIP

PRINTED IN THE UNITED STATES OF AMERICA

For my Mother
and the memory of my Father

Contents

Acknowledgments

Research for this book was generously supported by grants from the Georges Lurcy Foundation (through the Graduate School of the University of North Carolina at Chapel Hill) and the William Archie Fund (Wake Forest University).

My thanks to Aldo Scaglione, who got me started, as well as to Eugene Falk, Mallary Masters, Kenneth Reckford, and George Daniel, who saw this work through an earlier incarnation. For various encouragement, I am also grateful to Allen Mandelbaum, Dennis Looney, and Michel Simonin. I have profited from the comments of the anonymous readers for Fairleigh Dickinson Press, and from the guidance of the editorial staff there and at Associated University Presses.

Finally, I thank my wife Florence for her patience and belief.

The Gift
of Immortality

Introduction

Wozu Dichter . . .

At one point, Hector has paused from battle to enter Troy and command sacrifices. He meets Helen, who disparages herself and mourns the destiny of herself and Paris,

> hoisin epi Zeus theke kakon moron, hos kai opisso
> anthropoisi pelometh' aoidimoi essomenoisi.

> [on whom Zeus set an evil fate, so that hereafter we may become subjects of song for men of the future].[1]

She who is to become the most praised of all women sees that the perpetuation of her name will be the perpetuation of sorrow.[2] She also knows that the gods have willed disaster *in order that* immortal song may arise. The Muses remain indissolubly linked with mortality. The nine goddesses attend on Achilles' bier, singing a threnody that draws tears from all the Achaeans.[3]

We see the sorrowful power of poetry in the work of the two poets of the *Odyssey*. Phemius holds spellbound the suitors in Ithaca as he sings of the disastrous homecomings of the Greeks. The listening Penelope is moved to weep and commands him to sing a less gloomy song. But Telemachus defends the poet's choice: "Singers are not to blame; it seems that Zeus is to blame."[4] Likewise, when at the Phaeacian court Odysseus hears Demodocus sing of the fall of Troy, the hero weeps silently until the song is halted. These poets resume in their persons the misfortunes they evoke in verse. Demodocus, despite his courtly office, despite the silver-studded chair in which he sits, is blind, a model for the traditional picture of the poet who created him.[5] The Muse, though she loved him, bestowed upon him evil as well as good.[6] The bard Phemius sings against his will to the dissolute, violent suitors, and narrowly escapes sharing their fate upon Odysseus's homecoming. Odysseus, however, with his rich experience of sorrow, appreciates the poet's office. He listens to Phemius's plea to respect

13

and pity him and excepts him from the slaughter of the suitors. He is
not unimpressed by the poet's promise to sing of him as of a god.[7]
Demodocus too benefits from Odysseus's largesse. The hero sends the
poet part of his serving at a feast, dedicating it as a tribute from one
who is grieving. He comments: "Among all men upon the earth singers
have a share of honor and compensation."[8] The ambiguity of *time*
(honor and compensation) as the poet's reward underlies the poet's
social status. His reward is bestowed in exchange for the sorrow he
evokes through his commemoration of disaster.

Perhaps two and a half millennia later, the poet in exile addresses
his birthplace Zacynthus, an island neighboring Ithaca:[9]

Tu non altro che il canto avrai del figlio,
o materna mia terra.

(You will have nothing but a song from your son, o my motherland.)[10]

And, as he begins the final movement of his greatest poem, he invokes
the Muses as conquerors of time:

E me che i tempi ed il desio d'onore
fan per diversa gente ir fuggitivo,
me ad evocar gli eroi chiamin le Muse
del mortale pensiero animatrici.
Siedon custodi de' sepolcri e quando
il tempo con sue fredde ale vi spazza
fin le rovine, le Pimplèe fan lieti
di lor canto i deserti, e l'armonia
vince di mille secoli il silenzio.

(Let the Muses, resuscitators of mortal thought, call me to evoke heroes;
me, whom the times and a desire for glory chase, a fugitive among different
peoples. They perch as guards of the sepulchers, and when time's cold wings
sweep everything to ruins, the Muses gladden the desert with their song,
and their harmony conquers the silence of a thousand centuries.)[11]

As a compensation for the poet's own destitution and exile as well as
for the historical human misery (*i tempi*) that makes up the subject
of his song, the appeal is to the immortalizing power of poetry. But the
Muses do not merely overcome silence; the desert and the graveyard
are their dwelling place. *Custodi de' sepolcri*, their office is to elicit
glory from mortality.

From Homer to Ugo Foscolo (and beyond), the persistence of this
idea, the glorifying or immortalizing power of poetry, is a striking con-

stant in European literature. It is one of the most popular of topoi. Its use shows an exemplary richness.[12]

Sappho voices one of the earliest "pleas for the humanities" in these lines to a woman who neglects literary culture:

> When you are dead you will lie, and be remembered by none hereafter; for you do not partake of the Pierian roses. Unseen even in the dwelling of Hades, you will roam fluttering among the obscure dead.[13]

In a positive direction, Theognis assures Cyrnos, the addressee of his poem, that Cyrnos will take flight among the living:

> I have given you wings, with which you may be borne up and soar easily over the boundless sea and all the earth. . . . Even when you enter the much-lamenting abode of Hades beneath the depths of the dark earth, even dead you will not lose your glory, but will be cherished among men and possess an unwithering name forever.[14]

Theocritus's sixteenth Idyll presents a similar boast in a plea to honor poets:

> Who would know the best of the Lydians? Who would know the long-haired sons of Priam, or Cycnus with delicate skin, if singers did not rehearse the battlecry of those before us? Nor would Odysseus . . . possess lasting glory, the swineherd Eumaeus would be silent, like Philoetius, busy with his cattle, and great-hearted Laertes, if the songs of an Ionian man had not profited them. From the Muses noble glory comes to men, and the living squander the wealth of the dead.[15]

Propertius addresses his beloved Cynthia:

> fortunata, meo si qua es celebrata libello!
>   carmina erunt formae tot monumenta tuae.
> nam neque Pyramidum sumptus ad sidera ducti,
>   nec Iouis Elei caelum imitata domus,
> nec Mausolei diues fortuna sepulcri
>   mortis ab extrema condicione vacant.
> aut illis flamma aut imber subducet honores,
>   annorum aut ictu, pondere victa, ruent.
> at non ingenio quaesitum nomen ab aeuo
>   excidet: ingenio stat sine morte decus.[16]

(How fortunate, if you are celebrated in my book! My poems will be so many monuments to your beauty. For neither the Pyramids, built up to the stars; nor the temple of Olympian Jupiter, which imitates the heavens; nor the rich fortune of Mausolus' sepulcher, are free from the final state of death. Either fire or rain steal their honors, or they collapse, overcome by their weight and the blows of time. But a name sought through poetic talent will not fall; that glory remains without death.)

The topos is central to the self-image of Renaissance writers with regard to antiquity. Benedetto Accolti writes in a dedication to Cosimo de' Medici:

> Legenti mihi saepius eorum libros, qui ornate, copioseque Antiquorum res gestas, vitam ac mores descripserunt; felices multum illi fuisse visi sunt, quibus contigit ab his referri virtutes suas qui eas tradentes literis, magnam et immortalem eis gloriam pepererunt; quam consecuti sunt, ut nedum perennem in caelis vitam, sed in terris etiam, post corporis mortem, habuerint.[17]

(As I often read the books of those who elegantly and abundantly described the deeds, life and mores of the Ancients, those men seemed very fortunate who chanced to be revived by writers who, consigning their excellence to literature, created great and immortal glory for them. They obtained this in such a way that after the death of their body they had not only everlasting life in heaven, but on earth too.)

A royal character in one of Bandello's *novelle* excuses thus the homage she has done a poet (Alain Chartier):

> Gli scrittori sono quelli che perpetuano la memoria di tutti quelli che negli scritti loro a la memoria hanno consacrati; ché infiniti sono che oggidí sono nominati e vivono ne la memoria nostra perché i poeti e gli istorici hanno di loro fatta menzione, i quali forse sepolti ne le tenebre de la oblivione sarebbero se la penna degli scrittori stata non fosse.[18]

(Writers are those who perpetuate the memory of all those whom they have consecrated to memory in their writings. There are an infinite number who are named today and live in our memory because poets and historians have mentioned them, but who might be buried in the shadows of oblivion if it were not for the writers' pen.)

The great philologist Denys Lambin praises the usefulness of literature:

> Litterae posteritatis causa repertae, omnium rerum hominibus utilium ac salutarium a veteribus inventarum custodes, eas ipsas res universas complectuntur & continent, eas aeternas conservant, eas cum omni posteritate communicant, adeo ut omnia antiquitatis erga nos beneficia, quemadmo-

dum ea paullatim & singillatim in nos collata sunt, ita sensim iampridem oblivione sempiterna deleta interiissent, nisi litterae hominum oblivioni subsidio fuissent.[19]

(Literature was invented for posterity. It is the guard of everything useful and wholesome discovered by the ancients. It embraces and contains those things, it makes them eternal, it communicates them to all posterity. Indeed, all the benefits we have had from antiquity, bestowed on us slowly and gradually, would have long ago perished bit by bit into everlasting oblivion, had literature not supplied an aid to human oblivion.)

Moreover (lest Renaissance use of the topos seem too prosaic), Ariosto's *Orlando furioso* supplies a famous passage, including the declaration:

Gli uomini degni da'poeti
son tolti da l'oblio, più che morte empio.
Oh bene accorti principi e discreti,
che seguite di Cesare l'esempio,
e gli scrittor vi fate amici, donde
non avete a temer di Lete l'onde![20]

(Men who deserve poets are snatched from oblivion crueler than death. O princes prudent and sage, who follow Caesar's example, and make writers your friends; which means you need not fear the waters of Lethe!)

And, among innumerable occurrences in the works of Ronsard, his "Elégie à J. de la Peruse":

Aussi le Roy, quelque chose qu'il face,
Meurt sans honneur, s'il n'achete la grace
Par maints presens d'un Poëte sçavant
Qui du tombeau le deterre vivant,
Et fait tousjours d'une plume animée
Voler par tout sa vive renommée.[21]

(Thus the King, whatever he may do, dies unglorified if he does not buy the grace of a learned poet with many gifts. The poet digs him up alive from the grave, and with an inspired pen makes his living fame fly everywhere always.)

A catalog could go on and on. Topology runs the risk of being nothing but a catalog. But it is not at all immediately clear what ought to be done with topoi. A necessary first step is to define the term. I follow E. R. Curtius, the founder of the modern study of topoi, in taking *topos* to mean a literary cliché or commonplace. It has passed from a normative function in ancient rhetoric to a heuristic principle for interpreting literature.[22] But what does that heuristic power find? For Curtius, it is unity and continuity.[23] As a reaction against the compartmentalized myopia of literary history and the barbarous ideologies of his time, Curtius emphasizes the universality (Mediterranean and Western European, at least) of literary tradition. More specifically, identifying and tracing a topos through several texts means pushing to the forefront a tendency to identity which those texts may have. Such an emphasis is understandable as an antidote to vague received notions of originality. Yet Curtius has been justly criticized for neglecting the real importance of discontinuity and the creative use of tradition. Certainly, the lofty temporal perspective of topology should not lead to a leveling tendency and an excessively serene, Platonic contemplation of the constants of European literature.[24]

The nature of a topos suggests the double hermeneutic for which it is useful. A topos is both a specific occurrence in a given text and the tradition comprising such occurrences. A twofold aim of topology could plausibly correspond to this double nature: elucidation of individual works and of the tradition that contains them. Clearly, there must be a continuing dialogue between the two poles. Just as clear is the tension between them, which cannot be evaded. Topology naturally floats upward to irenic vistas of continuity in culture at the same time as it dwells among the nuts and bolts of the particular. The tension must be made explicit in order to avoid the idealism of a Curtius.

I believe the proper twist to topology may be a more concentrated use of it as an interpretive tool than has been customary. No doubt the pervasiveness of the boast concerning literary immortality is important, but a more interesting question concerns how that common denominator works in given cases. A topological method ought to consider a given topos not as a static thing sitting in a text, but as a dynamic, volatile power. Quintilian calls topoi *argumentorum sedes,* or the foundations of artistic representation.[25] Their use, therefore, does not simply constitute an unconscious homage to tradition. It may also have some of the fertile paradox inherent in all literary art. A method that remains true to its object would have implications about culture and the constants underlying a series of texts, but an attention to the particular that is as micrological as possible lends some ballast to speculation and eases the vertigo of vast historical distance. There is no escaping the commonplace that significant broader understanding can only be reached through attention to the particular. More pertinent, a dialectical topology regards textual detail as microcosms of the world. W. Benjamin is surely right that every exegetical idea contains in itself an interpretation of the world.[26]

Another possible approach worthy of consideration, which takes account of the tendency to both identity and difference in the use of topoi, would be a structural typology. The typical elements of a topos and their typical relationship (syntactical, etc.) might be determined as a paradigm, and the adherence or departure of individual uses from that paradigm could be gauged.[27] However, such an approach seems most helpful with topoi that are highly stereotyped and not especially conceptual; for example, the Petrarchist catalog of feminine beauty. The topos concerning literary immortality sprawls beyond the possibility of neat categorization. What is the power deployed? What is empowered? Remembrance, glory, immortality; for the writer, the text, the subject, the dedicatee; of a poem, a history, or any literary work? The terms of the boast are often combined. Moreover, as a highly intellectualized topos with literary-theoretical content, it may influence the development of a text in a pervasive way, and so resist isolation. This is not to deny that the topos in question possesses typical elements that can be identified, the creative variations of which can be studied. But a strict typology does not appear possible.

A productive approach seems more likely to derive from the double nature of this topos as topos, considered from another angle. What is common to the forementioned examples is the boast of a great power contained in literature. At the risk of belaboring the obvious: The topos concerning literary immortality claims that literature in general, and implicitly or explicitly the text where the topos is found, exercises power over reality. In particular, literature makes people live on or brings them back to life.[28] The topos claims an effective power for the poetic or eloquent word. Such a claim is essentially magical. A look at the powers attributed to language in archaic cultures reveals striking analogies. In such cultures (both contemporary "primitive" peoples and early civilizations), what is at play is mythical thought. I use *mythical* in the sense used by Ernst Cassirer, referring to one of the forms of thought by which humans organize the world.

> The original bond between the linguistic and the mythico-religious consciousness is primarily expressed in the fact that all verbal structures appear as *also* mythical entities, endowed with certain mythical powers, that the Word, in fact, becomes a sort of primary force, in which all being and doing originate.[29]

A belief in word magic results from the tendency of mythical thought to perceive substance where scientific thought perceives relation. Mythical thought effects "a hypostatization of properties and processes, or forces and activities."[30] In contrast to their function for theoretical-scientific thought, for mythical thought "word and name do not designate and signify, they are and act."[31] If it is true that "mythical and verbal thought are interwoven in every way," where "words and actions become absolutely equivalent," then to propose the topos of poetic immortality as an example of word magic does not seem far-fetched.[32]

The supreme power of the Word is deployed by both the gods, particularly in their work of cosmic creation, and by humans in magical ritual. In Egypt, for example, word magic was the force that, pronounced by the god Re, created the cosmos.[33] From that primordial moment, verbal power dominated the world. The god's powers included the power of resurrection; his voice could resuscitate the dead.[34] The Babylonian creation poem, *Enuma elish,* makes the origin of heaven, earth, and gods identical with their receiving a name.[35]

Significantly, the word can also descend from its divine office and maintain its power among humanity. The yearly human recitation of the *Enuma elish* was considered to renew the original divine creative act.[36] The maxims of a certain Egyptian named Djedefhor, which lived on in the world, assured him of eternity better than his tomb.[37] It seems that the word has an independent existence, to which all beings, even the gods, remain subordinate. We read in the *Vedas:* "On the Spoken Word all the gods depend, all beasts and men; in the Word live all creatures."[38]

The human use of word magic extends as far as magical practice itself. Without oversimplifying, it might be helpful to categorize the magical use of verbal power in literary terms: as praise and blame. "Knowledge of the name is true power."[39] Therefore, what the magician does with a name has a positive or negative effect on the person or object named. The negative role of language is abundantly attested in magical curses.[40] On the other hand, incantations for the survival of a person after death seek perpetuation and embellishment of the name of the deceased.[41] Cases that seem to fall into neither category, such as love spells, often turn out to be praise of the desired one.[42] Magic is performative language with invective and epideictic functions.[43]

It has often been claimed that magic presided over the birth of art.[44] What concerns us particularly is the kinship between magic and poetry. That kinship can be considered a quibble over the Latin word *carmen,* which means both an incantation and a song or poem. Likewise Greek *aoidos,* meaning both singer and enchanter, and analogous words in other languages.[45] When in an epode Horace writes of a witch and her books "carminum valentium refixa caelo devocare sidera" (of spells able to detach and call down stars from the sky), the magical sense of *carmen* is foremost.[46] But when Ovid boasts of the powers of *carmina* in a context that is unmistakably literary, including references to heroic poetry, and concludes with the claim that "di quoque carminibus, si fas est dicere, fiunt" (the gods themselves, if it is permitted to speak so, are created by poems), how clear is the semantic frontier?[47]

However, what is at issue here is a literary topos, a commonplace, not an element of magical practice. It would be chimerical to seek to explain the topos of literary immortalization anthropologically by scrutinizing possible "origins." Just as the origin of language and its original status have not traditionally been an object of linguistic study, so also with regard to the origin of topoi: It is not an object of literary study.[48] I assert not the ultimate historical derivation of the topos, but rather that this *locus communis* is a place where the proximity of *mythos* and *logos* becomes particularly striking. Whatever magical function art, including poetry, may originally have had faded long before those texts that mark the beginning of the Western literary tradition. In the topos we find hints and, as it were, a nostalgia for that original office. Poetry is haunted by the traces of primitive incantation.[49]

In the distance between real magical effectiveness and the metaphorical nature of the topos's claim to immortalize lies the pathos of that claim. The hypothetical unity of myth and language, where word magic dwells, inevitably dissolves in any literary tradition. Cassirer explains this dissolution as a consequence of the logical power inherent in language.[50] As this power gradually reduces words from forceful actors to mere signifiers, the boast of verbal effectiveness can no longer command faith. At the root of the traditional polemic against glory lies a rational belief in the separation of word and thing, a belief that there is no mythical commerce between them. Thus Montaigne:

> Il y a le nom et la chose; le nom, c'est une voix qui remerque et signifie la chose; le nom, ce n'est pas une partie de la chose ny de la substance, c'est une piece estrangere joincte à la chose, et hors d'elle.[51]

> (There is the word and the thing. The word is a sound which marks and signifies the thing. The word is not a part of the thing or of substance; it is a foreign piece attached to the thing, and exterior to it.)

The pretense of immortalization through words becomes only a literary fiction. The traditionalism inherent in topoi acts as a conservative, crystallizing element akin to magical formulas in early poetry.[52] In this way, art preserves something from the realm of myth while renouncing its claim to truth.

For Giambattista Vico, too, language is confounded with myth. When he states that every metaphor is a concentrated fable (*una picciola favoletta*), he means that all tropes recall the primitive force of language:[53] hence, the impossibility for Vico of treating the origin of literature separately from the origin of language.[54] What he understands as the origin and the primitive state of language is in several respects quite close to what Cassirer calls mythical thought. Vico calls it *sapienza poetica*. It is characterized by an awestruck misunderstanding of nature and an attribution to nature of anthropomorphic categories and, in addition, by the fact that it historically precedes and is clearly distinct from rational thought. Although Vico does not emphasize the effective power that Cassirer recognizes in mythical word magic, both concepts present language as active embodiment or hypostatization.[55]

Vico imagines a primal scene at the origin of language, religion, history, and poetry. This is the moment at which early humanity first hears thunder. Attributing a humanlike agent to the celestial phenomenon, the primitive mind interprets thunder as a language, a message from God. The frightful but innocuous sound is taken to be an expression of the divine power to destroy, withheld out of mercy. Jupiter was called *Soter,* or savior, because he did not destroy humanity. It is thus that Vico interprets Eusebius's phrase about the invention of the gods "ob terrorem praesentis potentiae" (from the terror of present power). But the same fear, relief, and gratitude for being spared, the same submission to authority, are also the foundation of literature. The attribution of a human body and human meaning to nature is what characterizes metaphor as the essential trope. When primitive humanity read thunderbolts as a divine language, this word of the gods was not only (literally) the first theology, but also the first poetry.[56]

Vico devotes a large part of the *Scienza nuova* to showing how the primordial *sapienza poetica* gradually civilized humanity and how philosophical knowledge followed metaphorical knowledge. Without plunging further into the subject, it is enough for now to note the similarity between Vico and Cassirer in (1) the human origin of language that imagines a divine origin, and (2) the evidence of that origin even after rational thought has obtained hegemony in the use of language. Vico, the heir of Renaissance humanism, and Cassirer, the heir of Kant and Humboldt, agree in recognizing the continuing element of myth or magic in language.[57]

However, an instructive difference also separates the two pictures of mythical thought and language. In both, we find portrayed a confusion of subjective categories with the workings of exterior reality, a confusion essential to the foundations of language. But for Cassirer and theories of magical language, that confusion is directed toward a domination of exterior reality through the faith in verbal effectiveness. For Vico, on the other hand, language (and poetry as language par excellence) is born from a different hypostatization of human power. That is, the menaces of nature are deified (which means anthropomorphized), and it is their awesome power, perceived in human terms, that provokes linguistic expression. Language born from fear signifies two things: human impotence before nature and the human will to dominate that humanity attributes to nature.

What both Cassirer and Vico recognize but do not probe is the importance of mythical thought's minority status after it has been eclipsed by rational thought. Both admit its continued, but diluted, existence in art. But how does word magic behave when confined to literature? To answer this question, it may be useful to introduce a third strange philosophical bedfellow. An important element of Theodor W. Adorno's *Aesthetic Theory* concerns the early kinship of art and magic and art's subsequent disenchantment.

> Art used to be part of a praxis that sought to affect nature. Subsequently, at a time when rationality came to the fore, art went its own ways, realizing that its expectations about having an impact on reality [were] no more than an exercise in self-deception.[58]

To understand what art's subsequent "own ways" were, it is necessary to examine the original pretense to "affect nature." Adorno expresses this as the "power and dominance of empirical reality,"[59] which I have called poetic effectiveness. When that pretense proved hollow, when rationality and not art/magic manifested real power over nature, art internalized the impulse to domination and made it a principle of form. The autonomous work of art is a closed, unified synthesis of its individual elements; it dominates and transforms them as it cannot dominate nature. Hence (to narrow the focus to literature), literary form grew out of literature's original situation, just as Vico sees poetic conventions as products of primitive *sapienza poetica*. "Postlapsarian" literature is thus inevitably of two minds and shows two faces, depending on whether it considers its (putative) original status and formal power on the one hand or, on the other hand, its fallen status and impotence before reality. From this situation comes the amphibole of the topos about literary immortalization, which is the paradigm of all amphiboles about poetry: its power/impotence, its immortality/caducity, its bounty/destitution, its virtue/amorality, its purity/venality, its truthfulness/mendacity.

Adorno introduces a further implication for this study. The necessarily vague expression rational domination of nature includes political power. The rationality that by its success showed the hollowness of poetic effectiveness includes political leaders, increasingly free from dependence on priests and *vates*. By this contrast I do not mean to posit kings as traditional embodiments of scientific thought. Rather, by force and organization, the political leader manifested a power over empirical reality not available to "mere words." Nor do I mean to posit a historical period when poets ruled until they were displaced by kings. This has been a potent myth, as witness the traditional popularity of an idea such as the Druids. But the primordiality is conceptual rather than historical, contained as an "as if" in poetry's self-awareness.

From such a point of view, the continued existence and proximity of poetry and political power take on a special significance. Their relationship acquires a dynamic interest. This relationship has traditionally been one of patronage. Yet modern notions of patronage are insufficient for understanding what is at issue. "The Gift of Immortality" suggests that, whatever the social profit of magic, a magical model is finally inadequate to explain by itself the gesture of bestowal.

Any reference to gift giving must take account of Marcel Mauss's *Essai sur le don*. What that work reveals is an extremely widespread system of archaic exchange. It precedes the development of economic rationality in the form of buying and selling and the use of money, yet it has its own constant principles. Obligation pervades the system of gift exchange, comprising an obligation to give, to receive, and to give a gift in return. Furthermore—and this departs most strikingly from modern notions of exchange—the purpose of bestowal is not an eventual desired profit, nor simple altruism, but the obtainment and exhibition of power. The exchange establishes friendship, but also rivalry that can come close to war. The extreme form of gift giving is potlatch, an extravagant outpouring of goods for no pratical use; expenditure in its purest form.[60]

Mauss's anthropological theorizing of the gift will prove useful to this study because it puts the poet-patron exchange in better perspective. Traditionally, the relationship has been seen in terms of the patron's paying as the poet praises. But that view makes it seem that only material and ideological self-interest is in play. What may appear in the poet's words as flattery or an inflated self-image is really structured exchange. The traces of the poet's vatic function include the reflex of archaic bestowal, including the obligatory giving, receiving, and rendering; generosity as manifestation of power; and the positive value of extravagance.

It may be that the poet is the only one dedicated to playing by the rules. In his rhetoric, at least, the poet typically needs to convince the patron to assume his proper role of receiving and rendering gifts. With this model, we will be better able to understand the copresence, in the poet's relationship with patron, of submission and self-assertion. Bestowal can be an agressive, even violent assertion of superiority.

Mauss's theory of the gift requires the same qualification as do the other anthropological concepts of mythical thought and verbal magic. We confront models based on archaic societies from the point of view of the highly advanced culture of Renaissance Europe and, more particularly, from the avant-garde of that culture, literary humanism. As previously indicated, there can be no obscuring of the social and temporal distance involved. But I do not assert a specific influence (even though the texts introduced earlier do show a continuing tradition available to the humanists).[61] Rather this: that the backward gaze of the Renaissance does not mean simply imitation of classical models or a longing for the golden age. It is also, and more fundamentally, atavism. We consistently find gestures that point back far beyond classical antiquity.

It is clear from Mauss and Adorno that, if the relationship between poet and prince/patron is anything, it is dialectical. That means for one thing that literary praise cannot be considered simply as ideology and measured against what it refers to. Even the most complete affirmation, what could be called base flattery, has its moment of truth. That moment lies in the fact of praise itself, in the poet's assertion of power, whether used to uphold or oppose the status quo. Praise may be considered fetishism, in the sense Adorno gives the term: as both a necessary (because constitutive) aspect of art and what founds art's peculiar power:

> It is this fetishism—the blindness of the art work to the reality of which it is a part—that enables the work of art to break the spell of the reality principle and to become a spiritual essence.[62]

The constitutive fetishism of art is the reason that a dialectical reading of the topical tradition does not mean contrasting the use of commonplaces against their social situation to reveal the former as ideological illusion. The illusory element will certainly be evoked in the following pages. But the fact, theorized by Adorno, that works of art are monads of society explains the relative concentration on immanent analysis of the texts discussed here.[63] While each text may be, in Maussian terms, a *fait social total*,[64] that means that it is not only engaged in the totality of social practice, but also represents that totality in its own artistic language. Because literature internalizes the relationship with power, the dialectic takes place within a given text. Quite a bit can be learned from the poet's voice alone. The boast of power is self-contemplation in a peculiar mirror; both flat and convex, reflecting both present and ideal past. The poet typically expresses both a claim to mythical effectiveness and a rational awareness that undercuts it. In the dialectic, never resolved, between the dream of power and waking disenchantment lies the truth content in the use of this topos.

Of course, the poet's self-contemplation includes the contemplation of the nature of poetry. The topos of literary immortalization belongs to the group of topoi that express poetry's self-awareness (other examples include the topoi of poetic furor and of inexpressibility). What this means is that each occurence of the topos presents a poetics. The writer who elaborates the claim of poetic power in a certain text thereby asserts: "poetry is essentially this. . . . "

Such a dialectical reading of the topos may serve as a corrective to one element of Cassirer's aesthetics. As already indicated, Cassirer sees the original unity of myth, language, and art fall apart as the power of logic in language asserts itself. The three become independent realms, each with its own laws. The connection of language with myth is maintained in art, but without the material pretense of hypostatization. Poetry for Cassirer is a realm where "word and mythic image, which once confronted the human mind as hard realistic powers, have now cast off all reality and effectuality."[65] This may be somewhat true, but it has an inaccurate implication. It is not true that poetry slips serenely into the condition of impotence with regard to reality. The idea of effectuality that adheres to words in mythical thought can never be entirely detached in the aesthetic realm. There always remains the pull of an effective relation, however illusory, to empirical reality. The subject of this study could be described as the various manifestations of that pull.

It might also be objected to Cassirer (and has been) that his picture of mythic thought unfairly deprives its possessors of all rational characteristics. After Lévi-Strauss, it must be admitted that, whatever differences may exist between archaic cultures and "advanced" ones, both sorts exhibit a genuine logic, and neither neglects the constraints of reality.[66] But if Cassirer misjudges mythic thought in stressing its shortcomings from the point of view of scientific thought, or, to put it another way, in seeing it as completely other because it is not what we have today, I would like to approach the question from the opposite point of view. Namely, to see the kinship of mythical and advanced thought not because of the presence of the latter in the former (as Lévi-Strauss does), but because of the presence of the former in the latter. However, there are dangers in proceeding thus. The danger, for example, of a cult of primordiality, of stressing the mythic substrata to modern texts; of falling into a Jungianism similar to that of Curtius.[67] The same risk might seem to exist in the use of Maussian gift exchange, except that a growing body of scholarship reveals how much the gift model exists and thrives today; the continued existence of archaic forms of bestowal does not simply constitute atavism (although it may also be atavistic).[68] No similar guarantee exists for the use of mythic-magical language. We need a way to follow this archaic tendency into a modern literary existence, without reducing that existence to the glow of a nostalgic aura. How this might be done is suggested by Vico and Adorno. They agree with a comment Wittgenstein made upon reading Frazer's *Golden Bough*: "In unserer Sprache ist eine ganze Mythologie niedergelegt" (a whole mythology is deposited in our language).[69] The task concerns a proper understanding of *Mythologie* in literary language and how to extract what is *niedergelegt*.

When we consider the contributions offered by each theorist, we find them connected to one another by something each lacks and something each can supply; hence, a mutual theoretical bestowal. For example: Cassirer supplies a model for understanding the power claimed for words. But what sort of verbal activity do we find taking place? These are not magic spells, not even literary imitations of magic spells. They are gestures of bestowal; hence, the contribution of Mauss. But he provides a model for archaic, precommercial societies. How are we to understand the continued existence of such elements in highly advanced societies, including early capitalism? Vico helps out with the proposition that later texts and language itself contain traces of the original state of humanity. We have only to look at that proposition in a different way (since our concern is not primarily to know that original state, but rather the later texts and language) and to see the *picciole favolette* that are metaphor (and figurative language in general) as inscriptions in literature of previous historical and mythic reality. But does not Vico's historical scheme suffer from its circularity? Not to mention its anthropological inadequacies and hermeneutical fantasies. We need a more sophisticated way of reading art in relation to society and a model of "progress" that brings us up closer to a present-day vantage point; hence, Adorno. He does not by himself prove a sufficient guide, being explicitly concerned with the relations between art and society in the capitalist era, rather than in the earlier periods that primarily interest me.[70] Hence, in turn, the usefulness of the ethnological examples of Cassirer et al. All this may give the appearance of a ring dance of theorists. But it is not a closed circle.

The element of time is worth dwelling on. My use of Cassirer and Mauss extracts from them two elements of an atavistic poetics, namely, poetry as mythical language and poetry as gift exchange. On the other

hand, Vico and Adorno provide two ways of seeing the historical duration of such poetics; namely, literary history as *corsi* and *ricorsi* and
literary history as the dialectic of enlightenment. We might consider
the first couple's contribution significant synchronically and the second couple's diachronically, but with a caveat. Following the lead of
Vico and Adorno, literary history appears as not simply something
taking place through time (*dia-*), but as dynamically and even violently
related to it: as a chronomachy.

A natural question: why Renaissance humanism? For several reasons, the interest of the topos concerning literary immortality seems
greatest in the Renaissance. First, by that time the topos has pro-
gressed further on the road to becoming, ideally, wholly topos; that is,
wholly literary. While in antiquity we find explicit remnants of a cultic
function in references to poetic power, and while in the Middle Ages
the use of the topos is hindered by its obnoxiousness to Christianity,[71]
the Renaissance pretends to take up the topos as pure artifice. Just
as the pagan gods have lost their numinous quality to become mere
mythological signs, so the topos in question appears as a matter only
of literature. That this appearance does not constitute the whole truth
will be seen later.

Second, the topos expresses a faith central to the Renaissance. Perhaps at no other time in European literature has the respect for the
eloquent word and the eloquent man been so high or, at least, been
expressed so persistently. The Renaissance forms the summit of Western "logocentrism." And if the epoch in general tends to cense the
logos, this tendency is heightened in those philologists called humanists.[72] Whether or not the *litteratus* has ever had a real opportunity
of being central to the *res publica,* it is at this time that he trumpets
his chance most boldly. At the same time, however, the Renaissance
sees the beginnings of the consolidation of absolute political power.
Such a trend will widen the gap between the private individual, literary
or otherwise, and temporal authority; in this way, the disparity between the "ought to be" of the topos and the "is" of actuality becomes
particularly dramatic.

Third, the commemorative or glorifying power of literature is, by its
nature, concerned with time. In particular, its praisers say that literature bears the remembered past into the present and preserves both
past and present into an unknown future. Moreover, the triumph over
death advertised for literary immortality celebrates a triumph over
time. Just as we find in few periods such acute awareness of the power
of poetic and eloquent language, so do we rarely find a sense of the
past such as the Renaissance manifests. It is well known that to this

period belongs the emergence of a modern historical sense, a realization of both the closeness and the distance of the past.[73] The topos of literary immortality provides a concentrated image of the resurrection of ancient glory. It means the establishment of an object to imitate and emulate, the establishment of community with the past. But in the simultaneous sense of discontinuity, of the past's real distance, there surfaces a sense of all that has been irredeemably lost. Here again, the amphibolic nature of the topos is typical of the Renaissance. We shall also see that the gaze the topos casts at the future, at commemoration assured by literature and at the possible relationship between literature and political power, is a utopian vision. This testifies to the faith of the age (or of a part of the age) in human, immanent reconciliation—not, however, without the qualification assuring us that such a utopia, although *ou topos*, not simply a commonplace, is also *ou topos*, no place.

The utopian longing refers to an ideal future state of things; the topos in action is addressed to the prince/patron with a hope of bringing about that state. For, characteristically, the topos of poetry's power to bestow includes an at least implicit request; that is, an admission of need. The utopia is founded on a balanced exchange by which the poet grants glory and is rewarded with material support. But it is necessary that this utopian exchange should take shape as archaic gift giving and should not be tainted by the form it readily assumes, the form of commerce. The dream contains the reconciliation of the ideal with material actuality: The poet fulfills the prince by raising him to the level of poetic ideality, while the prince makes possible the poet's existence in a material world that is, after all, the one he must inhabit. But the place of the topical utopia is not only the future. The writer constantly appeals to a past state of things, where the poet was central to society, where praise was natural and was never flattery. He localizes this mythical past through identification with the names of the earlier known poets. We shall see the prominent role played by the idealization of Homer. Throughout the topical tradition, Homer embodies the perfect poet, not only because of the power he possesses or inherits through inspiration, but also because of his role as dispenser of immortality in the *res publica*. This perennial invention of Homer by tradition testifies to the requirement that the power of the word be made flesh; that is, that the utopia of the topos be situated, preferably on the foundation of a primordial beginning. The Renaissance, with its pervasive cult of origins,[74] is here again resumed in the working out of the topos.

An introductory chapter on the development of the topos in antiquity is a necessity. Far from a survey of ancient occurrences of the topos, it will examine some of the more significant uses. As a proleptic antidote to later appropriation of Homer, I will indicate that, in fact, even he has a belated, mediated attitude toward poetic immortality. In Pindar, what may seem a more archaic poetic function turns out to be a dramatically divided sense of what poetry is and does. The selected figures of Roman literature, Cicero, Horace, and Ovid, show an enormous faith in literary power and various reactions to the beginnings of the unprecedented temporal power of the Roman Empire. Cicero's plea for poetry in his defense of Archias advertises both a personal passion for glory and an attempt to tie the fortunes of literary praise to the state he envisioned. Horace's successful embrace of the new dispensation under Augustus indicates a poet who knew how to convincingly present images of the poet's public role. However, the working out of those images suggests some of the contradictions of the Horatian pose. Ovid, who did not adjust, expresses in his poems from exile a wish of how the poet would like to fit in. Antiquity supplies a stock of motifs for future use of the topos, most striking among them the Ciceronian scene of Alexander at Achilles' grave, as well as the Horatian phrases about the enduring monument, strong men before Agamemnon, or the civilizing effect of poetry. But the working out of the topos in ancient texts also produces certain paradoxes that are not irrelevant to its working out in Renaissance texts.

The choice of the three principal figures in this study needs little justification a priori. Francesco Petrarca, Angelo Poliziano, and Guillaume Budé are well known as three of the greatest humanists of the Renaissance. However, something may be said about their complementarity. Given the impossibility of a thorough examination of the Renaissance, these three figures span it in a representative manner. Petrarca, the first great seminal humanist; Poliziano, the summit of the Italian Quattrocento; Budé, heir and rival of the Italian tradition and one of the "Evangelists" of its European diffusion[75]—they give us, if not a composite portrait of the age, at least an idea of its scope and variety. But the purpose is not merely to give some sharper lines to the concept "Renaissance." Each of the three central chapters presents a problem that is both self-contained and illuminated in the context of the study as a whole. In each, the problem grows from the investigation of neglected works by each author: Petrarca's *Africa,* two of Poliziano's *Sylvae, De Philologia* and other writings by Budé. A reading of each of these works shows the centrality of the topos concerning literary power. In each case, pursuit of this realization means a new interpretation, which reveals a greater poetic interest than has previously been perceived.

That the central texts are all in Latin has its own importance. This study takes seriously the use as a poetic language of what is called neo-Latin. To emphasize the Latin works of these writers does not in itself reveal a wholly new dimension; recent students of Petrarca and Poliziano have shown the importance of their Latin side, while Budé has hardly any other side to show. What may become apparent, however, is the real relationship between between "dead" language and vernacular. In his time, Petrarca's greatness as a poet and historian was embodied in the *Africa*. Poliziano was primarily a philologist, who occasionally wrote Italian poetry to order or for amusement. Budé's sole departure from the use of Latin and Greek was an unpublished treatise directed personally to the king. Moreover, the predominance of Renaissance Latin in this study is appropriate to what the topos in question claims. Neo-Latin by nature attempts to resurrect the glories of past literature. A faith in literary immortality underlies its very existence. It is a thoroughly bookish language; topoi are its lifeblood.

Petrarca, Poliziano, and Budé all illustrate in different ways various aspects of the topos. In all three, we find an imagined utopia for the relationship between poet and patron; connected with this, a dialectical relationship between literary and political power; and at the bottom, crucially and repeatedly, the glorifying and even deifying power of literature.

For Petrarca, the sense of time is especially important. The poet aims ideally to create an intimate relationship to past and future that can reverse or nullify time. The event in Petrarca's career that best encapsulates that desire is his poetic coronation in Rome in 1341. In the texts referring to that occasion, together with the poem that gained him that honor, the *Africa,* he reveals his desired intimacy as a relationship to power. In its working out, the poem of praise that is the *Africa* ends up as a lament for the poet's subjection to time and social isolation.

In Poliziano, we see the importance of origins and how the deified word founds literary history, whether in the apotheosized figure of Homer (*Ambra*) or in a survey of poetry *ab initio* (*Nutricia*). Poliziano marks the culmination of Quattrocento discourse on poetry, in particular of two currents: the essential category of praise as idealized gift exchange and the elevation of poetry to a position of sovereignty and primordiality.

Budé's defense of humanistic learning poses the problem of the behavior of literature in proximity to temporal power. He radicalizes the boast of literary immortalization by being attentive to the theological element of the Logos. Budé's attempts to make humanistic learning serviceable to nascent French absolutism make use of verbal power, but run up against the obstacle of his metaphoric style and its subversive potential.

Although one facet may be particularly striking in one author, it is certainly present to some degree in the other two, thus suggesting constants in humanism. For example, Petrarca, like Poliziano, bases his literary history on the traditional power of poetic praise, and, like Budé, is keenly interested in the existence of literature with temporal power; Poliziano's philological poetry is based, like Petrarca's, on an ideal of temporal reversibility; and so on.

In each of the three principal figures, there is a moment that draws our attention as a "scène de l'écriture."[76] At this moment, the writer's relation to his activity and subject stands out in a new, perhaps bizarre light. In Petrarca's *Africa* it is the dream of Ennius in book 9, which almost realizes the ideal of poetic community and a guarantee of the public function of praise. In Poliziano's *Ambra* it is the encounter of Homer and Achilles, which effects the composition of the Homeric poems, Poliziano's subject. In *De Philologia* it is the hunt narrated in book 2, represented both linguistically and metaphorically as an image of the usefulness of humanism to the purposes of power. None of these moments provides a hermeneutic key to the totality of the work in question. Just as no one would pretend that all previous readings are irrelevant, so I make no claim that meaning can be reduced to the function of the immortality topos—and so much the less to any single "scène de l'écriture." Yet the scenes provide concentrated images of what poetic invention, in all its paradox, means to these writers.

At the same time, I have brought to the foreground a concept in each writer. These concepts, at the same time idiosyncratic and representative, have required special names: poetic metempsychosis, poetic paleology, and mystical philology. Poetic metempsychosis, as manifested in the dream of Ennius in the *Africa,* encapsulates Petrarca's ideals concerning temporal reversibility, literary intimacy, and the service of glorification. Poliziano's *Nutricia* culminates a tradition of ancient and humanistic texts that meditate the role of poetry in civilizing primitive humanity; it is this tradition and Poliziano's use of it that I have called poetic paleology. Mystical philology refers to the theological tendency in Renaissance linguistic thought (or, conversely, the linguistic tendency in theology, broadly understood) that offers the possibility of a new interpretation of Budé's career and his *De transitu.* Again, these are not master concepts meant to arrange everything in the respective writers. They provide, rather, oblique entrances to the works in question and the means of formulating some effects of the topos concerning poetic immortality.

The structure that organizes the readings in each chapter is based on the interplay of the four "guides"—Cassirer, Vico, Mauss, and Adorno—who are most often left nameless. Just as my borrowings from each combine to help understand the immortality topos, so they can help to organize an interpretation of each principal figure studied here. The structure amounts to an itinerary in four stages—not chronological or hierarchical, but as dialectical parts of a (never complete) whole. To recapitulate: The Cassirer stage elucidates a belief in verbal magic and the effectuality of poetry.[77] The Vico stage projects from the present state of literary language to a primordial (or, it may be, ancient) situation, where the metaphorical nature of poetry supposedly held a central social role. The Mauss stage concerns the construction of a desired relation of exchange with a patron. And in the Adorno stage, the most ambitious, we find that social and historical contradictions have become "inner breaks" in the literary works themselves.[78] To the extent that the "guides" have very diverse interests and philosophical origins, their hermeneutic presence in the coming chapters should illustrate the complexity of the texts studied. Whatever differences may arise among them testify to the richness of meaning latent in the immortality topos, that cliché that at first glance seems so transparent.

A final, more specific recurring element is the sepulchral presence. As will become clear, the contemplation of mortality typically accompanies the evocation of immortality. The anecdote of Alexander at Achilles' tomb supplies only the most famous and widespread of the scenes that place poetry at the grave. Horace's monument, the destination of the *Africa*, the inspiration of Poliziano's Homer, the objective of Budé's hunt—far from a morbid thematics, the funereal goal of humanist poetics belongs intimately to the topos. After all, *locus communis* means both commonplace and grave. Like the literary *tombeaux* so popular in the Renaissance, the text itself is a tomb meant to preserve its subject, the deceased. Moreover, we may be convinced by Adorno that the formal law itself of works of art allies them with death. "The affinity of all art with death is most noticeable in the idea of pure form imposed by art on the living manifold, which is thus snuffed out. . . . While the idea of works of art is modelled on immortality and eternal life, the road to the destination is strewn with the annihilated life of particulars. . . . To that extent the success of art works is synonymous with decomposition."[79]

Like any topological study, this one will end up showing tradition, constants, and continuity. However, the interpretation of the elements of that tradition—texts where the topos matters—resists mere subsumption in the totality. A danger exists, especially great for topology, of losing from sight the uniqueness of the particular in the Great

Tradition. Literary humanism can be better understood, what remains alive in it better grasped, not through emphasis on the glorious constants of Western culture, but through recognition of what is discontinuous, different, and contradictory in that tradition. Such a need—the need to discover humanism through its alien nature—helps explain whatever role anthropology may play in this study. Still, the theoretical elements introduced from Cassirer, Vico, Adorno, and Mauss are not methodological precepts, but rather points of view from which to attempt interpretations of individual works. For this reason, even were a survey possible, it would not be desirable. Likewise, this is obviously not a thematic study (on the "idea" of glory, immortality, or whatever). The texts chosen may have the appearance of fragments snatched from the flood of topical tradition. That is not an inappropriate appearance. Those fragments must be studied for what they tell us of the common force bearing them along, but also questioned for the unique message each carries from the dead.

1

Antiquity

On me montrait le dieu rayonnant à la place du cadavre.

Toute poésie est la voix donnée à la mort.

HOMER AND POETIC GIFTS

POETIC preoccupation with the power to glorify or immortalize exists as far back as the historical eye can see. Scholarly attempts to infer some characteristics of Indo-European poetry have established the centrality of the idea of glory. Moreover, the epithet that often adheres to "glory" is "immortal" (unwithering).[1] The granting of such glory is equally basic to the concept of poet, because the most probable Indo-European word for poet conveys the idea of herald or singer of praise.[2] Such early formulaic expressions of undying fame, even outside the Indo-European tradition, suggest two things about the topos.[3] First, that it would be futile to search for concrete origins. But at the same time the idea of origin, of primordiality, grows up as part of poetry's awareness of its commemorative function.[4]

Already the Homeric poems express a sense of the fall from a superior past. That superior past is the world of the poems, contrasted with the poet's fallen present. In several well-known passages, a hero easily heaves a rock that two men of the poet's own day could not have budged.[5] Nestor's rambling memory also recalls a past of greater heroes, but what he alludes to is a still earlier time of heroes superior to Agamemnon and Achilles.[6] To find glorious deeds that merit song, the poet's gaze is drawn irresistibly to the past.

Glory itself is already a complex notion for Homer. The most common term, *kleos,* has three principal meanings. Most generally, it is good reputation, fame, and glory. By transferral, it also signifies the deeds that bring fame. Finally, the good report of glory can degenerate to mere rumor.[7] The semantic "fall" of *kleos* matches the degeneration of heroic deeds between legendary times and Homer's day. Yet that semantic fall is not chronological; if anything, the Indo-European root suggests rumor as the original meaning of *kleos*.[8] This last sense occurs in an important passage where the poet of the *Iliad* prefaces his catalog of the Greek ships with an invocation to the Muses. Homer admits his need of divine help because of his human limitations. He confesses: "You are goddesses, you are present and know all things, / while we hear only rumor and know nothing."[9] "Rumor" here is *kleos,* opposed to truth in the same way hearing (*akouomen*) is opposed to sight or knowledge (*idmen*). The poet asks for inspiration to transcend the realm of uncertainty, so poetry ought to belong to the Muses' domain of what is sure. "The gift . . . of the Muses, or one of their gifts, is the power of true speech."[10] And yet the poet's proper function is itself gift bestowal: the commemoration of *kleos* as glory. Glory as what is told or sung is condemned to a perpetual semantic vicinity to mere rumor, or what is false. The most common as well as vaguest Homeric sense of *kleos* thus balances between the insubstantial (rumor) and the palpable (great deeds), between verbalism and violence. Despite the loftiness of the poet's calling, it is based on this radical uncertainty. From this point of view, we may better understand why Vico places Homer in the third period of poetic history: not among the theological or heroic poets, but in a time already corrupted.[11]

Hesiod displays a similar ambiguity. As he reports it, his *Theogony* was directly inspired by the Muses as he tended his flock on Mount Helicon. But the Muses said to him:

> We know how to say many falsehoods so they appear true,
> And we know, if we wish, how to sing what is true.[12]

As in Homer's invocation, the veracity of what is sung does not lie within human power. But Hesiod goes further by stressing the inscrutability of the divine realm. The poet and his audience cannot know if he is inspired with (and so sings) the truth or only a specious image. When the Muses command Hesiod to sing "those things which are to be and those which have been, . . . and the race of the happy gods who always are," they grant him mastery over time.[13] But his singing or glorification (the verb is *kleioimi*) commemorates the past, future, and eternal without assuring or being assured that it is not all illusion.[14]

The poet who voices the beginning of poetry, whether through invocation (Homer) or narration (Hesiod), represents it as a divine gift. That commonplace is present in archaic Greek poetry in a somewhat stronger form than subsequently. Certainly, the presence in such archaic poets as Archilochus, Theognis, Solon, Alcman, Anacreon, and

Bacchylides of the expression "gift of the Muses" (*Mousaon dora* or something similar) suggests a formulaic use.[15] In what sense, then, do we find poetry as a gift in a "stronger form" in these early poets? Not primarily through an appeal to religious practice; no doubt the presence of the Muses was already experienced as less numinous than literary. Rather because the relations of endowment between gods and mortals mirror those between mortals. The transcendent grounding of poetry finds its model in the relations of exchange that bind society together.

The Homeric *Hymn to Hermes* represents the origin of poetry and poetic glory as the product of an exchange between two gods. Hermes, inventor of the lyre, charms Apollo with his performance; Apollo calls the instrument "a noble gift" and requests it of Hermes, promising in return "splendid gifts."[16] Just what the appropriate exchange might be, Hermes makes clear later when he offers his lyre, so Apollo may bestow glory (*kudos*) upon him with it.[17] In this way, the god of poetry equips himself and is prepared to inspire human poets. The interest of the story lies in the fact that what may seem like the divine legitimation of poetic performance—the plenitude of Apollo or the Muses that is bestowed on humanity—is itself made dependent on barter or gift exchange.[18]

Hermes thus became the patron of relations of exchange (*epamoibima erga*) among men.[19] And, in fact, early Greek society was pervaded by the network of gift exchange, from before the Homeric era until long afterward.[20] While in the *Theogony* Hesiod represents himself as a beneficiary of the Muses, in his *Works and Days* he sententiously posits gift exchange as a fundamental social rule: "Give to whoever gives, and do not give to whoever does not give."[21] Certainly the Homeric world is organized by the varieties of such a principle. We can agree with M. I. Finley that "gift-giving in the Homeric poems is . . . absolutely consistant with the analysis made by Mauss."[22] In the *Iliad* we have only to consider the importance of bestowal or its absence in Achilles' evolving role, from his anger at Agamemnon's violation of the norm, to the conciliatory embassy of Odysseus and Phoenix, to his divine endowment with new armor, to his acceptance of a ransom for Hector's corpse (the term is always *doron* or *dotine*).[23] Indeed, the entire *Iliad* develops in the interval between gifts refused and gifts accepted and rendered, that is, between Agamemnon's refusal of Chryses' ransom for his daughter and Achilles' acceptance of Priam's ransom for his son.[24] This epic may be read as elaborating the consequences of failure to maintain the system of exchange.

If the *Odyssey* marks a return from tragedy to some kind of restored social order, we might expect that restoration to be embodied in a reaffirmed system of exchange. And, in fact, such is the case with the well-known role of the *xeinos* relation. Odysseus's homecoming and the restoration of order in Ithaca finds a prefiguration in his stay at the Phaeacian court of Alcinous, where the guest finds himself loaded with gifts. The various other arrivals and departures that compose the structure of the *Odyssey* are likewise informed by the obligation to bestow, presided over (at least theoretically) by Zeus *Xeinios.*

The place of poets in such a system has already been suggested in the introduction. The *Iliad* represents one significant poet.[25] Thamyras finds a place in an anecdote squeezed into the Catalogue of Ships. We learn briefly how the Muses maimed and deprived him of poetic ability because of his boast to surpass even them in talent.[26] The anecdote obviously recalls other stories of gods' punishing mortal competitors such as Marsyas and Arachne. But what compels attention here is the fact that the Muses, daughters of Memory, made Thamyras forget his poetic/musical skill (*eklelathon kitharistyn*). They thus withdrew the gift that they ordinarily bestowed on him and other poets and undid the granting of the lyre that (in the *Hymn to Hermes*) established Apollo as the patron of poetry.[27] Thamyras had apparently violated the rule of gratitude and humility toward the goddesses who had endowed him. In these few lines we may find encapsulated the larger tragedy of the *Iliad;* both epic and anecdote as the story of divine retribution for the failure to reciprocate.

The representation of poets in the *Odyssey* too resumes the overall movement of the poem. Here the poets benefit from a reconciliation affirming their social role. However, the total picture is more complex. This is so because of a greater variety of setting and plot than in the *Iliad,* because of the greater prominence of poets, and because the later epic portrays a world in peacetime, where more exists than the immediate concerns of warriors. But most of all, the more complex picture of the poet's place in the *Odyssey* can be attributed to the role played by mythical elements in the poem.

Demodocus finds himself compensated with honor (*time*) as well as meat, or both spiritual and material sustenance. Phemius is spared as Odysseus recognizes the poet's essential innocence. Odysseus himself becomes a storyteller at the Phaeacian court and is amply rewarded for his skill.[28] In fact, since the Phaeacians are the ones who transport the hero to Ithaca, it could be claimed that Odysseus's poetic power makes possible the poem's central reconciliation, his homecoming.[29] But what are we to make of Odysseus's acting the roles of both patron (with regard to Demodocus and Phemius) and poet (in his own performance)?

Consider first the substance of Odysseus's narrative. He tells of his wanderings and harrowing adventures, including more or less fantastic encounters with the Lestrygonians, the Lotus-eaters, Polyphemus, Circe, and the Sirens. His tale makes a striking contrast with the rest of the *Odyssey;* scholars have long noted its mythical and folktale elements. So it would not be far-fetched to claim that Odysseus's assumption of the role of poet coincides with a movement backward in time. Indeed, the land of the Phaeacians itself, the setting for Odysseus's performance, is depicted as a fairy-tale land recalling aspects of the golden age. Considering Homer's use of the past as legitimation of poetic power and poetic social function, we may be justified in wondering what more or less poetic activity takes place during the mythical suspension that Odysseus's narrative effects. Moreover, we might be alert to the connection of gift bestowal with that activity.

In their famous chapter on Odysseus in *Dialectic of Enlightenment,* Horkheimer and Adorno point out the temporal reversion performed by the hero's wanderings. The Sirens' song displays an "archaic superior power"; the Lotus-eaters act out a regression to the epoch of "collecting the fruits of earth"; while Polyphemus and the other Cyclopes represent the later stage of herdsmen and hunters.[30] The hero moves through that world as a prototype of the traveling merchant, dissolving myth with his rational gaze. And yet, if Odysseus embodies "bourgeois reason," that *Aufklärung* itself is constructed by its mythical adventures.[31] But a further step is necessary to understand Homer's significance, not just for a fundamental history of subjectivity,[32] but for a literary tradition interweaving fame, bestowal, and mythical regression. What Odysseus tells of in his poetic performance is a series of quasi-poetic enunciations and their consequences.

Such enunciations direct several episodes. The magical effects of Circe are prefigured aurally when she is first heard singing at her loom.[33] All the danger and temptation of the Sirens derive from their irresistable song (*aoide*).[34] But the richest adventure is the encounter with Polyphemus. The Cyclops's name itself speaks of verbal effect, looking forward to the role played by a concern with fame at the end of the episode. *Polyphemos* is also an epithet applied to the poet Phemius.[35] Yet "much-famed" Polyphemus does not himself broadcast his name.[36] That is Odysseus's role, much to his own disadvantage. The hero, it will be recalled, can safely make his escape if he maintains the witty pseudonym *Outis* with which he has deceived Polyphemus. But Odysseus's magnanimity, meaning a desire for renown, makes him incapable of withholding his real name as he sails away. He refuses to remain "Nobody" and recommends that the Cyclops "say that Odysseus sacker of cities had blinded" him. The release of his name makes him vulnerable to the curse that his enemy promptly calls down upon him.[37] The hero's verbal ingenuity is what saved him, but his verbal self-assertion is what lays him open to mythical powers. Polyphemus then fulfills his own name and shows the perilousness of fame, broadcasting the hero's name in the form of a curse.[38]

But if the Cyclops episode narrates the dangerously double-edged power of speech, it also stresses the central role of gift bestowal in what may be considered a patronage relation. When Odysseus and his men arrive at Polyphemus's cave, Odysseus refuses to rob the absent master, looking forward instead to a legitimate profit through guest gifts. When the monster returns, the hero tries to initiate the kind of guest-host rapport, based on bestowal, which is the norm in the Homeric world.[39] He soon discovers that his host does not play by the rules, but rather flagrantly denies hospitality to the Greeks. Polyphemus even makes a mockery of the language of bestowal; when Odysseus, in return for a promise of a gift, tells his (false) name, the Cyclops reveals that that promised gift is the privilege of being eaten last of all the prisoners.[40]

Polyphemus's punishment, then, appears as a punishment for his refusal to observe civilized norms. Odysseus's encounter with him constitutes a reaffirmation *a contrario* of social order, just as the maiming (blinding?) of Thamyris in the *Iliad* reaffirms the principle of rendering to the divine realm its due. The Polyphemus episode and the sojourn among the Phaeacians which frames it figure two sorts of mythical societies, made possible by two sorts of temporal reversion performed by poetry. If the hero, who is the poet responsible for narrating the negative archaism evident in the Cyclopes, escapes from that menace and benefits from the positive archaism that Homer portrays in the Phaeacians, the credit must go to poetry. Verbal power threatens and saves Odysseus during his wanderings and charms his final hosts into a magnificent enactment of *xeinos* relation.

A figure of the patron in the Sirens episode, Odysseus is menaced by the irresistible charm of poetry but renders it ineffective by imprisoning himself.[41] A figure of the poet in the Cyclops episode, he overcomes the savage antipatronage of his host but falls prey to the temptation of quasi-poetic renown. His oscillation between the two roles illustrates the temporal instability of the hero's mythical wanderings. Poetic performance as a relation of exchange is caught up in that suspended and uncertain time.[42]

PINDAR: IMMORTALITY IN CIRCULATION

If it is true that "[a]ll Greek literature—song, poetry, prose—originates in *kleos,* the act of praising famous deeds, and never entirely loses that focus,"[43] *kleos* is, nevertheless, not monolithic. The glory of Homeric and Hesiodic poetry moves, as it were, in the sublunary realm. There is, certainly, much commerce between humans and immortals, and the latter make themselves felt in the works of men. But there is no confusing the two realms. Homer's gods often disguise themselves as humans to deliver advice or command, but before departing they nearly always let slip a sign that reveals them as divine. Poetry, a gift of the gods, nevertheless remains something thoroughly human. Born from human misfortune, it offers mortals duration in memory but no transformation of their state. It may appear otherwise in the poetry of Pindar, who seems in some ways a more archaic poet than Homer. For Pindar, the gods do not simply concern themselves with human affairs, as do the meddlesome Homeric gods. They are, first, mostly benevolent in their interaction with humans (while, despite exceptions such as Athena's patronage of Odysseus, Homeric characters more often suffer at the hands of the gods). Second, the mixing of the two realms comes about not only by descent from heaven—in both the aerial and genealogical senses—but also by man's raising himself to the status of a god. And this elevation is the work of poetry.

No doubt, Homeric heroes are qualified as *dioi,* godlike. But the epithet is consequent on their great deeds. They have no illusion of possessing godlike immortality. Death is an irreparable evil, as Achilles declares with the wisdom of a shade.[44] That fact results in large part from the Homeric conception of the soul.[45] The *eidola* which subsist after death are anemic images of life's plenitude. They have nothing to compensate the loss of mortal blood. Pindar, too, is concerned with heroes who have shown physical *arete.* His epinician odes commemorate victors in the great games at Olympia, Delphi, Nemea, and Corinth. But the poetic celebration is not tacked on to the athletic triumph; the two make up a whole that is the hero's deification. If "only the children of the gods are unscathed,"[46] the poet's office entails enrolling heroes in the divine family and so exempting them from mutability and its damage. Pindar recalls Homer's picture of the Muses gathered around Achilles' bier. What he has them sing is a "dirge of glory," *threnos poluphamos,*—that is, a song that both mourns mortality and overcomes mortality by making the object "much-spoken."[47]

The ensemble of a victory ode's performance was a religious event.[48] J. Duchemin has observed a thorough parallelism between funerary archeology and Pindar's poetry.[49] In general, both have in common the function of insuring an individual's survival after death. In particular, how is that end achieved? Both funerary art and epinician odes share the essential element of substitution. On a stele or sarcophagus, the deceased may be portrayed transformed into one of the Muses. By this identification, the deity's immortality is attributed to the mortal.[50] Pindar achieves something similar through his use of myths. A poem that starts as praise of a particular athlete's victory soon modulates into an account of some ancient hero's adventure. Those heroes (such as Hercules, Peleus, Cadmus, Castor, and Pollux) generally benefited from some form of deification; the present-day hero finds himself more or less tacitly admitted to their ranks and shares their reward. Pindar's abundant use of myth, sometimes to the point of almost crowding out the victor, is one of his most striking characteristics. Likewise, the jump within a poem between present and mythical past; it is the basis of the supposed Pindaric obscurity. But precisely that apparent lack of transition constitutes the effective part of mythical substitution. Because the poet moves freely between present and past, mortals and demigods, he can transform the victor he celebrates.[51] Duchemin observes the parallel between this sort of poetic substitution and the more general effect of metaphor, which transforms entities by effacing their differences:

De même qu'une métaphore, à la différence d'une comparaison, épargne la distinction des deux termes, de même le mythe inséré sans articulation visible, par simple juxtaposition, suggère l'assimilation du héros du jour au héros du mythe.[52]

In fact, funerary customs, poetic use of myth, and metaphor all share the same foundation. Their common use of substitution means a common movement toward identity that is finally magical. The characterization of magic as sympathetic (based on resemblance), at least in one of its important varieties, dates back to Frazer and was endorsed by Freud.[53] As a comprehensive theory of magic itself, it has been justly criticized.[54] But there is little question that the magical gesture does pretend to efface difference and to draw an effective power from that effacement. Pindar, who does not claim to be a magician, does claim to be able to do things with words. The poetic task that he establishes for himself is the effective deployment of narrative (myths) and tropes (metaphor) in a pursuit of identity—that is, immortalization.

And yet, if certain constellations of Pindaric metaphor represent his poetry as retaining a magical force and his social office as built on the lofty ground of that force, there exists another but not always distinct series of metaphors that figure the poem as gift. It would be misleading to leave Pindar with the appearance of a disembodied poetic voice, fluctuating only in the universal realm of the human condition. In the working out of the gift metaphor, Pindar's poetry performs not only the gestures of cultic function in a transhistorical realm, but also the gestures of economic exchange in a given social situation. It is the coexistence of both these tendencies that helps create his chiaroscuro.[55]

In an important book that draws significantly on Mauss, L. Kurke argues convincingly for a view of Pindar's victory odes as a "traffic in praise." The valuable object, namely, glory (*kleos*), circulates in the household (*oikos*), in the aristocratic community, and in the *polis* as a whole.[56] Pindar's figure of the poet thus appears socially central, not hidden by priestly vestments, but expressing the material life of his fellow citizens. The pervasive structure, or structures, of gift exchange penetrate the far from Homeric world of fifth-century Greece. One vitally important development lies in the representation of poetry itself as a gift. The human bestowal of poetry as a gift, which is not prominent in Homer, comes to the fore in Pindar.

Among the many developments of this metaphor, we might note the beginning of *Olympian* 7. There the poet calls his song a gift of the Muses (*Moisan dosi*[s]), echoing the numerous similar expressions in archaic lyric. A more elaborately developed metaphor has already compared the poet's gesture of bestowal to that of a bride's father who hands a golden goblet brimming with wine to his new son-in-law.[57] The festive occasion resembles the celebration of Olympic victory. But the occasion comprises both the sparkling glory of light on gold and wine and the conclusion of an economic deal: the marriage bargain.[58]

The slippage between gift and commerce becomes verbal in the easy transition between *dosis* and *kerdon* or *misthos*.[59] This indicates a period of historic transition, when metaphor takes up current economic categories and develops them side by side with other categories left over from an epoch now past. While his elaboration of gift exchange embeds Pindar in the material life of the *polis,* the uneasy frontier between gift exchange and commerce reveals the threat that that embedding may be compromised and mercenary. In *Isthmian* 2, for example, the poet laments a present day in which venal poetry has fallen from a past time of pure praise; the Muse has become *philokerdes,* profit loving.[60] But in the same poem, Pindar redeems his inspiration by changing the image of material benefit to one of gift exchange.[61] In a similar way, commercial metaphors may point back to more archaic phenomena; for example, in *Olympian* 10 Pindar mentions interest in such a way as to evoke poetry as potlatch. The poem that he calls his interest (*tokos*) for a debt later becomes an ocean wave washing away all economic obligations. Like potlatch, poetry attempts a relation of overwhelming superiority to its benefactor.[62] The excellence that Pindar recognizes in his poetry surpasses generic expectations and tends toward an imbalance of trade.[63]

Pindar's representation of poetry as gift (from gods to poet, from poet to hero/patron and thus to *polis*) is an attempt to maintain poetry's mythical social force. Nevertheless, he must face the contradictions inherent in an increasingly commercial world that tempts him with unavoidable metaphors. Pindar's position on the threshold of the fifth-century "Enlightenment" is paradigmatic both in historical/social terms and with regard to the literary enchantment that he attempts to maintain against economic disenchantment.

There is also a political side to the praise bestowed by Pindar on his historical moment. The games he commemorated were essentially the preserve of aristocrats, the only class with the necessary leisure and wealth.[64] However, Pindar's career corresponds to the passing away of aristocratic rule in the Greek world. His images of fleeting life and light imply the precarious position of a thoroughly aristocratic poet. He does attach himself to certain of the new class of tyrants; most notably Hieron, ruler of Syracuse, and Theron, ruler of Akragas.[65] The tyrants' courts were often sites of lively patronage; they have been compared with the Medici in their brilliance, but also in their artificiality.[66] The move of poetry to tyrants' courts holds considerable significance, and not just for Pindar. If we consider two of the common expressions of relations with the Muses, poetry as a "gift of the Muses" and the poet as "servant (*therapon*) of the Muses" we may naturally suspect some connection between the two.[67] The Muses may serve as prototype of the patron, whose function is to endow the poet. The poet serves the goddesses by disposing appropriately of their gift, namely, by rendering inspiration to them in the form of a poem. Pindar calls himself the servant of Apollo, god of poetry.[68] He thus establishes patronage in the divine realm in a double sense: by elevating the noble victor by means of myth and by portraying the gods themselves as "patrons" of humanity requiring glory as both *therapeia* and *xeinia*.[69] It is the profoundly ingrained poetics of bestowal that makes possible the celebration of a poetics of service. And it is the confusion of bestowal with service, like the confusion of bestowal with commerce, that accompanies the poet as he looks for protection to new sources of power.

The tenth Nemean ode presents a fable of the poet, portraying his simultaneous immortalizing and mourning function in a relation of exchange. Pindar begins this ode with praise of Argos, *polis* of the victor. He recalls the deification of Argive heroes and Zeus's dallying with the women to beget demigods. The central section reviews the victor's numerous triumphs, and the poem ends with a myth that helps explain those triumphs. Because of a connection of ancestral hospitality, the athlete enjoys the protection of Castor and Pollux. The myth chosen concerns the origin of their unique alternation of mortality and immortality. Here we may see an allegory of the poet's decision to serve human finitude by raising it to share the divine relationship to which he has a natural right. Castor was killed in battle. Pollux cries out in sorrow for his twin and calls to account the king of the gods. He asks that he may share the lot of mortals. Zeus answers: "You are my son," and so immortal. Castor was born of a mortal father. However, says Zeus,

> I grant you a choice of these two possibilities: if, avoiding death and hateful old age, you want to dwell on Olympus with me . . . , that is your share. But if you want to strive for your brother, and intend to share out all things equally with him, you may breath half the time beneath the earth, and half the time in the golden dwellings of the sky.[70]

Such is the poet's characteristic role, poised above the athlete's ephemerality like the Muses at Achilles' bier, yet determined to bring the hero to life by song. He raises the dead by affirming his own humanity.

> He felt no doubt in his mind, but released the eyes then the voice of Castor with the bronze belt.[71]

What Pollux assents to is an odd sort of immortality: an everlasting alternation of life and death. Only through an acceptance of material reality (gift exchange and the commerce it leads to) can the poet claim entrance to the transcendent realm of magical-religious function. Such an allegory would propose Castor and Pollux as two parts of the poet. But we may also see the poet as Pollux bestowing eternal life and death on the patron as Castor. That is, only through a compromised existence with (for example) tyrants can the poet attain his desired effect. In both allegories (the poet as both brothers, and the brothers as poet and patron), the death accepted in the myth represents an acceptance of the material realm, economic or political. Such acceptance serves as a means to the end of eternal life, that is, poetic self-legitimation through the boast of effective power.

CICERO, *PRO ARCHIA; RES PUBLICA,* POET

Man of action, man of involuntary *otium,* occasional poet and philosopher, Cicero manifests both sides of the dialectic of praise. In fact, there are two dialectics at work. One is the tension between desire for glory and awareness of its vanity. Cicero in his philosophical persona expresses the latter position in, for example, his *De re publica* (book 6) or the *Tusculan Disputations*.[72] The weight of the former position we shall see presently. The second dialectic functions within the realm of dedication to glory; its two poles are the man of action who desires glory for his reward and the *litteratus* who is capable of bestowing that reward. Cicero was intimately acquainted with both roles; it is, perhaps, this fact that gives the question of glory such central significance in his work.

Cicero theorizes the bestowal of glory, a fact that distinguishes him from the practicing poets who previously voiced the topos.[73] Nevertheless, the one who claims to "discuss" literary glory is inevitably implicated in pursuing and creating the same. Nor can this critical egoism be simply chalked up to the notoriously lofty opinion Cicero had of himself.

When as consul in 63 B.C. Cicero had defended Rome from the Catilinarian conspiracy, he claimed as his reward enduring memory in the minds of Roman citizens.[74] That such memory might be guaranteed by his own orations would seem plausible (and, in fact, has been the case), but the prestige of poetry as commemoration clearly surpassed harangues, no matter how accomplished. It is no doubt for that reason that some years later (in 55 B.C.), Cicero turned to a writer of his acquaintance, Lucius Lucceius, and in a remarkable letter begged him to grant literary immortality to his consulship. In his letter, Cicero makes bold to request what he was ashamed to mention in person, "epistula enim non erubescit" (for a letter does not blush). He soon comes to the point: "Ardeo cupiditate incredibili neque, ut ego arbitror, reprehendenda, nomen ut nostrum scriptis illustretur et celebretur tuis" (I burn with an unbelievable desire that is not, I think, blameworthy, that my name might be honored and glorified in your writings).[75]

The letter to Lucceius has considerable importance as an early example of the confusion of history and panegyric—a confusion that will have a long tradition. Cicero confesses he has no shame about subordinating truth to his praise.

Itaque te plane etiam atque etiam rogo, ut et ornes ea vehementius etiam quam fortasse sentis, et in eo leges historiae neglegas . . . amorique nostro plusculum etiam quam concedet veritas largiare.

(sec. 3)

(So I am begging you quite earnestly to dress things up, even more than you may feel, and in this to neglect the laws of historical writing; and to bestow on our friendship even a little more than truth may allow.)

However, he does not fear that this may turn out to be simply flattery. The politician's adventures have great dramatic potential, are *quasi fabula*. Moreover, he realizes that he can only hope for glory from a writer talented enough to glorify himself at the same time.

> Neque autem ego sum ita demens ut me sempiternae gloriae per eum commendari velim, qui non ipse quoque in me commendando propriam ingenii gloriam consequatur.
>
> (sec. 6)

> (I am not so insane as to wish myself committed to eternal glory by someone who cannot himself obtain glory for his own talent through praising me.)

This declaration of a harmony of interests between poet and subject brings with it the example of Alexander the Great, who only permitted himself to be portrayed by artists as great as Apelles and Lysippus.[76] It is also the reason for the introduction of Alexander's comment at Achilles' grave[77]—a scene that, as we shall see, Cicero had already introduced in the oration *Pro Archia*. Cicero emphasizes this point because he does not want to resort to writing in praise of himself. Literary self-praise has the obvious drawbacks of inferior credibility and a certain lack of taste. It seems, alas, that Lucceius did not come through and so drove Cicero to that expedient. He wrote a commentary in Greek and at least three poems on his consulship. However, as he puts it, these were not encomiastic but historical.[78]

In exposing his desire to be glorified in literature, Cicero implicitly argues the importance of the *litteratus*. In 62 B.C. he argued a legal case in which the question of the poet in society was explicit. So much of the oration *Pro Archia* is paradigmatic for the later topical tradition that it merits a close if selective examination.

The charge against Aulus Licinius Archias was simply that of enjoying the benefits of Roman citizenship while not being a citizen. What was aimed at was his expulsion from the *res publica*. Cicero's argument is twofold: first, that Archias is, in fact, a citizen, and second, even if he were not, he would deserve to be made one. The first is the properly legal argument and does not regard Archias's profession. The lawyer delivers it succinctly in the early part of the oration. In the other part of the plea, and especially in the weight given to it, Cicero is deliberately unconventional. At the start he asks indulgence for this new and *inusitatum genus dicendi* (2.3).[79] He will speak more freely than is his custom in court and will assume a *persona*, or dramatic mask, to make a special kind of plea. And, in fact, the oration that ensues "is undoubtedly the least typical speech of the Ciceronian corpus."[80] Why does Cicero introduce the second, unjudicial argument if it is unnecessary, even foreign to his case? He is arguing for himself as much as for Archias, for his ideal of the orator as man of letters in action. For this reason, he expands Archias's significance from simply that of a poet to the entire field of *studia humanitatis*. Cicero's strategy aims at a vindication of his own thirst for literary glory.[81]

It would be easy enough to show how that is the case. But what is more interesting and more influential in *Pro Archia* grows from where that self-centered itinerary takes Cicero. Briefly, the plea for the place of the poet (man of letters) in the *res publica* depends on (1) a reversal of debt, which becomes an ideal of mutual bestowal, (2) a temporal reversal, which becomes an archaic or even primitivist cultural ideal, and (3) a yoking of poetic purpose to imperial purpose. Each of these elements leads to and overlaps with the others.

From the beginning of the oration, Cicero casts Archias in the role of a benefactor, who deserves gratitude and reward. This means first of all a benefactor with regard to the orator himself.[82] From the start, the question of obligation is reversed; it is no longer a question whether the poet has obeyed the law, but whether he has been given his due. Cicero's praise of literature explains just what that benefaction consists of. What begins as a praise of literature as recreation after public action becomes a declaration that that same public action is directly served by literary training. Cicero himself has always placed at the disposal of the *res publica* the verbal skill he owes to literary study (6.13). No one could miss the speaker's allusion to his consulship of the previous year, where his verbal service had a resounding success in the Catilinarian orations.

In addition to rhetorical skill, Cicero describes how he has found in books virtuous examples, "quae iacerent in tenebris omnia, nisi litterarum lumen accederet" (which would all lie in shadow, if the light of literature were not added) (6.14). Just as literary examples compel imitation by their readers or listeners, so does Cicero use examples of past poets rightly rewarded to further his case. As he moves from the didactic value of *studia humanitatis* in general to poetry in particular, Cicero declares that poets are a gift from the gods.[83] The appropriate return for such divine bestowal evidently consists in quasi-religious veneration: "Sit igitur, iudices, sanctum apud vos, humanissimos homines, hoc poetae nomen quod nulla umquam barbaria violavit" (O judges, who are most humane men, accept as sacred this name *poet* which no barbarian ever dishonored) (8.19).

The allusion to barbarians' homage to poets introduces a strategic trope that Cicero pursues through several transformations. It consists of an example of poets' receiving their due, in a situation not as compelling as the present case. Hence the conclusion: so much the more should Rome honor poets, and Archias in particular. The first form of the trope is the most "primordial," introducing the effect of poetry as verbal magic:

> Saxa atque solitudines voci respondent, bestiae saepe immanes cantu flectuntur atque consistunt: nos instituti rebus optimis non poetarum voce moveamus?
>
> (8.19)

> (Rocks and wilderness respond to their voice, monstrous wild beasts are softened and brought to a halt by song. Shall we, with the finest education, not be moved by the poets' voice?)

The obvious allusion is to the power of Orpheus's song. The power of the poetic voice in general has a foundation in physical effectiveness, but that power grows as poetry addresses itself, in addition, to the mental faculties. Hence, the assumption that cultured men, *instituti rebus optimis,* should be all the more susceptible to poetic charms.

The next form of this "exemplary compensation trope" uses the first poet with a textual existence, namely, Homer. Cicero names several of the cities that traditionally claimed Homer as a citizen. Some went to the extreme of building a temple to the poet, as to a demigod; all fought vigorously to claim him as their own.

> Ergo illi alienum, quia poeta fuit, post mortem etiam expetunt: nos hunc vivum qui et voluntate et legibus noster est repudiamus, praesertim cum omne olim studium atque omne ingenium contulerit Archias ad populi Romani gloriam laudemque celebrandam?
>
> (9.19)

> (They even seek him out after his death, foreigner though he was, because he was a poet. Shall we reject him who is alive and is ours voluntarily and legally, especially since for a long time now Archias has devoted all his energy and talent to celebrating the glory and honor of the Roman people?)

Homer was rewarded posthumously as the benefactor of all Greece, simply because he was a poet. Archias, who is legally a Roman (as Cicero hopes to have already proved), who has dedicated himself to glorifying Rome explicitly, should reap at least Homeric honor. In both the foregoing comparisons, we see the establishment of a lasting strategy in the defense or promotion of poetry: The contemporary poet is evaluated in relation to the myths concerning the great archaic poets (Orpheus and Homer). Such figures, about whom nothing historical is known, grow into allegories of poetic power, their careers into allegories of poetry's service and reward.

From Orpheus to Homer to the foundational Latin poet; Cicero's logic leads him to the example of Ennius and the exemplary tribute paid to him by Scipio Africanus.[84] Cicero calls Ennius *noster,* making him a privileged figure. The poet's intimacy with Scipio and his office of praise both endure beyond death and are figured in the marble monument admitted to the tomb of the Scipiones. Later readers of the *Pro Archia* will recall this model of the relationship between *dux* and *poeta.*[85]

A non-Roman, Ennius was made a citizen as a reward for his poetic service. All the more should Archias find a place.[86] The desired embrace of the poet by the *res publica* finds a still more recent image in the scene of Pompey's granting citizenship to Theophanes of Mytilene, *scriptor rerum suarum.* This gift was a public ceremony, performed before Pompey's army, which warmly approved because they too had benefited from commemoration.

> Nonne . . . nostri illi fortes viri, sed rustici ac milites, dulcedine quadam gloriae commoti, quasi participes eiusdem laudis, magno illud clamore approbaverunt?
>
> (10.24)

> (Did not those men of ours, brave but rough soldiers, moved by a certain sweetness of glory, participants as it were in Pompey's praise, approve the action with a great cheer?)

We are thus brought around again to the first, most primordial example of exemplary compensation. The sweetness of literary glory has become the magic of Orpheus's lyre, moving the rudest things.

It is worth noting that Cicero repeatedly identifies the *populus Romanus* with the active Roman army. In the previous example, when Theophanes honored the army, he honored Rome; the soldiers' ratification of his citizenship resembled a decree SPQR. Likewise when Archias wrote of the Cimbrian and Mithridatic wars (9.19–21). The golden chain of glory's bestowal connects *poeta* to *dux,* thence to *exercitus,* and finally to *populus.* What this amounts to is a harmony posited, not just between poet and *res publica,* but between poet and Roman imperialism. Cicero equates the extent of Roman conquest with the ideal extent of literary glory, that is, of Roman literature:

> si res eae, quae gessimus, orbis terrae regionibus definiuntur, cupere debemus, quo manus nostrorum et tela pervenerint, eodem gloriam famamque penetrare . . .

(If those deeds which we do are bounded by the parts of the earth, we ought to desire that our glory and fame penetrate wherever our troops and weapons reach.)

The social use of glory becomes clear; it acts as incitement to further conquest: "hoc maximum et periculorum incitamentum est et laborum" (10.23).[87]

It is in this context that the exemplum of Alexander arises. The vignette of the conqueror at Achilles' tomb has become so familiar in the topical tradition that it may be hard to discern the fresh power of this first version.[88] Cicero presents the scene frozen, isolated from its context. But it clearly takes place during a pause, in Asia Minor, on Alexander's triumphant sweep to the East. His visit to his rival's tomb and his words there express admiration and envy of both Achilles' incomparable prowess and Homer's incomparable ability to glorify. Alexander's words voice an insatiable thirst for conquest and glory. Posterity will inherit these words somewhat one-sidedly as a simple confession of the prince's need for poets.

> Atque is tamen, cum in Sigeo ad Achillis tumulum adstitisset: 'o fortunate, inquit, adulescens, qui tuae virtutis Homerum praeconem inveneris!' et vere; nam, nisi Ilias illa exstitisset, idem tumulus, qui corpus eius contexerat, nomen etiam obruisset.
>
> (10.24)[89]

> (And yet he, as he stood in Sigeum at the grave of Achilles, said: "o fortunate young man, who have found Homer as herald of your excellence!" He spoke truly for, had the *Iliad* not existed, the same mound which covered Achilles' body would overwhelm his name too.)

The *tamen* in this passage refers to the fact that Alexander took many writers with him on his campaigns. Thus he showed not only an awareness of the writer's office, but also an understanding that only talented writers (Homer above all) can adequately fulfill that office. The introduction of this theme permits Cicero some lightly comic relief, as he recalls examples of even bad poets' finding patronage. Yet even here he continues the structure of his argument, "if . . . then so much the more"; if poetasters have been honored, then all the more should Archias be rewarded.

The revolutionary effect of Alexander the Great in antiquity includes his role as patron. The conqueror's personality cult created an unprecedented demand for art as a vehicle for propaganda.[90] This was most obviously true for the visual arts, but literature was not neglected. If the effect of the new demand was to make artists and writers

necessary functionaries attending on the conqueror, what Alexander
represents is an epochal change in patronage. That Cicero strategically
introduces his anecdote in a plea for the necessity of poets suggests
that for the Roman, too, poets are desirable as propagandists of conquest. This means the invention of a new Homer. Perhaps no one
before Simone Weil has read Homer as a consistent antiwar poet, but
the cult manifested for him by Alexander and consecrated by Cicero's
anecdote certainly departs from whatever previous ideological uses we
can discover for the Homeric poems.[91] Subsequently, the wide diffusion
of the anecdote in the Renaissance indicates a long tradition where
the poet's elevation matches his usefulness in a politic personality cult.
Alexander envies Achilles the job of legitimation Homer has done for
him: transforming the selfish, immature, treasonous, choleric warrior
into a perpetually shining tragic hero.

Cicero's promotion of Roman hegemony has as one foundation the
proto-Imperial ideology of universality. The anecdote concerning Pompey and Theophanes follows directly on Alexander and Homer, making
the same point for contemporary Rome. Even verbally there is an in-
terpenetration of the two cases, with *magnus ille Alexander* echoed
by *noster hic Magnus.* Pompey, who was certainly a prominent figure
in Roman imperialism,[92] follows Alexander also in the importance he
gives to poets. However, Pompey's poet (and by extension, Cicero's) is
alive. The Roman achievement should be to revive and pull from his
grave the singer of Roman conquest. A further difference lies in the
fact that Alexander is a solitary figure, whereas Pompey has the ovation
of the Roman people behind him.[93]

The final movement of the oration, a defense of the desire for glory,
should be understood as a variation on the same universalizing tendency. Even before Cicero turns with rhetorical flair to the judges and
accuses himself of an excessive desire for glory, he exculpates himself
by asserting that such a desire drives all of us.[94] Alexander holds a
lesson for Rome's destiny because the best of us share Alexander's
desires. The matching universality of the poet's office means that he
affirms *virtus* in the service of imperium. Such is the seed of a humanism that Cicero sows for posterity.

The orator claims that Archias has already begun a poetic celebration of his consulate.[95] We do not know enough to convict Archias of
ingratitude, but in a letter to Atticus the following year, Cicero mentions, in a somewhat disappointed tone, that after all Archias has still
written nothing in his praise.[96] The irony remains, that the poet would
be practically unknown were it not for Cicero's defense.

Horace

Something in Horace's work may provoke suspicion. It is perhaps his eager and opportune embrace of the powerful or his complacent self-portrait. "*Odi profanum vulgus et arceo,* said the son of the freed slave."[97] Horace's boasts of power and his vindication of poetry's office may ring hollow, echoing with the usual notes of imperial ideology; he who abandons the republic posits a republic of letters.

Nevertheless, it remains true that Horace has a coherent "thought" on these matters, expressed in poems of enormous influence. And perhaps more important, this fact remains: although the poet may be superior to time, he is rarely superior to his time. The figure of Horace represents a transformation that poetry underwent in his age and that marked all subsequent uses of classicism or antiquity. Naturally, there is no question here of charting the metamorphoses of ancient poetry, but of a sketch of some indispensable points.

E. R. Curtius sees a decisive moment of the topical tradition in the disappearance of judicial and deliberative rhetoric, at the time of the Roman Empire's consolidation.[98] That left only epideictic rhetoric, which was not necessarily bound like the other genres to public occasion, and which found its home in poetry. Of course, that is not to say that epideictic migrated from rhetoric to poetry; as we have seen, poetry had always contained the element of praise and, in fact, exercised its own influence on rhetorical convention.[99] The noteworthy change is the isolation of praise in "mere" literature, without an external occasion. Curtius attributes a crucial role to Ovid, who effected the metamorphosis of rhetorical tropes into poetic ones, which he passed down in great number to posterity.

A similar role can be discerned for Horace. By his own boast, he was the poet who brought Greek lyric into the Latin tradition.[100] This was not without bringing about a profound change in that lyric. If Horace "wanted to adopt a theme . . . he had no choice but to empty it of its substance of primary life and turn it into a bare topic of literature."[101] As we have seen, for Pindar, the Greek lyric poet par excellence, the occasion or "substance of primary life" holds the utmost importance. This is not to deny that the Greek poet possessed a technique heavily indebted to literary tradition. But the tradition itself resulted from the occasion of celebration. The poet's voice is present with the dance and the crowning. He does not draw back from the immediate. Even when he declares his unique power, it is not to set himself apart from the others, but to insist that his office is integrated in the social whole.

The difference we find in Horace may be explained as the expression of an evolution in ancient poetry's mode of existence, including the use of writing. According to E. Fraenkel, already in the classical age of Greece there existed an audience for poetry that was not immediately before them, that was reproduced or read. These readers

> were already separated by a considerable distance from the conditions out of which the poems had grown and they could not be greatly interested in the immediate purpose for which the songs were originally destined. What must have mattered most to these later readers could only be the more general and, as it were, timeless elements of the poems.[102]

The increased distance from occasion was, of course, gradual. In the next stage, the conventions of poetic composition came to reflect the conditions of its reception. In this later stage, which was Horace's situation, poems

> were no longer produced for a special occasion and addressed to a limited audience, but were from the outset composed to find their place in a roll of papyrus, where any reader, of the present or of some future generation . . . might pick them up. When the book had become the normal means for the transmission of poems, the emancipation of poetry from the conditions of the life of a definite society was complete.[103]

One may be skeptical about the possibility of emancipation from the conditions of social life. A pretended shift from the immediate to the eternal does not take place without influence on the immediate, in the form of a status quo maintained. To pass over the specific in favor of the "more general and . . . timeless" permits violation of the specific. Even where Horace's poetry takes on explicitly political themes, he develops them as a series of meditations on timeless values. As we shall see, Horace identifies the immortality of his poetry with the duration of *imperium Romanum*.[104]

The meters themselves reveal the distance traveled from the Hellenic world to Rome, as in Horace's use of the Alcaic strophe, most strikingly in the Roman odes (the first six odes of book 3). Alcaeus wrote political poetry that was clearly oppositional, as even Horace notes in the epithet *mina[x]* he applies to Alcaeus.[105] For Horace, on the other hand, what is at work in the Roman odes is service of the status quo dressed up as the eternal.[106]

Naturally, there is nothing incongruous in Horace's taking up elements of poetry from which his own differs so profoundly, elements that make claims for the immediacy and social importance of the poetic act. Those are precisely the "timeless, general" elements that become topoi. Indeed, the model of such topoi is the claim of poetic power to immortalize. That claim thematizes, first, the specific cultic function that the poet pretends to have originally held, and second, the time-lessness and literariness that make it possible to overcome that speci-ficity. Horace's use of the topos embodies both the nostalgia for a former mythical state of affairs and the admission of a thoroughly different situation for the present poet.

Horace naturally concerns himself with the poet's place in the *res publica*. His ideal becomes clearest in the late *Carmen Saeculare*, performed by a chorus of girls and boys at the *ludi saeculares* in 17 B.C. The *ludi* were a traditional Roman religious festival in which propitiatory offerings were made to the gods of the underworld. Thus the occasion gave the poet an occasion to exercise his archaic cultic function, and Horace shows his awareness of that throughout the poem. However, for this celebration, Augustus had changed the empha-sis from worship and propitiation to "thanksgiving for present bless-ings and ... prayer for the continuance of them forever."[107] The ceremony consecrates the imperial status quo; by the intercession of the immortals the poet desires a similar immortality for the state. And not only immortality but also size and power. To Apollo goes the prayer: "possis nihil urbe Roma / visere maius" (may you see nothing greater than the city of Rome) (11–12).[108] The poem moves in a world of collec-tives, allegories, and gods; there are no human individuals. For this, the use of a chorus is significant. Horace refers to himself and boasts of his skill in the singular ("doctus et Phoebi chorus et Dianae / dicere laudes" [skilled at speaking Apollo's chorus and Diana's praise] [75–76]), but the words were performed by a plural voice. The poet has tried to literally identify his voice with that of his fellow citizens. A similar effect may be observed in Pindar's choral lyric, but the point for Horace concerns a pretense of civic unanimity that simultaneously boasts the poet's superiority.[109]

The *Carmen Saeculare* includes an important element of moral reform. "Honos Pudorque / priscus" (57–58) posits an epoch of pristine virtue, the present rebirth of which the poet asserts.[110] A well-known technique that founds the legitimacy and grandeur of Rome is the appeal to origins. Horace recalls the legend of Aeneas and, further back, Rome's divine descent from Venus (37–52). This gaze into the past is also an essential strategy in founding the poet's office. The *locus classicus* for that latter strategy is in the *Ars poetica*, where Horace interprets the Orphic myths as allegories of poetry's civilizing power:

Silvestris homines sacer interpresque deorum
caedibus et victu foedo deterruit Orpheus,

dictus ob hoc lenire tigris rabidosque leones;
dictus et Amphion, Thebanae conditor urbis,
saxa movere sono testudinis et prece blanda
ducere quo vellet. fuit haec sapientia quondam,
publica privatis secernere, sacra profanis,
concubitu prohibere vago, dare iura maritis,
oppida moliri, leges incidere ligno.[111]

(Divine Orpheus, interpreter of the gods, deterred savage men from blood-
shed and their coarse food; for this reason he was said to tame tigers and
ferocious lions. Amphion too, builder of Thebes, was said to move stones
with the sound of his lyre and lead them where he wished with his persua-
sive prayer. Such was wisdom formerly: to distinguish public from private,
sacred from profane, to forbid promiscuity, to impose marital laws, to build
cities, to inscribe laws on wood.)

Poets were, then, the founders of civilization. The power of song drew
man away from his solitary bestial state to make him social.[112] However, Horace does not merely situate the matter in the past. One notices
the similarity between the primordial poets' reforms and the moral
crusade undertaken by Augustus. We know the strenuous efforts by
the Princeps "to forbid promiscuity, to impose marital laws,"[113] and the
disastrous consequences for a poet like Ovid who failed to realize the
importance of a "moral" poetry. The legendary poets who founded
primitive society acted in harmony with Horace himself; they prepared
for the present day.[114]

The term *vates* used immediately after this passage (400) had only
quite recently added the meaning "poet" to its primary sense "seer."[115]
There is no need to dwell on the obvious importance of such semantic
broadening for the task of poetry in Augustan ideology. The exemplarity of Horace concerns the rooting of his vatic collaboration at
the beginning of literary history, and the identification of that literary
history with the history of civilization itself. At that foundational moment, the poet performs two essential gestures: deterrance and construction. Orpheus frightens primitive humanity away from its nasty
habits, and Amphion erects the walls that enclose civic community
and foretell *altae moenia Romae*.[116] Poetry's magical effect as a movement of enclosure founds the poet's office within the *res publica*.

If the poet was originally the founder of society and now upholds it
as intermediary between humanity and the gods, nothing more can
be asked of him in service to the state. "Militiae quamquam piger et
malus, utilis urbi" (Although lazy and unsuccessfull at military service,
I am useful to the city).[117] The cares and duties of other citizens are
insignificant to the poet. He has something more important in hand.

Os tenerum pueri balbumque poeta figurat,
torquet ab obscenis iam nunc sermonibus aurem,
mox etiam pectus praeceptis format amicis . . .
castis cum pueris ignara puella mariti
disceret unde preces, vatem ni Musa dedisset?
. . . avertit morbos, metuenda pericula pellit;
impetrat et pacem et locupletem frugibus annum.
carmine di superi placantur, carmine Manes.[118]

(The poet molds the child's tender lisping mouth, even now he turns his
ear away from base language. Where would the virgin learn prayers with
chaste children, if the Muse did not bestow the poet? He averts disease,
drives away fearsome dangers; he obtains peace and the year's rich harvest.
By poetry the gods are placated and the spirits of the dead.)

As propitiator of the gods, from Olympus to Hades, the poet is endowed
with magical powers. His more real because vaguer powers concern
his educative and ethical function—the same powers that characterized his primordial predecessors. The present *torquet* and *avertit* recall the past *deterruit* that summed up Orpheus's action; *format*
recalls Amphion's construction. A continuity thus extends from poetry's mythical beginnings to its present situation. By this means, Horace hopes to show that the past ideal has not been abandoned.

All the same, despite the importance of such atavistic claims, the
Carmen Saeculare is not typical of the Horatian voice or situation.
More commonly, the Horatian ode or epistle poses as communication
from man to man (occasionally, to a woman), from poet to friend or
patron. It is on this personal level that glorification comes into play.
True, private patronage does have its own primordial grounding. The
hallowed authority of the Twelve Tables decreed a relation of fair exchange between patron and client.[119] Certainly Horace, like Pindar,
represents his poetry as a privileged element in gift exchange. However, the transformations already evident in the victory odes have pursued their course. The social significance of *xeinia* has evaporated
from Horace's world, so the Roman poet's images are affected by their
embedding in a society with different sorts of exchange. Although Horace repeatedly represents poetry as *munus* or *donum,* the term that
best expresses the value of that gift may be *opes,* meaning power both
physical and monetary.[120]

The *Odes* are full of allusions to the nature of poetry, and the eighth
ode of book 4 provides a particularly rich example of what it means to
bestow a poem. It is set apart by the Lesser Asclepiadic meter, used
only here, in 1.1 and in 3.30. One notices immediately that the promise
of glory beyond the material world is expressed in terms of material

gifts. Admittedly, the opening movement is a negated hypothesis ("Donarem pateras etc. . . . divite me" [I would give drinking bowls etc., if I were rich] [1–2]); the poet assures the addressee Censorinus that he would give him costly gifts if he had the means. He does not make such material gifts not only because he is incapable of it ("non haec mihi vis"), but also because Censorinus has no need of further luxury ("nec tibi talium / res est aut animus deliciarum egens" [9–10]). If patron and poet agree on the superfluity of material gifts from the latter to the former, they also agree on the alternative:

gaudes carminibus; carmina possumus
donare et pretium dicere muneri.

(11–12)

(You rejoice in poems; we can give poems and set a price on our gift.)

Through the happy agreement of patron's taste and poet's ability, it is possible to substitute poetry for material goods—presumably in return for gifts the poet has already received. Poetry thereby remains in the realm of material exchange, and although gift giving itself is not commerce, it is described here in commercial terms. When the poet claims his ability to *pretium dicere,* his reference to a *munus* is obscured, and it is treated as a commodity. Interestingly, the ancient commentators hasten to assure us that mercenary begging is far from Horace's mind and that the expression *pretium dicere muneri* only refers to the intrinsic value of poetry.[121]

In any case, setting a price on the poem does not only mean stating how much money it is worth. In the lines that follow, Horace evaluates poetry in terms of its superiority to physical memorials (13) in guaranteeing survival to great deeds. The choice of the Punic wars as the place of those deeds is not fortuitous, because they were to a considerable extent trade wars. The commerce between poet and patron (poetic gifts for material ones) is reflected in the hero's reward (glory for valorous deeds); Scipio returned from conquered Africa *nomen . . . lucratus* (having won the profit of a name) (18–19).[122] That Scipio Africanus's fame was his sole war profit indicates not so much his virtue in rejecting booty as the superior profitability of the word. As a rule, someone who acts without the recompense of poetry is cheated of his labor.

Neque
si chartae sileant quod bene feceris,
mercedem tuleris.

(20–22)

(If pages are silent about what you do well, you will receive no payment.)

Literature as the wage of heroism makes heroism a matter of commercial calculation. The metaphor is not absent in Pindar but becomes more powerful here through the variety of its repetition.[123] Among the examples Horace puts forth is the mythical Aeacus, *ereptu[s] Stygiis fluctibus* (snatched from the Stygian current). The hero was saved by his own *virtus* and by *favor* (popular applause, a marker on the way to true glory), but most of all by *lingua potentium / vatum* (the tongue of powerful poets) (26–27). Thus he was consecrated to the *divitibus insulis*. Surely it is no accident that Horace calls these mythical islands of ease "opulent" rather than the more common *Fortunatae*.[124]

In his ability to enrich the hero with immortality, the poet qualifies as *potens*. This takes up the epithet Horace applies to himself in *Carm.* 3.30: "ex humili potens / princeps."[125] There poetic power acquires an imperial dignity; in 4.8 poets' largesse makes them omnipotent magnates. And "omnipotent" is no exaggeration in the light of what follows.

> Dignum laude virum Musa vetat mori
> caelo Musa beat.
>
> (28–29)

(The Muse forbids that a man worthy of praise should die; the Muse enriches him with the heavens.)

Here the first line looks back at the examples just given of literary rescue from death and oblivion. The hemistich (*caelo Musa beat*) looks ahead to a further aggrandizement that concludes the poem. This line and a half acts as a hinge in the passage from durable commemoration to apotheosis.

>   Sic Iovis interest
> optatis epulis impiger Hercules,
> clarum Tyndaridae sidus ab infimis
> quassas eripiunt aequoribus ratis,
> ornatus viridi tempora pampino
> Liber vota bonos ducit ad exitus.
>
> (29–34)

(Thus tireless Hercules is present at the welcome banquets of Jupiter. The bright star of Castor and Pollux snatches battered ships from the depths of the sea. Bacchus, his temples adorned with the green vine, grants a favorable outcome to prayers.)

The three cases of Hercules, the Dioscuri, and Bacchus present examples of heroes raised to the state of immortality. The poet represents himself as another Jupiter, able to hoist his favorites out of the flux of existence into the Olympian domain of glory.[126] The picture of Hercules at *optatis epulis,* along with the figure of Bacchus, takes us back to the beginning of the poem and the festive exchange of such gifts as tripods and libation-bowls. Even though Horace claims superiority to such a world, he promises only a hyperbolic form of that world. The poet as magnate surpasses the patron's ability to give gifts; finally, as the king of the gods, the poet is the most powerful of magnates and the most generous of patrons.[127]

The poem that follows, ode 9, expands on the poet's boast of power. The poetics developed there may be characterized as ahistorical and antimimetic. That is: We know nothing of the past except what literature has saved, and moreover, both in past and present the essence of things is given to them by literature. Horace begins by way of a defense of the lyric Muse. In 4.8 the principal figure of the immortalizing poet was Ennius, with his epic commemoration of Roman history. At the beginning of 4.9, Horace hastens to add that he himself shares that power even though a lyric poet. Nevertheless, he draws the subsequent examples of poetic immortality from Homer. Helen was not the first to burn for a Paris, Troy not the first unfortunate city, Hector and Deiphobus not the first to take up arms for their wives and children. . . . These culminate in the most striking formulation, and the most influential:

> Vixere fortes ante Agamemnona
> multi; sed omnes illacrimabiles
>   urgentur ignotique longa
>   nocte, carent quia vate sacro.[128]

(25–28)

(Many powerful men lived before Agamemnon, but all are unknown and unwept, oppressed by a long night, because they lack a sacred poet.)

History is imagined as a chaos, where recurrent great deeds and misfortunes lie obscured save where poetry has cast islands of light. The poet's office, what rescues the dead, does not consist of praise but of mourning. The forgotten heroes are not called unsung but unwept. But, of course, the poet's office cannot dissociate praise and mourning, as worthy deeds are inseparable from misfortune. As we have seen from Homer (whose presence here is not accidental), the poet commemorates the past as the immortalization of disaster. The poet may illuminate in defeating oblivion, but this is only to cast light on the darkness of sorrow.[129]

The leap Horace makes from the defense of lyric to examples of epic commemoration may be taken to imply the unity of all poetry from the point of view of its office. All good poets are *vates sacri*. The other leap, from the survival of ancient poets to the creation of history, springs from the pessimistic view of history described above. The only things that survive from the past are relics: monuments artistic (the inferiority of which was asserted in 4.8) and literary. So the survival of poets *is* all we have of history.

This fact leads further, to the realization that all we know of the past is the phenomena, how things appeared to poets, and not how they were in themselves; hence, a transition to the last part of the ode, praise of the addressee M. Lollius. The hinge here is formed by the lines

paulum sepultae distat inertiae
celata virtus

(29–30)

(There is little difference between hidden excellence and buried indolence),

which follows upon the exempla concluded by Agamemnon. It operates on two levels. It explicitly introduces praise of Lollius because he must be praised in order not to suffer the long night of oblivion. Virtue without a herald lies as if in the grave (in an image reminiscent of Cicero's comment on Alexander and Achilles). But there is another sense to the transition and to the praise of Lollius. Given the conclusions on history implicit in what precedes and the absolute power of poetry to create, there appears a relativity in the values of that power. If great men have no existence apart from that which poetry bestows on them, their goodness or badness entirely depends on the writer's praise or blame. Thus *virtus* and *inertia* are determined not by their presence in the person, but by whether or not he is sung and how.[130] In this way, the movement to praise Lollius provides an example of poetry's ability to create the moral character of whomever it commemorates. If we believe Velleius Paterculus and other historians, the character of Lollius was precisely opposite to the qualities Horace attributes to him. While Horace calls him

vindex avarae fraudis et abstinens
ducentis ad se cuncta pecuniae

(37–38)

(a punisher of criminal greed, not covetous of money which draws all things to it),

to Velleius he is "hom[o] in omnia pecuniae quam recte faciendi cu-
pidior" (a man always more desirous of money than of doing the right
thing).[131] It is as if Horace took up a particularly challenging subject
as a handicap to show more clearly the autonomous power of literary
praise. In fact, we doubt the veracity of his account of Lollius only
because there exist other literary documents, and these weight the
scale on the side of blame.

As in the preceding ode, economic considerations reenter the picture despite their explicit dismissal. In 4.8 the rejected golden gifts
are smuggled back into the poem in the form of panegyric opulence.
Horace's praise of Lollius in 4.9 admires his immunity to *dona nocen-
tium* (the gifts of the wicked) (42), but also his prudent use of *deorum
muner[a]* (the gifts of the gods) (47–48). Base material considerations
are sublimated through their contact with poetry, just as the tainted
patron may find his reputation polished.[132]

The poet's creation of the object of his praise means both the creation of history and the creation of the present patron. This is the
larger phenomenon that explains the evolution and reversal of the
relationship to the patron (particularly Maecenas) in the *Odes*. Literary
patronage in ancient Rome was a microcosm of social relations generally. What we call patronage was one manifestation of the larger institution of *amicitia,* which bound together patron and client in a
multitude of relationships.[133] In a reversal that Horace operates by
means of poetry's glorifying power, it turns out that "it is not the poets
who are the clients, but the patrons."[134] Now, such a reversal is naturally helped by the reversibility of the term *amicus,* which refers to
all participants in *amicitia,* the great man as well as his hangers-on.[135]
In the same way, *xenos* or *xeinos* in both Homer and Pindar means
host as well as guest.[136] Consequently, *xeinia* are gifts bestowable in
either direction.[137] In Horace's case, as seen, for example, in *Carm.*
4.8, the poet's self-fashioning sets his own sublimated gifts above anything he may receive. Such sublimation is already built into the ideology of *amicitia,* where relations of material interest are verbalized by
a term based on the intangible feeling *amo.* In contrast, *xenos* refers
first of all to an objective relation, the situation of a foreigner in need
of hospitality. The Latin pretense of spiritual equality, at least within
the limits of the common denomination *amici,* enables Horace to address a familiar verse letter even to Augustus, reminding the Princeps
of just how high poets' power raises them.[138] After all, he refers to
himself elsewhere as *Musis amicus,* meaning, of course, beloved by
the goddesses, but also a model parasite.[139]

All that has as a consequence the apparent (relative) modesty in the
first three books of the *Odes*. In this earlier collection, the poet rarely

boasts of his ability to glorify others.[140] Generally, Horace only stresses his own glorification. This is most in evidence in two crucially placed odes, those that close books 2 and 3.

In 2.20 the poet describes his metamorphosis into a bird.

Non usitata nec tenui ferar
penna biformis per liquidum aethera
   vates, neque in terris morabor
     longius invidiaque maior
urbis relinquam.

(1–5)

(I shall be borne as a poet, with a double nature, by no ordinary or feeble wing through the clear sky. I shall no longer dwell on earth and, superior to envy, I shall abandon the cities.)

The opening picture of ethereal flight prepares for the poet's declaration of his freedom from death ("nec Stygia cohibebor unda" [I shall not be held by the Stygian current] [8]). But he also shows a clear aversion to society, as when he declares he will abandon cities and the earth itself. This picture occupies the antipodes from the one evoked by the *Carmen Saeculare*. Here, the poet dreams not only of his release from earthly ties, but also of release from his own human form. The verses that describe the metamorphosis ("iam iam residunt cruribus asperae / pelles, etc." [Right now a rough skin is settling onto my legs . . .] [9–10]) are usually dismissed as tasteless by modern commentators.[141] But the grotesqueness of the transformation suits well the career effort it describes. Apotheosis, or at least metamorphosis, turns out to be the poet's only chance for social advancement.[142] One might expect his self-promotion to trumpet the social importance of his office, but here just the opposite takes place. In his aspiration to pure sovereignty, the poet's power takes him out of the world altogether. It also sets him above the patron. Horace declares: "non ego quem vocas, / dilecte Maecenas, obibo" (I shall not die, the one you summon, dear Maecenas) (6–7), and puts a distance between himself and the aristocratic but mortal Maecenas.[143] Exempt from mortality, the poet can scorn funerary convention. He follows Ennius's famous epitaph in forbidding mourning after his corporeal death.[144] The poet's name will soar, freed from the confines of time and space. He has set himself apart from the fortunes of Rome, but his fame obtains for him a similar imperium. Horace passes in review, from a bird's-eye view, the lands that will know and recite his poetry, from Spain to Scythia, from Africa to Hyperborea (which is itself a land of immortality). The poet justifies his superiority to the *amicus* and caps his boast of autonomy by internalizing the Roman Empire.

Carm. 2.20 represents one extreme of the poet's claim to power, by which he contradicts his claim of integration in the *res publica*. On the other hand, the last ode of book 3, which may appear similar, appears to attempt a step back to greater equilibrium. This poem, "Exegi monumentum," is, along with the golden passages of *Pro Archia*, perhaps the most famous of the ancient *loci* for the poet's immortalizing power. However, it should not be viewed as an isolated poem but in its context as epilogue to the first three books of odes. It gains meaning from its architectonic function. Odes 1.1 and 3.30 frame the entire work. They are the only odes in the collection written in the Lesser Asclepiadic meter. Along with 2.20, they are the odes that raise the issue of poetic immortality. In 1.1 it is in the form of a request to Maecenas: If the poet receives the benefits of patronage,

> si me lyricis vatibus inseres,
> sublimi feriam sidera vertice.

(1.1.35–36)

(If you include me among the lyric poets, I shall strike the stars with my sublime head.)

But by 3.30 Maecenas has disappeared from the scene. What has become of him? The collection he inaugurated (his name is the first word in 1.1) has left him behind.[145] We have seen in 2.20 how Horace's faith in his poetic powers takes him beyond the world of Maecenas. That is the evolution evident in all the odes addressed to Maecenas in books 1 through 3. What begins in book 1 as the poet's respect for his patron and recognition of material dependence is reversed by book 3 to expression of the patron's spiritual dependence on the poet.[146] While he begins by invoking the patron, "atavis edite regibus" (the offspring of ancestral kings), the poet eventually decides that he is the one with a more deeply atavistic legitimation. This shift climaxes in the pair 3.29 and 3.30. The former poem is the last where Maecenas is mentioned, but there he is forced to hear Horace lecture him on the vanity of his way of life. The poet calls on Maecenas to follow the example given in 2.20 and flee the city (3.29.11–12). By the poem's end, Horace makes bold to offer himself in his modest self-sufficiency as a positive model.

After the self-possession of *vixi* (3.29.43), the most obvious declaration of 3.30 is *vivam*, "I shall live" (*non omnis moriar* [6]).[147] The previous ode's aquatic imagery is replaced by the *monumentum aere perennius,* and the didactic tone disappears. The poet speaks of himself to a timeless audience. He compares his poem to the pyramids, those pharaonic tombs where the great attained immortality. There is, to be sure, a measure of hubris in this poem that contrasts with the Epicurean modesty of the preceding poem, but not to such an extent as may appear. It is an exaggeration to say that this ode "is basically uncertain and diffident in tone,"[148] but there is no mistaking the progressive rhetorical reduction of the opening boast. In lines 1–7 the poet brags of his immunity to the elements and to time,[149] which obviously amounts to immortality:

> Non omnis moriar, multaque pars mei
> vitabit Libitinam.
>
> (6–7)

(I shall not die altogether, and a large part of me will shun the funeral goddess.)

But already an attenuation appears in *non omnis* and *multa pars*. Soon, the claim shrinks from an outlasting of nature to a longevity matching that of Rome:

>   dum Capitolium
> scandet cum tacita virgine pontifex.
>
> (8–9)

(As long as the priest climbs to the Capitol with a silent virgin.)

The spatial domain, too, dwindles to the Roman world. The third stage produces a further limitation, when Horace boasts of his honor to come (*dicar*) in his native Apulia. Here he makes no mention of long-lasting fame, and the region of glory has shrunk to an imperial province. Why this dramatic decrescendo in such a critically placed boast?

The decrescendo provides only half the truth. There is a simultaneous growth in power through increasing specificity. The opening trumpet blast about the enduring monument moves in the vague world of natural elements and the *innumerabilis annorum series* (incalculable series of years) (4–5). But when he comes to evoke Rome, Horace gains a point of reference as well as a revered image. To last as long as Rome's most hallowed rites means something. Something similar results from the subsequent concentration on the region where the poet himself has his roots. Ode 2.20 also effects a movement from abstract hyperbole (albeit with the brief graphic account of metamorphosis) to a specific naming of names. But there it is less satisfactory, since the poet's survey of the lands he will fly over maintains the same pitch as

the earlier part of the poem. In 3.30 Horace has discovered in variety
the secret to successful self-promotion.

However, variety here is more a matter of complexity than of simple
copia. The intersection of the two opposite movements just described
(from larger to smaller claims and from lesser to greater specificity)
maintains a tension that benefits the poem. At the center of those
movements and of the ode itself is the poet's identification of his posthumous survival with Rome. It may be worthwhile to dwell briefly on
this point. The trope is not unique to Horace. It turns up in the *Aeneid,*
and Ovid will give his version of it.[150] In Horace's case, identification
with Eternal Rome acts as a palinode to his utterances elsewhere urging escape from the city, as in 2.20 and 3.29. Of course, there are
numerous odes expressing concern for the Roman state, most notably
the Roman Odes which begin book 3. But the significance of 3.30 lies
in the fact that here the *res publica* has a part in the poet's highest
aspirations. He does not put in a word on civic matters just because
he knows men like Maecenas and Augustus, whom he leaves behind
in his more individual, autonomous flight. Rather, as high as he flies,
he finds before him the image of the *res publica.*

On the other hand, the role reversal with the patron is here carried
even further. The introduction of Rome as well as the monument's
regali[s] *situ*[s] (2) gives an inevitable imperial flavor to the subsequent term *princeps,* which Horace applies several times elsewhere to
Augustus, but here to himself:[151]

> princeps Aeolium carmen ad Italos
> deduxisse modos.
>
> (13–14)

(The first to have converted Aeolian poetry into Latin measures.)

The first in time becomes the first in power. The *translatio* of Greek
poetry to Italy becomes a conqueror's triumphal procession. Thus,
when at the poem's end, Horace invites the Muse to crown him with
laurel, this could be the *imperator*'s reward as well as the poet's. After
all, a triumph would ascend to the Capitol as do the priest and virgin
of lines 8–9. So in that way, too, a movement of aggrandizement offsets
the reduction of scope in the ode. As the last piece in the original
collection of odes, 3.30 holds a special significance. The poet's assurance of his immortality, his use of Rome to establish both his civic
roots and his poetic imperialism, reflect back on the great variety of
lyrics that precede.

Nor is the issue of exchange absent. *Aere perennius* means superior not only to bronze monuments, but also to money. *Aes* is tainted as the commercial form of exchange that Horace condemns throughout his works. Nevertheless, as we have seen, his promotion of poetry's dealings as purified bestowal cannot escape commercial metaphors. Yet the poet's sovereign boast cannot not claim that purification. Assuming the persona of *princeps* has among its other attractions the attainment of an elevation where money poses no problem—elevation higher than a pyramid, which is a treasury as well as a tomb;[152] elevation coexisting with ascent to the Capitol, where war booty was sanctified.

Still, there is no getting around Horace's representation of his poetry as a supreme tomb. The pyramid holds not only riches, but also a corpse. Words construct a monument superior to one of bronze, but a monument all the same.[153] Horace's heritage to his innumerable literary posterity will consist prominently of this monumental tomb and its rapprochement of poetry with the death it claims to overcome.[154] Finally, let us take the pyramid, as Hegel did, as a prime image of archaic art itself.[155] Then the heritage of Horace's boast will also include an atavistic retreat from the very heart of classicism.

The contradictions observed throughout Horatian poetry, between integration in and abandonment of the *res publica,* between a purer form of exchange and commercial calculation, between the poet as servant of virtue and as *amicus* of the powerful, find formal expression here in a simultaneous increase and decrease of the boast for poetic power. The increase ascends with Roman hegemony; decrease dwindles into death. In the final image of this ode, closing the most influential lyric collection of antiquity, the poet imperiously commands the Muse to crown him with laurel: "et mihi Delphica / lauro cinge volens, Melpomene, comam" (15–16). Yet the goddess he names, Melpomene, is the Muse of tragedy.[156]

OVID AND LITERARY EXILE

Horace and Ovid are complementary figures. If for the former the topos of poetic immortalization represents his ticket to reconciliation with temporal power, for Ovid it provides consolation in disgrace and exile. Moreover, if Horace's attempt at a harmonious use ends as a metaphorical reversal of the status quo, Ovid's exiled verses are also a bid for reintegration in Rome.

That is not to say that Ovid boasts only in exile of poetry's power. One of the classic expressions occurs in the final lines of his *Metamorphoses:*

Iamque opus exegi, quod nec Iovis ira nec ignis
nec poterit ferrum nec edax abolere vetustas,
cum volet, illa dies, quae nil nisi corporis huius
ius habet, incerti spatium mihi finiet aevi:
parte tamen meliore mei super alta perennis
astra ferar, nomenque erit indelebile nostrum,
quaque patet domitis Romana potentia terris,
ore legar populi, perque omnia saecula fama,
siquid habent veri vatum praesagia, vivam.[157]

(I have erected a work which neither the anger of Jupiter, nor fire, nor the
sword, nor voracious old age will be able to destroy. That day, which has
authority over nothing but this body, will finish when it will the uncertain
span of my life. Yet I shall be borne immortal in my better part above the
lofty stars, and my name will be imperishable. Wherever Roman power
extends over conquered lands I shall be read out loud by human lips, and
in my fame, if poets' prophecies hold any truth, until the end of time I
shall live.)

The influence of Horace's ode 3.30 is unmistakeable. In both passages,
repeated negation opposes the elements that normally consume things
in time.[158] In both, the poet asserts that only his body will die.[159] And
both Horace and Ovid join their posthumous fate to the extent of the
empire. However, while Horace's *dicar* maintains the the pretense of
oral immortality, Ovid's *legar* illustrates the progress of a book culture.

Another Ovidian element that Horace does not share is the poem's
declared exemption from *Iovis ira*. The expression may serve as not
only a periphrasis for thunderbolts, but also an allusion to imperial
wrath. The identification of Augustus and Jupiter is not at all far-
fetched, especially since the lines immediately preceding this passage
have described the emperor's anticipated apotheosis. Without secure
information about Ovid's later troubles, one can only speculate.[160] But,
to say the least, the *Metamorphoses* has its antiauthoritarian moments. Its moments of adulation did not provide a sufficient counter-
weight, and this meteorological self-assurance was equally vain. The
poet later alludes to his disgrace as a thunderbolt descending from
Augustus's Palatine hill onto his head.[161] Ovid ought to have paid closer
attention to the warnings of his older colleague, Horace. The latter
portrays Augustus more than once as a fulminating divinity aiming to
restore traditional virtue and religion.[162]

However that may be, the exile of Ovid in A.D. 8 is of primarily
literary interest because it provides the principal theme of his later
poetry. The aspect that draws our attention here is the nature of the
immortality topos as consolation in exile. Although this poetry is most

obviously characterized by its insistently querelous tone, the poet's exile has a more interesting effect. The personal crisis becomes a crisis of poetry, which circulates repeatedly around expressions of its nature and powers. His actual impotence compels the poet to radicalize his boasts and concomitant despair. In the long poem constituting book 2 of the *Tristia,* Ovid declares that he has been punished for two crimes: *carmen* and *error.*[163] What that *error* may have been we are unable to know. The question must concern the other term; what makes possible the equivalence *crimen/carmen*?[164]

The poet's wretchedness upon banishment from Rome is, among other things, a linguistic wretchedness. Exile was his only punishment, but it was sufficiently harsh.[165] In Tomis, on the shore of the Black Sea, and so on the edge of the empire, even the Latin language was a tenuous possession. Curiously, Ovid anticipates Renaissance humanists in his awareness of how precarious the glory of Latin may be, surrounded (and corrupted) by barbarian tongues. It seems to him sometimes that he has unlearned his native language and is menaced by silence.[166] But exile did not deprive him completely of the one compensation that made life possible. When he felt poetic inspiration, he was elevated above suffering.[167] The gifts of the Muses were *solacia, curae requies* (rest from anxiety), *medicina.*[168] The poet's body pined on the Danube, but his spirit was borne to Helicon.[169] In this way the portrayal of poetry as hypostasis, with its magical healing and other powers, becomes subjectified. What this leads to is the central role of glory. At the end of an important autobiographical poem in the *Tristia,* Ovid goes on to thank the Muse for having made him famous in his lifetime and to anticipate his posthumous glory. He echoes his words from the *Metamorphoses:*

> si quid habent igitur vatum praesagia veri,
> protinus ut moriar, non ero, terra, tuus.[170]

(If the prophecies of poets hold any truth, as soon as I die I shall not be yours, o earth.)

While the boast of the earlier poem resounded in a timeless realm, here the poet of a specific situation is foremost. The posited duality of body and spirit gains poignancy from present pain. The confined body has already loudly voiced its suffering, and the promised escape from earth, which is here the land of exile, becomes the more pathetic for that.

The final poem *Ex Ponto* contains a similar assurance. Against the menace of the envious, Ovid asserts:

non solet ingeniis summa nocere dies,
famaque post cineres maior venit.[171]

(The final day is not apt to harm talent; after the ashes comes a greater
fame.)

There follows a list of earlier Latin poets, in whose tradition Ovid takes
his place. (The irony is that these poets would be unknown were it not
for their mention here.) This poem closely resembles the last poem of
the first book of *Amores*. There, too, are listed poets (Greek and Latin)
whose fame survives. In both, as in Horace's ode 4.9, a "literary history"
is adduced as evidence of poetry's enduring glory. In the *Amores* Ovid
defends himself against the accusation that he has misused his gift of
eloquence. He responds that, on the contrary, to use that gift in the
courts or in the forum would have been to prostitute it. Poetry alone
is superior to time and so to the taint of commercial actuality.

Mortale est, quod quaeris, opus; mihi fama perennis
    quaeritur, in toto semper ut orbe canar.[172]

(What you request is a mortal work. I seek an everlasting fame, so that I
will be sung always all over the earth.)

The extratemporal superiority of poetry should ultimately make kings
admit their subjection to it: "cedant carminibus reges regumque triumphi" (let kings and the triumphs of kings yield to poetry).[173] This
does not refer openly to contemporary Rome, since the Romans
shunned with ostensible horror the title of king. But in the *Tristia*,
one of the exile's consolations derives from the immunity of his poetic
ingenium to Caesar's power:

ingenio tamen ipse meo comitorque fruorque:
    Caesar in hoc potuit iuris habere nihil.[174]

(I accompany my talent and reap its benefits; Caesar has no authority over
it.)

One is reminded of what the *Metamorphoses* boasts, the poem's secu-
rity from imperial thunderbolts.

However, the exile who has not completely renounced his past does
his best to win readmission to the *res publica*. Ovid's declarations of
autonomy form part of an argument that the state really needs him.
Ex Ponto 4.8, the central part of which is addressed to the imperial
heir Germanicus, pleads the necessity of the poet's office of praise.

That plea comprises a number of familiar arguments. First, the poet declines to bestow material memorials, both because of his poverty and because of the superiority of his verbal monuments.[175] The poet then makes explicit what he has suggested with the gesture of bestowal: his obligation to render gifts (*reddi munera* [35]) for the favors he hopes to receive.[176] Moreover, in vindicating his little gift of verse, he compares it to humble offerings made to the gods (39–44). The imperial patron thus finds himself cast as a divinity; as does his grandfather, when Ovid mentions the apotheosis of Augustus while referring to his poems in the emperor's praise (63–64).[177] We find a movement similar to that of Horace in this portrayal of sublimated exchange. It is capped by the revelation that Germanicus himself is a poet, and so an ally in the poet's plea to him. Ovid can even introduce *pretium*, purified into ethical value by its contact with the prince:

> non potes officium vatis contemnere vates:
> iudicio pretium res habet ista tuo.
>
> (67–68)

(Yourself a poet, you cannot despise the poet's office; this matter receives its due by your authority.)[178]

The twin tendencies—aggrandizement of the addressee (with a correspondent self-abasement) and the poet's self-aggrandizement (with the addressee correspondingly portrayed as dependent)—interweave continually. On this shifting foundation Ovid attempts to erect the monument of poetry's self-praise. The value of poetic praise swells through several stages. First, the abstract declaration of its enduring power:

> carmina vestrarum peragunt praeconia laudum,
>   neve sit actorum fama caduca cavent.
> carmine fit vivax virtus, expersque sepulcri
>   notitiam serae posteritatis habet.
> tabida consumit ferrum lapidemque vetustas,
>   nullaque res maius tempore robur habet.
> scripta ferunt annos.[179]
>
> (45–51)

(Poems declare your praises, and ensure that the fame of your actions will not be transitory. Excellence is brought alive by the poem, is free from the tomb and known to distant posterity. Wasting old age consumes iron and stone; nothing is stronger than time. What has been written bears up against the years.)

Next come epic historical, mainly Homeric, examples of what poetry has preserved.

> Scriptis Agamemnona nosti,
> et quisquis contra vel simul arma tulit.
> quis Thebas septemque duces sine carmine nosset,
> et quicquid post haec, quicquid et ante fuit?
>
> (51–54)

(Through what has been written you have known Agamemnon, and whoever bore arms against him or with him. Who would know Thebes and the seven chiefs, and whatever happened before and after, without a poem?)

Finally comes the most daring assertion: poetry creates not only history, but even the gods themselves.

> Di quoque carminibus, si fas est dicere, fiunt,
> tantaque maiestas ore canentis eget.
>
> (54–55)

(The gods themselves, if it is permitted to speak so, are created by poems, and even such great dignity needs the voice of their singer.)

There follow examples from "sacred" history—the chaos at the world's beginning, the Gigantomachia, the triumphs of Bacchus and Hercules—which illustrate the literary creation of myths.

The structure of that monument of poetic self-praise appears, then, as a conceptual elevation. From the tomb planted in earth, the poet's gaze rises to heroic, that is, literary history and, finally, to the gods in their celestial dwelling. But there remains the application of that sublimating movement. If any doubt existed that the Olympian pantheon exists as an allegory of the imperial one, it is dispelled when, at the end of the enumeration of demigods, Augustus follows on the heels of Hercules.

> Et modo, Caesar, avum, quem virtus addidit astris,
> sacrarunt aliqua carmina parte tuum.
>
> (63–64)

(And now, my lord, poems have deified in some way your grandfather, whose excellence has placed him among the stars.)

Although it is Augustus's *virtus* that has put him among the stars, poetry has enshrined him there and made him *divus*, an imperial

Jupiter who, the poet hopes, may be more inclined to thunder than to hurl lightning bolts.[180] Ovid presents this accomplishment as a climax to his argument and an unmistakeable case where *di quoque carminibus . . . fiunt.* The claim to glorify is both an offer of service and a reversal of the hierarchy. The exile's submission is his proudest, defiant boast, his bid to take part in a Roman triumph.[181]

However, Ovid died in Tomis. As he foresaw, his poetry, like Horace's, is his sepulcher, *monimenta.*[182]

Ovid is a significant figure with which to leave antiquity. According to Curtius, his poetry marks the absorption of rhetoric into literature.[183] That means the abstraction of eloquence from praxis, the apparently complete establishment of "mere" literature, where the poet no longer overthrows tyrants, like Alcaeus, or moves rocks and trees, like Orpheus. The transition harmonizes with the emblem of Ovid as poet in exile. It is as if Cicero had lost his case for Archias. The poet finds himself banished from the *res publica.* His claims that his office is essential are not heeded. As Roman imperium rises to its zenith, its greatest living poet languishes far from Rome. Roman military-political power, which laid one sort of foundation for the enduring Latin tradition, divorces from itself the other foundation—the literary root of the topical tradition. Centuries later, the Renaissance humanists take up Ovid's attempt to repair the cleavage of poetry and power. In various ways, the Renaissance will try to return the poet to Rome.

2

Petrarca

The threshold, Rome, and that more merciful Rome
Beyond, the two alike in the make of the mind.

BEING A POET, AND TIME

FEW writers have been as aware as Petrarca that time is the element of poetry. That means not simply that verbal art unfolds in duration, but that the work once written maintains an intimate relationship with the past and future. Petrarca's community with the ancients and posterity is a passion, perhaps his major passion.[1] For him the literary present is, to use Leibniz's words, "chargé du passé et gros de l'avenir."[2]

Book 24 of the *Familiares* sharply articulates the distance of ancient authors from the modern world. Among the letters to Roman writers, the famous valediction of the first letter to Cicero (24.3) may serve as typical:

> Apud superos, ad dexteram Athesis ripam, in civitate Verona Transpadane Italie, XVI Kalendas Quintiles, anno ab ortu Dei illius quem tu non noveras, MCCCXLV.[3]

> (Among those in the upper world, on the right bank of the Adige, in the city of Verona in Italy beyond the Po, on 16 June, in the year 1345 since the birth of that God whom you did not know.)

Despite the Roman terms used to locate himself in space and time, Petrarca begins and ends the formula by emphasizing the impossibility of intimacy: Cicero is dead and Petrarca is alive, their embrace blocked by the barrier of Christianity and time.

And yet Petrarca pursues the company of those shades.[4] What he seeks and finds in their community he expresses in the letter to Livy (24.8): "vite solatium et iniqui temporis oblivio" (consolation for my life and obliviousness of an unjust time).[5] He flees from an unbearable

74

present to find a place among kindred spirits in a friendship exempt from time. Thus to Asinius Pollio (24.9): "amicitie lex . . . qua clarorum omnis evi hominum cineri ac fame non aliter ac presentium obstringor" (the law of friendship, by which I am attached to the ashes and fame of illustrious men of every age, as well as to those who are present). A friendship, then, but not immune to the pathos of time, or from dissent, as Petrarca's harsh criticism of Cicero's political meddling shows (24.3).

There is a complementary movement to embrace the future in the *Epistola posteritati,* which belongs to the poet's later years.[6] The letter, a voice from the grave, begins with an admission that survival for posterity is a tenuous possibility:

> Fuerit tibi forsan de me aliquid auditum; quanquam et hoc dubium sit: an exiguum et obscurum longe nomen seu locorum seu temporum perventurum sit.[7]

> (You may perhaps have heard something about me, although even this is uncertain, whether a slight and obscure name can penetrate far in space and time.)

This introduction of an *exiguum nomen* is not based on modesty, but on a recognition that the relation of posterity to him will be the same as his relation to antiquity.[8] He may be a Varro of the future, a name whose works lie buried.[9]

This *ego-tu* address to a future reader results from dissatisfaction with the present. Just as he has sought the ancient to escape the contemporary,[10] so he raises his voice to posterity to overcome the empty effect of common fame.[11]

More positively, however, the relationship to posterity is founded on love. Petrarca depends on this love to make him live in the future, just as his love for the ancients has brought them to life in his day. In his preface to *De viris illustribus,* addressed to the reader, he expresses this desire and faith:

> Nullum a te aliud premii genus efflagito, nisi ut diligar, licet incognitus, licet sepulcro conditus, licet versus in cineres, sicut ego multos, quorum me vigiliis adiutum senseram, non modo defunctos sed diu ante consumptos per annum millesimum dilexi.[12]

> (I demand no other sort of reward from you than that I might be loved; unknown, hidden in the tomb, turned into ashes though I may be—just as I have loved many not only deceased but long annihilated a thousand years ago, by whom I have felt myself encouraged in my studious wakefulness.)

In this connection, we may better understand the central importance of the Latin language for Petrarca—not as an erudite or antiquarian habit, but as the only way of expression endowed with literary endurance. Latin is a door of access from the present to the past and from the future to the present.[13] It has long been a critical commonplace to consider Petrarca's greatest work his Italian poetry, particularly the *Canzoniere*.[14] The concomitant tendency, which has weakened only recently, has been to consider Petrarca's Latinity as a mistake a priori, as an aberration common to all humanists. De Sanctis expresses this well in his *Storia della letteratura italiana* where he writes of the arid work of imitation performed by the Renaissance Latinist: "Dice non quanto o come gli sgorga dal di dentro, ma ciò che può rendersi in quella forma e secondo quel modello."[15] From this romantic point of view, the Renaissance was to find the true voice of self-expression in the emergence of a national vernacular, welling up out of subjectivity like the spring of Vaucluse ("sgorga dal di dentro"). Leaving aside that larger issue, I mean only to suggest that the use of Latin based on classical models was not necessarily cold pedantry. Croce, for example, opposes the idea that Latin had become a dead language by the Renaissance: "Diventava una sorta di lingua sacra, profanamente o laicamente sacra, circonfusa di amore e di riverenza."[16] This is, of course, a sort of language quite different from the vernacular, but perhaps not less vital. A language of the dead, for conversation with the dead; but for that very reason Latin was undying.

Such talk about reverence for a "sacred language" may lead us to suspect a mythical substratum to Petrarca's attitude toward language and time. And indeed we find in Cassirer's treatment of mythical thought a crucial role for time consciousness. The relevant elements of that consciousness may be summarized as follows: a lack of sharp distinction between past, present, and future; contemplation of the essential role of origins; and a certain malleability at the hands of individual subjectivity.[17]

It is the first element that is most evident in Petrarca's symmetrical relation to past and future. "The stages of time—past, present, future—do not remain distinct; over and over again the mythical consciousness succumbs to the tendency and temptation to level the differences and ultimately transform them into pure identity."[18] For the humanist, it remains only a tendency, resisted (as we shall see) by a growing historical sense. Yet the temptation of temporal reversibility is a constant presence for Petrarca; it is the foundation of his greatest passions.

For mythical thought, the contemplation of the past and thus of time generally, is organized by a belief in ultimate origins. The gods are only to be understood through theogony, the world only through cosmogony. The present can be known from its history, but that history is only conceived primordially. "The true character of mythical being is first revealed when it appears as the being of origins."[19] Moreover, and perhaps more important, the mythical relation to origins is not simply a relation of knowing, but also of acting—most notably through the effectiveness of magical speech.[20] Of course, the anthropological sense of Petrarca and of all Renaissance humanism has a limited reach. In particular, the Greekless Petrarca cannot gain more than a scattered sense of the *mentalités* of any gentile culture before the early Romans. It is thus those Roman forefathers who become hallowed with the aura of primordial founders and the Latin tradition as a whole that is informed by its foundations.

The subjectivity of Petrarca's "historical" sense does not at all mean that it is limited to idiosyncrasy. It is in the nature of mythical thought to perceive time as dictated by a particular limited point of view and not abstractly or universally.[21] Moreover, causality is understood according to the principle of post hoc, ergo propter hoc.[22] Since individual needs and desires determine temporal relations, or what is post hoc, it follows that causation (propter hoc), and in particular historical causation, is essentially subjective. This, too, may help us understand Petrarca's expression of his overwhelming Romolatry.

As explained in the introduction, word magic provides evidence of a (relatively) unified mythical consciousness, or a basic category of perception. For Petrarca, as for other humanists, the trace of archaic magical attitudes persists in the topos of literary immortalization. More particularly, this chapter follows the itinerary that that topos devises for our poet. The element of mythical thought on which I am concentrating, namely, time consciousness, is intimately tied up in Petrarca's varied uses of boasts for poetic effectiveness. The complex thus introduced leads us along lines suggested by the other theoretical guides. The appeal to foundational origins suggests the *sapienza poetica* of Vico and the role of poetry in founding human culture and ultimately the *res publica*. That primordial civic function places the poet in a relation of patronage, based on the principle of gift exchange as elaborated by Mauss. And the pursuit of such remembered roles into the contradictory work of art will lead to a dialectical reading of the epic *Africa*.

In Petrarca's career, we can see the constellation of temporal-linguistic concerns—the passion for the past and future of the Latin tradition as compensation for the present—fixed in one central event: his coronation as poet laureate in Rome on 8 April 1341.[23] The event is central not just for Petrarca the man, but for everything he wrote. It is comparable in importance with the first sight of Laura, another drama on another day in April that also promised victory over time.[24] The coronation was a ritual that realized, for Petrarca and his contemporaries, the vindication for poetry of a place in the *res publica.* When we consider the staged, literary nature of the event and the enormous distance separating fourteenth-century Rome from the ancient city, we may consider the ritual purely symbolic and somewhat hollow. But, as we shall see, the poet was not insensitive to the pathos of historical distance and to the futility, in a sense, of his endeavor.[25] I shall here consider the coronation for what it reveals of Petrarca's thought on the ideal function of poet and poetry and to introduce the poem where that ideal is embodied: the *Africa,* the epic whose conception principally earned the poet his crown.

Roman Honor (*Privilegium, Collatio*)

The facts of the coronation, insofar as they can be determined, are the following.[26] After some maneuvering, Petrarca received in late 1340 offers of the poetic crown from both Paris (the Sorbonne) and Rome. He soon chose the latter, both for the reminder of ancient Roman custom and for the opportunity to meet King Robert of Naples. Having set out in February 1341, Petrarca went to Naples and there spoke with the king, or was examined by him, for three days. Robert was satisfied and issued the order for Petrarca's honor. Neither the king nor his representative could be present in Rome, so the Roman "senator" Orso dell'Anguillara conducted the ceremony. There were two speeches delivered. Petrarca made an oration, known to us as the *Collatio,* which was probably followed by the *Privilegium laureae* read by Count Orso. The former is naturally Petrarca's work, and he had at least a substantial part in composing the latter.[27] Both documents make explicit the meaning of the coronation for Petrarca as the ideal of temporal reversibility, made possible through the power of poetic language.

The *Privilegium* is a short document that officially confers the laureate honors on Petrarca. The *Collatio edita per clarissimum Franciscum Petrarcam Florentinum Rome in Capitolio tempore laureationis sue* shows a more systematic structure and greater attention to style.[28] The two works stress a number of the same points: the duality of man (body and soul) and of his glory (military and literary); the power of poets to immortalize themselves and others, and thus the need for them to save worthy men from oblivion; the parity of *cesares* and *poete* in the laureate triumph; the long desuetude of this custom; and the significance of the laurel.[29]

The public realm provides the point of departure and culmination of the *Privilegium*. The poet's triumph is made possible by the fundamental equivalence of military and intellectual glory, asserted from the start. At the conclusion, there is recorded an appeal to the Roman people, who unanimously voiced their approval of the poet's admission into the *res publica*. "De quibus omnibus et singulis interrogatus, P. R. solemniter ut mos est, nemine protinus adversante, placere sibi omnia acclamando, respondit" (When asked about all this, the Roman people answered solemnly, as is its custom, declaring unanimously by acclamation that it approved everything).[30] The poet's partnership with *duces* and his admission as a Roman are both due to his poetic office, that is, to the temporal and supratemporal nature of poetry. The poetics of this document reduces to essentially an emphasis on the immortalizing, memorializing power of literature; that is, what turns out to be poetry's social function.[31]

Although Petrarca trains the spotlight on literary men, the place of the ceremony makes it inevitable that he should refer to ancient Roman military glories at the receiving end of writers' largesse. Only because of such writers do we have any knowledge of the founders of Rome and its empire and of all great men and their mores. The classical past is the place of the proper functioning of that dynamic. On the other hand, the lack of literary memorials in the present day condemns men to oblivion. There thus ensues the paradox that we can be ignorant of worthy contemporaries, although familiar with past heroes: "Hinc sepe contingit, ut laudes eorum hominum, qui nobiscum vixerunt ignorantes, mira res dictu vetustissimorum certam notitiam habeamus" (Hence it often happens that, while we are unaware of the praiseworthiness of men who have lived with us, we amazingly have reliable knowledge of some from long ago) (1254). What this means more generally is that poets are free to move in the past and future, lighting up realms otherwise obscure: "Et poete quidem preteriti gloria temporis pariter illustres sunt, et futuri, quoniam ut diximus, immortalitatem, et sibi et aliis querebant" (And indeed poets are brilliant with the glory of past time as well as future, since, as we said, they sought immortality for themselves and others) (1254). For this temporal mobility they deserve the honors they have received in the past, and particularly the laurel crown. The laurel's evergreen foliage represents the perpetuity of literary glory; that the tree is never struck by lightning indicates literature's immunity to the passage of time, "que more fulminis cuncta prosternit" (which like lightning strikes down all things) (1255).[32]

However, this tradition of rewarding poets has been interrupted for thirteen hundred years.[33] Such a lack of reverence for poets is due to an ignorance of the real nature of poetry. Poetry is not, as many affirm, an art of beautiful lies, but rather (true to allegorical tradition) a veil concealing wisdom. In opposition to the vulgar disregard for poetry, Petrarca has desired to revive in his own person the ancient custom. Thanks to the endorsement of the appropriate *dux*, King Robert, the poet now receives his various privileges. Petrarca is crowned by the *comes et senator* Orso and is granted in addition the right to teach, dispute, and live like a poet ("in actu atque habitu quolibet Poetico, et publice solenniter exercere" [1256]) in Rome and elsewhere. Finally, and not least important, he is made a Roman citizen.

In the *Collatio,* Petrarca proceeds by interpreting a passage from Virgil's *Georgics* (3.291 f.): "Sed me Parnasi deserta per ardua dulcis / raptat amor" (But sweet love carries me away up the bare slopes of Parnassus) (1). Such a strategy shows that the triumph proceeds, not from a historical reality, but from intimate contact with a previous text.

The poet alleges three reasons for the difficulty (*deserta, ardua*) of his ascent: the nature of poetry, the opposition of Fortune, and the baseness of the present day (2–4). If the first concerns poetry as divine endowment (with a significant citation of *Pro Archia*),[34] the arrows of Fortune amount to no more than the poet's lack of a fortune and so become part of the third obstacle, the cursed present time. Parnassus thereby takes on alpine dimensions. The poetic mountain climbing that Petrarca proposes, then, is an effort to combat the gravity of time and the material injustice associated with it.[35]

The motive of ascent, love (*dulcis amor*), also has three roots: the honor of the state, the beauty of one's own glory, and the desire to spur on other's literary efforts.[36] In the combination of these elements, Petrarca follows the same strategy as Cicero in *Pro Archia.* The pursuit of glory, common to all humanity, becomes compatible with both patriotism and intertextual benefaction. That harmony of literary and political is encapsulated in the introduction of the Virgilian line: "Vincet amor patrie laudumque inmensa cupido" (7).[37]

The poet's just reward is likewise threefold, consisting of personal glory, immortality of name, and the laurel (10). The poet's immortalizing power obviously comprises two varieties, as its object is either the poet's own name or that of someone else. Petrarca brings forth the *loci classici:* for self-immortalization, Ovid and Statius; for another's name, Virgil and Statius again; and for both at once, Lucan (10).[38] What follows from this is the need for poets, so great deeds may live on. Inarticulate greatness is not enough. In Horace's (slightly altered) words, "Vixere multi fortes ante Agamemnona, sed omnes illacrimabili nocte premuntur" (Many powerful men lived before Agamemnon, but all are

oppressed by a tearless night) because they lacked poets.[39] This naturally introduces the *Pro Archia* again and its scene of Alexander at
Achilles' tomb. The ideal repeated here is the harmony of the leader
and the poet he supports, imagined by Claudian as the marriage of
virtue and the Muses:

Gaudet enim virtus testes sibi iungere Musas;
  Carmen amat quisquis carmine digna gerit.

$$(10)^{40}$$

(Excellence rejoices to join the Muses to itself as witnesses; whoever
achieves deeds worthy of a poem loves poetry.)

It is clear that, just as the laureate ceremony realizes Petrarca's ideal
of the place of poetry, so the laurel itself reduces all that has been said
to an object of great symbolic significance. The laurel as expounded in
the *Collatio* (11) possesses the following qualities: (1) the laurel is
fragrant (like good repute), (2) it is shady and lends a resting place to
laborers (as to caesars and poets after their exertions), (3) its leaves
are incorruptible and preserve whatever they touch (books, for example), (4) it is a sacred tree, to be held in awe, (5) when a sleeper is
touched by laurel, his dreams come true, (6) it is evergreen, (7) and
immune to lightning.[41] Throughout this explication of the laurel Petrarca repeatedly refers to the fact that *cesares* and *poete* together are
so honored. As in one of his sonnets, the laurel is "sola insegna al
gemino valore."[42]

What the two ceremonial documents show is how the various commonplaces on poetry belong together. The glorifying power of poetry
cannot be declared without its defense against the calumniators of
poetry as lies.[43] The celebration of the poet's indispensability to *res
publica* and *dux* is accompanied by bewailing the long-lost awareness
of this. For Petrarca, the praise of poetry is dialectical; it thrives on
and even exists through opposition. The poet's triumph on the Capitoline has sense only as a vindication of poetry; the opposition still
remains, however, with Parnassus still steep and barren. The dialectic
persists even in what would seem the moment of full affirmation in
Rome. Moreover, with time Petrarca's doubts about the meaning of the
honor grow. In the *Epistola posteritati,* he confesses that the laurel
brought him no wisdom, only envy.[44] Other later passages declare a
similar disaffection with youthful vanity.[45] As we shall see, those
doubts darken the poet's bright faith in the power and value of poetry,
making a Petrarchan chiaroscuro of the noontime triumph.

But what is particularly worth retaining from the *Privilegium* and

Collatio is how the image of temporal power remains insistently present for poetics. Whether it be the will of the Roman people or the poet's imperial partner in laureate triumph or the performers of great deeds who give the poet his calling, the image is not external, but part of poetry itself. If, then, Petrarca portrays his coronation as an ideal moment of reconciliation with past and future through literary glory, it is also an essentially social and political moment. The poet's meditation on his art is always also a meditation on his place in the *res publica*. A declaration of the powers of poetry brings with it an awareness of the other powers in the world where poetry exists. Even Petrarca's orchestration of the laureate process makes that much clear. His preference of Rome over Paris as the bestower of his honor was based on the greatness of ancient Rome and on his desire to meet King Robert.[46] His three-day examination by the king gave Petrarca a royal patron and a guarantee that what he planned was not merely literary. It was King Robert's proxy, Giovanni Barrili, who was supposed to crown the poet in Rome; only his difficulties on the trip from Naples made necessary the participation of Orso dell'Anguillara—who in any case symbolized the power of the ancient Roman Senate. If the poet's Roman triumph can be considered as a ceremony that inaugurates the Renaissance,[47] it also provides the inaugural expression of an ideal relationship between poets and *duces,* which is itself central to the Renaissance.

"Patronage" concerns: Cola di Rienzo

Petrarca's personal search for an ideal place in some *res publica* coincides with his many dealings with the powerful figures of his world. It is neither possible nor appropriate here to fully consider that search or those dealings; not to keep the life distinct from the work (which is finally impossible with Petrarca), but because it is a search largely identical with the poet's whole career. There are, however, two episodes that deserve a brief mention because of the light they throw on Petrarca's literary-political concerns. These are. Petrarca's involvement with Cola di Rienzo and his dealings with the Visconti family, namely, Giovanni, Luchino, and Brizio. Put together with the Roman coronation and the case of King Robert, they form a paradoxical portrait of the man of letters in the world.

Despite appearances and his own words, the restlessness of Petrarca's career cannot be reduced to a desire for freedom from all worldly entanglements. He does, of course, express that motive whenever he indulges in a more or less secularized monastic discourse (more in *De vita solitaria,* less in *De otio religioso,* for example). But I think it is more helpful to consider Petrarca's movements as determined not so much by the pursuit of diluted Franciscan ideals or even of some premodern urge toward personal authenticity as by political motives; in the sense, naturally, of politics as a relation with the *polis* real or imagined. The relation he seeks throughout his career, both within and outside books, is a satisfying structure of intimate exchange. The Maussian model can help us understand several things about that desired exchange; for example, the need for reciprocity, the assertion of power with the agressiveness that accompanies it, the difficulty of distinguishing public from private friendship, and the opposition to contemporary (economic) reality. The atavistic pull on Petrarca manifests itself in relations of power, where literary and political authority meet each other uneasily.

Petrarca has Augustine say to him in the *Secretum:* "Quia cesaream sperare fas non erat, lauream poeticam ... concupisti" (Because you could not hope for the imperial laurel, you longed for the poetic laurel).[48] Despite the poet's lofty conception of his calling, one occasionally senses that he would rather be exercising "real" power. It is an ambition for just such a public role that characterizes his relationship with Cola di Rienzo.

Petrarca first met Cola di Rienzo only two years after his poetic coronation. The persistent image of Cola before his rise to prominence is of the reverent decipherer of epitaphs among the Roman ruins.[49] Like Petrarca, his enthusiasm aimed at a restoration of ancient Roman wholeness and power. Cola's brief period of prestige is portrayed by his early biographer as a return to Rome's ancient glory.[50] Petrarca never wavered in his support for Cola's ideal, which was his own dream of a golden age of Roman hegemony.[51] The development of the poet's attitude follows his conception of himself as a literary ally.

On the one hand, Cola was the man of action who was to realize what Petrarca evoked and legitimized in words. Both before and after the Tribune's moment of power, Petrarca sounds the same. "Delectat ... , quia facta non possum, ad auxilium libertatis saltem verba conferre" (Because I cannot contribute deeds, I would like at least to contribute words in the service of liberty).[52] Even more than exhortation, the poet supplied "lyricus apparatus tuarum laudum" (a lyrical supply [or embellishment] of your praises); poetic immortalization for the tribune and the Roman people.[53] The poet's service to the state is thus a triumph over time: resuscitation of ancient models of *virtus* goes hand in hand with undying commemoration of present glories.

On the other hand, Petrarca emphasizes at various times the literary character of this man of action. The poet's account of their first acquaintance emphasizes Cola's eloquence, characterizing the Roman as an oracle.[54] When late in his career Cola had some hope of being released from the Pope's prisons, Petrarca attributes that fact to the traditional immunity of poets. He compares Cola with Archias, although he promptly denies that the ex-tribune is a poet at all. That such a defense could be made for him at all is due, says Petrarca, to the stupidity of the present day, which takes the least hint of eloquence for true poetry.[55] In Petrarca's eyes, Cola has shrunk from an oracle preparing to bring Livy's world to life, to a prisoner narrowly escaping punishment under false pretenses, through a privilege extended even to poetasters. The implication resembles Cicero's logic in his oration: If even bad poets or men with the reputation of being poets are so respected, then so much the more do true poets deserve honor.

This is not the place to consider at length precisely what was important to Petrarca in Cola's undertaking. It might be worth noting, however, that republican liberty was not what inspired the poet. Petrarca agrees with Vico in seeing the similarities between Cola and the *eroici antichi,* and he values a similar elitist capacity for violence in his hero.[56] While he calls vigorously for the expulsion of Roman oligarchs, particularly the Colonna and Orsini families, Petrarca's accusations against them are illuminating. A repeated and prominent element of his indictment is the foreign origin of the oligarchs.[57] They do not deserve power because they are not really Roman. The honorary citizen-poet dons a republican mask to drive out the tyrants, when it is really Romolatry that compels him. Certainly his message for Cola in the latter's hour of need is clear. Success would be possible with maximum ruthlessness.[58] That means elimination of Cola's enemies, foremost among them Petrarca's old friends and benefactors the Colonna family. The dream of reawakened Roman power, with the poet's playing an essential role, is stronger than any other loyalty.

PATRONAGE CONCERNS: THE VISCONTI

In 1353, Petrarca left Vaucluse for good and settled in Milan, where he spent the better part of the next eight years. When the poet left France, he apparently did not know where he would make his new home and was convinced to choose Milan only by the insistent and generous invitation of its ruler, Giovanni Visconti.[59] As word of Petrarca's decision spread, he received protests from friends and acquaintances in other parts of Italy and France, reproaching him for settling down with a tyrant. The accusation of Milanese tyranny was hardly disinterested, coming as it did largely from citizens of Florence, Milan's rival for hegemony.[60] However, Petrarca was also accused of inconsistency. His friend Giovanni Boccaccio wrote him an allegorical letter, which represented a past Petrarca vigorously condemning the aggressive foreign policy of Giovanni Visconti.[61]

In defending himself, Petrarca insisted that his autonomy was not in danger, although he also praised the putative tyrant's *humanitas.* When asked what he wanted from the poet, Visconti replied thus: "nichil ex me velle respondit nisi presentiam meam solam, qua se suumque dominium crederet honestari" (he answered that he wanted nothing from me but my presence alone, by which he believed himself and his rule were honored [or made respectable]).[62]

Petrarca has several "deeper" excuses for his presence in Milan, offered with varying degrees of explicitness, or consciousness. In a letter to his Florentine friend Francesco Nelli, Petrarca begins and spends most of his space discursing "quam cara res sit tempus."[63] However, the familiar laments about how quickly and irrevocably time slips away turn out to be an introduction to a description of the poet's situation in Milan. Nelli was one of those in whose eyes Petrarca wanted to justify his move, and the matter was clearly still fresh in this letter of August 1353. Although there is no open plea in the latter part of the text, the opening movement seems to be an oblique apologia. What most concerns us in life is the flight of time, and that flight justifies any step one can take to use time most profitably. The tendency Petrarca follows here and elsewhere is to generalize and radicalize his personal situation, so that any objection to his specific choices may seem superficial and petty. He presents his dealings with Giovanni Visconti as an episode in a lifelong struggle with time. The pathos of that struggle is the main issue.[64]

Moreover, Petrarca elaborates the opening reference to time as *cara res.* As he asserts a direct relation between rarity and value, comparing time to pearls and balsam, persistently using financial metaphors, it becomes clear that the *pretium* of time is not only psychological. In the context of this apologia for his patronage situation, Petrarca makes time a commodity apt for exchange.[65] If, in fact, the extreme fugacity of time gives it a value *inextimabile,* that pricelessness cannot be irrelevant to the poet's material situation. Naturally, Petrarca obscures the relation between commodified time and the tyrant's patronage in the transition between the two parts of the letter to Nelli. Nevertheless, the poet's privileged access to time (although by no means a secure possession) does seem to constitute the wealth on which he draws in exchange for the patron's support.

A brief report in that same letter about how he is faring in body and soul suggests another tack, which Petrarca develops elsewhere. In

1355, he wrote an *Invectiva contra quendam magni status hominem sed nullius scientie aut virtutis,* which is partly a defense of his Milanese sojourn. He defends his dwelling with tyrants by stressing the radical distinction between his body and soul. The body, admittedly, is subject to the lord in whose territory it happens to dwell. In that sense, no one is truly free. However, the soul is what counts, and does exist free from the contingent and material realm. "Animo quidem sub nullo sum" (with my soul I am subject to no one)—to no one except to God or those like me, to whom I am subjected by love.[66] "Ita . . . melior pars mei vel est libera, vel iucundis atque honestis ex causis libertate carens aliter libera esse non vult" (So that my better part either is free, or else, losing its freedom for pleasing and honorable reasons, does not want to be free in any other way). The soul-body dichotomy can be deceptive. It would be inaccurate to see Petrarca's argument as based on a distinction between the enchained body and the autonomous soul.[67] The body is indeed chained, but so is the soul—yet voluntarily. In this way the courtier-poet has a double defense. He considers the political details of his situation insignificant, because they refer only to the corporeal, while the remainder concerns the virtuous subjection of friendship with the so-called tyrant. Poet and prince are thus essentially equals, each subject to the other, since friendship must be reciprocal.

Such a line of reasoning explains the tone of Petrarca's dealings with the powerful. His letters even to popes and emperors have the boldness that results from a conviction of spiritual equality. In 1348, Petrarca sent a pair of letters, one in prose, the other in verse, to Giovanni's brother and predecessor as ruler of Milan, Luchino Visconti.[68] Taken together, the letters evoke an equality based on an exchange of gifts. Luchino Visconti has sent the poet some fruit trees for his orchard in Selvapiana. Petrarca replies with a verse letter to the trees themselves, exhorting them to grow and bear fruit in honor of their bestower, that "greatest of Italians." The Milanese lord appears ultimately as the dominator not only of the political life of the peninsula, but also of nature itself. He is, moreover, the one who has brought the golden age, carrying out the sacred injunction for Roman greatness: "Parcere subiectis et debellare superbis" (Spare those who submit and subdue the proud).[69]

The epideictic elevation that Petrarca operates for his benefactor in the verse letter is rationalized by its prose companion, the subject of which is *principes literati.* Armed with a supply of classical examples (and first of all Julius and Augustus Caesar), Petrarca argues that to be a good prince one must cultivate literature. A ruler who is truly human desires fame, which is the product of personal excellence (*virtus*), but requires literature to live on.[70] To encapsulate the natural link between the prince's power and literary patronage, Petrarca cites the passage from Claudian that has already turned up in the *Collatio*:

Gaudet enim virtus sibi testes iungere Musas;
Carmen amat quisquis carmine digna facit.

For the gift that Visconti has given him, Petrarca draws on the treasury of literary time to offer something incomparably superior. In exchange for a contribution to the poet's *otium* and sustenance, he renders the gift of immortality and proof that the lord of Milan is a true prince. It appears, then, that the praise in the verse letter is at least partly proleptic. The golden age will return if a lord as powerful as Luchino Visconti cultivates poets and historians. True to Mauss's model of archaic exchange, the poet outdoes his benefactor's gift and thereby asserts his power.

It is in this context that Petrarca's invective against Luchino's illegitimate son Brizio Visconti should be considered. The invective texts are two *Epistolae metricae* (2.10 and 2.17), probably written in 1344.[71] The addressee is called simply Zoilus to recall the ancient "scourge of Homer."[72] The real anonymity that Petrarca imposes on his opponent is in keeping with his practice in all his invectives. He means to withhold the fame his writings can bestow and, thereby, annihilate those he combats.[73] In the case of the powerful Brizio Visconti, there was probably also a motive of political prudence.[74]

What provoked Petrarca's self-defense was his opponent's doubt that he had really received the laureate crown in Rome, plus the declaration that he did not deserve the honor anyway.

There are two parts to the first verse letter, by far the more significant. Petrarca's effort at self-justification is followed by a praise and defense of poetry, a structure that makes the poem a sort of *Pro Petrarcha poeta*. The first part includes his most important defense of the poetic coronation. Petrarca responds to his attacker for the laurel's sake, "laurea perrarum decus, atque hoc tempore soli / Speratum optatumque michi" (the laurel, that rarest honor, hoped for and desired at this time by me alone) (6–7).[75] As in the two coronation documents, the laurel is the privilege of those powerful in either words or arms.[76] Hence, an alliance with rulers provides the guarantee of Petrarca's honor. To his opponent's complaint that he has seen no sign of poetic accomplishment, the poet replies that only the happy few have been his readers. The first and most important among these has been King Robert, "Concivis meus egregius" (my illustrious fellow citizen) (30), whom Petrarca also calls his *autor* and *iudex* (88, 90). If the Roman ceremony has turned out to be an obscure occurrence, that is only because Petrarca has no desire to be read or admired by the vulgar.[77] Petrarca follows the alliance and makes it more intimate at a later moment when he answers the reproach of poetic folly. Besides asserting that poetry is necessarily a divine madness, he brings forth the examples of Julius and Augustus Caesar, who both wrote poetry and ruled the world (159 ff.). The overt argument is that poetry is a serious matter because it has been practiced by such men. In the larger movement of the polemic, however, Petrarca avoids isolation by recruiting the most prestigious and powerful of *concives*.

Still, the question of citizenship remains complex. Petrarca's rejection of vulgar praise is related to his ideal of solitude. What is clear throughout his work, for example, in the invectives against Avignon and in *De vita solitaria,* is that literary *otium* can only be found away from the city. One of Petrarca's excuses for settling in Milan was that his house was hardly in the city at all. His antiurban stance is largely matched by an anticivic one. The poet shows little sense of community with the inhabitants of those cities where he unwillingly dwelled. Rome provides the only exception to this profound bias in Petrarca. Of course, the exception is only apparent. Rome for Petrarca is literary Rome. The crowds supporting Cola di Rienzo become the defenders of republican liberty. Those applauding the laureate ceremony are *populus Romanus* exercising an ancient prerogative. Ideal community exists only in epistolary friendship and in the relationship to past and future that is the natural dynamic of literature.[78] It is in that sense that we can also accept as paradoxically true the assertion made earlier about Petrarca's enduring concern with the *polis.*

There is, then, no real contradiction in the poet's assertion of a place at the heart of the *res publica* at the same time that he deserts the cities. In this way, Petrarca is able to parry in an unusual way his opponent's appropriation of the Platonic ejection of poets from the state.

> Media nos pellis ab urbe,
> Sed paulum expecta. Iam sponte recedimus omnes.
> Et nemorum secreta placent, turbamque nocentem
> Odimus, ac leti campis spatiamur amenis.

(173–76)[79]

(You drive us out of the city; but wait a moment. We have already left by our own choice. We love forest solitude, we hate the harmful crowd, and stroll happily in the pleasant fields.)

The fact that some emperors wrote verse and that some rulers like Robert approved of Petrarca may seem a rather slender argument for poetry's place in the state. Perhaps for that reason, Petrarca brings out his and humanism's favorite argument. The anaphora and parallelism of the following passage create a crescendo to emphasize the message.

> Quis preclarissima bella
> Heroum, moresque graves et nomina nosset?
> Quis stimulis animos ageret per mille labores
> Perque altum virtutis iter? Quis tristia vite
> Demeret implicite dulci fastidia cantu?
>
> (193–97)

(Who would know of heroes' glorious wars, of solemn mores and names? Who would spur the spirit on through a thousand hardships along the lofty road of virtue? Who would remove the sad weariness of a complicated life with sweet song?)

The subjunctive of the parallel rhetorical questions is answered by the subjunctive of what dreadful world could be imagined without poetry to link present to past and future and thereby teach virtue. Yet there follows a confident indicative, first present, then future, to show the truth about the effect of literature: its symmetrical relationship to past and future.

> Ora forent quasi muta hominum si spiritus orbi
> Deforet Aonius; virtus ignota lateret
> In se clara licet, studiosique impetus omnis
> Torperet; lingue nam fundamenta Latine
> Nulla forent, quibus egregie fiant sedibus artes,
> In quibus omne procul vobis ostenditur evum
> Nostraque venturis longum servabitur etas.
>
> (199–205)

(The human voice would be almost mute if the Muse's spirit were absent from the earth. Excellence, although bright in itself, would lie obscure. The impulse of anyone zealous would become inert. All this because the foundations of the Latin language would not exist, on which basis the arts are made illustrious, in which every distant age is shown to you, and our own age will be preserved for those far in the future.)[80]

The reward awaiting all true poets follows directly from its service: "Est michi fame / Immortalis honos, et gloria meta laborum" (Immortal honor is mine, and glory is the goal of my efforts) (254–55).

What finds comprehensive expression in the letter to Zoilus/Brizio

Visconti is an echo of the coronation speeches, delivered now as the attacks on poetry seem more palpable and more menacing. Petrarca did not know when he wrote that his opponent was the dangerously powerful Brizio Visconti, so the polemic cannot be read immediately as a battle between poet and a member of the ruling class. However, after Petrarca learned the identity of his correspondent he pursued the invective in *Epistola metrica* 2.17 and, more curiously, recalled the exchange in two longer works that he composed during his stay in Milan.[81] In the *Invective contra medicum* and particularly in the *Invectiva contra quendam* . . . , Petrarca represents the exchange with Brizio Visconti as a courageous and principled stand taken despite the personal danger.[82] In both, the poet names envy as the motive for the attack, echoing the end of *Epistola metrica* 2.10 (286–87) with its triple repetition of the verb *invidere* in reference to his opponent. Attacks on his Roman honor, which he could only conceive as envious attacks on poetry as such, provoked Petrarca to imagine an alliance with the powerful in an ideal literary state. His dealings with the Visconti family in the 1340s and 1350s cast them in various roles of intimate exchange, both positive and negative, in relation to the poet.

THE IDEA OF THE *AFRICA*

One of the characteristic puzzles about the Roman triumph is just what it rewarded. It seems unlikely that Petrarca's poetic output in Italian, although already significant by 1341, was considered in the bestowal of such a classicizing honor.[83] The Latin poetry published by then amounts to little more than a dozen *Epistolae metricae*. Apart from those minor works, the only poetic composition that can have motivated the coronation is the then-unpublished, incomplete *Africa*.[84] In this poem, Petrarca himself associates it with his coronation (1.65–66). As he narrates in the *Epistola posteritati* the first inspiration to begin the *Africa,* which came upon him on a Good Friday, Petrarca immediately follows with the narration of the offers of the laurel and his journey to receive it. In describing his meeting with King Robert in Naples, Petrarca says he showed the poem to the monarch, who was so impressed that he asked that it be dedicated to him. This passage implies that Robert's official approval of Petrarca was due to the poem as well as to the three-day examination. And, as we shall see, the matter of that examination was not foreign to the *Africa.* After retelling his Roman triumph, Petrarca dwells on the new inspiration to finish the poem that seized him in Selvapiana on his way back to Vaucluse. Thus in the most comprehensive account, that of the *Epis-*

tola posteritati,[85] Petrarca closely associates the genesis, composition, and "conclusion" of the epic with his coronation. In his own mind, Petrarca *laureatus* was the poet of the *Africa*.

He was so, too, to his contemporaries.[86] It may be worthwhile to briefly consider here two later texts by younger humanists inspired by Petrarca: Giovanni Boccaccio and Coluccio Salutati. They are important not only for the belief they show that Petrarca was crowned for the *Africa* (which is, after all, not such an important point), but also for what they reveal of the immense importance of the very concept of the *Africa* to its contemporaries. They also introduce the poem's post-humous fate, a fate ironically appropriate to it.[87]

After Petrarca's death in 1374, the manuscript of the *Africa* came into the possession of a group of Paduan acquaintances. Just as Petrarca had refused to publish the poem during his lifetime (with one exception: the last thirty-four lines of book 6, shown to Barbato da Sulmona in 1343 and diffused by him),[88] so after his death was this Paduan "tribunal" hesitant to release the poem. In a letter of 1376 to Lombardo della Seta, the Florentine chancellor Salutati asked for a copy of the work.[89] He presented as his argument a poem already written during Petrarca's lifetime and addressed to the poet, the *Metra . . . incitatoria ad Africe editionem*. Boccaccio, in contrast, had seen the poem and so was able to discuss it more pertinently, in his *Versus domini Iohannis Boccaccii ad Affricam*.[90] As the title indicates, this latter work is addressed to Petrarca's poem itself.

Both poems operate in a hortatory mode, urging the *Africa*'s publication. Not surprisingly, Salutati and Boccaccio build their panegyric of poetry, and of Petrarca's poem in particular, on similar lines. Both declare the *Africa* his greatest work and the reason for his Roman coronation.[91] More significant, they evoke a pathetic relation to the dead, a literary duty to revive and illuminate their greatness. Salutati pictures the hero of the epic, Scipio Africanus, longing for the poem that will release him from obscurity into his proper heroic light:

> Iam claro carmine poscit
> In lucem prodire tuo, secumque gravatur
> Tempore iam clausum sub nocte teneri.

$$(232.7–9)$$

(Now he seeks to come into the light through your illustrious poem, and is oppressed by being held confined in darkness by time.)

Although he has been remembered eloquently by historians, and especially by Livy, he has not yet been *sung* as he deserves. Here is implicit a disdain for Scipio's contemporary, Ennius, whose crude art could not do justice to his friend. To at last "laudes / Instaurare suas", Scipio "Carminis eternos optat melioris honores" (To begin his praise, Scipio prays for the eternal honor of a superior poem) (232.15, 19).

Boccaccio's poem includes a moving lament from the urns holding the ashes of those great men whom Petrarca has sung. They pray for rest, to not be subjected to a second pyre when their name has the chance of rescue from oblivion (71 ff.). A parallel voice of the dead comes from the late King Robert, who asks that Petrarca's promise be kept and the poem be dedicated to him, "ut sua sis nomenque suum per secula serves" (that you may be his and preserve his name through the ages) (83).

The pathos in the prosopopoeia of the dead abandoned without song moves into the contemporary public realm in a *mise-en-scène* of the *res publica*'s need for poetic illustration. The great poem also rescues the state. Florence appears in Boccaccio's poem as a squalid widow praying for death to end her misery unless the published *Africa* can give her life (85 ff.). This longing of a city for her poet becomes more understandable in light of the competition Boccaccio presents between Rome, Paris, and Bologna for the honor of the poem (110 ff.). The classical allusion is clearly to the claims of cities in the Greek world to be Homer's birthplace.[92]

Salutati and Boccaccio hold forth a similar promise for the efficacy of the *Africa*. Salutati declares that the epic, if released, will immortalize not only the poet and the hero he has sung, but also his country and his age ("nostre etati patrieque daturus / Perpetuum nomen" [241.3–4]). Boccaccio goes further, associating the epic not only with the laurel coronation, but also with the rebirth or resurrection of Latin literature and of all Italy. The poem is

Ytalie renovatus honor museque latine,
laurea tarpeia digitis assumpta sub arce, etc.

(39–40)

(The renewed honor of Italy and the Latin Muse, the laurel possessed on the Tarpeian height . . .)

The people of Rome eagerly desire the *Africa* because it can recreate the city's ruins and the names of its forefathers (69–70). If the poem is published, a new golden age will arise: The cities will become a pastoral paradise blooming with song, the laurel grown pale will recover its green, people will think "in priscos rediisse dies" (that they have returned to the earliest days) (137). Scipio will rise from his

exile's grave, return to Rome, and ascend the Capitoline in a new triumph: "Scipiades Romamque suam sanctumque senatum / consurgens
repetet" (Scipio will rise up again and seek his Rome and the sacred
Senate) (141–42). In short, the poem will make ancient glory live
again: "Patrie decus omne resurget / sospite te" (The glory of the father-
land will revive, if only you are safe) (146–47).[93]

The underlying ideal of both hortatory poems, like Petrarca's, is temporal reversibility. Both texts hover around the tomb, trying to pull
something (the hero, glory) forth from the past into a shining future.
In addition, while power to immortalize belongs explicitly to the poet,
these texts recognize the importance of the editor. The power of Petrarca's poem will be null if it is kept secret; it will remain a prisoner
of oblivion like the unsung dead. Salutati shows his awareness of this
in a letter written after he had finally received a copy of the *Africa*.
"Ecce," he says to himself, "Francisci nomen et fama in manibus tuis
erit" (Look, the name and fame of Francesco will be in your hands).[94]
Thus the editor is to the poet as the poet is to the hero.

Clearly, the laureate ceremony and the *Africa* are central to Petrarca
and to early Renaissance humanism, for their emblematic importance
and for the commonplaces they diffuse about the place of poetry. But
what, after all, is this poem that was to bring back the golden age, that
revealed its author as a rival of Homer and Virgil?[95] The history of the
Africa's fortune has yet to be written, but there is no doubt that its
fate has been a decline of understanding and interest almost from the
moment of its appearance, in 1395 or 1396.[96] Its first editor, Pier Paolo
Vergerio, can be said to have been its last true admirer.[97] The fact that
by the early fifteenth century Niccolò Niccoli could call the poem a
ridiculus mus indicates how quickly its reputation fell as tastes in
Latin style changed.[98] Such a judgment also shows a distinct sense of
the disparity between Petrarca's ambitions and his achievement in the
Africa. Apart from the favorable judgments of a few modern special-
ists, the situation today is not much different. It is less a case of negative criticism than of indifferent acceptance of the received opinion
that the *Africa* is an ambitious failure. At best its selective reading
may be recommended, through its famous anthology passages.[99] My
purpose here is not to argue the poem's excellence or to excuse its
defects. But if the very idea of the *Africa* was so stirring for Petrarca
and his contemporaries and seemed such an opportune expression
of the concerns of nascent humanism, we may possibly profit from
reopening the poem as a whole to see what evidence there is of its
passionate inception.[100] Although "the ponderous volume" of the *Africa*, in Gibbon's words, "be now abandoned to a long repose," its re-

pose may not be an eternal sleep and perhaps not lack instructive visions (*somnia*).[101]

The Hero's Dream: *Africa* 1–2

I propose that the "deep structure" of Petrarca's unfinished epic is the working out of three aspects of the topos concerning poetic power. Mythical thought as temporal reversibility, civic function, and gift exchange with the patron are those aspects that run through Petrarca's career and underlie his would-be masterpiece. All three interact most intensively in the final book, book 9, particularly in Ennius's dream, but they also inform the architecture and meaning of the whole poem. What makes the epic unfold as it does is its status as epideictic poetry.

Even a superficial acquaintance with the *Africa* recognizes it as a poem of praise. It is most obviously a panegyric of Scipio Africanus.[102] This is evident not only in the title, modeled on such classical titles as the *Aeneid, Odyssey,* or *Achilleid,* but also in the first lines of the poem. Virgil's "Arma virumque cano," Homer's "Andra moi ennepe,"[103] Statius's "Magnanimum Aeaciden . . . refer" are echoed in

Et michi conspicuum meritis belloque tremendum,
Musa, virum referes.[104]

(To me too, o Muse, you will recall the man famous for his virtues and fearsome in war.)

However, while the classical exordia immediately indicate the context of action where the hero's heroism becomes apparent, Petrarca's interest lies elsewhere. Certainly, Aeneas is repeatedly characterized as *pius,* Odysseus as *polutropos,* but on the whole, their adventures define their character. Scipio, on the other hand, is a surprisingly static hero. He is, in addition, a hero most evident in his absence, as a glance at the structure of the *Africa* will show.

After the exordium and dedication to King Robert, books 1 and 2 are occupied by Scipio's vision, in which he ascends to the heavens to be granted revelations from his father and grandfather concerning his own destiny and that of Rome. In books 3 and 4, Scipio's great friend Lelius travels to the African court of Syphax and, to convince this king to become an ally of Rome, delivers a long panegyric of Roman greatness and of Scipio. Book 5 is dedicated to the passion of Massinissa (another African ally) for Sophonisba, and the latter's death. In book 6, the preparations for a climactic confrontation between Rome and

Carthage permit a glimpse of Scipio in action. However, rather more action takes place elsewhere, and by far the most eloquent passage is the lament of the dying Mago, Hannibal's brother. The decisive battle between Hannibal and Scipio near Zama provides the matter of book 7. Here is where Scipio appears most and to the best advantage. But after the capitulation of Carthage at the beginning of book 8, he again becomes a luminous figure in the background, as the awe of the Carthaginians, come to Rome suing for peace, is the center of interest. Scipio converses with the poet Ennius at the beginning of book 9, but the attention quickly shifts to Ennius's account of his own vision. Upon their arrival in Rome, general and poet celebrate a triumph together. But as we shall see, the poet's participation in this triumph has the greatest importance; moreover, the glory of Scipio's presence is undermined by subsequent reference to his future disgrace and exile.

To note Scipio's scarcity in the poem does not mean to deny that he is its hero; rather, it suggests a suspicion that the poem's emphasis lies elsewhere than in exclusive attention to one hero. No doubt Scipio was for Petrarca a figure without peer among ancients and moderns, at least at the time of the *Africa*'s composition. The homage he receives in the *Africa* parallels to some extent the *Vita Scipionis,* by far the longest of the biographies in *De viris illustribus.*[105] There is nothing contrived about Petrarca's devotion to Scipio, as we might suspect if the object were a contemporary. And yet, as I shall try to show, the real panegyric in the *Africa* concerns the power of panegyric. That is, the poem does not so much glorify Scipio as it glorifies its ability to glorify him. This is the essence of what has been called "the birth of humanism's dream."[106] Petrarca, that most self-conscious of writers, could have no illusions about an immediate relationship to his matter (simply praising what is great). The example of Scipio is significant above all because it illustrates the poet's powers and the ideal relationship between political/military power and poetry.

The first two words of the poem encapsulate Petrarca's approach. *Et michi* makes the poet the first character introduced in the *Africa.* More important, the conjunction *et* links Petrarca and his endeavor to something outside the poem, something preceding it. It may not be necessary to insist on the extent to which the *Africa* exists intertextually, making sense only as a constellation of the poet's humanistic culture. But it is a particular variety of intertextuality that *Et michi* introduces, and that, as will be seen, the rest of the poem specifies. Petrarca immediately sets himself in a position of belatedness in relation to previous praisers of Scipio. The invocation to the Muse is not a prayer for the success of his poem in itself, but for success in time, relative to a poetic tradition.[107] The similarity of *Et michi* to the *Sed me* of the Virgilian passage that begins the *Collatio* is no accident.

We have seen in the hortatory poems of Salutati and Boccaccio the idea that Scipio awaits resurrection in Petrarca's poem. Petrarca had already introduced the same idea in his first Eclogue, *Parthenias*, written about 1347. It is a dialogue between Silvius (Petrarca, according to the poet's own exegesis) and Monicus (his brother Gherardo).[108] At the end, Silvius excuses himself from the discussion of sacred and profane poetry, claiming that an urgent task awaits him: "Urget amor Muse" (Love of the Muse spurs me on). A youth waits on the shore of Africa, where he has done great deeds, worthy of greatest praise. But "Carmine fama sacro caret hactenus, et sua virtus / premia deposcit" (His fame has lacked a sacred poem until now, and his excellence seeks its reward) (120–21).[109] Scipio, here a contemporary of his singer Silvius, is destitute without the literary honor he merits. That means that not just any praise will do. "Hunc simul italidesque nurus, puerique, senesque / attoniti adverso certatim a litore laudant" (From the opposite shore Italian women, children and old men compete with each other, stunned, to praise him) (118–19)—but not fittingly. The historians have remembered him, and Ennius has written of him with his crude art.[110] Here is the belief that poetry gives higher praise than prose (even Livy's prose), as well as the denigration of Ennius that plays an important role in the *Africa*. Thus Scipio is clearly represented as dependent on Petrarca for his fate.

The *Africa* too represents the hero's need of his poet in the strongest terms. The narrative is framed by two great visions, in books 1–2 and book 9; what we may call respectively *somnium Scipionis* and *somnium Ennii*. The first is, of course, based on Cicero's account in *De re publica* 6 of Scipio the Younger's vision of Scipio Africanus the Elder. Petrarca changes the characters, so that it is Scipio Africanus, the hero of the poem, who sees his deceased father, Publius Cornelius Scipio, and is guided by him in a tour of the heavens. Young Scipio has been divinely granted the privilege of overstepping the bounds of mortality, both in entering the celestial realm and in knowing the future (1.173–79).[111] The purpose of his privilege is that he may be encouraged to carry on the war against Carthage to its destined conclusion. To this end Scipio hears described his father's brave death in battle and sees the souls of other great Romans dead during the war. Then, that his mind may turn wholly to his virtuous task, Scipio's father impresses upon him the vanity of the earthly realm.

This simultaneous attention to both imperium and *vanitas* is only apparently paradoxical. It provides the contrast that underlies Scipio's vision, but it becomes more understandable when the poet enters into the picture. Schematically, we may say that books 1 and 2 represent a double aporia of glory that receives a promise of resolution from the imagined convergence of the poet and the republican hero. That double aporia comprises, first, the portrayal of Roman hegemony as supreme virtue and the pinnacle of earthly honor, and yet doomed to an inglorious decadence; and second, the introduction of the poet as a culture hero whose works, however, are also ultimately mortal.

If Scipio is waging a war of transcendent importance, his commitment to military victory can harmonize with disdain for earthly vanity.[112] However, time provides the element that troubles such serene assurance of purpose. In book 1, Scipio has seen a procession of Roman heroes of the remote and recent past. Book 2 opens with a new privilege, that of prophecy. After learning the destined outcome of the war with Carthage, Scipio hears from his father's mouth (this time without the spectacle of luminous souls) the great figures of future Roman history. As the narrative progresses into the empire, Publius Cornelius must necessarily refer to the ultimate decadence and fall of Rome. To his son's consternation, he paints Rome's final sorry state, with only a vague hope of renewal (2.294–95).

> In finem, quamvis ruinosa, dierum
> Vivet et extremum veniet tua Roma sub evum
> Cum mundo peritura suo.
>
> (2.324–26)

(Your Rome will live on, although in ruins, until the end of time, and will reach the last age to perish with its world.)

Subsequently, Scipio's father generalizes this future nadir of Roman fortunes and declares the vanity of all earthly glory.

Publius Cornelius's final speech mounts an attack on the human thirst for glory. To a great extent, the attack is built on commonplaces drawn from the Old Testament as well as from Cicero's *Somnium Scipionis*. The pursuit of earthly fame is vain because of the empty and fugitive nature of life in the world.

> Tempora diffugiunt; ad mortem curritis; umbra,
> Umbra estis pulvisque levis vel in ethere fumus
> Exiguus, quem ventus agat.
>
> (348–50)

(Time flees. You are running toward death. A shadow, you are a shadow and light dust, or meager smoke which the wind chases into the sky.)

The gusts of his passions keep man from realizing just how limited are his chances for fame, both geographically and temporally. A brief consideration of the globe shows how most of the earth is either uninhabitable or inaccessible to us or uncomprehending due to differences in language and mores. Men hope to prolong their existence in the memory of posterity:

> libet ire per ora
> Doctorum extinctos hominum, clausosque sepulcro
> Liberiore via per mundi extrema vagari.
> Vivere post mortem, violentas spernere Parcas
> Dulcia sunt, fateor, sed nomine vivere nil est.

> (410–14)

(There is a desire in the deceased to travel from mouth to mouth of learned men, and in those enclosed in the tomb to wander by a freer route to the ends of the earth. It is sweet, I admit, to live after death, to scorn the violent Fates; but to live through one's name is nothing.)

Only in the other world after death is there permanence; here all physical trace of us soon disappears, even our epitaph. A name consigned to literature lasts somewhat longer, but it, too, is mortal:

> Clara quidem libris felicibus insita vivet
> Fama diu, tamen ipsa suas passura tenebras.

> (433–34)

(Certainly, illustrious fame planted in fertile books will live a long time, yet even this will suffer its own night.)[113]

What this development in the vision seems to do is doubly negative: to chasten Roman triumphs past and future and to proleptically dismiss the figure of Petrarca, which has yet to be introduced. If all worthy deeds are doomed to fail in time and cannot be rescued even by literature, then the twin glories of the *Africa,* embodied in its hero and its poet, appear canceled—or at least crippled. Now, no reader of Petrarca would hesitate to characterize him as ambivalent about nearly everything under the sun and about glory most of all.[114] Certainly, a large florilegium could be gathered from Petrarca's works, illustrating his contradictory attitude toward literary glory.[115] But it would be inaccurate to reduce the *Africa* to a wrestling match between the laureate and the penitent or, worse still, between medieval man and Renaissance man. While the commonplaces pro and contra glory do pervade his career, what is more important in particular cases is what the clichés of ambivalence contribute literarily. In *Africa* 1 and 2, they result in an alliance and mutual rescue between poet and *dux*. This comes about in several ways.

First, immediately before his father's attack on earthly vanity, there occurs an extraordinary adjustment of the machinery of Scipio's vision. His interlocutors have repeatedly stressed the shortness of time for what they have to say and show.[116] At the beginning of book 2, Publius Cornelius announces that it is time for his son to descend from heaven (2.2). But at his son's plea he prolongs the privileged moment to present Rome's future. When he has sorrowfully finished, day is coming, the morning star has risen, and the sun is about to appear. But Scipio's guide halts the cosmos by the power of his voice:

Hic iterum genitor sacro veneranda resolvit
Ora sono. Stetit eximia dulcedine mundus
Captus et eternos tenuerunt astra meatus.

(2.334–36)

(Now his father opened his venerable mouth again with a sacred voice. The cosmos stood still, captivated by the exceptional sweetness, and the stars held back their eternal course.)

Whereas previous postponements of the conversation's end had been at Scipio's request, now his father adds a further delay on his own initiative. And while the previous part of the vision was set in the framework of the advancing night hours, the passage that ensues here for more than two hundred lines is freed from the pressure of time.[117] Thus what Scipio's father has to say in his last speech is strikingly emphasized by the departure from the vision's convention. The sudden freedom from time is perfectly appropriate to what he has to tell his son on the need for transcendence, summed up in the succinct admonition: "Sine tempore vivite" (Live without time) (2.422). Moreover, what has halted time and the cosmos is a verbal command. The enormous power thus illustrated in word magic contradicts the subsequent skepticism about literature.

Then, too, there is Petrarca's entry into the poem. After declaring that glory entrusted to books will also perish one day, Scipio's father abruptly resumes prophecy to consider his son's posthumous fortune.

Cernere iam videor genitum post secula multa
Finibus Etruscis iuvenem qui gesta renarret,
Nate, tua et nobis veniat velut Ennius alter.

(2.441–43)

(I seem to see a youth born after many centuries in Tuscany who will retell your deeds, my son, and will come to us as another Ennius.)

Here Petrarca first introduces himself into his narrative, as a figure divinely prophesied, destined to do justice at last to Scipio's great deeds. He will be like Scipio's friend and poet, *Ennius alter*. The two poets occupy complementary positions in the history of Latin literature, which Petrarca views as a unity from Ennius's crude beginnings to his own function as renewer:

Iste [sc. Ennius] rudes Latio duro modulamine Musas
Intulit; ille [sc. Petrarca] autem fugientes carmine sistet.

(445–46)

(Ennius introduced the uncultivated Muses into Latium with his harsh music; but Petrarca will stop their fleeing with his poem.)

In fact, Publius Cornelius prefers Petrarca. First, because of his remoteness in time: "Multo michi carior ille est / Qui procul ad nostrum reflectet lumina tempus" (He is much dearer to me who turns his gaze back on our time from afar) (449–50). This can refer to the greater difficulty inherent in writing about the distant past. But we have also seen that time is a medium that establishes affection between those who have a common interest yet are remote—an advantage denied to the contemporary Ennius. Another consequence of Petrarca's removal in the future is the second reason for cherishing him more: "In quod eum studium non vis pretiumve movebit, / Non metus aut odium, non spes aut gratia nostri" (Neither force nor reward will compel him to this zeal; neither fear nor hate, neither hope nor our favor) (451–52). The praise of the fourteenth-century poet will be untainted by the possibility of material reward by his subject or by the passions that disturb contemporary judgments. What then will move him to write? "Magnarum sed sola quidem admiratio rerum, / Solus amor veri" (Only the admiration of great things; only love of what is true) (458–59). This is the love of the past that cleanses epideictic poetry from the stain inherent in what is present. It is the ideal of a pure poet-patron relationship.

When the speaker interrupts himself with an abrupt "Sed quid tamen omnia prosunt? / Iam sua mors libris aderit" (And yet what good is all this? Even then death will attend on books) (454–55), the passage introducing Petrarca may seem parenthetical. But in declaring its own uselessness, the poem at the same time establishes the foundation of its pathos. And more pertinent, that great self-centered parenthesis cannot be canceled by its surroundings. The association of literature with caducity and death is not a crippling ambivalence for Petrarca but, on the contrary, an inspiration. When the poet declares in a letter that true glory begins only after death,[118] this may mean that death is a presence in the pursuit of glory mocking its vanity. But it also means that the literary relation to glory is necessarily a relation beyond the grave. That relation, which negates time and mortality, provides the poet's source of invention. Another passage from the *Familiares* gives extreme expression to the proximity of death to the acts of both writing and reading.

> Continue morimur, ego dum hec scribo, tu dum leges alii dum audient dumque non audient; ego quoque dum hec leges moriar, tu moreris dum hec scribo, ambo morimur, omnes morimur, semper morimur, nunquam vivimus dum hic sumus. . . .[119]

> (We die continuously: I while I write this, you while you read, others when they hear or do not hear it. I shall also be dying while you read this, you are dying as I write this; we both are dying, we all are dying, we are always dying, we are never alive as long as we are here. . . .)

We have only to compare a passage like this with Petrarca's comments elsewhere on his *insanabilis scribendi morbus* (incurable disease, writing)[120] or on his passionate determination not to waste time—which means reading and writing as much as possible[121]—to understand that for the poet "écrire, c'est apprendre à mourir" in an unexpected way.[122] The experience of literature (and so of glory) coincides with the experience of death—which is a stronger way of saying that the pursuit of immortality must go through mortality.

Hence, the dialectic never resolves itself.[123] The aporia of glory reveals itself as an amphibole: both . . . and. *Africa* 2 concentrates the aporia in a double attitude toward the present moment. The present is both a punctual prison and timeless transcendence. Scipio's father summarizes the first version as he exhorts his son to dedicate himself to the celestial realm of virtue: "Annorum, nate, locorumque / Estis in angusto positi" (My son, you are all placed in the narrow straits of time and place) (470–71).[124] The human condition consists of imprisonment in the infinitesimal point of here and now. With regard to now, the point of time: The introduction of Petrarca into the poem is what holds forth a promise of escape. Even if literary memorials are not immortal, they possess a longevity greater than anything else.[125] Consigned to the care of the poet, Scipio will at least find an exit from the *angustum* of his own time.

On the other hand, however, the present not only is a negative concept, but also presents a transcendent positive face. This is perhaps clearest in the *Trionfi*, where time, which has devoured all immanent things, is in its turn defeated by eternity. Clearly, such a resolution constitutes the unattainable ideal of literary memory. For what else does Petrarca scrutinize past and future, but for a state where

> non avrà loco "fu" "sarà" nè "era",
> ma "è" solo in presente, ed "ora" ed "oggi"?[126]

> (There will be no place for "was" or "will be," but "is" only, in the present, and "now" and "today.")

Thus the supratemporal power portrayed as superior to poetry in *Africa* 2 is not really of another sort altogether. It is a sanctification of the essential literary ambition. The sense in which literary glory is "canceled" by transcendence is perhaps best expressed by the Hegelian ambiguity of *Aufhebung*: both suppression and elevation.[127]

The mission of Rome as *virtus* means that only poetry among worldly things can be its ally and, to a certain extent, its savior. Poetry can extend Rome in time. And yet what about the poet? He, too, is sentenced to the strait prison of time and space, the here and now. Of course his métier permits him the same relative freedom in time as it does his subject. But then there is the *angustum* of space. How does the poet escape the confines of the here? That is where we find a rather less transcendent solution of the aporia of glory. Part of the senior Scipio's diatribe against glory is based on the flight of time and the passing of all worldly things. That element of the aporia is addressed, as in the *Trionfi*, by an appeal to a transcendent, timeless present. But another part of the antiglory polemic is based on the vastness of the earth and the improbability that one man's name could be known in more than an insignificant region. Such an obstacle as this can be overcome by the main subject of Publius Cornelius's discourse: the progress of Roman imperialism. Petrarca has Scipio's father prophesy the universal authority of Rome. In such a world as the one promised, unified linguistically, culturally, and administratively, glory could seem not so clearly mortal after all. Petrarca's *romanitas* provides not only the loftiest examples of literary glory; it even comes as close as imaginable to defeating glory's enemies through the institution of a Latin empire. With such a gift does *dux* reward poet.

THE POET'S DREAM: *AFRICA* 9

One plausible reason for the discomfort of readers with the *Africa* lies in its extraordinary beginning, with the main character's passivity and the apparent self-destruction of the poem's project. The two books recounting Scipio's vision precede any but the most cursory reference to the Punic War or even to the hero's character. Military trumpets blare at the end of book 2, awakening Scipio, dissolving his vision, and calling him to action. Here we might expect to enter the business of war and so to see evidence of the hero's *virtus*. But instead, Scipio calls his confidant Lelius and, taking counsel with him as advised by his father (2.518–20), sends Lelius to the African court of Syphax. There his friend will attempt to recruit that king as an ally. Books 3 and 4 are thus devoted to a description of the adornment of Syphax's palace; an African bard's praise of Carthage followed by Lelius's praise of Rome; and finally, Lelius's praise of Scipio. Thus, the poem's indirectness continues. What is the meaning of that fact?

Conversation has a central importance in the poem. Like Petrarca's epistolary conversations with antiquity and posterity, the conversations in the *Africa* are charged with pathos. These become lengthy scenes, themselves of almost epic proportions, presented as islands of eloquent exchange in the world's profound momentary quiet. Such is the description of Scipio's colloquy in heaven; likewise the exchange of Lelius and Syphax. Likewise the dialogue between Scipio and Hannibal before their climactic battle; as well as the words of Scipio, Lelius, and Massinissa, relaxing the evening after the battle; and, finally, the conversation of Scipio and Ennius on the ship returning from Africa, and, within the vision Ennius recounts, his conversation with Homer.

Two observations may be made about the *Africa* as a poem of conversation. One is that the dialectic of conversation provides a model for the relationship between the present and past tradition.[128] The meaning of a dialogue cannot be reduced to what one of the interlocutors says. Thus, for example, the meaning of the *Secretum* lies somewhere between the words of its two main characters, Augustinus and Franciscus. Despite the oratorical (that is, relatively impersonal) character of parts of the dialogues in the *Africa,* they remain dynamic. In the same way, what lies in the past can neither be consigned to oblivion nor carried unscathed into the present. Literary engagement with past *virtus* is an intimate exchange that aims at ideal resurrection—but ends as recreation of the past.

The concept of conversation is important in a second way, also relevant to glory. The use of dialogue in the *Africa* shows the mediated nature of all glory. The *Africa* differs from previous epics in its incessant awareness of its task. The poem cannot forget itself, as it were, and narrate great deeds with a pretense to immediacy. Scipio cannot be shown "as he really is"; rather he is presented from different angles: in his father's harangue, his friend's panegyric, the curse of his enemy

Sophonisba, in contrast with Hannibal, in relation to his poet Ennius. The poem's indirectness in presenting its hero makes a statement on the nature of poetry and provides an explanation why *duces* need *poete.*

On the other hand, the *Africa* is more than a series of conversations or speeches. It is, like the *Divina Commedia,* "un poema al quale ha posto mano e cielo e terra."[129] Suspended between the two great dreams that begin and end it, the poem spans the entire cosmos. The beginning of book 6 represents Sophonisba's descent to Hades, after she has killed herself through frustrated love for Massinissa. As the battle of Zama rages in book 7, the scene rises to heaven where the figures of Carthage and Rome plead before Jupiter. The celestial realm is also the subject of the artwork in Syphax's palace, which is described upon the arrival of Lelius in book 3. Besides jeweled representation of the planets, he finds sculpted figures of the Zodiac and the divine pantheon. There, too, is the whole cosmos: from Jupiter to Pluto on their respective thrones, with the earthly birth of Venus in between. The significance of that ekphrasis gains in scope if we accept the plausible but unprovable theory proposed by the poem's editor about the lacunae in books 3 and 4.[130] According to N. Festa, the description of the palace in book 3 does not belong to the episode of Lelius's visit to Syphax. Rather it is a misplaced fragment from a lost or unwritten episode, in which Scipio himself comes to Africa to meet with Syphax and visits a "Palace of Truth," the existence of which in the *Africa* is indicated at the beginning of the *Secretum.*[131] In this palace, then, Scipio would observe the figures of the planets, Zodiac, and gods, which allegorically represent truth about the moral and physical world and about the liberal arts. The episode would thus represent Scipio's initiation into wisdom, complementary to his instructive conversations in books 1–2 and 9. Even if we do not adopt this tempting suggestion, it indicates a characteristic of the remainder of the poem: namely, how much Scipio receives instruction in hidden wisdom, pointing toward universal authority. One of the poem's peculiar tensions lies between Scipio as masterly *dux* and as neophyte seeking to be taught. The two aspects are reconciled if we see Scipio as Petrarca's model for the Renaissance prince: the leader whose authority is based on virtuous knowledge taught by his men of letters—and particularly by his poets.

This brings us to book 9, the one part of the *Africa* that ranks with Petrarca's greatest work. In it we see once more the contemplative Scipio, after he has briefly shown his excellence as a man of action. He has resolved the tragic passion of Massinissa and Sophonisba (by recalling the former to his duty to Rome, which causes Massinissa to require suicide of his forbidden bride). In the battle of Zama he has faced Hannibal for the first time, decisively defeated him, and thus cleared the way for Roman hegemony. At this point we can see ahead centuries of incomparable imperium.[132] The view resembles that at the victorious moment of the *Aeneid*. There, Roman destiny had gained a foothold in Italy. Here, that same destiny begins to climb to its zenith, while Roman *virtus* is already at its most admirable. And as in Virgil's poem, the poet looks ahead to the physical glory of the city of Rome. When in book 8 of the *Aeneid* Evander shows Aeneas the sites that will become the Tarpeian rock and the Capitol, "aurea nunc, olim silvestribus horrida dumis" (now of gold, formerly bristling with wild thorns), Virgil purposefully reveals the difference and identity of Rome bridging the abyss of time.[133] Petrarca is less explicit. When Carthaginian ambassadors arrive in Rome, seeking peace from the Senate, they are awestruck at the architectural wonders that were actually built many years after Scipio's era.[134] The anachronism is too obvious to be the poet's oversight.[135] In fact, Petrarca's most typical movement is literally anachronistic. By reascending the current of time, he creates a fictive entity, a composite Rome, which has existed nowhere else. The poet displays his power to build an artifice superior to time, partially fulfilling the promise made for him in book 2.

When, therefore, the issue has been decided and Rome's destiny assured, there falls a contemplative lull. After the Roman fleet has set sail for Italy, the sea itself is calm.

> Non rauca procellis
> Equora fervebant; ventisque silentibus undas
> Victorem sensisse putes.
>
> (9.2–4)

(The waters did not seethe harshly in a storm; with the winds fallen silent, you would think that the waves were aware of the victor.)

The sea and all the elements do homage to the victorious Scipio. Several times earlier in the poem a sea voyage has been the occasion for important conversation or soliloquy: by Hannibal and an old sailor in book 6, by Hannibal alone in book 8, and by his dying brother Mago at the end of book 6. Here, as Festa expresses it,

> L'attività della memoria e della fantasia s'intensifica; lo spirito si sente quasi a contatto con l'infinito e contempla le cose umane da un'altezza meravigliosa.[136]

Thus in this last book, as in the first two, the narrative is elevated, the flux of human violence and time falls calm as the windless sea, and men speak eloquently of essential matters.

Ennius sits on deck on the commander's ship, lost deep in thought. Petrarca first introduces him personally here, described as "assiduus rerum testisque comesque" (the constant companion and witness of his deeds) (11). Petrarca follows Claudian in making Ennius a companion of Scipio in war, a poet who commemorates what he has himself seen.[137] Scipio addresses the silent poet as "solamen dulce laborum" (sweet comfort for my labors) and asks for some words to quiet his cares. His request that the poet break a long silence ("Nunquamne silentia rumpes . . . ?") reveals a certain momentous undercurrent in the situation. Here at last the poet appears and speaks, no longer eclipsed by his future rival and his present detractors.

One way of ordering an interpretation of this scene and its extraordinary richness lies in the structure of Ennius's discourse itself. What he has to say falls into three parts, each prefaced and followed by words of encouragement or reaction from Scipio. The subject matter of each part is clearly distinct. It may be summarized thus: (1) Ennius first speaks of his role as praiser of the deeds of Scipio (24–64), (2) then, of the nature of poetry (78–123), (3) and finally, recounts a dream he had recently (133–289). It is possible, without forcing the pattern, to see each of those stages of the poet's discourse as corresponding to an element of the general pattern we have pursued: (1) gift exchange, (2) poetics as civic function, and (3) temporal reversibility. Book 9 would thus seem to stage a fulfillment of the archaic longing of humanist poetics and summarize Petrarca's ideals. It remains to be seen, however, whether the conclusion of the poem maintains the elements in their positivity as they are first given.

Although Ennius finally speaks for himself, the preoccupation evident in his reply to Scipio's inquiry is the same one previously expressed by other characters: the concern that his own poetry cannot do justice to Scipio's *virtus*. His "peritia fandi . . . Nuper ab exiguis radicibus orta" (eloquence recently sprouted from meager roots) (45, 47) is too primitive to adequately fulfill its office of commemoration. This judgment has already been expressed by Publius Cornelius Scipio in the passage from book 2 (445) cited earlier and also by Lelius in book 4 (37–40). In the latter passage, part of the panegyric of Scipio is a comparison between him and Achilles. Scipio deserves a poet as great as Homer to sing his deeds; the *insanus iuvenis* Achilles, on the other hand, deserved no better than *rusticus Ennius*. Now Ennius raises his own voice to echo those judgments. He, too, recalls the relationship between Homer and Achilles by evoking Alexander before Achilles' tomb (51–54) and agrees with Lelius that no one is more deserving of Homer than Scipio (58–59).[138] He does not, of course, neglect the more general point:

> Non parva profecto
> Est claris fortuna viris habuisse poetam
> Altisonis qui carminibus cumulare decorem
> Virtutis queat egregie monimentaque laudum.
>
> (54–57)

(It is no little good fortune for illustrious men to have a poet who can amass the glory of outstanding excellence and the monuments of praise with high-sounding poems.)

The subjunctive *queat* means that few poets are capable of *altisona carmina* and that it is only poetry of such quality that can store up or increase (*cumulare*) the glory of greatness. Given this situation, Ennius (like Scipio's father) can only hope the hero will find a more worthy poet in the future.

> Currentibus annis
> Nascetur forsan digno qui carmine celo
> Efferat emeritas laudes et fortia facta.
>
> (60–62)

(As the years run by, there will perhaps be born one who with a fitting poem will bear to the heavens your deserved praises and powerful deeds.)

As we shall see, Ennius's hope is not uninformed.

In declaring the primitive nature of Ennius's art, Petrarca follows certain classical judgments. Ovid calls his predecessor "ingenio maximus, arte rudis" (greatly talented, but technically crude).[139] But an emphasis on the poet's limitations in a work that glorifies poetry requires some explanation. Petrarca's negative judgment of Ennius can be attributed partly to his sense of competition with a forerunner. Petrarca did not know Silius Italicus's *Punica* and so was unaware of any previous poem on Scipio besides what he knew of Ennius's fragments.[140] The only place, besides the *Punica* and his own work, where Ennius appears as a character is briefly in Claudian's *De Consulatu Stilichonis*,[141] so Petrarca had considerable freedom in portraying him. But it is not enough to invoke the "anxiety of influence"; Petrarca's love for ancient writers surpasses his jealousy of them. In addition, the portrayal of Ennius in the *Africa* has a pronounced positive side. As the principal figure of poet here, he must embody Petrarca's ideal of the function of poetry. Therefore, Ennius may fall short as poet of the greatest of heroes, but he is at the same time the credible bearer of truth about poetry.[142]

It is some such truth about the nature of poetry that Scipio urges

Ennius to reveal. The logical progression of the conversation becomes clear as the general assures his poet that he wishes to be sung by no other. Once he has agreed to the mutual relation that poetic praise institutes, Scipio desires initiation into the mysteries of poetics. Assuming the role of student or initiate that he has played earlier, Scipio asks to learn "que sint permissa poetis, [et] . . . quid laurea signet" (What is allowed to poets, and what the laurel means) (70–72). He declares that he is not undeserving of such secrets. When Scipio represents himself as a man of action with an appreciation of beauty ("nobis animum dulcedine quadam / Pulcra movent" [beautiful things move my spirit with a certain sweetness] [75–76]), he reveals himself as the ideal Renaissance patron-prince.[143] However, a man of action permits himself such pleasures only as respite from his real business, as *otium*. When the taste for beauty exceeds certain bounds, it becomes pernicious and enervates; that is the lesson of the Massinissa episode.

We find in the reply of Ennius further proof that poetics is at least partially constituted by a relation with temporal power. Ennius prefaces his explication of the nature of poetry by recognizing the importance of Scipio's last words, but goes further: The pleasures of the Muses have always pleased leaders, no matter how rough; Scipio merely surpasses all in this virtue as in every other. The poet tends to increase the place for poetry, overstepping the bounds of *otium*. Delight in the Muses is, after all, just as natural as the love of glory.

> Errasset, si cui dederat [sc. Natura] cupidissima fame
> Pectora, Musarum non ingessisset amorem.
> Quisquis enim se magna videt gessisse, necesse est
> Diligat eternos vates et carmina sacra.

> (85–88)[144]

> (Nature would err if it did not bestow a love of the Muses upon someone to whom it had given a heart avid for fame. Whoever sees that he has accomplished great things necessarily loves eternal poets and their sacred poems.)

Great deeds and the thirst for fame would be inadequate without the immortalizing power of poetry.

When Ennius takes up the nature of poetry, he repeats a number of the same points raised by Petrarca in the *Collatio* and *Privilegium*. In fact, the circumstances are similar. Although some terms hint at a defense of poetry, the scene presents poetry triumphant. Ennius the soldier has shared in Scipio's victory, and as poet he will share the leader's triumph and laurel coronation in Rome, on the same Capitoline where Scipio's other poet will be crowned in 1341. Ennius's exposition of poetry is the *Collatio* to his own coronation.[145]

Ennius emphasizes the factual basis of poetry somewhat more than the laureate Petrarca. If the latter rejects wholly fictitious invention, the former seems to restrict further the freedom of poets: "Non illa licentia vatum est / Quam multis placuisse palam est" (Poets do not have that freedom which many evidently desire) (90–91). The restriction is understandable under the circumstances; if Petrarca conceives of epic as essentially panegyric, then the story of Scipio (whether told by Petrarca or Ennius) must appear to be based on Scipio's real qualities. "Scripturum iecisse prius firmissima veri / Fundamenta decet" (It is necessary first of all for a writer to lay the perfectly sound foundation of truth) (92–93); on this foundation the poet will spread the traditional veils that make the attainment of the truth more satisfying. Ennius stresses the paradox inherent in the commonplace, between a factual basis that hides as a central kernel of truth and the deceptive play of appearance on the surface.

> Quicquid labor historiarum est
> Quicquid virtutum cultus documentaque vite,
> Nature studium quicquid, licuisse poetis
> Crede: sub ignoto tamen ut celentur amictu,
> Nuda alibi, et tenui frustrentur lumina velo,
> Interdumque palam veniant, fugiantque vicissim.
>
> (97–102)

(Believe me: poets are permitted any effort in history, any devotion to excellence and example for life, any inclination of nature—provided these things, otherwise bare, be hidden with an unfamiliar mantle, and sight be frustrated by a light veil, as they alternately come and flee from view.)

Thus, at the same moment that Ennius calls poetry truth,[146] he asserts the autonomy of its illusiveness; his poetics holds the two aspects in tension.

When Ennius turns to the significance of the laurel, he takes up the familiar ideas of its immortal green, its sacredness to Apollo, and its immunity to lightning. On this latter point, the limits of poetry's victory over time (as asserted by Publius Cornelius Scipio in book 2) are forgotten as poetry stands fearless:

> Iam fame quod fulmen erit, nisi sola vetustas
> Omnia prosternens? Hunc gloria nostra pavorem
> Non habet, atque ideo spernentis fulmina frondis
> Serta gerit.
>
> (120–23)

(What would be a thunderbolt to fame, if not age alone, which strikes down all things? Our glory does not have this fear, and bears the garland of leaves which scorn thunderbolts.)

Nor does Ennius neglect the familiar idea that *vates* and *duces* share the laurel triumph (111). As in the case of the *Collatio,* the public, political ceremony of laurel coronation is made the culmination of poetics. Just as the laurel symbolizes the greatest powers of poetry (foremost among them immortality), so do the various excellent qualities explicated by poetics reach their definitive recognition in the Roman triumph. What this amounts to is in a sense a palinode to the discussion of poetry in book 2.

The desired harmony with the public realm, figured in the first two parts of Ennius's discourse, is based on the dream of temporal reversibility. That much becomes apparent in the vision that Ennius recounts to satisfy Scipio's desire for more *dulcia verba.* There is significance even in the words with which the general urges his friend to "kill time" by continuing to speak.[147] The subsequent passage is emphasized in a way similar to the speech in book 2 introducing Petrarca amidst the vanity of literature. There, the heavens stopped time. Here, too, there occurs a universal lull, albeit less cataclysmic. Scipio in his request mentions the circumstances: No land is in sight, the sun has just passed its zenith. The calm of wind and sea that greeted the start of the conversation evidently continues. As Ennius begins, everyone aboard becomes attentive: "Hic omnes tenuerunt murmura naute / Et comites siluere ducis" (At this point all the sailors held their voices and the general's companions fell silent) (132–33).[148] This last passage shows that while what preceded was only a conversation between Scipio and Ennius, the following possesses greater and more impersonal interest, addressed to all.

The vision Ennius recounts is briefly this: As a result of his loving cultivation of Homer, Ennius dreams of Homer the night before the battle of Zama. After reverently greeting the poet's squalid image and learning the reason for his blindness, Ennius learns of the successful issue of the next day's battle. A lacuna ensues, then the two poets are looking upon Petrarca in Vaucluse. Homer explains who this is and the poem he intends to undertake; at these words a great affection for the future poet takes hold of Ennius. He starts to greet Petrarca but at that moment is awakened from his dream by battle trumpets. What is there in this brief passage that makes it seem to hold the secret of the *Africa?*

"Je n'ai pu percer sans frémir ces portes d'ivoire ou de corne qui nous séparent du monde invisible."[149] Nerval's words describe well the awe with which Petrarca, or any of his predecessors in the classical tradition, would regard the passage in and out of the realm of sleep with its myriad revelations. What the words also indicate, however, is the difficulty of that passage. Difficulty of knowing the precise relationship between the two realms; of estimating what one carries into sleep or what of real value one carries away. The well-known ascent of Aeneas, through the ivory gates that release him from the underworld, dramatizes the doubt in which one must stand upon waking. For this reason, the *frémissement* connotes fear as well as awe and expectation.

It is also worth suggesting that the passage into the dream-world represents a typically humanist retrieval of certain habits of mythical thought. Freud has proposed the similarity of dreams to archaic forms of language. He claims that they share an amphibolic nature, or the refusal to observe logical principles of contradiction and opposition.[150] It thus seems that dream experience tends in a direction similar to the ideal of humanist poetics. What we would then observe in Petrarca's oneiric regression in time is a movement beyond his classical sources to a yet earlier time of magical effectiveness.[151]

And yet, E. Benveniste has justly criticized Freud's too-hasty parallel between dreams and archaic language. In addition to the linguistic problems, what is at issue is a mistaken appeal to origins. Language as such does not evolve from amphibolic roots. As Benveniste points out, it is rather discourse as *style* that achieves the contradictory movement analogous to dream experience. That means that rhetorical and poetic tropes, rather than any imagined pristine origins, are what manifest the most profound expression of opposition.[152] Petrarca and humanists after him stage a variety of atavistic movements through the very artificiality of literary convention. The coincidence of dream with a poetics of cultural belatedness in the *Africa* makes those movements all the more powerful.

Petrarca would have read in Cicero's *Somnium Scipionis* the pretext for his own *somnium Ennii,* illustrating the power of literary hypostasis:

> Fit enim fere ut cogitationes sermonesque nostri pariant aliquid in somno tale, quale de Homero scribit Ennius, de quo videlicet saepissime vigilans solebat cogitare et loqui.[153]

> (It happens as a rule that our thoughts and words produce something in a dream, in the way that Ennius writes concerning Homer, about whom he plainly thought and spoke very often when he was awake.)

Petrarca presents Ennius as someone like himself, a devoted seeker for companionship in the recesses of antiquity, looking back even beyond the reach of fame. Whomever he found shining with merit, he embraced:

illum
Amplexu tenuisse animi michi gloria summa est
Inque locum cari semper coluisse parentis.

(139–41)

(It is the highest glory to me to have held him in a spiritual embrace, and cherished always in the place of a beloved ancestor.)

He cherished the poets above all,[154] and Homer first among the poets. As a consequence of his loving study of Homer's work, day and night, both spent in this study, and sleep and waking became indistinguishable to Ennius. The identification of antithetical states signals a movement backward in time—here, the time of literary history. As a consequence, Homer appeared to Ennius one night: "michi ... Affuit in somnis" (158–59). Yet Ennius immediately retracts the suggestion that he was asleep: "Quis somnum dixerit illum? / Pervigil astabam" (Who says it was sleep? I was awake) (159–60). He claims that he was kept awake that night by concern for the climactic battle about to take place the following day. The description of Homer's approach ("Aspicio adventare senem" [I observe an old man approach] [167]) is as of the meeting of two people in the same waking realm. Yet at the end of his narrative, Ennius describes his awakening from a dream: "Excutior visis, somnusque recessit inanis" (I am shaken out of the dream, and vain sleep withdrew) (287). That last word on the dream, *inanis,* stands in contrast with what the poet sees upon opening his eyes: the full living figure of Scipio moving his troops to battle.[155]

Moreover, *visum* is a technical term in the typology of dreams. In the list that Petrarca knew from Macrobius's commentary to Cicero's *Somnium Scipionis, visum* is the lowest sort of dream, referring to apparitions that come to someone between sleep and waking who thinks he is awake; they have no truth value for divination.[156] In the chapter on dreams in his *Rerum memorandarum libri,* Petrarca even denies the necessary truth value of dreams in general and considers their occasional verification as coincidence.[157]

Something similar might seem to be true of Scipio's dream earlier in the poem. At the beginning of book 2, his father reminds him how uncertain the vision will seem to his waking mind (2.7–10). However, the defect lies not in the dream experience itself but in the very different state of mind that will judge it. There is no doubt that Scipio is asleep or that he owes his privileged moment to divine permission. And the word his father uses is *somnium*, which, according to Macrobius, is enigmatic but does have a claim to truth. In contrast, the status of Ennius's vision (strictly speaking, *visum Ennii* rather than *somnium*)[158] remains ambiguous; has he passed through the ivory gates or the gates of horn?[159]

One fact, at any rate, is clear about the vision of Homer: It is based on love. Ennius's love for Homer brought the dead poet into his presence. Homer greets him as "care michi Latie telluris amice / Unice" (my dear only friend from the Italian land) (173–74), and upon learning the old man's identity, Ennius falls to embrace the feet of the shade—vainly, in a manner familiar from the *Aeneid* and *Divina Commedia*: "Umbra fuit nudeque heserunt oscula terre" (He was a shade, and my kisses fell on the bare earth) (179).[160] This love against time can only be frustrated.[161]

The pendant of love is the pathos of destitution. Homer appears as a beggar "quem rara tegebant / Frusta toge et canis immixta et squalida barba" (covered by the scant rags of a toga and a filthy white beard) (167–68). True to tradition, he is blind (169–70). Ennius cannot understand how a blind man could have known and described the world with such mastery. What Homer replies to this can be taken as a more general statement on his poverty: "Qui michi corporeos Deus abstulit, ille nequibat / Restituisse alios quibus hec archana viderem?" (Did the God who deprived me of corporeal eyes not know how to repay me with others, by which I might see these secrets?) (201–2) The poet's privilege with respect to *arcana* more than compensates his physical nullity.

Ennius accepts the proposal of his sightless guide to proceed. The only indication before the lacuna of what Homer intends to show him is in the phrase "Fortasse videbis / Multa animo placitura tuo" (Perhaps you will see many things pleasing to you) (211–12). Several scholars have argued that Petrarca intended to fill the lacuna with a procession of the great poets of antiquity.[162] The spectacle would thus somewhat resemble the *Trionfi*. This hypothesis finds some support in Petrarca's tenth Eclogue, *Laurea occidens*. In that poem the shepherd Silvanus (the figure of Petrarca) describes his voyages to cultivate the laurel; meaning allegorically just such a literary journey in pursuit of ancient poets as Ennius describes in the *Africa*. Silvanus's most important encounter is with Homer, who greets the Italian poet affectionately and leads him to where he can see the crowd of poets.[163] The remainder of the poem is devoted to a literary-historical list, which identifies each poet by periphrasis. Finally, Silvanus himself obtains the laurel, aided by Argus (King Robert). This is not the place to discuss the laurel's double significance of poetic glory and Laura (the sorrow of Silvanus is due to the laurel's death); what is relevant is the similarity of certain elements to book 9 of the *Africa*. Those elements are the narrator's cultivation of ancient poets, his affectionate encounter with Homer, and the importance of the laurel as a goal. It might then be a reasonable suggestion that the main feature of the eclogue (a *Triumphus poetarum,* we might say) resembles the missing or unwritten part of book 9. Homer would thus show Ennius the great poets who had written between their two ages and after Ennius (these would indeed be *multa placitura*). The procession would end with the last poet of the Latin tradition, Petrarca.

Like Festa's suggestion about the Palace of Truth, this is an attractive hypothesis, but unprovable and, what is more, not indispensable to understanding what is important in the poem. What joins Homer, Ennius, and Petrarca in the vision is a myth of literary continuity based on a community of love and on a victory over temporal distinctions. To convey this, Petrarca has turned to his own use elements already present in the poetry of the true Ennius. The most important element may be called poetic metempsychosis.

Petrarca's vision of Ennius uses as its point of departure the vision that begins Ennius's own epic, the *Annales*.[164] The *Annales* exist only fragmentarily, as citations in other works. Petrarca knew enough of these other works to have some idea of how Ennius began his poem.[165] This epic on the history of Rome was apparently introduced by an invocation of the Muses and an account of an apparition. Cicero in his *Academica* and *De re publica* relates that Homer appeared to the poet in this vision or dream. Ennius heard the exclamation "O pietas animi," which was probably addressed to him by Homer. Otherwise, the only surviving words of Homer to Ennius are "Memini me flere pavum" (I remember that I became a peacock).[166] After this fragment the poem proper begins. What could Petrarca make of these enigmatic pieces?

Both Lucilius and Horace call Ennius *alter Homerus*.[167] What may seem only metaphorical homage becomes more precise in light of an obscure passage in Persius (6.9–10) referring to Ennius: "postquam destertuit esse / Maeonides, Quintus pavone e Pythagoreo" (After Ennius had dreamed that he was Homer, from the Pythagorean peacock). Petrarca knew Persius; he may or may not have known the ancient scholiast who tried to explain the passage by introducing an ancient genealogy of a soul's various incarnations. Misinterpreting the *Quintus* of Quintus Ennius as an ordinal number, the scholiast presents the poet as the fifth possessor of one soul. The order of incarnations is Pythagoras, peacock, the Trojan Euphorbus, Homer, and Ennius. The obvious chronological absurdities apparently did not hinder this genealogy from becoming a commonplace in antiquity. Lactantius Placidus, the fifth-century scholiast of Statius's *Thebaid,* makes only minor adjustments.[168] It is not certain that Petrarca knew these versions of the genealogy, although he did read Statius as well as Persius, if not their commentators. He did, however, know a third version, found in pseudo-Acro's commentary on Horace. In an ode (1.28), Horace introduces Pythagoras who claimed to possess the same soul as Euphorbus formerly. The scholiast elaborates thus:

[Pythagoras] praedicavit se . . . Euphorbum . . . fuisse, qui interfectus . . . iterum revixit, factus Pythagoras . . . hic ante et in Homerum dicitur renatus, postea in pavonem, postremo iam in Ennium poetam.

(Pythagoras declared that he had been Euphorbus, who, after his death, lived again and became Pythagoras. He is also said to have been reborn first as Homer, then as a peacock, and finally as the poet Ennius.)

The main point here is the descent of Ennius from Homer; that is what is at issue in the proem of the *Annales.* To legitimate his epic undertaking, Ennius claims for himself Homeric inspiration of the most intimate sort possible. In this way, he makes clear his preeminence as the first true epic poet in Latin, eclipsing such predecessors as Livius Andronicus and Naevius. The peacock, too, has a major role, perhaps especially in pseudo-Acro's version where it intervenes between the two epic poets. In the *Annales,* "Memini me flere pavum" means that Homer knows his soul existed in a peacock before passing on to Ennius. The significance of the bird lies in its acceptance in antiquity as a symbol of immortality.[169] Petrarca was aware of the tradition that considered the peacock's flesh to be incorruptible.[170] Ennius's invocation of divine inspiration (from the Muses) and intertextual inspiration (from Homer) amounts to an affirmation of the immortality of his poem. This affirmation reappears more openly a few lines later ("Latos [per] populos res atque poemata nostra [clara] cluebant") and at the beginning of book 16, making Ennius's boast the first explicit reference to literary glory in Latin literature.[171] Finally, the other incarnations are not negligeable: neither the "first philosopher," Pythagoras, nor Euphorbus, a Trojan character in the *Iliad.*[172]

Thus, we can place Ennius's fragments in an ancient tradition where metempsychosis combines with a genealogy of poetry and wisdom. It is both these elements that help to understand Ennius's epitaph, which Petrarca knew from Cicero and may be the text he cited and imitated most often:

Nemo me lacrumis decoret nec funera fletu
Faxit. cur? volito vivus per ora virum.[173]

(Let no one honor me with tears or celebrate my funeral with weeping. Why? I fly living from mouth to mouth of men.)

Ennius's survival after death is not simply in his poetry, which lives on when spoken. The breath of his *psyche* too will enter into a successor in the series of poets. As for Petrarca, he was aware of this succession—most important, from Homer to Ennius and of a possible succesor to Ennius. As a serious Christian, Petrarca would not retain in his work the full force of a literal metempsychosis. Rather for him the transmission of a soul becomes the image of an ideal evident throughout his work: that the present can ultimately be joined with past and future through the identity of one soul.[174] The mythical tendency to not distinguish logically separate temporal domains is matched here by the effacement of the ego, or the identity of subject and object. Petrarca's dream experience portrays him as about to melt into a composite with his poetic kin.

And yet, paradoxically, that tendency to self-effacement results in an almost hubristic self-affirmation. In the triad of poets, Petrarca may be seen as the linear successor to Homer and Ennius, the poet of the "last age" (*Africa*, 9.223) who closes the Latin tradition begun by Ennius and perhaps the broader poetic tradition begun by Homer. But Petrarca also considers himself a synthesis of Homer and Ennius. This becomes clear in the passage in Lelius's speech mentioned earlier (4.37–41). Homer sang Achilles, a defective hero; the greatest hero, Scipio, was first sung by Ennius's insufficient art. Petrarca's undertaking in the *Africa* is to be an *Ennius alter* (and thus an *alter Homerus*), but better, because his art will establish a harmony between the poem and the object of its praise.

When Ennius and Homer come upon him in Vaucluse, Petrarca is seated in a laurel grove, preparing to crown himself. He is also about to begin the *Africa*.[175] As Homer describes the undertaking and triumphs of Petrarca that rival those of Ennius, the latter, far from feeling jealousy, is seized by a strong affection. Ennius says to Scipio: "Iam michi carus erat te propter et alta relatu / Cetera" (Already he was dear to me on your account and the other lofty material in the narrative) (272–73). He is breathless with desire to see and talk to the future poet; he even goes so far as to wish Homer would be silent to make possible communication with the other! This preference expressed by Ennius is not simply evidence of Petrarca's egoism, but shows the essential importance of the poet's task. Ennius turns from Homer to Petrarca not because the latter is a novelty just revealed to him, but because Petrarca will fulfill his own task of honoring Scipio. Ennius's joy comes from learning that Scipio's glory will not be obscured by the years, but rather augmented. Likewise, the new poet's light will brighten the old age of Rome. Thus, at the heart of this poetic succession lies the poet's task of praise.

The ancient poets have drawn closer to where Petrarca is seated. Ennius marvels at all he hears from Homer, when Petrarca becomes aware of their presence, "auditaque salute / Sustulerat gravis ille oculos et dicta parabat" (and when he heard our greeting he solemnly raised his eyes and prepared to speak) (284–85). At this sublime moment Petrarca flirts with the impossible. What would it mean if the modern poet greeted his forerunners in his own poem and could for once speak with them face to face rather than *aenigmate*? How would humanism's dream come true? How would Petrarca and Ennius join hands in their common glorification of Scipio, establishing the poet's rightful place in the *res publica*? It is a view of paradise, although barely glimpsed. Barely glimpsed because, though their eyes have met, Petrarca is left with his mouth open about to speak:

> vix . . . dicta parabat,
> Cum matutino litui clangore repente
> Excutior visis, somnusque recessit inanis.
>
> (284–86)

(He was just prepared to speak when I am suddenly shaken out of the dream by the morning blare of the battle-trumpet, and vain sleep withdrew).

Like Scipio's dream, that of Ennius is dissolved by a military blast. The abrupt shifts in verb tense emphasize the disorientation that results from both waking and temporal dislocation. All the epic passions in the *Africa* pale to insignificance beside the pathos of that moment of missed opportunity. (And yet, had Petrarca had the time to rise and go to embrace Ennius, which one would have yielded? Which would be the insubstantial shade?)[176]

Despite his dream's failed consummation, Ennius has infected Scipio with his enthusiasm for what he has seen. Still, the great man recognizes the uncertainty of what has been retold. Is it a true vision or poetic invention? "Seu sunt, seu talia fingis, / Dulcia sunt, fateor, sensusque et pectora mulcent" (Whether it is so, or whether you are making it up, I confess that all this is sweet and charms my senses and heart) (302–3). More important, Scipio declares his love for his future poet, whether that poet is to exist or not.

> Illum equidem iam nunc iuvenemque novumque poetam
> Complector, tibi nunc visum quondamque parenti,

Promissumque michi gemino sponsore profecto
Diligo, quisque erit; si nullus, diligo nullum.

(304–7)

(Already now I embrace that new young poet, seen now by you and previously by my father; and, promised to me by a double sponsor, I love him, whoever he may be. If he is nothing, I love nothing.)

Although Ennius's words are guaranteed by the more trustworthy prophecy of Publius Cornelius, Scipio does not commit his faith entirely to dreams. Yet he embraces the idea of his own praise all the same. In this declared embrace some critics have seen the climax of the poem.[177] That climax, of course, cannot be a plenitude, located as it is in the dubious realm of Ennius's dream and in Scipio's words for his unborn and perhaps imaginary glorifier. But—following that interpretation—precisely here lies the poem's (and poet's) triumph. When Scipio says, "si nullus, diligo nullum," he declares his faith, not in a historical Petrarca, but in the power of poetry.

So it would seem that the scene between Ennius and Scipio represents a realization of the ideal poetic situation. Even the apparently inconclusive dream finds redemption in the verbal embrace between the hero and his present (re)creator. The natural culmination of all this ought to be what we, in fact, find later: the laurel triumph of Scipio and Ennius on their return to Rome, followed by Petrarca's reminder that he, too, has experienced the same honor.[178] Yet a closer look at the remainder of book 9 shows that the poem concludes with a negative reversal of each of the elements introduced thus far. The *Africa* thus reveals in its self-reflexive epideictic character the emergence of an original genre: tragic panegyric.

Each of the elements that underlie the poem and find their most concentrated expression in Ennius's discourse (poet-patron exchange, civic function of poetry, mythical time) shows a negative sign to complement its affirmation. First, it may seem that Ennius's modesty about his ability to do justice to Scipio is reassured by Scipio's acceptance of him and the promise of the future Petrarca. However, what appears in all of this is an indefinite postponement of a harmonious match between poet and *dux*. Words are the medium of Scipio's and Petrarca's embrace, and that is not nothing, but there remains an unsatisfied yearning for real presence. Moreover, Ennius's position points out a more general truth about the poet-patron relation. When a poet describes his task to a willing patron, he normally falls back into a confession of incapacity; the virtuous leader is too good for his words. In contrast, it is the reluctant patron who gets to hear the bold boasts of poetic power, since he is the one who must be convinced to reciprocate in the exchange promoted by the poet.[179] Thus, it is Scipio's putative excellence itself that postpones his proper tribute.

Second, if the laurel coronation affirms poetry as ideal civic service, the narration of Scipio's and Ennius's common triumph ought to be the narrative clinching of that affirmation. And indeed, Petrarca begins his account as a model of victorious plenitude. He prefaces his description by invoking Calliope for additional inspiration (322–23) and to set off the the scene that ensues. Never was there so beautiful a day; Apollo presides in all his solar glory (324–29).[180] Scipio appears looking like a god ("generisque ferebat / Etherei frons alma fidem" [his gracious brow bore proof of a celestial lineage] [340–41]). An immense and varied array of conquered peoples and booty attests the establishment of Roman imperium. Scipio ascends the Capitoline hill to place the booty in the temple of Jupiter, contenting himself with a verbal acquisition, his new cognomen Africanus (391–92).[181] However, as he turns back from the Tarpeian rock, Scipio is suddenly revealed as "coronatus lauro frondente" (crowned with the leafy laurel) (398). He wears the laurel crown, but with no mention of a coronation. The importance of this omission increases when we find Ennius laureate at Scipio's right hand and when the implications of their common triumph are declared:

> Ennius ad dextram victoris, tempora fronde
> Substringens parili, studiorum almeque Poesis
> Egit honoratum sub tanto auctore triumphum.

(400–2)

(Ennius at the victor's right hand, his temples bound with a similar foliage, celebrated the honorable triumph of his studies and gracious Poetry, on the great example of Scipio.)

What Petrarca asserted in the *Collatio* and the *Privilegium* as the parity of the glory of *dux* and *poeta* is here realized in Ennius's triumph at Scipio's side.[182] This triumph of poetry and learning, their establishment in the *res publica,* has Scipio as author or authority. The different terms among which Petrarca hesitated in his revisions— *auctor, princeps, iudex, consul*—show what importance attaches to the precise nature of the Scipio-Ennius relationship at this moment.[183] Yet with the absence of a ceremony, the triumphant moment gapes as a lacuna.

That it is a necessary lacuna becomes clear when we reconsider the third and most important element. The dream of Ennius appears as a

successful *mise-en-scène* of temporal reversibility, its inconclu-
siveness redeemed by Scipio's acceptance of its significance for him.
However, the emptiness of that embrace (similar to Ennius's greeting
of Homer) also emphasizes the inextricably verbal nature of the vision.
That verbal nature founds the basic uncertainty of Ennius's experience, as indicated above. The only power that might rescue the dream
from its shaky epistemological status appears in the laurel that Ennius
and Homer saw Petrarca about to place on his own head (218–19). In
the *Collatio laureationis* (11), Petrarca mentions as one property of
the laurel its power to make dreams come true if the sleeper is touched
by it. Here a character in the dream is the one touched, but a character
who is also ultimately its author. The dream's unusually self-
referential nature complicates the issue. Petrarca is character and
"real" author; Ennius is narrator, character, and intertextual source of
the dream through his *Annales;* Homer is character but also orchestra-
tor of the dream as well as its psychological cause, in the sense that
Ennius's assiduous reading of him led to the dream. What all this
indicates is that both the uncertainty and the possible recuperation of
Ennius's dream derive from its status as a poetic contrivance: inspired,
conceived, and populated by poets, and guaranteed by the poetic fiction
of the laurel. Scipio's dream possesses far greater certainty, dreamed
and populated by men of action and inspired by a work on the public
realm by Cicero the political philosopher. The dream of the poets is so
much a matter of literary history that the referential world hardly
finds a place in relation to it. That world appears only through the leap
of faith by which Scipio deigns to extend his patronage to the unborn.

The absence at the heart of each of those developments leads to the
poem's logical "conclusion": the ultimate absence that is death. The
search that the *Africa* embodies, of a place and time for poetry, finds
its goal thus: Its place is the grave, its time the past, present, and future
of tombs. The thoroughness of such negation may no longer appear
unprepared. It only remains to consider why that particular resolution
is appropriate and what besides biographical accident and historical
subject matter could motivate it.

A POEM'S DESTINATION

Only when we consider both *somnium Scipionis* and *somnium Ennii,* those twin poles about which Petrarca's poem describes its eccen-
tric orbit, does the conceptual structure of the *Africa* become clear.
What emerges from Scipio's vision is an assurance of continuity
through filial and national *pietas.* His god-given task is ratified by the

assurance he receives of a glorious national destiny and the place of his family in it. On the other hand, book 9 presents a poetic community founded on literary *pietas* that ratifies the celebratory undertaking of Ennius. The action of the poem, such as it is, is framed by Roman political imperium and by a far less assured image of Latin literary imperium,[184] each based on its proper sort of *pietas*. The link between the two is, of course, the relationship between *dux* and poet. The harmony of the two Latin traditions ought to be accomplished in the verbal embrace between Scipio and the poets. Petrarca aimed at the same accomplishment in his own Roman coronation. What both symbolic actions, embrace and coronation, depend on is the possibility of temporal reversibility, the transformation of historical time into mythical time. If Roman *virtus* can inform the contemporary world, if the poet can retrieve his ancient honor through intimacy with those he finds in books, then the exercise of supreme power, poetic and military, may yet be realized.

Immediately after the description of the victorious homecoming and Petrarca's self-introduction, triumph plunges into destitution. The poet renounces the pursual of Scipio's career, admitting its fall from this pinnacle of success to public disgrace and exile:

> Nunc ego non ausim vos hinc ad tristia, Dive,
> Materiamque trucem post tot modo laeta vocare.
>
> (410–11)

> (Now, o Muses, I shall not dare call you from such glad matters to what is sad and cruel.)

The poet dismisses the Muses; he leaves to others the commemoration of the wrongs done to Scipio and the great man's bitter epitaph.[185] Nevertheless, to say, "I shall not pursue sorrowful matters" is already to pursue them. Rather than leave Scipio in his glory without a mention of what befell him later,[186] Petrarca has begun the coda that will end the poem in a minor key. The question is *why*?

The most obvious element of an answer lies historically in the death of King Robert in 1343. Most likely he did not represent a political ideal to Petrarca, unlike Cola di Rienzo.[187] But whatever the real Robert may have been, the poet's expressions of sorrow declare that with his death all virtue has departed from the world.[188] The king was not merely the official bestower of Petrarca's crown. Their conversations in Naples acquire a special significance in representing the ideal friendship between princely patron and poet, an embrace similar to the one that links the Roman hero and his modern praiser.[189] When

Petrarca granted Robert's request and dedicated the *Africa* to him, the *alter Ennius* thereby established a *Scipio alter*.[190] Even more, Petrarca added poetic power to the king's endowments. In a letter immediately preceding those letters that narrate the events leading to his laureate coronation, the poet praises a eulogy that Robert presumably delivered for his recently deceased granddaughter. The effect of this opuscule, says Petrarca, has been to make the deceased live on in the world just as Christ has immortalized her in heaven. He imagines people who will echo Alexander at Achilles' grave by exclaiming, "o fortunatam, que talem preconem tue virtutis invenisti" (o fortunate girl, who found such a herald for your excellence).[191] King Robert thus provides a supreme example of a prince who supports poetry—not only through patronage, but also through being a poet himself, and even assuming Homer's role. In this he resembles Petrarca's conception of Augustus, who only needed *otium* to become a supreme poet.[192] The poet's crafting of an ideal relationship of exchange sublimates the patron to the point where both parties are poets.

However, just as King Robert is only one of the powerful with whom Petrarca sought to establish a satisfactory relation of patronage, so the crisis of Robert's death has a more representative significance. The intellectual of the Trecento is a figure caught between two worlds. No longer securely in the bosom of the Church as cleric and university teacher, the man of letters moves progressively into the milieu of courts. With secularization comes, more pertinently, a division of labor and an aristocratization of intellectuals.[193] We may see the prevalence of this humanist claim of nobility in such details as the title of Boccaccio's poem on the *Africa, Versus domini Iohannis Boccaccii*.[194] The humanist's designation as *dominus* both sets him squarely in the princely court and claims a parity with those more traditionally called *domini*. The movement toward such a rapprochement operates as nostalgia for a mythical past when such parity existed. As in the utopian verbal embrace between Scipio and Petrarca, patron and poet become indistinguishable.

More generally, it is also true that the reaction of Italian élites to the various crises of the Trecento—banking crises, monetary stagnation, decreased agricultural production, numerous economically based revolts, demographic contraction causing cycles of famine and epidemic[195]—was a perverse imitation of temporal reversibility. In Italy more than elsewhere, the response to those crises was an effort to turn back the clock through the restoration of feudal structures, while admitting the influx of the inevitable nascent bourgeois elements.[196] The maintenance of power thus manifested itself as a simultaneous looking backward and forward. Like the humanists gazing at the past, the élites would have liked to find there an ultimate ground for their claim to power. The duality of their situation, however, explains the tentative and contradictory nature of much political activity of the time. The irresolution, or realism, of someone like the Emperor Charles IV in his reluctance to take truly imperial steps in Italy enraged Petrarca.[197] *Litteratus* and prince execute a similar movement against time—that is, against history—but the prince's is necessarily less thoroughgoing. King Robert, characterized by later nostalgia for his reign as a return to the golden age,[198] could seem an exception to princely limitations and a figure more in harmony with Petrarca's desires.

Finally, the simultaneous loss of Scipio and Robert in the poem is significant because of a kinship that has deeper roots than may at first appear. Certainly, Petrarca cherishes Robert because the king recalls a better time. But it is also true that that "better time," embodied in Scipio, is not stable and self-possessed. The most heroic moment of Roman *virtus* requires confirmation in the earlier roots and later ramifications shown to Scipio in books 1 and 2. The aristocratic republic of the Second Punic War is based particularly on an earlier state of affairs. This last point is argued by Vico, who sees the Roman republic as based on oppression of the plebeians by the nobility. The latter based their claim to power on an appeal to a primordial state of heroic authority due to alleged heavenly genealogy.[199] The epochal significance of the Punic Wars lies in the fact that, until the elimination of Carthage, the Roman patricians hesitated to go to war for fear of arming the lower classes. Likewise, the celebrated custom of not taking booty derived from the desire to not enrich the plebeians. Hence, honor came to count as payment for military service.[200] So that two details that Petrarca presents as among Scipio's most superlative qualities— his rumored divine descent and his satisfaction with nothing but a name as a reward for his generalship—turn out, from a Vichian point of view, to be evidence of regression and class warfare. Not only is Petrarca's conception of his own role in the *res publica* ideological and atavistic, but also is his ideal historical example turned in that direction.

At the end of the *Africa,* when the poem should be achieving a triumphant conclusion, its foundations (dedicatee/patron and hero) are destroyed. That destitution may be understood at least in part as the surfacing of the poem's historical contradictions, or its bad conscience. Although the faith in poetry's immortalizing power may not be canceled out, that in itself is not enough to provide legitimation. Left without social roots and wealth at the death of its supporters, impoverished poetry finds itself cast out of the *res publica.*

It is to just such a destitute figure, his poem itself, that Petrarca

turns in the extraordinary *envoi*. It is here that the *Africa* reveals
itself as tragic panegyric, combining what Petrarca considered the two
highest literary modes.[201] The beginning of his apostrophe, "O mea non
parvo michi consummata labore / Africa!"[202] (O my *Africa,* finished by
me with no little labor) (421–22) is modeled on the conclusion of Statius's *Thebaid.* However, Statius expresses modesty about his epic's fortune because of the huge shadow of the *Aeneid*.[203] In contrast,
Petrarca's doubts about his poem's survival are due to the vicissitudes
of time and the public situation of all poetry revealed by King Robert's
death. Now that the one exceptional figure has gone, poetry's normal
existence in the world is clear.

The civic function of poetry, boasted in the laureate texts and represented "historically" in the situation of Ennius, has collapsed into exile. The poem has no place in the state. Its itinerant fate leads it to
wanderings that match its uncertain claims to truth.[204] The convention
of the *envoi* in lyric tradition consists of a personification of the poetic
text, as the words become flesh are set in motion to seek effectiveness
(typically, compensation from the beloved). Petrarca's adaptation of
that convention sets the hypostasis of the poetic word in contrast with
its present impotence. Such a contradiction dramatizes the final development in the relation of patronage and exchange.

While the poem would normally be told to betake itself to an addressee, here the patron's death closes off the expected *iter* (426). No
money and protection are to be found that way. Impoverished in both
senses, material and political/social, the poem is nevertheless directed
to a road ("Quo tramite perges, / Infelix? Monstrabo viam." [By what
path will you travel, unhappy one? I shall show you the way.] [426–
27]).[205] The *via* is now to Robert's sepulcher. There the poem will
dedicate itself in fulfillment of the promised exchange (432–33). The
poem's journey is based on trust in Robert's side of the exchange, his
love for Petrarca,[206] even when the former is now an immortal soul,
like Scipio's father, looking down from the heavens on human error
with nothing else to bestow.

Faced with impoverishment and exile, the poet expresses a familiar
longing for temporal reversibility:

> Felices quos illa prius meliora tulerunt
> Tempora! Nosque utinam . . .

(446–47)

(Happy those whom a better time bore! Would that we too . . .)

But that impulse to an impossible leap, which the rest of the poem
attempts, is immediately repressed with the realization

            Nequicquam vana precamur!
Non licet ire retro.

                                                    (447–48)

(In vain we are praying for what is empty! It is not permitted to go back.)

Because the past is unattainable and the present is unbearable, the
only route with hope lies in the direction of a possibly better future.
To that utopian hope, Petrarca commits his poem's posthumous fate:

    At tibi fortassis, si . . .
    Es post me victura diu, meliora supersunt
    Secula: non omnes veniet Letheus in annos
    Iste sopor!

                                                    (453–56)

(But perhaps, if you are to live on long after me, better times will greet you;
that Lethean sleep will not last forever!)

While Boccaccio, in his verses *ad Affricam,* predicted a return of the
golden age because of the poem's appearance, Petrarca here submits
his poem's fate to a possible golden age independent of it. Of course,
he thereby perpetuates myth; despite its rejection in the previous "Non
licet ire retro," temporal reversibility returns through the backdoor
that is utopia. The images are familiar: the future return from shadows
to a pristine radiance, the restoration of Helicon, the reflowering of
the laurel with poetic inspiration.[207] Hoever, even that world, which
will be the world of the *Africa*'s true existence and effectiveness, is
imagined as organized around an essential lack. The poem will travel
to one more grave.

    Tu nomen renovare meum studiosa memento:
    Qua potes, hac redeat saltem sua fama sepulto
    Et cineri reddatur honos.

                                                    (462–64)

(Remember to ardently renew my name. As much as you can, at least let
his fame return to one who is buried, and let glory be rendered to ashes.)

This last instance of self-glorification in the *Africa* is a sepulchral
moment in keeping with the rest of the *envoi.* The grave of poet as
well as patron is the place of poetic immortalization. And the poem
must spend its period of waiting for renascence in a dark and narrow
dwelling that resembles a tomb ("repostum / Angustumque precare

locum sub paupere tecto" [request a remote and narrow place beneath a poor roof] [471–72]). Such will be its exiled existence for posterity until the golden age comes, and time can be reversed for the poem become eternally young.

Tum iuvenesce precor, cum iam lux alma poetis
Commodiorque bonis cum primum affulserit etas.

(476–77)

(Then, I pray, become young again, as soon as the light which nourishes poets and a time which favors the virtuous shines forth.)

The poem ends thus, with a promise, or a vision.

MORTAL POETRY

A consideration of the poem's conclusion should include a detail of the revision that Petrarca pursued. The line that describes the poet at work in Vaucluse, raising his eyes at the approach of Homer and Ennius ("Sustulerat gravis ille oculos et verba parabat" [285]) did not satisfy him. In a marginal manuscript note, he told himself: "attende Eneyda 4, in fine."[208] The reminder *attende* means to check a passage in a classical writer to see if its echo in the *Africa* is too close. In this case, Petrarca refers to *Aeneid* 4.688–69, which describes Dido's vain attempt to speak further while dying from her self-inflicted wound: "illa gravis oculos conata attollere rursus / deficit" (striving again to raise her heavy eyes, she failed). What is remarkable is that the words for the poet's grazing encounter with his poetic forefathers (and we have seen in how strong a sense they are his forefathers), which should be a transcendent joy, are similar in the poet's mind to the most pathetic moment of a lover's tragic death. Of course, the subjects are *graves* in obviously different ways, but there is a sense in which the poet's concentration and studious inspiration draw near to bloody suffering. Death remains an intimate part of the poet's genius because its negativity, although resisted, works as the dialectical corrective to his mythical affirmations.[209]

The *Africa,* like the texts concerning the laureate ceremony, voices an attempt to represent the life of poetry in the *res publica,* based on its office of praise and intimate relationship with temporal power. And yet as the epic ends, poetry's place is among the dead, a dwelling indicated by many other Petrarchan texts as well.[210] Such a phenomenon might be simply explained: Petrarca's ideal past, the sole period worthy of poetry, has receded, as has the sole modern leader worthy of mention in the same breath. Quite true; but a more important point concerns the working of poetic praise itself. What is at work is an exercise of verbal power, aiming at commemoration and purification of military and political power. That which is present can never be free of taint. Historically, that taint seems evidence of more or less violent domination. For Petrarca, however, the taint is due particularly to the mortal enemy of glory, envy. Envy thwarted the greatest men, Scipio and Julius Caesar. It is also the greatest enemy of the poet's glory.[211] Only after death can envy be defeated and the perfect power of *dux* and *poeta* have a chance to flourish. But, of course, beyond death lies impotence for all those not aided by literature. Yet literature requires support and legitimation from living temporal power, is thus subject to envy, and cannot escape from the vicious circle in which its praise of *virtus* sets it. The victory over envy and the full exercise of power can only be imagined as a victory over time. The impossibility of that victory, played out by the end of the *Africa,* is evidence of the humanist mystifications and partial self-correction of which Petrarca provides the first great example. There is no patronage but intimacy with the dead in their grave; no republic but what one finds rising from one's own mortality to flutter on the lips of those to come; no victory over time, only the dream of an eternal present. Such is the setting of Petrarca's work of glorification.

The inevitable failure of temporal reversibility brings with it an inkling, unrealized, of the meaning of history. Expressed as a formula: that encounter of myth with history constitutes poetry. Literature is the elaboration of mythical thought's eloquent failure in its historical working out. The failure—and persistance—of myth, and the victory—yet complicity—of history find their most powerful image together in Petrarca's final scene. The poet meets the past and its imagined virtue in the intimacy of the grave, where he embraces what he loves in all its vanity. The *Africa* ends with the personified poem circulating as an exile in history among the different tombs: of the hero/patrons present and past and of the poet to come. Poetic immortalization is no triumph. Its crown is heavy with the pathos of a losing struggle against death and forgetfulness, compromised by its necessary dwelling with what it opposes.

3

The Quattrocento and Poliziano

Can Honour's voice provoke the silent dust,
Or Flatt'ry sooth the dull cold ear of Death?

VIRGIL CONTRA MALATESTA: VERGERIO AND SALUTATI

THE most important defense of poetry in the Trecento is, undoubtedly, that of Boccaccio in the last two books of his *Genealogie deorum gentilium.* As he approaches the end of his argument, the author makes a final appeal to the enemies of poetry, so that they, defeated by his reasons, may be reconciled to poetry. That this conversion may not seem a humiliation, Boccaccio gives the example of King Robert, who was convinced by conversation with Petrarca to change hostility to love of poetry. The conversation alluded to is the laureate examination of 1341 in Naples.

Boccaccio characterizes Robert before his conversion thus: "clarus olim phylosophus et medicine preceptor egregius, atque ... insignis theologus" (an illustrious philosopher and preeminent authority on medicine, as well as a famous theologian).[1] The only example of his scorn for poetry is directed against Virgil: "cum ... parvi pendisset Virgilium, illumque cum reliquis more vestro fabulosum diceret hominem et nullius fore precii ornatu subtracto carminum." (He did not think highly of Virgil, and, among other things, in your manner [the enemies of poetry], called Virgil a storyteller who was of no value once the adornment of his poetry was removed.) This is the theologian's familiar charge of poetic mendacity. The content of Petrarca's discourse with Robert must have resembled his coronation oration because, as Boccaccio reports, he revealed to the king that profound truths lie hidden beneath the surface of poetry. King Robert, to whom this possibility had never occurred, was immediately convinced and regretted that he had begun so late in life to understand poetry. He began at

128

once to cultivate poetry, "ut plenum e Virgilio sensum sumeret" (so that he might embrace Virgil's full meaning).

Boccaccio thus adds an element of adversity overcome to Petrarca's attainment of the laurel crown. Robert was not always the ideal patron but had to be formed, or reformed. Boccaccio portrays him as an intellectual already possessing the equipment of the dominant professions (medicine and theology); his acceptance of poetry only depends on his realizing its philosophical substance. When the poet provides him with the allegorical key, Robert's about-face concentrates on the figure of Virgil. What was formerly worthless the king now adopts with a promised embrace (*ut . . . sumeret*) both intellectual and affectionate.

This version of Petrarca's verbal triumph may be compared instructively with an event that, although it happened in 1397, may be taken to mark the beginning of Quattrocento discourse on poetry. The first actor is Carlo Malatesta, lord of Rimini. The Malatesta family had been among the most valued protectors of Petrarca's later years.[2] He addressed to Pandolfo Malatesta a sonnet of warm praise emphasizing his ability to make permanent the virtues so evident in the prince. The poem concludes with a contrast between memorials of bronze or marble and poetry's greater durability: "ma'l nostro studio è quello / che fa per fama gli uomini immortali" (but our activity is the one which makes men immortal through fame).[3]

In 1397 Carlo Malatesta was leader of the Venetian league aiding Francesco Gonzaga in his war against Milan. After a victory at Governolo on 28 August, Malatesta arrived in Mantua; as somewhat of a conqueror, although it was the city of his ally Gonzaga. The victorious prince objected to a statue of Virgil in the city that was held in perhaps superstitious honor by the people. The circumstances of the event remain somewhat murky, like Malatesta's motives. But it seems that his devoutness was offended by what appeared a concession to paganism. Hence, he had the statue pulled down and thrown into the Mincio.[4]

Among the reactions to this insult we have two important contemporary documents. One is a letter of 18 September 1397 from Pier Paolo Vergerio to Lodovico degli Alidosi, papal vicar of Imola. The other is a letter of 23 April 1398 from Coluccio Salutati, chancellor of Florence, to Pellegrino Zambeccari, chancellor of Bologna.[5] Both letters protest Malatesta's action, and both take the defense of Virgil's statue as the point of departure for a more general defense of poetry. They have their place in a long series of disputes about Virgil lasting two centuries.[6] What is significant here and what marks the entry into the fifteenth century is that in both cases the defense of poetry does not finally depend on allegorical interpretation. The humanist no longer hopes for a simple about-face as soon as poetry's double nature is revealed to its enemy, as in the case of Petrarca and King Robert. What the defense does depend on is the power of poetic praise. The varieties and dilemmas of that power in the Quattrocento will be the subject of this chapter.

The relation between Carlo Malatesta and Virgil, and its contrast to the relation between King Robert and Virgil—as well as the relation between Malatesta and the humanists, and its contrast to the relation between Robert and Petrarca—reintroduce the ever-present pairing of patron and poet/humanist. This chapter develops the convergence of two aspects of poetic praise: its function in an exchange relation of patronage and the transcendent power claimed for it based on its mythical status. These two aspects find their full development in texts by Poliziano. That is, I will read his *Ambra* as the play between the mythical power of poetic language and the poet-patron dialectic; and *Nutricia* as the play between the primordial social role of poetry and, again, the poet-patron dialectic.

Pier Paolo Vergerio's letter provides a good example of how a particular situation of "patronage" directly influences discourse on the nature of poetry. In this case, the situation comprises both an immediate negative relation between Virgil and Carlo Malatesta and the ideal positive alternative. Vergerio is careful not to isolate himself in opposition to the prince. He appeals to Lodovico degli Alidosi to speak to Malatesta as one prince to another, "principem princeps hortare" (202) for the reestablishment of the statue.[7] Vergerio praises Lodovico at the beginning of the letter as the only contemporary prince who cultivates poets and orators (189). In addition, he blackens Malatesta's action by comparing it with the favor granted to poets by greater princes such as Augustus, by King Robert, even by Malatesta's own ancestor Pandolfo. Thus, Vergerio attacks the present example of princely abuse of a poet by appealing to an ideal, yet historical, harmony between poet and prince.[8]

In this insult to the greatest poet, Vergerio sees a triple scandal.[9] It consists first of the disparity between what one prince has done and what any prince ought to do, next in the disparity between intention and result in the conflict between prince and poet, and finally, in the disparity between what this poet in particular suffered and what he or any poet deserves. Vergerio's poetics here are thus structured by a concentration on the ideal and the actual nature of the prince, the nature of the poet, and the exchange between them.

The scandal lies first in the incongruity of Malatesta's person and his action. For a plebeian to scorn poetry is insignificant, because the *vulgus* has nothing in common with literary glory (193). Likewise, someone content with the consciousness alone of virtuous deeds could afford to neglect any trumpeting of fame. But a prince must not only be, but also seem; for this reason, he should have *in pretio* not only *virtus,* but also *gloria.* Multiple examples of patron-princes come forth to show how wise leaders cultivate their glory through literature (193).

The scandal lies also in the unintended irony of Malatesta's vandalism. By destroying a monument, he evidently hoped to obscure Virgil's honor and consign him to oblivion ("obscurare laudem ... delere memoriam" [191]). But, in fact, just the opposite will be the case; he has consigned himself to infamy and has not affected the immortality of poetry, which does not depend on statues. Vergerio boldly compares the prince to the ancient criminal who sought fame by setting fire to the Ephesian temple of Diana.[10] That Malatesta's infamy will last forever is due, of course, to the nature of literature. "Que potest esse, non dico eterna, sed vix lunga ullius rei memoria sine scriptorum ope?" (What memory of anything can be long, let alone eternal, without the power of writers?) (192)[11]

Verbal power does not simply record; otherwise, we would have *nomina nuda.*[12] Rather, the poets hypostatize unseen places and men so vividly that readers "interfuisse rebus ipsis videantur" (seem to be among the things themselves) (193). From this ensues the same paradox introduced in Petrarca's *Privilegium,* that things remote from us in time can be known better than what is more recent, if only they have the benefit of *clari auctori.* The poetic word is the necessary supplement to perishable human memory.

> Memoria namque hominum facile perit, et vix unius seculi vivit etatem, nisi libris et memorie litterarum commendetur. errat ergo qui sibi gloriam querit et scriptores negligit, quando non potest partam gloriam famamque tenere sine beneficio litterarum.
>
> (193)

> (The memory of men perishes easily, and lives scarcely a century, unless it be entrusted to books and the memory of literature. Whoever seeks glory for himself and neglects writers goes astray, since he cannot hold on to newborn glory and fame without the benefit of literature.)

The scandal lies finally in the identity of the victim: Virgil. All the excellence and powers of poets are found in Virgil to their highest degree; Malatesta's error is thus all the greater. Mantua, the object of the recent military action, owes its prestige to the poet; indeed, Mantua is more glorious for its citizen Virgil than Rimini is for its prince. The familiar commonplace of Homer's birthplace(s) turns up here, used as in the *Pro Archia:* fortunate Homer, whom Greek cities competed to claim as a native son! (196)[13] Virgil, in contrast, is exiled from his true birthplace: "Virgilius patria sua pulsus est" (195). This greater Archias does not even get the chance to defend himself.

Vergerio's defense of poetry, like Boccaccio's (and Petrarca's), is both a panegyric of poetry and poets and an invective against the enemies of poetry. The primary purpose of poets, according to Vergerio, "est virtutem laudare, vitio turpitudinique detrahere" (is to praise excellence, and to draw away from vice and shamefulness) (202). He resorts to invective when the prince shows himself unworthy of panegyric, that is, when the prince hinders the establishment of the right relationship between poetry and power. The victorious *dux* has felt himself threatened by a poet, rather than seeking a collaboration. The embrace of poetry that should have followed upon military victory (as in the *Africa*) has been replaced by a blow. Malatesta's attack on the venerated statue has something atavistic about it. It harks back to mythical days when *vates* had magical-religious power to compete with kings. Vergerio replies with similarly atavistic gestures, sketching a poetics based on those good old days when power recognized power. Even when his positive alternatives of patronage to Carlo Malatesta are historical and not too distant, they acquire meaning as approximations to an archaic ideal. In his attempt to restore the fallen idol of poetry, Vergerio evokes with a dense network of commonplaces the power imagined and lost.[14]

While the isolated humanist Vergerio allies himself with a tradition of good princely patrons, Salutati, a member of the ruling class, proceeds with an ironic confusion of praise and blame. That confusion works both in the immediate context of the writer's attitude toward Carlo Malatesta and in the idea of poetry that he elaborates there.

Salutati's procedure is to deny that the act of vandalism ever took place. He expresses disbelief that a man as intelligent as Carlo Malatesta could be capable of such a thing (294).[15] Salutati chides his correspondents for their credulity. But his disbelief is simulated.[16] His strategy is to attack the action while denying it was committed. The argument goes: "Malatesta is far above such a foolish deed, which is foolish for these reasons. . . . " Thus Salutati can bind together the two versions of Malatesta, syntactically distinguishing but implicitly confounding defense and accusation, praise and blame. For example, he says his correspondents have called "dominum illum, virtutibus multis perspicuum atque clarum, hostem infestissimum musis contemptoremque" (that lord, brilliantly conspicuous with many virtues, a furious enemy and despiser of the Muses) (288), as he puts the antithetical predicates of *dominum illum* on the same grammatical level. The lengthy defense of poetry concludes with a hope that Malatesta may see it, "non ut corrigat errorem suum, in quem, ut arbitror, non incurrit, sed ut se firmet in recte proposito, si, prout est credibilius, non erravit" (not so that he may correct his error, which, as I believe, he did not commit; but rather that he may be strengthened in his upright intention if he did not err, as is more believable) (294). On this play of ambiguity Salutati builds his defense of poetry.

A substantial part of that defense is composed of a familiar network of concepts, usually considered medieval: poetry as hidden truth, justified by its presence in the Bible and its use by the church fathers. This allegorical way of thinking is constant in Salutati, as a look at his correspondence or his vast treatise *De laboribus Herculis* will show. But here, at least, something more is at work.[17] First, he gives a particular twist of emphasis to the commonplace of poetry as veiled truth, where *illa* (*divina*) contrast with *ista* (*humana*):

> ut sicut in illa veritas ex veritate processit, sic in ista non ex veritatibus solum, sed ex fictis et humanis inventis ipsa veritas oriatur, et quasi lux in tenebris lucens et ex falsitatum abditis immaculata procedat.
>
> (293)
>
> (Just as in the divine realm truth has appeared from truth, so in the human realm truth may arise not only from what is true, but from fictions of human invention, and may appear unstained from the hiding-places of falsehood and like the light shining in darkness.)

The old paradox of poetry's deceptive surface concealing truth stretches to become something subtly different. Here the image no longer presents truth as kernel or veiled *arcanum,* but as a creation that arises or is produced (*oriatur*) by the power of poetic falsehood. Invention is active, no longer merely concealment. Moreover, the obvious allusion to the *Logos* at the beginning of St. John's Gospel ("quasi lux in tenebris lucens") raises the argument to a yet higher plane. Salutati boldly compares the truth produced by the poetic word with the truth of the divine Word. And the light of that word is immaculately conceived in the nooks of falsity. Although Salutati may elsewhere separate static truth as independent from poetic surface, here the whole appears dynamic, and poetry claims its own peculiar autonomy.

The other notable element of Salutati's defense is meant to refute the accusation attributed to Malatesta (also cited by Vergerio) that poets are *histriones.*[18] To answer the condemnation of poets for their excessive praise, Salutati takes as his point of departure two *loci classici.* First, there is Horace's definition of the poet's twin function: *prodesse . . . aut delectare.* Then, Salutati reads Aristotle through Averroes to assert that "poete sit ... laudare vel vituperare" (288).[19] Now, whether a poet praises or blames, he profits or pleases or both; so far nothing new. But Salutati's argument centers on the idea that a poet still profits and pleases whether or not his praise be true. "Nam si vere sint laudes . . . prosunt atque delectant" (if the praise is true, it profits and pleases); obviously, since all men enjoy praise and are incited by it to live up to their praise. "Sin autem falsa fuerit poete laudatio . . . tenendum est commendationes, quas false scripserat, vel acerrimam criminationem esse vel sincerissimam doctrinam" (However, if the poet's praise is false, his approval, which he wrote falsely, should be considered either bitterest indictment or perfectly straightforward instruction) (289). It thus turns out that praise can actually be blame. What may seem shameless flattery is actually an ironic comment on the prince's lack of those same qualities, or else, and perhaps at the same time, it is a didactic presentation of those qualities the prince should acquire. With the matter expressed thus, poetry can do no wrong in fulfilling its nature, to praise. The question of truth becomes irrelevant, although the ethical purpose of poetry is never lost from sight.[20] If in this light we again consider Salutati's attitude toward Malatesta, to whom he later wrote praising the prince's *humanitas*,[21] the entire letter appears an example of what he theorizes in this last passage: the author is at once praising and blaming, praising falsely in order to blame and make the prince worthy of true praise.

The reality of Carlo Malatesta's insult to Virgil's statue is obscure and fairly insignificant. But it may be clear now why the literary reactions to that pretext are not insignificant. The letters of Vergerio and Salutati introduce commonplaces central to Quattrocento discourse on poetry. Those commonplaces form a constellation that can be characterized thus: The poet bases his plea for a place in the *res publica* on his necessary office of praise and glorification (with its necessary partner, invective). This self-promotion, in turn, is based on a growing awareness of the aesthetic autonomy of poetry and an ever loftier idea of the poetic word. Such ideals force a gaze at the past, both mythical and (literary-) historical, for their previous realization.

PATRONAGE AND POETIC EXCHANGE

At issue here is the traditional bad reputation of Renaissance humanism. Literary historians used to condemn the absurd pretensions of humanists, as if those pretensions could be separated from a positive contribution to the progress of letters.[22] Humanists have traditionally been seen as purveyors of a cult of fine phrases, of appearance without substance. They have been compared with the Greek Sophists; for both, as J. A. Symonds puts it, "Phrases and sentences supply the place of feelings and convictions."[23] This matter is not unrelated to the question of Latinity touched on in the previous chapter. By most accounts, the humanists erred in joining their fate to that of a dead language and in preferring to imitate tradition rather than stepping out of their books. The underlying idea is that the humanists ought to have been sincere, expressed themselves and the world around them. The obvious corrective to such a one-sided view of literary history lies in a recognition of the intertextuality of humanism. "Phrases and sentences" are indeed the heart of the matter. But that also means that a kernel of truth remains in the traditional view; it needs only to be cultivated in a different way. Perhaps the pretensions of the humanists, their worst "sophisms," are inseparable from their real contributions to the Renaissance.

Like the sophists, the humanists have been traditionally discredited for their venality. Since Socrates, a taint has adhered to words exchanged for payment. That taint has seemed to fall not so much on humanist pedagogy as on the literary milieux of princely courts. Yet it might be worthwhile to ask just what sort of poetics grows up in such "compromised" circumstances, where exchange constitutes a fundamental structure.

In their letters in defense of Virgil, both Vergerio and Salutati refer to what poetry deserves in terms evoking a material debt. Salutati mentions *commendationis preci[um]* (the price of [poetry's] recommendation) (292), but Vergerio's vocabulary especially is significant.[24] He, too, writes in terms of a *pretium* owed to poets (198), but, more important, suggests a structure based less on commerce than on gift exchange with reference to the *benefici[um] litterarum* (the benefit of literature) (193) and to poets as *celorum munera* (gifts from the heavens) (201).[25] Vergerio, moreover, insists on a reciprocity (which Carlo Malatesta has refused): The statues granted to such poets as Virgil are a *munus* (196), analogous to the many things that Augustus bestowed (*donavit*) upon Virgil (200).[26] The protests against the injustice done to Virgil's statue take up some of the images, familiar from antiquity, evoking the poet's proper existence as a participant in gift exchange. Quattrocento humanism evolves a series of variations on those images.

The figure of Francesco Filelfo presents an extreme yet exemplary case of humanistic venality and inflation. V. Rossi succinctly characterizes his "impudente pieghevolezza di carattere e . . . ciarlatanesca prosopopeia."[27] During a long career, Filelfo sold his praise to any prince who would pay and directed his invective against anyone who would not.[28] The most notorious example of his panegyric is his epic *Sforziade,* meant to immortalize Francesco Sforza, lord of Milan. Filelfo made it known that he, as dispenser of immortality, was ready to sell a place in his poem to anyone who wished to purchase a glorious survival into posterity.[29] Such a character seems to display the self-seeking use of commonplaces that have long lacked real meaning. What is the relationship between such a careerism and a more sober humanism, a more general discourse on poetry?

At a point when Filelfo was encountering a certain measure of ingratitude from his patron of the moment, a letter from Theodore of Gaza to Antonio Beccadelli shows concern about this *res Philelphi*.[30] The two prominent humanists are evidently concerned with Filelfo's problem principally as it indicates a more general problem of the times for them and their colleagues and how it may be remedied. If a poet or philologist is not rewarded by his patron as he deserves, Theodore proposes a series of approaches to be tried until one is successful. One (here, Filelfo) should first reveal to the prince one's need, and remind him of the ideal submission of arms to wisdom and of the fact that poets and *viri docti* are those "penes quos est nomen, laus et perpetua memoria principum" (in whose power is the name, the praise and the lasting memory of princes) (336). The reasoning continues:

> Tamdiu enim principes vivunt quamdiu nomen eorum in scriptis hominum doctorum servatus et predicatus. Rogari etiam, honorari et laudari principes ab hominibus doctis officium est.
>
> (336)

> (As long as princes live, so long is their name preserved and proclaimed in the writings of learned men. Indeed, it is the duty of princes to be begged, honored and praised by learned men.)

By this account, the customary role of the poet is simply to praise and to ask remuneration. The word used for the prince's obligation, *officium,* declares the binding nature of the exchange. That exchange is a contract modeled on the Roman formula *do ut des* (I give that you may/must give).[31] Moreover, it is in the conventional nature of bestowal that the bestower thereby establishes his superiority. Someone who accepts a gift without rendering another gift falls to a position of dependence and servitude.[32] The humanist's strategy is to try to convince the patron of that danger, to encourage him to assert his superiority through a generous one-upmanship.

Moreover, honor has a doubly important role in the relation. Honor is naturally the substance of the humanist's gift, as in the above passage where *honorari* and *laudari* are roughly synonymous. But, in addition, a patron who does not reciprocate will by that very fact lose his honor, which is the most important "profit" of gift exchange properly performed.[33] Honor, or glory, is both immediate enunciation and the patron's future self-transformation within the structure of exchange that the humanists want to institute. Hence literary praise, as the rhetoric that aims at glory, comprises two stages: poet's (verbal) action and patron's (material) reaction. And hence, the humanist's interest in the effect of praise on the prince's character. In his letter to Zambeccari, Salutati considered praise sufficient to honor or correct the prince. Likewise Theodore of Gaza: "Decet id (sc. praise) enim, si virtus in principe est; iuvat, si virtus desideratur" (Praise is fitting if there is excellence in the prince; if this is lacking, then praise benefits or pleases) (336). *Iuvat* can mean either "benefit" or "please"; in this fusion of the Horatian *delectare* and *prodesse* lies the problem. Will the prince merely delight in false praise or will he be improved by it? Theodore seems to believe the latter: "aluntur namque honore ac laude non modo artes, verum etiam ingenia, indoles et animi principum" (for not only the arts are nourished by honor and praise, but also the natural abilities, character and mind of princes) (336).[34] Praise, then, regardless of its truth or untruth, will improve the prince's character and hence the poet's material condition. Only if this approach fails ought one to resort to extraordinary means, to the other *genus emendandi* ("alterum in laudando positum, alterum in reprehendendo" [one sort based on praise, the other on blame] [337]). Then one may proceed with a just harshness, as a physician with his cautery when other remedies have failed. All that harshness does is confirm the abasement the patron himself has accomplished by refusing to reciprocate.

Elsewhere, Antonio Beccadelli imagines an exchange of epigrams between a prospective patron (the humanist Pope Pius II) and a needy and hopeful poet (probably Paride Ceresara). The patron claims to deal with the poet on his own terms, in an exchange of verses, and so to be relieved from the commercial transaction of paying for the poetry he has received:

Desine pro numeris nummos sperare, poeta;
  mutare institui carmina, non emere.[35]

(Poet, do not hope for money in exchange for meter. I undertook to trade poems, not to buy them.)

The reply that Beccadelli attributes to the scorned poet attempts to correct the patron's faulty conception of the exchange relation.

Desine tu vitae laudem sperare, sacerdos,
   modo pro verbis, verba referre studes.
Sis licet Aeneidos vates, sis alter Homerus,
   malumus abs te nos munera, quam numeros.
Pauperis est proprium versus dare, divitis aurum.
   Dives, habe versus, munera, pauper, habe.
Augustus Musas ac doctos doctus amavit
   et posset versus cum dare, lucra dedit.[36]

(Priest, do not hope to be praised if you now want to return words for words. Even if you are another Virgil or Homer, we would rather have presents than poems from you. It is natural for a poor man to give verses, and for a rich man to give gold. Rich man, here are verses; poor man, here are gifts. Learned Augustus loved the Muses and learned men and, while he could have given verses, he gave money.)

The poet echoes the beginning of the patron's epigram but immediately asserts the dissymetry that does not permit words to be rendered for words. The rich man, *dives,* must give what properly belongs to him; whatever poetic talent he may have, it is not essentially his. Like Vergerio, Beccadelli brings forth Augustus as an ideal example of the right relationship with poets, even though, like Petrarca, Beccadelli admits the Princeps' poetic talent. While the patron's epigram associates the verse-for-money exchange with a tainted commercial model (*emere*), the poet rebuts that association through the long and honorable tradition seeing such an exchange as gift exchange. *Munera* become synonymous with *lucra.*[37]

The needy poet who, nevertheless, bestows his great gift is thus rich and poor, both dependent and independent. The poet's independent superiority, like the superiority of letters to arms, is based on his primacy in bestowal. His dependence on the princely patron is a dependence both on his necessary material sustenance and on the ratification of the exchange relation that the true patron performs. The other side of the coin, which justifies the dependence and explains the independence, is the need princes have of poets. It is an elemental need; as the wind to sailors, as the rain to farmers, so are poets to princes. Beccadelli puts it thus in a letter recommending himself to Filippo Maria Visconti, Duke of Milan.[38] The prince requires immortality more than money, power, or even—Beccadelli lingers on his audacity—virtue:

Quo per immortalem Deum Princeps indigere potest, nisi immortalitate, quam non pecunia, non potentia, non denique virtute ipsa comparare quis potest, absque poetarum auxilio?

(1v)

(What, by immortal God, does the Prince need, if not immortality? Who can obtain it through wealth, or power, or, finally, virtue itself, without the aid of poets?)

As water and fire are indispensible in life, so are *monumenta literarum* after death.[39] There is thus a tendency to portray as second nature what is eminently artificial. When, at the end of the century, a far greater humanist writes to a far greater prince, Erasmus assures Prince Henry of England (the future Henry VIII) that the poet's gift of immortality surpasses all material gifts because it is part of him: "non aliena, sed propria largiatur" (he bestows nothing that is not his own).[40]

This emphasis on the writer's autonomy may be less paradoxical where the work in question is not directly panegyrical. Such is the case in the domain of historical writing, although it remains true that many histories are more or less subtle panegyrics of one prince or another.[41] The greatest pedagogue of the age, Guarino Veronese, wrote in 1446 to Tobia Borgo, the designated historian of Sigismondo Malatesta (grandson of Carlo), "de historiae conscribendae forma."[42] Although Guarino dwells on the power of books to immortalize great deeds and does not forget the ubiquitous commonplace of Alexander at Achilles' tomb, he believes that the best way to achieve this victory over fate is the historian's independence.[43] Guarino's characterization of the historian may be taken more generally as an eloquent expression of the humanist's ideal of autonomy:

Sit enim scriptor intrepidus incorruptus liber licentiosus verus, non odio non amori non misericordiae quicquam tribuens, non pudibundus, iudex aequus, cunctis benevolus, hospes in libris, nullis adscriptus civitatibus, suis vivens legibus.

(462)

(The writer should be fearless, uncorrupted, free, unrestrained, true; making no concession to hate, love or pity; not shamefaced, an evenhanded judge, well-disposed to all, a guest/host in books, belonging to no city, living by his own laws.)

This is a portrait of subtle shadings, which reveals not quite all the freedom claimed. The writer is literally autonomous, *suis vivens legibus,* but only at the price of homelessness or exile, *nullis adscriptus civitatibus.* Rather, he finds his homeland in books. The twin sense of *hospes* expresses well the situation: As guest, the writer finds asylum in books and community with the great minds of the past; as host, he is the custodian of these realms of permanence to which he admits the worthy few whom he inscribes there.[44] The writer constructs his own home, which only exists through literary activity. And that activity is both reading and writing: reading the ancients as guest and writing contemporaries as host. Despite his proud attitude toward them, the historian depends on those whom he writes and for whom he writes.[45]

In the same letter, Guarino makes it clear that poetry goes even further than history in its freedom. In addition to the various liberties of the historian, he permits the poet the liberty to stretch the truth, thereby pushing to an extreme conclusion the Aristotelian distinction between history and poetry.

> Haec (sc. poetica) enim vel intempestive laudare et plus quam verisimilia licenter proferre profitetur et alatos equos effingere et in deos mortales vertere nil veretur.
>
> (461)[46]

> (Poetry claims to praise, even in an untimely manner, and to utter without restraint what is improbable, and does not fear to fashion winged horses and transform mortals into gods.)

Although Guarino's tone here is not necessarily approbative, he claims that the power and autonomy of poetic praise depend on the ability to surpass what is true, to violate nature.

In asserting the writer's freedom from the laws of Fortune, princes, and nature, a further step can be taken: to assert that poetry and eloquence are intrinsically violent and lawless. Poggio Bracciolini writes plainly, in a polemic against jurisconsults. In his argument, literature benefits from and resembles military aggression. The greatness resulting from Alexander's conquests, from Athenian hegemony or Roman imperialism, would have been impossible without the initial lawlessness in each case.

> Silerent literae, muta esset eloquentia, conticescerent bonae artes, omnis liberalis doctrina obdormivisset, praeclara opera, ingentia edificia cessassent omnia, si obsequendo vestris legibus suo quisque contentus, aetatem in ocio absumpsisset.[47]

> (Literature would be silent, eloquence would be mute, the liberal arts would hush, every branch of learning would fall asleep, all illustrious works and mighty constructions would pass away, if everyone obeyed your laws and squandered his life in ease, content with his own.)

The more general statement follows: Everything worthwhile is a consequence of violence and injustice.[48] The *ingenium*, like the Aristotelian soul interpreted as *endelecheia,* creates through its continuous rest-lessness;[49] it follows and imitates the violence of the princes who support it.[50] And the rejection of the principle of equity (*suo quisque contentus*) becomes, strangely enough, the basis of literary patronage.

If in the preceding Poggio seems to submit literature to the primordial lawlessness of arms, he expresses the matter differently in a letter exhorting Leonello d'Este to *studia humanitatis.* Although traditionally there have been two ways to glory, arms and literature, in our day, Poggio claims, the former is no longer a source of solid praise; great deeds disappear if not committed to literature. One side of the exchange is left in silence; the unreciprocated gesture of literary bestowal affirms its supremacy.

> Iacerent enim sepultae atque obrutae perpetua oblivione Regum atque Imperatorum res gestae quantumvis illustres atque magnificae, quippe quae raro aetatem hominis excederent, nisi doctissimorum virorum industria immortalitati dedicarentur. Consenescunt enim omnia et vetustate conficiuntur, quae doctorum hominum ingenio carent.
>
> (344)

> (The deeds of kings and rulers, no matter how famous and magnificent, would lie buried and overwhelmed by lasting oblivion, and would in fact rarely last beyond one man's lifetime, unless they were committed to immortality through the effort of most learned men. For everything which lacks the talent of learned men grows old and falls apart.)

Poggio supports this claim with the novel example of Tamerlane, a leader of almost unprecedented greatness, but who has already slipped from most minds for want of literary memorials. Likewise recent Italians, who may have been Achilles but lacked Homers.

> Quanti ergo extimanda est literarum facultas, quae gloriam praestat rebus gestis, et reddidit homines immortales. . . . Sacra igitur quaedam res cultu et veneratione digna sunt humanitatis et bonarum artium studia, quorum ope et beneficio mortui vivunt gloria et fama hominum sempiterna.
>
> (345)

> (How great we should consider the power of literature, which bestows glory on deeds and makes men immortal. Therefore, the pursuit of humane letters and the liberal arts is something sacred and deserving of worship and veneration; by the help and benefit of these arts the dead live on in glory and the fame of men is everlasting.)

As in Guarino's declaration that poetry can make men into gods, so here Poggio elevates poetry by attributing to it similarly divine powers.

The equilibrium sometimes claimed between arms and letters, poet and prince, dissolves as an apotheosized entity looks down on a humanity that should simply worship it. Such a move is, of course, part of an elaboration of the patron's role. When he declares the *studia humanitatis* deserving of a *cultus,* Poggio means both religious ceremony for a mythic power and the cultivation that is patronage.

To supplement his reasons for the young prince to persevere in his studies, based on the abstract sublimity of those studies, Poggio adds a glimpse of the perfect man Leonello can be when prepared to step into the public world:

> Tunc illud in te oriatur quod refert noster Cicero in oratione pro Archia poeta, asserens: Cum ad naturam eximiam atque illustrem, qualis tua est, accesserit oratio quaedam confirmatioque doctrinae, tum illud praeclarum nescio quid existere atque singulare.
>
> (346)

> (Then something may appear in you which our Cicero mentions in his speech *Pro Archia,* when he claims: "When to exceptional and outstanding natural gifts, such as yours, there is added a certain faculty of speech and corroboration of instruction, then there arises a certain indefinable and singular excellence.")

Poggio's citation of the Ciceronian passage (*Pro Archia,* 7.15) is almost exact except for one small change that makes a great difference. Where Cicero has *ratio* ("accesserit ratio quaedam . . . "), there Poggio gives *oratio.*[51] The added *o* may, of course, be merely a slip. But, in fact, several contemporary (fourteenth and fifteenth century) manuscripts of the *Pro Archia* have the reading *oratio.*[52] This fact suggests that scribes of that time (among whom Poggio was perhaps the greatest) could make sense of *oratio* in the context.[53] Such a preference has a paradigmatic significance: the belief that eloquence, training in words, would be the ineffable completion of an ideal man of action—as it is what *reddidit homines immortales.* This usurpation of *ratio*'s place by *oratio* represents the aggressiveness and comprehensiveness of claims for the power of the eloquent word in the Quattrocento. At the same time that the humanist boasts the transcendent benefits that literature bestows, by his very generosity he declares his superiority to his rival, the patron, and all earthly things.[54]

THE SUPREMACY OF POETRY

The preceding pages have concerned the relationship of humanist with prince. In what follows I shall consider a current that also regards the power of poetry and eloquence, but with respect to the elevation of poetry in an academic and ontic hierarchy.

The age of humanism has been called *aetas ciceroniana*.[55] This refers to the Ciceronian ideal of the central position that poetry and rhetoric should hold in the *res publica*. To a considerable extent, the claims made for eloquence can be made for poetry (although not always vice versa). However, later humanist poetics tends to emphasize poetry's independence from rhetoric.[56] An important element in the promotion of poetry is its elevation in the traditional scheme of disciplines. This elevation has begun already in the Trecento.[57]

In the third book of his *Invective contra medicum*, Petrarca responds to his opponent's claim that poetry is not one of the seven liberal arts and so of no great importance. He introduces an anecdote from that favorite source, the life of Scipio. When Hannibal was asked who were the greatest generals in history, he answered Alexander, then Pyrrhus, then himself. When asked why he omitted Scipio, who had defeated him, Hannibal said that this omission was not neglect, but rather the highest praise, considering the Roman "incomparable among the greatest."[58] Petrarca leaves his readers to draw their own conclusion, but the application seems clear. Poetry's absence from the curriculum of the seven liberal arts is due to its supreme status, above all other disciplines. What appears to be its lack is, in fact, when interpreted correctly, poetry's highest praise.[59]

It is impossible to ignore the most obvious point about Petrarca's metaphor: the similarity it declares between intellectual disciplines and victorious generals. He suggests a view of education not as the process of harmonizing the various arts, but as emulation, each specialty trying to prove it is the best. Poetry is preeminent because on the one hand, like Scipio, it has directly defeated some of its competition (one thinks of the present invective, crushing medicine), while on the other hand, also like Scipio, it benefits from the glory of an argument from silence. Poetry is the most liberal of the liberal arts because it is even free from the taint that results from mention in the academic curriculum.

A tendency to elevate poetry is also evident in the first book of Coluccio Salutati's *De laboribus Herculis,* which mounts a defense of poetry prefacing the allegorical task of the rest of that work. However, the basic gesture Salutati performs is not so much emulation as absorption. Briefly, poetry by its nature combines all the liberal arts: "ex omnibus scientiis et liberalibus artibus facultas ista (sc. poesis) collecta est" (the poetic faculty is built up of all fields of knowledge and liberal arts) (1.3.11).[60] Likewise, in a letter Salutati encourages a friend to study *poetica,* "que super omnia, que sciri possunt, sedem habet et sola de Deo loqui potest" (which has a place above all things which can be known, and can alone speak of God).[61] The supremacy of poetry is evident in its ability to range freely among all disciplines, using them *iure suo* and dominating them.[62]

Salutati also expresses this supremacy cosmologically. Discussing the music of the spheres in *De laboribus Herculis,* he decides that that harmony does not physically exist; rather, with this idea the ancients were referring allegorically to poetry. Just as the spheres represent all the arts and sciences, so is poetry the harmony of their relationships which completes and contains them ("tum exigere, tum etiam continere" [1.9.3]). Salutati is following medieval precedent in assigning the various disciplines to the heavenly spheres.[63] But his distance from that tradition becomes clear when he proposes another description of the cosmology of learning. Here the spheres begin with the earth, so the ninth and highest is the *celum stelliferum.* Whereas for Dante in the *Convivio* the cosmic mover is the *primum mobile,* to which ethics is assigned, Salutati makes the *pulcra sonoritas* of the *celum stelliferum* rule the movements of the cosmos.[64] *Pulcra sonoritas,* of course, refers to the harmony of poetic composition. The effective power of verbal magic becomes a universal category, and poetry thus rules the cosmos. Salutati investigates the analogy of poetry and cosmos more particularly in an explanation of how the proportions of poetic meter, especially the hexameter, are identical to the Pythagorean proportions of earthly and celestial music (1.5–7).[65] In the end, nothing can escape the pervasive analogies of such conceptual imperialism.[66]

Salutati's poetics is substantially the same as that of early Quattrocento figures (Bruni, Poggio, and Valla), with the qualification that these successors develop Salutati's view of poetry as a divine (yet civic) immortalizer of worthy deeds but emphasize less and less its allegorical aspects.[67] A good early example of this transition is provided by the treatise *Contra oblocutores et detractores poetarum* by Francesco da Fiano (ca. 1400). While the author does not ignore the allegorical analogy of pagan poetry with Scripture, he dwells with greater enthusiasm on poetry's autonomous power. Among the numerous passages where the glory of poetry is situated in its ability to immortalize, in what follows Fiano argues from that fact to poetry's supremacy over the other disciplines (even theology):

Quam divinum quam ve pretiosum hoc hominum genus (sc. poetarum) esse putemus, qui quia promittere et dare fame immortalis eternitatem et quoscunque virtutum claritate prestantes, possunt nomine perpetuo et pariter honorato immortales efficere, quod neque theologis, neque medicis, neque sacrarum legum, neque decretorum seu ecclesiasticorum canonum interpretibus contingere potuit, eos tanquam deos venerari priscorum merito sanxit auctoritas?[68]

(How divine and how precious must we consider this class of men, who, because they can promise and give the eternity of immortal fame, and make immortal with a lasting and honored name whoever is outstanding for distinction of excellence—something impossible for theologians, for physicians, for interpreters of civic or canon law—were deservingly revered as gods through the authority of the ancients.)

Here poetry triumphs not over the liberal arts, as Petrarca would have it, but over the major professions. It is notably superior to the *artes quaestuariae,* those venal professions that are medicine and law. And the criterion of that superiority? Poetry's preeminence results from Fiano's praise of the power of praise. Doing is always preferable to knowing, which is apparently all the competition is capable of—a surprising argument, which opposes poetry as effective action to those professions usually considered exemplary of the active life. As if in defense of the putative worship of Virgil's statue, Fiano makes the immortalizing power of poets the basis of their own immortality. Their ability to deify (namely, men of action) is what makes them gods, or did so in a past time that rewarded them as they deserve.

Poetry may be supreme because it possesses greater power (effectiveness) or else greater primordiality. All knowledge is verbal, and all use of *verba* originates in poetry.[69] Humanist considerations of the place of poetic discourse end up as declarations of its preeminent authority. We thus see a direction that complements the one in the previous part of this chapter. There, humanists' articulation of the relation of *litteratus* to patron ended up as a poetics. Now we find that explicit discourse on poetics ends up as an assertion of power and thus implicitly positions poetry with relation to the patron.

After all, the convergence of "social" and "literary-theoretical" discourse about poetry should come as no surprise. The hidden result of the tendencies just reviewed is to make poetry and poetics a microcosm. If poetry is the source of all discourse and hence of all reality, there is then no realm not subject to literary language. For that reason, the way one sees poetry will be the way one sees the world.

Situation of the *Sylvae; Raccolta Aragonese*

Perhaps these considerations will help to understand better some of the later work of Angelo Ambrogini, called Poliziano. What has traditionally been considered a paradox is that the greatest Italian poet of the Quattrocento is also the greatest philologist and, particularly, that the mature Poliziano appears to renounce poetry for more purely philological work. V. Branca has shown the error in drawing a too strict division (at about 1480) between Poliziano the young poet of the Medici household and Poliziano the master at the Florentine Studio.[70] The scholar did not repudiate his youthful compositions, nor even (despite appearances) resist their publication. On the other hand, philological research was not foreign even to the adolescent Poliziano. But with this qualification, the relative contrast persists.[71] After Poliziano assumed his chair at the Studio in 1480 and until his death in 1494, his poetic production was practically limited to the four *praelectiones* in verse delivered as introductions to certain of his courses.[72] The courses themselves show a movement away from poetry, as in the courses on Homer from 1485 to 1490, to an ever greater concentration on Aristotle's *Logic,* to which Poliziano devoted the last years of his life.[73] Everything indicates an at least relative renunciation of poetic creation for erudition. How can we reconcile this fact with the celestial preeminence recognized for poetry in Quattrocento discourse?

Moreover, the subjection of poetry to erudition seems to define Poliziano's late poetic production itself, in the form of his verse *praelectiones.* These appear constructed primarily for pedagogical ends, and the elaboration of the academic material at hand threatens to submerge a more easily recognizable poetic voice. The four poems in question are known as *Sylvae.* Poliziano borrowed the term from Statius, referring to variety of subject matter.[74] He delivered these compositions at the beginning of his courses at the Florentine Studio:[75] *Manto* for the course on Virgil's *Eclogues* in the academic year 1482–83; *Rusticus* for Virgil's *Georgics* and Hesiod's *Works and Days* in 1483–84; *Ambra* for the first course on Homer, in 1485–86; and *Nutricia* for the first course on poetry in general, in 1486–87. The two that have attracted my attention, *Ambra* and *Nutricia,* have the most to say on the nature and value of poetry. The greater part of each of the four works consists of a survey of the classical texts in question: In particular, *Ambra* provides synopses of the *Iliad* and *Odyssey,* and *Nutricia* sketches a history of poetry. Such a formal emphasis poses an obstacle for the modern reader. The pedagogical usefulness of such material is obvious, but a reader whose interest lies in Poliziano the poet may be disappointed by what seems a mere show of erudition.

Finally, both *Ambra* and *Nutricia* end with abrupt and fulsome praise of Poliziano's protector, Lorenzo de' Medici. The insertion of the patron into a context that holds no obvious relevance for him seems one more example of humanistic courtly flattery. Does the patron not

remain foreign to Poliziano's task, whether considered from its pedagogical aspect or from any other as well?

In short: Is it true that in these late texts the poet is overwhelmed
by the philologist, the professor, and the client? An answer begins with
the awareness that, as I have claimed, the championship of poetry in
the Quattrocento is indissoluble from an ever higher regard for the
eloquent word in general. Further, the traditional insistence that the
poet must be learned refuses to make *poeta* and *doctus* two distinct
types;[76] on the contrary, there is a tendency to fuse them. Poliziano's
Sylvae exemplify the poetry of erudition or, more precisely, the "history of poetry," in the tradition of Ovid (*Amores,* 1.15, *Ex Ponto,* 4.16)
and Petrarca (*Laurea occidens*). As such, they invite the reader to
enter their special world without preconceptions about what may or
may not be poetic.

A similar imperative holds true for the poems' status as occasional
pieces with a practical end and for their inclusion of the patron's figure.
While the *Sylvae* boast of the supremacy of poetry, they announce
their own lack of autonomy. The meaning of the poems grows from
the elaboration of that contradiction.

The traditional scheme of the academic *praelectio* or *prolusio* consists of two parts, *laus* and *cohortatio:* praise of the author(s) at hand
and exhortation to the students about to begin study.[77] Part of Poliziano's originality in his use of the genre lies in the reduction of the
cohortatio until it is insignificant or only implicit and in the concomitant amplification and enrichment of the *laus.* The *Sylvae* are unmis-
takeably panegyrics. Poliziano begins both *Ambra* and *Nutricia* with
a declaration of his obligation to praise. "Primitias . . . quisque sui fert
muneris auctor" (every originator bears the first fruits of his gift) (*Ambra* 7),[78] so Homer deserves the homage of a poet inspired by him, just
as Bacchus is offered the first fruits of the vineyard and Ceres the
harvested grain.[79] *Nutricia* too presents the law of gratitude as universal and everlasting:

> Stat vetus et nullo lex interitura sub aevo . . .
> Quae gratos blandae officio nutricis alumnos
> Esse jubet.
>
> *(Nutricia* 1–3)

> (An ancient law stands, never to pass away: it commands children to be
> thankful for the service of their sweet nurse.)

Here the poet pays the reward of praise not to a single human like
Homer, but to Poetry itself (21). Poetry has been his nurse, *nutrix,*
hence the title: *Nutricia* are the nurse's wages.[80]

Most notably, the poet represents praise as obligatory bestowal in a relation of exchange. Each poem begins with a cluster of important terms. *Ambra* stresses *donum* (2) offered for *munus* (7), in the mutual generosity of gift giving between mortals and gods.[81] In *Nutricia,* on the other hand, the commercial form of exchange is foremost, at least at first. *Merces* and *compendia* as well as the verb *penso* (7–8) refer to relations of buying, selling, and remuneration.[82]

The same commonplaces appear, more programmatically, in the epistle dedicating the *Raccolta aragonese* to Federico of Aragon. Lorenzo de' Medici presented as a gift this anthology of Italian lyrics, from the Duecento to Lorenzo's own day, in 1476 or 1477.[83] The question of the authorship of the dedicatory epistle is controversial. The two candidates are Lorenzo and Poliziano.[84] From the evidence, it seems likely that Poliziano is the author, writing in Lorenzo's name. But the important point is that the contents of the letter could have been written by either Lorenzo or Poliziano or by another member of their circle, for that matter. As I. Maïer (herself a partisan of Poliziano) puts it, "L'épître à Frédéric d'Aragon, écrite sous les auspices et au nom du Magnifique est, sans doute, l'expression fidèle des aspirations et des goûts du cénacle."[85] As an expression of shared commonplaces, the letter introduces Lorenzo as a dominant presence in Poliziano's poetics and poetic history.

The author of the letter begins by considering which is the most admirable characteristic (*laude*) of antiquity. He decides that it is this fact:

Che nessuna illustre e virtuosa opera né di mano né d'ingegno si puote immaginare, alla quale in quella prima età non fussino e in publico e in privato grandissimi premi e nobilissimi ornamenti apparecchiati.

(3)

(That no illustrious and excellent work, either physical or intellectual, can be imagined which was not in ancient times publicly and privately provided with the greatest rewards and the noblest adornment.)[86]

Here, too, we find allusion to an ideal structure of exchange: *opera* were compensated with *premi* and *ornamenti.*[87] From the familiar appeal to the equilibrium of a past time comes the general Ciceronian rule: Honor nourishes art.[88] "L'onore è veramente quello che porge a ciascuna arte nutrimento; né da altra cosa quanto dalla gloria sono gli animi de' mortali alle preclare opere inflammati" (Honor is truly what provides nutrition to each art; the human spirit is inflamed to conspicuous works by nothing as much as glory) (3). The metaphor of nutrition may seem to diverge from the initial one of material exchange, but it looks forward to the same metaphor evoked by the title *Nutricia*. In addition, the important role of food in archaic exchange turns back the clock on the apparently commercial or monetary emphasis of the initial terms (*premi* and so on).[89]

If the desire for glory innate in all men, a productive force when glory is forthcoming, was the cause of the greatness the ancients achieved "col senno e con la spada" (with the intellect and the sword), then the fortunes of the exchange structure determine historical periods. The absence of reward (*premi mancati*) brought about the Dark Ages (5). Formerly, to receive this reward of glory, the great men turned to those who could bestow it: the poets. "I quali potessino i valorosi e chiari fatti delli uomini eccellenti con la virtú del poetico stile rendere immortali" (Who could immortalize the brave and illustrious deeds of excellent men with the power of their poetic style) (4). The classic exemplum of Alexander at Achilles' tomb turns up here once again, told as Cicero tells it, except that Alexander's exclamation is expressed in Petrarca's words (*Canzoniere* 187):

Oh fortunato che sí chiara tromba
trovasti, e chi di te sí alto scrisse.

(Oh fortunate one, who found such an illustrious trumpet, and someone who wrote of you so loftily.)[90]

Lorenzo/Poliziano pursues the example of Homer. There is in his case a double rescue from oblivion. Just as Homer immortalized Achilles, so did Pisistratus revive the dispersed Homer by ordering the collection and edition of his work.[91] The greatness of the prince lay in his gathering of Homer's limbs scattered like Osiris:

Tutto il corpo del santissimo poeta insieme raccolse, e sí come a quello dette perpetua vita, cosí lui a se stesso immortal gloria e clarissimo splendore acquistonne.

(4)

(He gathered together the entire body of the sacred poet, and just as he gave him everlasting life, so did he win for himself immortal glory and a most illustrious splendor.)

This new twist to the tradition reveals the ideals of both Poliziano and Lorenzo. For Poliziano the philologist and faithful collator of manuscripts, the work of Pisistratus is a paradigm of the humanist rescue of antiquity. For Lorenzo, as the ideal patron/prince, the case of Pisistratus provides a model of how much the patron can do to repay the poetic gift of glory and to win immortality for himself. Moreover, the analogy between Pisistratus and Federico of Aragon is explicit. When he and Lorenzo met in Pisa in 1476, Federico asked for an anthology of Italian poets. In introducing the promised anthology, "Lorenzo" briefly passes in review the poets included, then turns to Federico:

> Questi tutti, signore, e con essi alcuni della etá nostra, vengono a renderti immortal grazia, che della loro vita, della loro immortal luce e forma sie stato autore.
>
> (7)

> (All of these, my lord, and with them some from our own day, come to give you immortal thanks, because you have been the author of their life, of their immortal light and form [beauty].)

That is, Federico has become an "author" and given immortal life to these poets (including Lorenzo) by causing them to be edited, put in a book. The dedicatee may enjoy the semantic richness of Latin *auctor*, as he is credited with both temporal authority and literary effectiveness.[92] The bestowal is reciprocal, though, as the *immortal grazia* given by the poets to Federico indicates.

What the dedicatory epistle of the *Raccolta aragonese* does for vernacular poetry, *Ambra* and *Nutricia* do for the classical tradition.[93] All three texts elaborate the equivalence *carmina-munera*.[94]

AMBRA

Ambra is a poem in praise of Homer that follows in several respects Poliziano's prose *Oratio in expositione Homeri*. One central element in the prose *praelectio* is the idea that Homer, as the ideal poet, is the origin of all wisdom and of all science.[95] The *Oratio* portrays Homer's wisdom as both supreme and primordial.[96] In his poems, Homer reveals himself a master of rhetoric, medicine, divination, jurisprudence, arithmetic, and music. He anticipates future revealed doctrine on God and the soul, and all philosophical sects have their origin in him.[97] It goes without saying that the poet also contains all literature in him. He uses all three genera: *sublime, tenue,* and *medium* (479); he also introduces all literary forms (489). Through Poliziano's words, Homer becomes an immeasurable natural force, whose stories are contemplated with wonder, like constellations, by remote barbarians (491). In the figure of Homer there is concentrated the aggrandizement of poetry evident throughout the Quattrocento.[98] *Ambra* assumes this fact and, more important, dramatizes it.

Ambra is a poem of praise. But, like Petrarca's *Africa,* it does not simply praise its subject, Homer. Rather, it makes a dramatic narrative of the act of praise itself, objectifying the complications in the matter. Moreover, Poliziano presents the Homeric poems themselves as essentially epideictic. The need for glorification is set out in a network of relationships among four figures: the poets ancient and modern (Homer and Poliziano) and the patron/heroes ancient and modern (Achilles and Lorenzo). What holds this network together and sets the story in motion is the relationship between verbal magic and patronage.

As previously mentioned, the poem begins with a recognition of the duty to repay homage for benefits conferred. Homer's supreme status as poetic model must be repaid with praise. As in the *Oratio,* Homer's power takes on cosmic proportions. Not only is he the revealer of the gods and of virtue ("Ille deûm vultus, ille ardua semina laudum / Ostentat populis" [He shows the face of the gods, and the difficult seeds of praise, to all peoples] [21–22]), not only does he span the entire universe ("Pervolitat chaos immensum coelum aequora terras" [He flies through the vast chaos, sky sea and land] [23]), but also his poems are the voices of things themselves:

> vocesque refundit
> Quas fera quas volucris quas venti atque aetheris ignes
> Quas maria atque amnes quas dîque hominesque loquantur.
>
> (24–26)

(He pours forth the voices which wild beasts, which birds, which the winds and heavenly fires, which the seas and rivers, which gods and men all speak.)

The word of Homer is supreme because it comprises all languages, natural and divine. He acts as the embodiment of verbal magic. In this way Homer is the inevitable source of any subsequent poetry. But he is not a model to be imitated; Poliziano scorns direct imitation.[99] Homer communicates inspiration to those in contact with him: "cuius de gurgite vivo / Combibit arcanos vatum omnis turba furores" (from whose living waters the whole crowd of poets drinks up hidden furors) (12–13). In what follows, the allusion to Plato's *Ion* is clear: Homer constitutes the link in the chain of poetic inspiration that connects the celestial realm to the earthly.

If all this is so, with what kind of praise can a modern poet repay Homer? Despite his sublime status, Homer requires this service because he is a victim of time. His remoteness from the present day has condemned him to silence.[100] At this point in the growth of humanism, when Greek had been taught regularly in Italy for less than a century, three years before the first printed edition of the Homeric poems,[101] Poliziano could still present the possession of Homer as a task to be achieved. But in addition to his philological intent, Poliziano's proposal to remedy Homer's lack of fame refers also to another aim of this poem. The task here is to bring Homer alive, to communicate the power of his poetry—in short, to extend the chain of inspiration to the pupils listening in the Florentine Studio. Poliziano will thus have numerous company in rendering the gift of life to Homer in return for benefits conferred. To this end Poliziano introduces a myth on the origin of the Homeric poems.[102]

The myth is this: The gods are enjoying one of their Ethiopean feasts when a tearful Thetis comes before Jupiter. She bewails the premature death of her son Achilles and begs the father of the gods to avert this destiny. Jupiter's reply begins with the recognition that fate is immutable and, thus, that the effects of mortality and sorrow are everywhere; nearly every one of the gods mourns the death of a mortal child at Troy. All Jupiter can offer is a recompense for mortality. First, he promises Achilles a blissful existence in Elysium. More significant, Achilles will also have undying fame: "Nulla virûm gens, nulla dies, nusquam ulla tacebit / Posteritas" (No race of men, no day, no posterity will ever be silent) (162–63). This will be effected by the divine Homer (for whom Poliziano has just proposed an identical reward):

Quippe deûm sancta nascetur origine vates,
Qui lucem aeternam factis immanibus addat.

(164–65)

(For a poet will be born of divine origin, who will add eternal light to those frightful deeds.)

Even Alexander will call Achilles fortunate in having such a herald. At this promise Thetis is consoled and joins in the celestial feast.[103]

The birth and maturing of Homer show the incarnation of a divine logos. He is the son of an unnamed god and Critheis, conceived illegitimately, *furtivo . . . foetu* (218). His first wail upon coming into life constrains nature:

Vagitu horrisoni sternebat murmura ponti,
Pacabat ventos, mollibat corda ferarum, etc.

(221–22)[104]

(With a wail, he struck down the roar of the horrible-sounding sea, he
calmed the winds, he softened the hearts of beasts.)

After an early cultivation of rustic pipes, adolescent Homer turns to
the poetry of the Apollinian lyre. Here his power to move nature is
joined with an immortalizing power, expressed as exemption from Avernus and Jupiter's thunderbolts:

Carmen amat, carmen (proh maxima numina vatum!)
Carmen apollineo tantum modulabile plectro,
Carmen caucaseas silices cautemque sicanam
Quod trahat, et rigidi leges infringat Averni,
Exarmetque Jovis minitantem fulmine dextram.

(255–59)

(Poetry he loves, poetry—ah great divine power of poets!—poetry which can
only be performed with the Apollinian plectrum, poetry which draws forth
the rocks of Caucasus and the cliffs of Sicily, and breaks the laws of unyield-
ing Avernus, which disarms of its thunderbolts Jove's threatening right
arm.)

The anaphora of *carmen* makes it clear that the divine power at work
belongs not to the individual Homer, but to the poetic Word manifested
in him.[105] The domination of nature (*trahat*) is combined with an
even more violent opposition to the supernatural realm (*infringat,
exarmet*). Poetry is not only autonomous, but also antinomian; it
breaks laws, it disarms Jupiter in personal battle. As will be seen in
greater detail in *Nutricia*, these are images central to the force of poetic
effectiveness.

The violence of poetry's effect is matched by the violence of its inception. This is evident in the description of Homer's encounter with his
subject matter, Achilles, and his inspiration to create the *Iliad*. An
insana vis and Achilles himself inspire the poet to prepare an *altum
opus*. Homer burns with a desire to know Achilles' appearance, to *see*
him immediately. Poliziano's parenthetical "(ah nimius voti!)" (265)
comments the excessiveness of this desire. To achieve such an intimacy, Homer hauls Achilles from his grave while speaking the words
of his poem. Creation and violent sacrilege are simultaneous: "Vio-
lentaque fundens / Murmura, terribilem tumulo ciet improbus umbram" (Pouring forth a violent mutter, he presumptuously stirs up the
terrible shade from its grave) (265–66). In his encounter with the
shade of Achilles, Homer is characterized as *improbus,* which can be
"indomitable," but also "wicked," "shameless," or as rendered here,
"presumptuous."[106] This rescue and desecration produces its desired

effect. The Troad is shaken; Achilles appears at his most terrible as he prepares to enter battle, seeking to avenge Patroclus upon Hector. The world of the *Iliad* comes to life as a shadow-battle takes shape.[107] The materialization of Homer's all-embracing world is expressed by Achilles' shield. As in the *Iliad,* his divinely built weapon portrays the entire cosmos of humanity and nature. Indeed, at this point Poliziano imitates the beginning of that Homeric description.[108] But the previous warning that Homer desired too much is here justified. As Homer contemplates the shield before him, he is struck blind: "dum lumina figit, / Lumina nox pepulit" (while he stares, night drives away his sight) (283–84).[109] Terrified, he also loses his voice ("Vox . . . repressa metu" [His voice is checked by fear]) (285).

Such is the encounter of the poet with his subject. Blindness and desecration appear as constitutive parts of inspiration. As the ideal poet, in a moment representative of all poetic creation, Homer resurrects the dead and evokes the famous shield. Word magic, as dramatized here, finds its most typical tasks in the accomplishment of immortality and the ordering of the cosmos.[110] Yet the poet alone is insufficient. The disaster that accompanies creation declares his need for help. It is here we see the dual role of Achilles: He has been the passive subject matter brought to life, and now he becomes a figure of the patron come to Homer's rescue.

Achilles pities his poet and, although, like Jupiter, he cannot undo disaster, he bestows upon Homer a compensation. This is twofold. First comes the consummation of inspiration: "Clypeo excipit, oraque jungens / Inspuit augurium" (He snatches him up on his shield, and joining their mouths spits the power of prophecy into him) (288–89). This violent kiss, where Achilles spits prophecy into Homer, summarizes the love and violation of their encounter.[111] Achilles next gives the poet the staff that once belonged to Tiresias. It is the staff of prophecy, but also the staff of destitution, which helps the homeless poet to make his way as a beggar through the world. At this, Homer overcomes his momentary muteness, "sacro instincta furore / Ora movet, tantique parat solatia damni" (he moves his mouth [or utterance] roused by a holy furor, and obtains the compensation for such a great loss) (293–94). Now he gratefully assumes his proper office. Homer unifies the disparate Achilles of tradition, unifies the hero and raises him to the celestial realm of poetic immortality.

> Aeaciden tamen, aeaciden coelo aequat et astris,
> Aeaciden famae levat arduus alite curru,
> Unum Dardanidis unum componit Achivis
> Aeaciden, unum ante omneis miratur amatque.
>
> (295–98)

(Yet Achilles, Homer raises Achilles to the heavens and stars, Achilles he elevates loftily in the winged chariot of fame, one Achilles he composes for the Trojans and the Greeks, one above all he admires and loves.)

We see here in all its richness the dialectic of poetic glorification: His violent love of the past impoverishes and redeems the poet so he can, in turn, redeem the past. There are reciprocal elevations, of the poet on the warrior's shield, of the hero in the chariot of fame. The structure of gift exchange lies beneath the surface of the narrative. One notes, however, that the hero's initial destitution is a result of death and the natural course of things; on the other hand, the poet suffers from the necessary hubris of his contact with the hero. Poetic invention is unnatural, both as a refusal to let the dead remain dead and as a violation of burial customs. The antinomian force of poetry ends up as necrophilia, is punished, then partially compensated by the patron's generosity. Given the aggressiveness and violent prodigality of Homer's actions, it might not be far-fetched to call poetic bestowal potlatch, as "prestations totales de type agonistique."[112]

The direct consequence of this encounter is the composition of the *Iliad;* an epitome of the epic ensues (299–404). When at the end of this Odysseus spontaneously appears in a vision (*in somnis* [405]), he echoes Achilles in instigating a poem for himself. He, too, appeals to Homer's immortalizing power:

> O magnae qui princeps debita laudi
> Praemia persolvis, qui lenta oblivia saeclis
> Excutis et seros famam producis in annos.

(411–13)

(O prince who pays the reward due to great excellence, who casts off slow oblivion from the centuries and prolongs fame for many years to come.)

And, like Achilles, Odysseus presides as a patron over the composition of the epic that is his panegyric: "Incipe, namque adero, et praesens tua coepta juvabo" (Begin, for I shall be present and aid with what you start) (431).[113]

Homer's apotheosis, represented after the synopsis of the *Odyssey* (434–56), shows that the composition of the poems deifies poet as well as heroes.[114] The laureate Homer transcends the earth:

> Ergo tegunt geminae victricia tempora laurus
> Vatis apollinei; geminis ergo arduus alis
> Fugit humo, celsumque altis caput intulit astris,
> Par superis ipsique Jovi.

(457–60)

(And so the twin garlands of laurel cover the victorious brow of Apollo's poet; and so he flees the earth, sublime with twin wings, and bears his lofty head among the highest stars, a peer of the gods and Jove himself.)

The poet invades the realm of the gods and claims parity with them. And yet that aggression contrasts with a more benign characterization:

> Sic eminet extra
> Liber et innocuus, toto sic ille sereno
> Perfruitur gaudens.

(462–64)

(Thus he rises above and beyond the world, free and harmless, thus he rejoices and enjoys the entire sky.)

Homer, free and autonomous, belies the force of his inspiration to attain a sublime innocence (*innocuus*).[115] He has become an Epicurean sage. This impression is reinforced by the comparison of Homer to Olympus, rising high (*purus ... procul ... tutus*) above earthly storms (464–66).[116] At this point he has become the all-embracing figure introduced at the beginning of *Ambra* and in the *Oratio in expositione Homeri*. Here, too, his poems are the ocean, an inexhaustible source for posterity. "Omnia ab his et in his sunt omnia" (Everything comes from them and exists in them) (481). His supremacy concerns not only *verba*, but also *res*.[117] As in the *Oratio*, Homer founds all disciplines and all literary forms. He is, in fact, the creator of all things human and divine:

> Heroûmque idem facies, et celsa potentum
> Ora deûm, variisque horrenda animalia formis,
> Diversasque urbes positusque habitusque locorum
> Innumeros, sensusque animorum, carmine pulchro,
> Naturamque omnem, illa ipsa mirante, figurat.

(570–74)[118]

(The same man portrays, in his splendid poem, the faces of heroes and the lofty heads of powerful gods, the dreadful animals in their various shapes, diverse cities, the disposition and state of innumerable places, the consciousness of minds, and all Nature as she herself marvels.)

The verb *figurat* here is not simply "portrays," but also "forms" as well as "utters." A previous reference to poetic creation of the gods ("olympiaco quin is dedit ora Tonanti" [he gave a face to the Olympian Thunderer] [565]) shows how mimesis—Homer represents all things—can shade over into autonomous creation—he made all things.

After the episodes illustrating his generosity to Achilles and Odysseus, Homeric bestowal is once again directed toward all humanity and all time. The wealth (*divitias* [467], *opulentior* [493]) that he lavishes on posterity calls for corresponding universal tribute. And it is only natural that such a godlike figure should receive worship in return: "Huic aras huic templa dedit veneranda vetustas" (venerable antiquity gave altars and temples to him) (575). Just as Homer portrayed the gods, so is he himself the object of cult statues. Poliziano briefly indicates the tradition of reverence for Homer, particularly among princes such as Alexander and Ptolemy, who thus become analogous to Achilles as patron.[119]

Homer is honored throughout as the bearer of, or rather one borne by the poetic Word. His immortalization of Achilles and Odysseus and his own apotheosis are directly consequent on his poetic composition. The actions and destiny of Homer are those of an agent of the Word at its most powerful. This fact helps explain what might otherwise seem grossly inflated praise. *Ambra* is the praise of poetry at its most extreme.

Nevertheless, the situation of that agent commands attention. The "plot" of *Ambra* coheres as a series of exchange relations: between Homer and Poliziano (with his students), between Thetis and Jupiter, between Homer and Achilles, between Homer and Odysseus. The terms *munus, donum, praemia,* and *merces* recur throughout the poem with reference to those relations, but also with reference to the action of the Homeric poems themselves.[120] All the examples bring us back to the figure of Homer. After all, there is no abstracting the poet's mythical powers from his commerce with others—a commerce that we can call patronage in a broad sense. Like Homer elevated on Achilles' shield, the boasts of word magic depend on the support, of various kinds, which is bestowed upon it. And yet that support, like the shield, has a debilitating as well as a sublimating effect.

The final section of the poem (590–625) is dedicated to praise of Lorenzo de' Medici's villa at Poggio a Caiano, where Poliziano wrote *Ambra*.[121] The poet honors Lorenzo's works of construction in the area as well as the variety of his livestock. In such homely details here as the grunting Calabrian hog rooting up a meal, is there not a dissonance with the lofty style and matter that precede? Moreover, what is the justification for this change of scene, this jolt from the timelessness of poetry and myth to the solid present? What kind of unity exists in the poem?

The preceding discussion should suggest some answers. What integrates this final passage into the poem is the introduction of Lorenzo. He is both the patron who grants Poliziano the *otium* necessary to poetry and a poet himself: "Mea gloria Laurens, / Gloria musarum Laurens" (My glory Lorenzo, Lorenzo glory of the Muses) (599–600).[122] This double aspect corresponds to the double aspect of the earthly paradise that is Poggio a Caiano. On the one hand, it is a place of cultured, rural ease; it greets a Poliziano *liber et innocuus* who cherishes there his Epicurean ideal of the good life. On the other hand, it is also the place of Lorenzo's energetic domination of nature. Poliziano enumerates his ambitious projects: an aqueduct,[123] levees on the Ombrone, the villa itself. This paradise has been won from nature. The catalog of agriculture, craft, and livestock begins, oddly, to resemble the lists of the riches in Homer's poems.[124] Poliziano presents Lorenzo obliquely as an ideal patron, as he presents Homer explicitly as the ideal poet.

In addition, as I began by stating, a complex relationship links Homer, Achilles, Poliziano, and Lorenzo. The modern hero is not presented here with the pathos of destitute Achilles; on the contrary, he appears in the plenitude of his works. For his part, Poliziano is self-effacing. He makes none of the claims to power that he shows in Homer and that are inherent in poetry itself. While Homer embodies the autonomy of poetry, Poliziano presents himself as a beneficiary of Lorenzo's generosity, which has made this poem possible. At first glance, then, there seems to be a chiastic structure: Copious Homer benefits needy Achilles; needy Poliziano is benefited by Lorenzo. But as we have seen, things are more complex. Homer raised Achilles from the grave to the heavens of fame but in doing so made himself destitute. It was only Achilles' pity that compensated him for his blindness and exile and even made his poetic activity possible. The sense in which Poliziano benefits Lorenzo is not as explicit here, but present nevertheless. The final lines in praise of Homer before the change of scene to Poggio a Caiano are devoted to the honor done to Homer by people everywhere, especially by great leaders such as Ptolemy and Alexander. There is no transition before we find Poliziano at Poggio a Caiano enjoying the honor Lorenzo has done him. This juxtaposition implies that the poet's reward in both cases is well deserved. Poliziano's evocation of rural life is an exercise in creating a poetic world and an understated imitation of Homer's creation of the cosmos (517–33). Moreover, not only Lorenzo, but Homer too (and, by extension, Achilles) is a beneficiary of Poliziano's art. As mentioned earlier, Homer's *fama tacet* (34) and depends on Poliziano to haul him from the grave as he himself did Achilles. Finally, it should be noted that Poliziano's philology and pedagogy are hardly separable from his purely poetic task here.[125] The resurrection of Homer will be achieved by a year of studying his words as well as by the present Latin verses. As for Lorenzo, he may draw as much glory from his reputation as promoter of classical studies as from being the friend of poets.[126]

As in the preface to the *Raccolta aragonese,* art depends on honor for its existence. In that preface, however, *artes* are arts both poetic and heroic, great achievements "e col senno e con la spada," and the honor granted them could be a triumphal procession as well as material reward. So that *honos alit artes* can mean both "the state supports the arts, particularly poetry," and "literary fame nourishes the achievements of men of action." The same reversibility underlies *Ambra.* Homer's poetic achievement is born from contact with the patron/hero Achilles. The effect this has on the poet is a mixed blessing: poetic success but material abjection, as embodied not only in the shield, but also in the patron's gift that is the staff of Tiresias. Poliziano's story inflates poetry mythically by boasting of its magical effectiveness, but at the same time chains it to commerce with a patron/hero. The patron bestows the physical world on his poet, whether in the form of Lorenzo's country estate or the cosmos represented on Achilles' shield. This means an extreme tension between autonomy and dependency and directionally between an ascent to the heavens and a dwelling among earthly matter and death. Homer's itinerary takes him from the grave to the temple of his own adoration, but his dwelling is nowhere. Poliziano, who may be luckier, does have a place in the earthly paradise of Poggio a Caiano. The emphasis on material reality in the last part of the poem, while it ends the *praelectio* on a benign note, lends the poem a final image of the dialectic that organizes it: the poet down to earth after his mythical flights, reminded of his real obligations to the patron.

THE TRADITION OF POETIC PALEOLOGY

Like *Ambra, Nutricia* treats poetry with the commonplaces of primordiality and bestowal. However, unlike the earlier *praelectio,* which dwells mainly in the timeless realm of poetic inspiration and the Homeric poems' action, the structure of *Nutricia* is based on a roughly chronological progress, from prehistory to the present.[127] While *Ambra* specifies Homer as the poet par excellence whose power is the power of poetry itself, *Nutricia* operates more generally in two senses. First, the poem's point of departure is what might be called *poetic paleology.* By this term I mean a representation of the primordial role of poetic language in forming individual and social humanity. Second, Poliziano presents all of ancient poetry, both as the historical succession to the primordial Word and as concrete examples of poetic power.

Despite these differences, both *Ambra* and *Nutricia* conclude with homage to Lorenzo the Magnificent.[128] In *Nutricia* this comes about because the survey of ancient poetry extends to the great modern Italian poets, of whom Lorenzo is the last. Thus, while the Lorenzo of *Ambra* is chiefly the ideal patron who permits Poliziano his necessary poetic leisure, in the later poem he is a summit in the range of poets that includes Homer, Virgil, Dante, and Petrarca.

Poliziano's use of poetic paleology in *Nutricia* is the culmination of a tradition of related commonplaces in Italian humanism. Defenses of poetry and attempts to define poetry's place are drawn back irresistably to a few tantalizing allusions in ancient literature. The humanistic obsession with origins seeks the true nature of poetry in its original function. The implications of that obsession may be better understood through a classification of attitudes.

The classical tradition concerning early humanity falls into two general tendencies, according to whether the development of civilization is seen as ascent or decadence. If the golden age existed in the beginning, then the ages of baser metals that ensued show the fall of humanity. Hesiod's *Works and Days* (109–201) and the beginning of Ovid's *Metamorphoses* (1.89–150) constitute two classic expressions of this primitivistic view. On the other hand, there is also an evolutionary scheme, by which humanity grew out of an original bestial state through a gradual acquisition of the techniques of civilization. The two sorts of development in time thus display respectively a falling or a rising curve and, at the same time, a positive or negative picture of primitive humanity. The latter tendency (progress from a negative original state) is antiprimitivism.[129]

Within antiprimitivism and its progressive view of humanity, there are again two general tendencies, which might be characterized as "realist" and "poetic." The first finds its most eloquent spokesman in Lucretius, in book 5 of *De rerum natura;* it also informs Vitruvius's *De architectura* (2.1). Their story concerns a humanity pulling itself up by its own sandal straps out of subjection to nature. In contrast, the second tendency posits the faculty of language, in the form of poetry or eloquence, as the motive force behind human progress. In this latter narrative the central role naturally belongs to the first poets and the relation they established with humans and gods.[130]

A final distinction can be made between the two varieties within poetic antiprimitivism, or poetic paleology. We can observe them already in two early Greek writers. Herodotus asserts that Homer and Hesiod were the first to distinguish and characterize the gods and compose their genealogies—in short, to invent the gods.[131] But through a comic use in his *Frogs,* Aristophanes presents an older tradition that places Orpheus and Musaeus before Homer and Hesiod. Considering the role of poets from the beginning (*ap' arches*) should convince us how useful (*ophelimoi*) they have been in the civilizing process. Orpheus inculcated reverence for life, Musaeus's verse had oracular and healing power, Hesiod taught proper use of the earth, and Homer directed military heroism.[132] Thus, the primordial poets founded the three elementary functions of Indo-European civilization: priesthood, agriculture, and war.[133]

The attitudes expressed by Herodotus and Aristophanes—of poetry as, respectively, directed toward the gods and directed toward humanity—become the two main currents of poetic paleology. They may be best labeled through the Latin writers whose texts are most important to the tradition; I will thus refer to the Suetonian and the Horatian/Ciceronian currents.

One entrance of the commonplace into Roman literature is through Cicero. In the late *De Oratore* as well as the early *De Inventione*, Cicero, in keeping with his cultural program, emphasizes the civilizing power of oratory:

> quae vis alia potuit aut dispersos homines unum in locum congregare aut a fera agrestique vita ad hunc humanum cultum civilemque deducere aut iam constitutis civitatibus leges iudicia iura describere?[134]

> (What other force could bring together scattered humanity into one place, or draw them from their savage and boorish way of life toward this human and civil state, or once cities were established prescribe laws, legal proceedings and codes?)

What seems a shift from poetry's preeminence to oratory's is not so pronounced after all if we consider what Cicero subsequently declares to be the close similarity between the two forms.[135]

At any rate, Horace in his *Ars poetica* makes the same claims but reintroduces Orpheus, Musaeus, and Homer in a hymn to the power and high seriousness of poetic form.[136] His allegorical interpretation of the primordial poets' magical power exercises an enduring influence. The poetic domination of nature, as exemplified in Orpheus's power to tame lions and tigers, works as an obvious sign of the domestication of primitive humanity. As observed in chapter 1, the civilizing force of Horace's poets is a movement of elitist delimitation ("publica privatis secernere, sacra profanis") and the repression of uncivilized urges ("concubitu prohibere vago").[137]

However, the text that is perhaps most pregnant for humanism is a fragment of Suetonius's *De poetis,* preserved in Isidore's *Etymologiae.*

As will be seen, in contrast to the Horatian current, Suetonius places greater emphasis on a religious function of the first poets.

> Cum primum homines exuta feritate rationem vitae habere coepissent, seque ac deos suos nosse, cultum modicum ac sermonem necessarium commenti sibi, utriusque magnificentiam ad religionem deorum suorum excogitaverunt. Igitur ut templa illis domibus pulchriora, et simulacra corporibus ampliora faciebant, ita eloquio etiam quasi augustiore honorandos putaverunt, laudesque eorum et verbis inlustrioribus et iucundioribus numeris extulerunt. Id genus quia forma quadam efficitur, quae *poiotes* dicitur, poema vocitatum est, eiusque fictores poetae.[138]

> (When men had first cast off their savagery and begun to possess a rational principle of life, and to recognize themselves and their gods, alleging that a moderate cult and language were necessary to them, they contrived majesty of both for the religious observation of their gods. Therefore, just as they made temples more beautiful than their homes, and statues larger than life, so they felt the gods were to be honored with a somewhat loftier sort of utterance, and expressed their praises with more distinguished words and more delightful rhythm. Because this type came about through a certain form called *poiotes,* it is called a poem and its inventors poets.)

Apart from the somewhat obscure etymological reasoning, there are at least three noteworthy elements in this passage. First, the invention of both religion and poetry follows the discovery of reason. This distinguishes the Suetonian heritage from Vico's paleology. Then, the intertwined exercise of poetry and religion is founded on exaggeration and removal from ordinary life. The accumulation of comparative adjectives (*pulchriora, ampliora, augustiore, inlustrioribus, iucundioribus*) defines poetic language as something only known through its excess, in contradistinction to ordinary language. Finally, the verbs that introduce the first, decisive step in this civilizing process, *commenti* and *excogitaverunt,* both strongly suggest the contrival of something false. If Suetonius is expressing skepticism about the invention of the gods, it is understandable that such subversion of paganism would be welcome in the Catholic bishop's pious encyclopedia. However, what is more important than Isidore's appropriation of this story for his book of origins is the tone that turns up again in the numerous Renaissance humanist uses. There appears to be something fraudulent about the origins of poetry. The suspicion lurks that its pristine function may be tied up with a Great Lie.

Petrarca, who knew Isidore's work from an early date,[139] adapted the tale of poetry's origin to a defense of poetry in a letter to his brother.[140] In addition to accentuating the aesthetic hedonism of poetry's beginnings, Petrarca portrays its opposition to the *vulgus*. Paradoxically, social function coincides with opposition to society.

Petrarca also introduces most clearly what will become a crucial element of the Suetonian current. The honor done to the gods consists primarily of material gifts, which implies a relation of exchange.[141] By their offerings, men hoped to constrain the gods to reciprocate. The essential step for this humanist version of cultural history lies in the primordial decision not to let that gift bestowal remain mute ("ne mutus honos fieret"). Poetic language originates as the sublimation of sacrifice. It results from a desire for the most effective exchange relation with the gods.

Boccaccio was probably influenced by Petrarca in his two significant uses of the commonplace, where he develops the position of the poet in primitive society into one of domination. In both the *Genealogie* and the *Trattatello in laude di Dante,* Boccaccio narrates the evolution of religious cult through the invention of temples, priesthood, statues, and other sacred objects, culminating in the invention of poetic language. That language is characterized by both its removal from mundane communication[142] and by its use as an instrument of power.[143] From awe at nature there grew a belief, which could also be gullibility (*credulitas*), in a Supreme Being. The primordial priest/poets subjected the *vulgus* through the specious loftiness of poetic allegory and style. Boccaccio's emphasis on the *mirabile* at work in this process recalls Aristotle's assertion that wonder (*thaumazein*) was at the origin of philosophizing.[144] But the essential difference lies in the fact that, from a similar starting point, Boccaccio makes wonder put an end to inquiry. It is in the nature of poetry to obscure the truth and, thereby, to dominate. The awe provoked by poetic form, awe of the gods; such a connection throws new light on the verse by Statius to which Petrarca, for one, paid special attention: "Primus in orbe deos fecit timor" (Fear first created the gods on earth).[145]

Moreover, Boccaccio's specification of the priest/poets' privileged role, "da ogni altra mondana sollecitudine rimoti" (removed from every other wordly care), provides a foundation for the *otium* necessary to poets.[146] As in Petrarca's letter, the deity appears to receive flattery (*lusinghe*) from his priests as a prince receives poetic flattery.[147] The magical effectiveness of poetry, its ability to make the gods propitious,[148] or rather to give an appearance thereof, was the basis of its social power in primitive culture.

Suetonius, Petrarca, Boccaccio, and their imitators all make the birth of poetic language the cause of social distinction and the division of labor. Although poetry is only one of the ways to propitiate the gods in a *recherché* manner, it is always represented as the culmination and sublimation of material worship of the gods. We thus see the relation between the Horatian and Suetonian currents. The simultaneous accomplishment of poetry lies first in the separation of humanity from nature (as in the Horatian topos), through a rescue from barbarism, and second in a division of human society (the Suetonian heritage). Through poetry, not only is the priestly/literary caste freed from the masses who remain closer to a barbaric state, but that caste's proper language also distinguishes itself from practical language. While everyday language works in the material realm through a mundane process of signification, poetic theology and the poetry that grew from it are transcendent forms of language possessing a unique effective power.[149]

Numerous humanists throughout the Quattrocento use either variety of the topos concerning poetry's civilizing power, often allied to the topos of poetic immortalization. Beccadelli follows Petrarca, Boccaccio, and even Herodotus in asserting the poets' role as introducers of the gods.[150] Salutati, too, stresses the necessary origin of poetic fictions in the act of speaking of a god, verbalizing the ineffable; similarily, Pontano in his *Actius*.[151] In the preface to his *Elegantiae linguae latini,* Valla adopts Cicero's more secular picture of the services of eloquence. He compares the Latin language to the primordial divine bestowers Ceres, Bacchus, and Minerva with their gifts to humanity of grain, wine, and the olive.[152] Landino makes similar claims but, moreover, shows the fluidity of the boundary between eloquence and poetry where mythical claims for them are concerned. In the *Disputationes Camaldulenses* and *Prolusione petrarchesca* he writes of eloquence, mixing the Ciceronian and Horatian topoi. In his *Proemio al commento dantesco,* Landino repeats himself and elaborates again on the figures of Orpheus and Amphion, but this time as examples of poetic power.[153]

Bartolommeo della Fonte, like Landino, was an acquaintance of Poliziano, a fellow Medicean and Florentine academic. His *De poetice,* written between 1490 and 1492, is a formal poetics that presents, also like Landino, in a less brilliant way the literary commonplaces they share with Poliziano.[154] Although it is already clear from other humanists that the assertion of poetry's civilizing role is fundamental to poetics, this fact becomes explicit in della Fonte's treatise.

The first book of *De poetice* comprises a defense and praise of poetry and poets. It is the necessary preparation for book 2, an *ars poetica* indebted mostly to Horace, and for book 3, which classifies the genres of ancient poetry with the poets who practiced each one. Generally speaking, *De poetice* has a structure similar to that of *Nutricia*. The praise of poetry as a supreme category, based on a myth of transcendent origins, makes possible the consideration of actual poetic practice.

Poetics and literary history are based on an ontology of poetry, which is first of all poetic paleology. In his first chapter, "De poetices origine et dignitate," della Fonte follows Suetonius, Petrarca, and other predecessors in asserting that the first poetic utterence was the praise of a divine power finally understood as supreme in the ordered cosmos. However, della Fonte introduces a single, anonymous individual as the one who made this double discovery, rational and verbal. Only afterward did this man turn to his fellows to teach them to adore in the same way. The language used was, of course, choice.

> Neque vero communibus et vulgatis deum orasse et laudasse verbis credendum est, sed quotiens illi sacra operaretur meditatis ac numerosis vocibus esse usum.

> (It is not to be believed that they praised and prayed to their god with common and vulgar words, but rather that they used well-pondered and harmonious utterances whenever they performed rites for him.)

After the dissemination of worship, there followed the dissemination of poetic-religious inspiration. Like Boccaccio, della Fonte emphasizes the power that these *prisci poetae* asserted over the masses:

> Ac quo maiorem auctoritatem apud multitudinem obtinerent, excelsa divinitatis mysteria figmentis poeticis occlusere.

> (And, so that they might obtain greater authority over the common people, they shut up the lofty divine mysteries in poetic fictions.)[155]

As in most of his predecessors, in della Fonte's text the prominence of religious practice and the theological nature of original poetic language are obvious. However, that is not where his interest lies. The Promethean figure of the Ur-poet is important not for what he said about the gods, but for what he instituted among humanity. Even earlier in the treatise, in the dedication to Lorenzo de' Medici, della Fonte reveals that the establishment of divine worship was a necessary foundation for the supremacy of poetry in human affairs.

> Nam cum sapientes primi poetae fuerint, deorum cultus ostenderint, res gestas heroum scripserint, ab iis postea fere omnia assumpsere qui caeteras facultates celebravere.

> (Since the first poets were wise men, who introduced [or represented] the worship of the gods and wrote the deeds of heroes, those who afterwards exercised the other faculties borrowed almost everything from them.)

The supremacy of poetry over the other disciplines, an essential argument in humanist poetics, is possible because of the domination to which poetry has been accustomed since its inception.

Contrary to what may have been thought, the main point of the topos of poets as founders of civilization does not concern poetry as theology, but rather the social and political role of poetic language. Such a generalization holds true whether we consider the Horatian current of poetry as civic organization or the Suetonian current of poetry as cultic praise. What is at issue is the power of poetic language—the power to revolutionize humanity at an early moment and redirect its destiny. That power is based on knowledge but does not communicate knowledge except to the happy few who can penetrate poetic fiction. It works through the agreeable coercion of poetic form. The topos is an anthropological fantasy of a moment before the establishment of traditional social power—namely, monarchy.[156] In this view, poets preceded kings, laid the foundations for them, and performed a purer, more transcendent social role. Humanism is drawn to the image of the poet at that supreme moment before the advent of kings. There poetry is at its highest, most effective among humanity and closest to the gods. Humanistic nostalgia for republican Rome or classical Athens and their literature longs for them as the remnant of that earlier primordial moment.

That is to say that Vico had the right idea in his interpretation of the fables of *poeti teologi* as primarily political.[157] The significance of Vico, anachronistic though it may be, lies not only in his recognition of the role of poetic language in constituting civilization, but more particularly in his analysis of primordial social domination. There is no question that for Vico, as for his humanist predecessors, poets founded human culture. He is uniquely systematic about this point, stressing the derivation of everything, from logic to geography, out of the experience of the first poets and their *sapienza poetica*.[158] But the all-embracing effect of those poets is not simply their heritage to subsequent progress. True, all later knowledge has its roots in the primordial situation. But the poets themselves exercised an all-embracing function, acting as fathers, sages, priests, and kings.[159] They thus presided over what Vico calls the heroic age of the world. The decisive event of that age was the arrival of vagabonds to put themselves at the mercy of the already settled heroic giants and the protection that the latter extended in exchange for service. With this distinction of two classes, society was born. Vico discerns the event's literary significance in the derivation of *famulus,* or slave, from *fama.* The heroes' fame was what constituted the servile state of their inferiors.[160] And it must not be forgotten that the heroic class included preeminently the *poeti teologi.* There thus developed an intimate relation between poetry and the social domination at the beginning of all history. Vico even considers the primordial poetic instrument as, first of all, an instrument of discipline. The lyre (*fides* or *chorda*) originated as the cord that chastised unruly subordinates; only later did it become musical.[161] Hence, the civilizing force of the Orphic lyre (as Vico specifies) appears in another light. When Vico asserts that the end of poetry is "d'addimesticare la ferocia del volgo" (to tame the wildness of the masses), he means more than the cliché about soothing the savage beast.[162] He pushes to its extreme the paradox underlying humanist poetic paleology: The original human society was just the opposite of innocent, and yet it possessed the purest and greatest poetry.[163] The same superstitious violence that led to human sacrifice (and so forth) also made possible the most powerful use of metaphor. So that the praise that recognizes poetry's role in hauling humanity out of barbarism and setting history in motion must also recognize poetry's complicity in the barbarism that persists in history.

Part of the significance of *Nutricia* in this setting lies in Poliziano's, like Vico's, introduction of a "historical" element. He combines the frozen anecdote of poetry's first effects with a chronological narrative of literary history. The third book of della Fonte's *De poetice* (written after *Nutricia*) points in the same direction, but Poliziano pays less attention to defining generic categories and more to the character and power of individual poets. In this way, the supreme moment of power is prolonged in time—significantly, a time concluding in the present day of Lorenzo de' Medici. Likewise, the lesson of primordial social domination is not to be neglected by the listening students, future members of the ruling elite.[164]

The "historical" dimension of *Nutricia* represents subsequent poetry as a working out, not just of that primordial power, but also of the contradictions inherent in all poetic language (because inherent in the original poetic situation). Poliziano's last *Sylva,* in its striving for totality, combines the strains of poetic paleology and unfolds as several intertwined dialectics: between the Horatian and Suetonian currents, or the political and cultic functions of poetry; within the Horatian current, between poetry's domination of nature and its domination of humanity; within the Suetonian current, between the civic service of sacred poetry—freeing humanity from the fear of a supernatural unknown—and poetic mystification in the pursuit of authority.[165]

A READING OF *NUTRICIA*

Those various functions of poetry, both primordial and historical, require a motor that drives them together. The pervasive relation of

bestowal provides that motor. As already mentioned, *Nutricia* begins
with a recognition of the obligation to reward one's *nutrix,* or nurse.
The exchange relation is expressed in commercial terms (*merces, compendia,* and *pensare*). However, as befits a poem rooted in mythical
origins, the introduction of *munus* (28) prepares a structure of archaic
gift exchange. Or rather structures; one fact that integrates the catalog
of poetic history with the opening narrative is the common element
of bestowal. Poliziano introduces an important modification into the
tradition of poetic paleology by giving poetry not a human, but a gratuitous divine origin. Poetry is a gift from God; Poetry showers benefits on
humanity; and the series of poets abounds with examples of exchange
relations, whether with gods, with disciples, or with the *res publica.*

The initial recognition of an imperative to repay sets the stage for
all subsequent developments. The poet compares his situation with
that of gods such as Bacchus and Jupiter, who rewarded their nurses
by deifying them. But what can a human do, who is "nec fulminis
auctor, / Nec thyrsi sceptrique potens" (neither the source of lightning
nor endowed with the thyrsus or sceptre) (24–25)? Nevertheless, in
introducing his benefactor, *Poetica,* Poliziano has characterized her
thus: "humanas augusta Poetica mentes / Siderei rapiens secum in
penetralia coeli" (Majestic Poetica, ravishing human minds with her
into the innermost part of the starry heavens) (21–22). Poetry by its
nature snatches men into the realm of the gods. And just as Poliziano
voices his uncertainty of rendering appropriate praise, he recognizes
the signs of nascent inspiration. By this divine gift he will be able to
repay the divine gift of poetry. Yet one notices how, right from its
inception, inspiration aggressively invades the *penetralia coeli.* The
poet's mind is *improba,* his *pietas, temeraria* (25–26). The immortality of the poem he now conceives even sets him above the gods. For
while Jupiter himself is traditionally subject to the Fates, the poet now
claims to pour out "Carmina nunquam ullis parcarum obnoxia pensis"
(Poems never subject to the Fates' spinning) (31). Not only *pietas,* but
furor, too (32–33), characterizes the poet and his gift as he sets out to
write the history of poetry.[166]

In Poliziano's scheme, all human existence can be divided into two
epochs: before and after the introduction of poetry. Or rather, humanity did not truly exist before its poetic endowment. Man as divinely
created was a being of infinite potential, but his capacities lay dormant
(48–49). He dwelled in the shadows of profound ignorance (45–46).
The poet enumerates all that primitive man lacked: *relligio, pietas,
officium,* friendship, marriage, justice, and a sense of *commune bonum.* Perhaps more fundamentally, selfishness was the rule: "Sua commoda quisque / Metiri . . . sueti" (Each one accustomed to calculate his

own benefit) (57–58). That is, none of the functions of human society existed yet because these depend on an overcoming of egoism, on each individual not hoarding *sua commoda.*[167]

Poliziano extends this ignorance of the common good to other areas of "primitive mentality," drawing on book 5 of *De rerum natura.* He makes creative use of Lucretius in describing how men in their ignorance considered the succession of day and night. Lucretius says explicitly that they were not upset by the setting sun, having been taught by experience to expect a new day after the darkness.[168] The primitives of *Nutricia,* on the other hand, have no sense of continuity and so are desperate at the daily loss of light:

> Et nunc, ceu prorsus morientem, vespere sero
> Ignari flevere diem; nunc, luce renata,
> Gaudebant ceu sole alio.
>
> (59–61)[169]

> (Now they ignorantly mourned the day as if it were dying altogether in the late evening; now, when the light was reborn, they rejoiced as if for another sun.)

As in their egoism, where each is a monad, so in their experience of time, primitive men are limited to the present moment. Nor do they understand the succession of seasons. *Causarum inopes* (66), destitute of causality or origins, they experience a world of isolated moments and unconnected things.[170]

A comparison with the essential moment of progress in Lucretius's poem may be instructive. According to Lucretius, humanity discovers community spontaneously as the result of a natural evolution. The development can be explained as necessary for humanity's continued existence.[171] Language enters the picture at the same time, but not as a cause. It originates naturally:

> At varios linguae sonitus natura subegit
> mittere et utilitas expressit nomina rerum.[172]

> (Nature drove man to emit the various sounds of his tongue, and usefulness elicited the names of things.)

Poetry itself is only invented at a yet later stage of culture.[173]

All this happens differently in Poliziano. Man is saved from his brutal state through personal intervention by God (referred to vaguely as the Olympian *genitor*). The divine agent is Poetry.[174] Now if Poetry is to be represented as something other than a *machina ex deo,* there must be some harmony between her nature (the nature of all poetry) and her subsequent activity. And indeed such is the case. Poetry, which comes to dominate nature, first dominates human nature. The art that measures and coerces words acts as charioteer and mistress (*auriga* and *domina;* 70).

> Tu flectere habenis
> Colla reluctantum, tu lentis addere calcar,
> Tu formare rudes, tu prima extundere duro
> Abstrusam cordi scintillam . . .

(70–73)

(You are the first to steer with your reins the necks of those who struggle, to spur on those who are slow, to mold those who are uncultivated, to strike a hidden spark on their hard heart.)

The first image evidently alludes to Plato's myth of the soul in the *Phaedrus*. Its direction, however, is different. Whereas Plato's dark horse must be reined in to control its impetus, Poliziano's primitive man must be spurred out of his indolence. Poetry must overcome his apathy (*socordes animos, marcentia pectora;* 68–69). On the hard heart of man's ignorance, Poetry strikes to ignite his enlightenment.

This new phenomenon gathers the wondering primitives around it. What holds them spellbound is its measured, contained nature: "Numerosque modosque / Vocis et arcanas mirati in carmine leges" (They marvel at the number and measure of her voice, and the laws hidden in the poem) (78–79). The immediate effect of poetry is the inculcation of such law, which means the birth of morality (81–89). As this poetic science of right relationships grows within them, the newborn human faculty, *vis provida veri* (91), gathers strength. It is the will to know. It makes man human by dominating his animal passions, but also by being aware of its own possible *imperium* (90). This passion to know and to control is a gift of the gods, but it results in cosmic hubris. It is this *vis* in man

> celsa quae sic speculatur ab arce,
> Ut vel in astrigeri semet praecordia mundi
> Insinuet, magnique irrumpat claustra Tonantis.

(92–94)

(Which observes from its lofty stronghold, so that it may work itself into even the heart of the starry realm, and burst through the bounds of the great Thunderer.)

The culmination of human potential is conceived as invasion of the divine realm.

That may seem an odd return for the supreme gift of poetry. It is true, nevertheless, that Poliziano dwells repeatedly on the hubris that seizes "poetized" humanity. Even when he characterizes the as yet unredeemed primitives, he looks ahead to what they have the latent capacity to do: invade the heavens with their knowledge and dominate nature.[175] The newly invented human arts culminate in scrutiny of the heavens, expressed as domination: "etiam aethera curis / Substravêre avidis" (they even cast down the heavens for their eager study) (109–10).[176] And, once more, the will to know is the will to enter the heavens:

> Etiam famulantibus altum
> Inseruêre apicem stellis, animoque rotatos
> Percurrêre globos mundi.
>
> (110–12)

(They even thrust their lofty head up among the subject stars, and surveyed with their mind the world's whirling spheres.)

Even the stars have become servile (*famulantibus*) and admitted man as their master. Moreover, we have already seen that the present example of poetic activity, Poliziano's avowed inspiration that sets *Nutricia* in motion, promises a similar invasion of heaven (20–22). When we add to all this the repeated introduction of Prometheus into the poem (5, 74, 202), it becomes clear that, to say the least, humanity's thanks for its gift does not consist of humble gratitude. But at least the power of divine endowment provokes a reaction of comparable ambition.

This myth makes the king of the gods himself a Prometheus. He is responsible for the gift of intellectual fire that enables humanity to compete with the gods. But the gift must be understood not as an object or faculty added to man; rather as the light that acts as a catalyst. It reveals and sets in motion what is already within. The men standing around gaping at Poetry are enlightened about their true nature.

> Agnôrant se quisque feri, pudibundaque longum
> Ora oculos taciti inter se immotique tenebant.
>
> (95–96)

(Each of these savages knew himself, and for a long while they kept their eyes cast down in shame, silent and unmoving.)

Agnôrant se: they recognize both what they can be and the bestial life they have lived up to this point. Their embarrassed silence is both shame for their past indolence and *pudeur* at the first sight of their potential. Like Adam, they are ashamed because they know what they have lacked. And, more significant, to put it in Vico's terms, they recognize the secret kinship between divine poetry and their own ignorance.[177]

After that moment of suspension, human history is set in motion.[178] The primitives have condemned their bestial style and revealed humanity: "protinus exseruere hominem" (99). In addition to its other senses ("stretched forth," "exercised"), *exseruere* connotes something exhibitionistic as well. Poetry apparently bestows both the faculty of shame and the urge to reveal what is *pudendum.*

And, in fact, the exercise of humanity in history turns out to be paradoxical. Thanks to the Horatian culture-heroine, Poetry, man is enlightened and begins to realize his potential. However, the way to becoming human is the way of constraint. In a variation on the charioteer image, man willingly bows his neck to the yoke of law (118–19).[179] He is soon surrounded by the walls of community (101–2). The law of reward and punishment, the repression of promiscuity ("desultoria certis / Legibus est adstricta venus" [106–7]) make their entrance. Along with this rational ordering, cosmic hubris turns up repeatedly. It may seem as if men make peace among themselves only to make war on the gods. But, in fact, both drives obey a common impulse in Poetry. Poetic form invites the human subjection of humans to measure and law as well as the urge to subject the nonhuman in a similar way.[180]

Like humanity, the world itself achieves its proper form under the rule of Poetry; the gods owe to it their just adoration. As the restoration of what was latent or lost, Poetry sparks the self-discovery of the cosmos:

Sic species terris, vitae sua forma, suusque
Dis honor, ipsa sibi tandem sic reddita mens est.

(114–15)

(Thus beauty is restored to the earth, form to life, honor to the gods, and Mind to itself.)

The semantic richness of *species* and *forma* here is not incidental. Both words mean on the one hand beauty, natural or artificial, and so stress the aesthetic awakening that is Poetry's effect on the world. But *species* and *forma* are also both translations of the Platonic *idea*. When set beside the similarily Platonic *mens* in its crucial position, the terms suggest the prompting of a vast, primordial anamnesis that is cosmic as well as social and individual.

As Poliziano makes clear in representing his own inspiration in *Nutricia,* poetry is both gift and madness (*munus* and *furor* [28–32]). As gift, poetry establishes a relation of exchange as the principle of social and cosmic order. However, that same gift simultaneously opposes its ordering impulse and throws humanity into contradiction with itself and the world. *Furor* is the key term in the transition from the primordial scene to poetic history.[181] *Furor* is also central to a more detailed description of inspiration, which sets the scene for the review of individual poets. That inspiration, explicitly sent from God, reiterates the original bestowal of Poetry. The histories of individual poets are thus so many variations on the first paradoxical gift.

The metaphors that Poliziano uses to represent inspiration deserve some attention. The initial simile may be deceptive:

> Ceu tralucet imago
> Sideris in speculum, ceu puro condita vitro
> Solis inardescit radio vis limpida fontis;
> Sic nitidos vatum defecatosque sonori
> Informant flammantque animos modulamina coeli.
>
> (158–62)

(Just as the sun's image shines in a mirror, just as, hidden in the flawless glass, the transparent force burns in the ray of its source, the sun; so the musical heavens' modulations mold and inflame the shining and purified minds of poets.)

The parallel *ceu ... ceu* makes appear as two similes what is only one. It distinguishes the two aspects of the picture: reflection (*tralucet imago*) and warming (*inardescit ... vis*). Likewise in the tenor: the effect of heavenly melody on the poets' spirit is to represent (*informant*) and impassion (*flammant*). These two elements of poetic furor must be considered together: There is no mimesis without madness, no madness without a claim to truth. At the same time, the twin actions of reflection and warming suggest the two inseparable aspects of poetry as exchange. On the one hand, reflection is the imperative of reciprocity, pointing toward a balanced principle of order. On the other hand, the sun's warming effect means the addition and agonistic rendering of more than was bestowed. So that, again in the amphibolic mode, poetry involves both an ideal of reciprocity and the excess that subverts that ideal.[182]

The inspired poet becomes a battleground for the conflict that is poetry. Poliziano describes the experience as a naval battle or storm at sea, where the rational mind is sunk:

> Fluctu . . . furoris
> Mens prior it pessum: tum clausus inaestuat alto
> Corde Deus, toto lymphatos pectore sensus
> Exstimulans.

(163–66)

(The former mind is sunk by the surge of madness. Then God seethes, enclosed deep in the heart, goading the frenzied senses throughout the soul.)

A struggle thus develops between the divine (Poetry) and human within man. The divine drives away the human *ad imas latebras,* to the underworld—slays it, in fact. We see generalized here the initially fatal effect that Achilles' inspiration had on Homer in *Ambra.*[183] As the conqueror of a besieged city, poetry takes over the corpse of the vacant poet to direct what is now a musical statue like the legendary Memnon.

> Vacua ipse potitus
> Sede, per obsessos semet tandem egerit artus,
> Inque suos humana ciet praecordia cantus.

(167–69)

(Taking possession of the empty site, it moves through his besieged limbs, and excites its song in the human breast.)[184]

The song emitted by the inspired human poet is said to surpass the power of the gods' own sounds (176–80). Thus divine poetry overwhelms man only to raise him above the gods. This is the opposite movement corresponding to the human invasion of heaven. The movement of poetic power from macrocosm to microcosm is again evident, but the power of inspiration is not an ordering but a derangement. Poliziano accentuates the Platonic paradox that madness is the greatest good, provided it be a gift from the gods.[185]

There may be in this rapprochement of madness and verbal power a deeper kinship than at first appears. Our analysis may gain by elaborating a suggestion by M. Foucault concerning the birth of the concept of madness in early modern Europe. He observes a historical passage in consciousness and practice from a magical *domaine d'efficacité* to a mad *domaine d'illusion.*[186] If we take that passage more narrowly as representing the transition from one image of the poet to another, it means that the poet as vatic purveyor of word magic makes way for the mad poet, cultivator of chimeras. Only, of course, poetic madness is a complex matter, both diachronically and synchronically. First, madness may be roughly divided historically into the literary fiction of poetic furor (where we find Poliziano), followed by the unreason of which Foucault traces the history. So it could be said that the long tradition of poetic furor maintains the positive transcendent function of word magic inherited from archaic culture, before slipping into the status of mere illusion with the advent of modern madness.[187] But on the other hand, and to return to "no mimesis without madness," poetic madness is not really subsequent historically to verbal magic. Particularly when they are considered as literary topoi, each requires the other. The "passage" just mentioned is one more case where, in a Vichian manner, the appearance of historical development is compressed in poetic convention. Just as for Vico metaphor tells about the original state of humanity, so we may take the copresence of poetic furor and immortality in Poliziano as the allegory of a history of poets.

Of course, Poliziano invents little in his description of poetic inspiration. He draws on a supply of well-known classical commonplaces that identify poetry as a kind of madness.[188] But the familiarity of a topos does not mean that every use of it is banal. His pretext, a praise of poetry as such, leads Poliziano to the limit of his clichés. In the present case, the complex of metaphors concerning inspiration moves from solar generosity to the image of poetry as allied with death.[189] In other words, it follows an itinerary from the transcendentally positive tradition of neo-Platonic emanation to the constitution of poetry through the absolute negativity of death.[190] The latter notion becomes particularly evident in the figure of Orpheus.

Orpheus receives the most attention of any poet in the survey, apart from Lorenzo. He is introduced among his usual peers, Amphion, Musaeus, and Linus. These mythical poets do not begin the survey, but rather follow the literally divine and semidivine poets as well as the special case of Biblical poets. However, they do come first in the culture of pagan antiquity and are introduced by a recognition of their magical effectiveness.[191] It is perhaps not surprising, given his starting point, to find Poliziano treating legendary poets as he subsequently does historical ones. What may be more surprising, given the pedagogical occasion, is that he does not distinguish those poets whose texts exist from those of whom nothing survives. This becomes more comprehensible when we recognize the predominantly anecdotal character of Poliziano's survey. Even such poets as Lucretius (487–91) and Lucan (499–519), for example, whose principal works are readily available to the professor and his audience, receive treatment that concentrates as much on (more or less fantastic) biographical details as on allusions to their texts. This tendency to represent all the poets as equally real has a double effect. On the one hand, it passes off each of the legendary poets as an actor in a given, quasi-historical situation. On the other hand, it tends to archaize even the later poets by placing them in circumstances that recall their mythical predecessors. In this light, Orpheus appears as a figure both privileged and representative, who encapsulates in his career the nature of poetry and poetic history.

Orpheus embodies the copresence of law and hubristic lawlessness in poetry. On the one hand, he tames wild animals as Poetry tamed bestial men.[192] His use of the lyre in song means the submission of voice to number and proportion. But on the other hand, and as the greatest triumph of poetry, Orpheus violates (for a short while) the laws of Hades. However, these alternatives are perhaps not so opposed. Orpheus's ability to move nature shows the power of poetry to dominate, to submit all things to its law. But that law itself is unnatural: Rocks and trees were created to sit still, not to dance; lions naturally roar, and so on. The domination of nature, the giving of laws, is at the same time the violation of nature.[193]

In Poliziano's day Orpheus is a figure who represents the ideal poetic predecessor, authorizing later literary endeavors. In the first *Sylva, Manto,* Orpheus begins the poem as a character singing to his fellow Argonauts. His song suspends nature and encourages the young Achilles to take up the master's instrument next and praise, in a crude unlearned style, "tantae murmura magna lyrae" (the mighty hum of Orpheus's great lyre). The rest of the audience hears this tribute with derision, but Orpheus warmly accepts the young hero's *pietas.* Subsequently, Poliziano compares himself with Achilles; and Virgil, the subject of praise in *Manto,* with Orpheus. Thus the great primordial poet is the model for a loving acceptance of later poetic efforts, particularly when those efforts are songs of praise.[194]

On the other hand, near the end of his *Morgante,* Luigi Pulci represents Poliziano himself as Orpheus, adding to his attributes the city-building power of Amphion:

> E i monti sforza come il tracio Orfeo,
> e sempre intorno ha di Parnaso il coro,
> e l'acque ferma e i sassi muove e glebe,
> e a sua posta può richiuder Tebe.[195]

(He moves mountains like the Thracian Orpheus, and always has the Parnassian chorus around him, and stops rivers and moves rocks and clods, and can enclose Thebes on its site.)

Finally, in his dedication to Lorenzo de' Medici of his translation of Homer's *Iliad,* book 2, Poliziano makes a similar identification. He addresses his patron/poet as one possessing Orphic powers: "Auritas ducere quercus / Cantando rabidasque potes mulcere leaenas" (You can lead the attentive oak-trees, and soothe frenzied lionesses with your singing). And he concludes the dedication by praying for inspiration, not from Apollo or the Muses, but from Lorenzo.

> Solus tu carmina nobis
> Ismarium possis afferre aequantia plectrum;
> Te duce, vel priscis ausim certare poetis.[196]

(You alone can bring an Orphic plectrum to my rival poem. With you as a leader I dare to contend even with archaic poets.)

All these Orpheuses exemplify an authority that makes poetry possible. Each one lends his primordial power to a poetic novice. And what is common to the variations on that role is the element of bestowal. Orpheus's gift consists of both promoting the process of civilization and stimulating subsequent poetry; most likely the former through the latter.

The central anecdote of the Orphic myth, namely, the retrieval and second loss of Eurydice, unites the threads of bestowal, inspiration, and death that wind through *Nutricia*.

> Tum primum et lachrymas, invita per ora cadentes
> Eumenidum, stygii conjunx mirata tyranni,
> Indulsit vati Eurydicen; sed muneris usum
> Perdidit: heu durae nimia inclementia legis!
>
> (294–97)

(Then the wife of Hell's tyrant, marveling at the tears flowing for the first time on the Furies' reluctant faces, bestowed Eurydice upon the poet. But he lost the profit of his gift—alas, such strictness of a harsh law!)

In the most important ancient literary versions of the myth, those of Virgil and Ovid, Eurydice is also called a gift.[197] The verb that expresses Proserpina's bestowal of the resurrected Eurydice, *indulsit,* recurs in *Nutricia,* describing the Muses' gift of poetry to Hesiod (383). The Orphic myth, which has always represented the not-quite-supreme power of poetry, here reveals an additional aspect. Orpheus's song coerces not only nature generally, but especially the queen of the dead. Moved by poetic law, she grants the poet a promise of earthly happiness. Proserpina's patronage is the culmination of the civilizing effect of poetry. The promise that her patronage holds forth, however, is not of consummated immortality, but only a restoration of the status quo—

and that only at the price of abstention from contemplating the reward, which is a price too dear for the poet. Eurydice as the gift that
poetry receives in exchange for its charm, but is forbidden to enjoy,
figures the ambivalent poetics of humanism. M. Blanchot has found
in the Orphic myth an allegory of the constitutional impossibility of
poetry.[198] Such an interpretation takes on complementary meaning
with the added element of patronage as Poliziano presents it. The *furor*
of Orpheus is both what enables him to bewitch the world and what
prevents him from a measured use of his reward from the dead.[199]

The other episode of the myth that Poliziano emphasizes is the poet's
posthumous activity. After he has been dismembered by the Maenads,
his lyre serves as a vessel for Orpheus's head and appears to prolong
his voice.

> Cum lyra divulsum caput a cervice cruenta
> Heu medium veheret resonans lugubre per Hebrum,
> Relliquias animae jam deficientis amatam
> Movit in Eurydicen, tamen illam frigidus unam
> Spiritus, illam unam moriens quoque lingua vocabat.[200]

(301–5)

> (As the mournfully resounding lyre bore his head, torn from a bloody neck,
> down the middle of the river Hebrus, it impelled what was left of a failing
> breath toward beloved Eurydice—her alone, her alone his cold spirit and
> dying tongue called.)

The plaintive repetition of *illam unam,* which echoes a similar effect
in the Virgilian and Ovidian passages, accentuates the object of the
poet's final apostrophe.[201] Not surprisingly, it is what he has won and
lost as reward for his song. The uncertain meaning of *vocabat* reflects
the uncertain function of poetry: Is he summoning her with an effective spell or is he simply calling her name in an elegiac mode? In any
case, the insistence on mortal adjectives and adverbs (*cruenta, lugu-
bre, deficientis, frigidus, moriens*) emphasizes the miracle of living
poetry, arising from death through the lyre's office.[202] Moreover, this
forms the prelude to the adoption of Orpheus by a people more pious
than the Thracian women. The inhabitants of Lesbos recover the poet's
head and grant him a permanent public role by setting up a statue to
him in a holy place.[203]

The career of Orpheus thus tells, most obviously, a story of poetry's
power extending beyond mere individual death and sorrow. And yet
death is not merely an enemy of poetic invention, but a collaborator,
too. Orpheus's itinerary to the underworld reiterates the direction of
inspiration, *ad imas . . . latebras,* as previously described (166–67).

As in the case of Homer in *Ambra,* the poet's hubris, driving him beyond limits, makes his work what it is. That excessiveness also informs the poet's relationship to the patron, which, as we find consistently in other contexts, is an essential element in poetry's self-image.

Poetry evidently has two symmetrical moments of effectiveness: when it enters man as inspiration and when it departs from him as poems. Following a familiar scheme, poetry descends from the divine to help humanity reach the divine. Man is, it seems, only fully human in his instability; his nature realizes itself in the movement from beast to divinity. In this, as E. Garin has noted, Poliziano's Orpheus is analogous to Pico della Mirandola's Adam.[204] They are both capable of partaking of the eternal. One important difference is that Adam's capacity lies in his god-given human nature, while Orpheus's power and potential, his humanity, is a consequence of the gift of poetry.[205] Moreover, the relation of Adam to the rest of humanity is representative, while Orpheus's role is effective; Adam merely shows what everyone is capable of, while Orpheus works a change upon his fellow humans with his song.

Adam and Orpheus may also be understood as complementary allegories of the humanist's social role. The ontic instability of Pico's Adam presents a purified image of the social mobility that could characterize a literary life. Poliziano himself provides a striking example of a provincial of indifferent birth whose power with words led him ultimately to a comfortable existence.[206] Likewise, the tenacious self-promotion of a Filelfo is the materialist version of Adam, obeying the divine command to raise himself up.

Orpheus, on the other hand, is the primordial poet who founds civilization based on his magical efficacy. As noted above, this foundation is troublesome and contradictory. Humanists' ambition to be legislators (and preferably acknowledged) of humanity is based on an Orphic image of verbal power. Moreover, the literary history of *Nutricia* pretends to prolong the genealogy of that power. And just as the passage on Orpheus shows him exercising his spell over various audiences— animate and inanimate nature, Proserpina, the Maenads, and the Lesbians—so does Poliziano portray later poets in relation to what may be called patrons. That is, in relation to not simply listeners, but listeners who manifest their powerful approval (and disapproval) through a reciprocal relation.

A number of poets in the survey are identified with regard to imperial or military authority: Stesichorus and Phalaris (601), Thespis and Solon (664–65), Eupolis and Alcibiades (680–81), Ennius and Scipio (466–70), Terence and Scipio (693–94), Catullus and Caesar (483), Lucan and Nero (502), Silius Italicus and Nero (523), Bassus and Vespasian (526–27), and Oppianus and Antoninus Pius (421–22). On the other hand, some poets are remembered for their commerce with a god or some quasi-divine figure: Branchus and Apollo (214–15), Linus and Hercules (321–27), Hesiod and the Muses (382–85), Pindar with Apollo, Pan and Proserpina (572–79), Stesichorus and Helen (599–600), and Simonides and the Dioscuri (606–7).

The most obvious cases where paleological civilizing function becomes "historical" civic role are the examples of poets paired with temporal rulers. Reaction to the poet can be oppression from a tyrant (Alcibiades, or Nero against Lucan) or else a tyrant's respect (Phalaris). A good leader can exercise material generosity (Vespasian, Antoninus Pius), magnanimity in return for invective (Julius Caesar), or a genuine friendship, as when Scipio shared his tomb with Ennius. The variety of those examples is based on the twin powers of epideictic poetry: praise and blame. To illustrate the latter, Poliziano retells the story of the Greek satirist Archilochus, who was spurned as a suitor and composed such powerful invective as to drive the girl and her father to suicide (644–47). While the satire of Archilochus appears to operate only in the private realm, Poliziano's other examples make attractive Vico's interpretation of that episode as a trace of early class warfare.[207] Such poets as Alcaeus (595), Stesichorus (601), and Greek tragedy in general (653–54) were able to overthrow tyrants. They thus exercised the double functions, religious and political, which combine the Suetonian and Horatian currents of poetic paleology. Moreover, the sacred poet manifests a special power even apart from immediate performance and even beyond his lifetime. A military commander desecrated Simonides' tomb to build a tower; the poet was avenged when the commander was defeated from that very tower (609). Likewise, a flock of cranes avenged the death of Ibycus (616). The house of Pindar in Thebes and his descendents were unharmed by the fires of the victorious Alexander (580–84). Here, too, poetic effectiveness has a predominantly civic, and a predominantly oppositional role.

However, the poet may not always be so neatly vindicated in this world. Ovid, for example, ennobled Rome but was repaid with exile, to the city's dishonor (434–39).[208] His compensation lies only in Poliziano's defense of him here and in the recognition that Ovid himself has saved many poets from oblivion in the last of his poems *Ex Ponto* (537).

If we turn to the relations between poets and gods or demigods, one injustice in particular stands out, both because it remains uncompensated and because of the identity of the criminal. That is the murder of Linus by his pupil Hercules. There is no need to dwell on Linus's traditional place with the great primordial poets Orpheus, Musaeus, and Amphion (he was the son of Apollo and Terpsichore),[209] nor on the immense symbolic importance Hercules had in the Renaissance. As a hero, ultimately deified, Hercules' murder of the poet takes on a paradigmatic character. He was driven to this act by impatience with the authority, the *imperium,* of his teacher:

> quondam triste perosus
> Doctoris magni imperium, veneranda rebelli
> Contudit ora lyra, et clamantem plurima frustra
> Tendentemque manus obtestantemque peremit.

> (323–26)

(Once, bitterly loathing the authority of his great teacher, he crushed that venerable head with a rebellious lyre, and slew him as the victim called out, stretched out his hands and implored him in vain.)

Triste, rather than referring to Hercules, may qualify Linus's authority as severe and thus give a motive for Hercules' hostility.[210] Nevertheless, poetic power merits reverence (*veneranda*), even from such a hero. The worst of the impiety lies in the murder weapon. Hercules cracks the poet's skull with his lyre; the life-giving instrument (one remembers Orpheus, only a few lines away) becomes a tool of death. Poliziano exclaims: "Heu non ista piae meritum sibi praemia linguae!" (Alas, this is not the reward he deserved for his virtuous tongue!) (327). In fact, Hercules has been forgetful of the benefits received from poetry (322); he has flagrantly violated the universal law of gratitude to one's *nutrix.*

The space that Poliziano allows this anecdote compels attention to it as a negative exemplum. It is as if Odysseus refused to have mercy on the poet Phemius.[211] The pathetic depiction of the poet's murder, in the context of an affirmation of poetic domination and immortality, provides an outsized reminder of the real way of the world. Hercules, the man of action par excellence, may have previously assumed the role of pupil in the manner of a good Renaissance prince. But in the realm of force, the humanist's *imperium* is rudely revealed to have been only metaphorical. The reversal of the lyre, the instrument of domination, as well as the pathos of the hypotyposis (*clamantem . . . tendentemque manus . . . obtestantemque*) suggests a certain masochism on the part of the humanist/poet. The anecdote anticipates certain sixteenth-century comedies in which a pedant is brutally humiliated.[212] The difference is that the comic use is satirical and does not necessarily implicate the author. What surfaces here is rather a mythical self-correction.

Admittedly, in *Nutricia* the relations between gods and mortal poets are more often benevolent. A god may protect a poet, as the Dioscuri did Simonides, or, more often, he may bestow poetic talent. The transition from the first divine poets (Nereus, Prometheus, Themis, Jupiter, Pan, and Apollo) to the human tradition is effected erotically. Apollo gave to the shepherd Branchus the gift of poetry in exchange for a kiss. Hesiod's famous inspiration is similar. Among later poets, Pindar had perhaps the most frequent commerce with the gods. After his death he was honored in the manner described earlier, so that, in contrast to so many poets excluded from their native cities, Pindar's home was the one part of Thebes immune to the conqueror's ravages. The mention of his death ("tacita rapuit Proserpina dextra" [Proserpina snatched him up with a silent hand] [579]) refers to a story related by Pausanias in which Proserpina appeared to the aged Pindar in a dream.[213] She complained that she alone among the gods had not been honored in song by the poet but assured him that he would compose an ode when he came to her. Soon afterward he died. Here the goddess, like all divinities, requires poetry. The poet, recalling Orpheus, is at the same time her benefactor and subject to her realm of death. The god Pan, on the other hand, was seen singing the poems of Pindar in the forest (574–75). And the height of the poet's glory on earth was the decree that assigned to him a part of the offerings to Apollo at Delphi (572–73). He thus participated in the rewards of deity, as is only right for one who benefited the gods so well in their respective infernal, terrestrial, and celestial realms. As we have already seen, Pindar conceived of unusually close links between gods and great humans.[214] Here and elsewhere, Poliziano makes the relation even closer, elevating poets to divinity rather than Pindar's athletes and nobles.[215]

By now, one of the most striking characteristics of Poliziano's literary history should be clear: its immobility. Although the survey unfolds as a narrative *ab ovo* and covers a vast sweep of time and genres, it contains no hint of literary development. Beneath all the anecdotal varieties of its manifestations, Poetry's divine essence remains independent of history. If Poliziano's account of poetry's existence in time corresponds to none of the traditional metaphors of literary history (the plant's organic growth, the kaleidoscope's rearrangement of traditional elements, the dialectic of night and day),[216] then is there another metaphor that will do? Perhaps, partially, this one, which captures poetry's unchanging nature as well as the poet's hieratic posture: literary history as a series of archaic statues.

The logical extension of the commerce of poets with gods may be seen by returning to the figure of Homer. We have already found that the *Oratio in expositione Homeri* and *Ambra* present Homer as a creator of godlike primordiality and range. There exists yet a third *praelectio* to Homer, this one to a course on the *Odyssey* and probably delivered around 1489.[217] This brief text takes up a number of the themes developed in the earlier *praelectiones*: "that [Homer] formed the voices of all things, that from him alone every renowned philosophical sect flowed and every poet originated," and so on.[218] The passage on Homer as source of all benefits of the Word concludes thus: "sic ut eum quasi divinitus ortum divinis honoribus affecerint" (so that they endowed him, as someone of divine descent, with divine honors). *Ambra* too alludes to such honors (575). Both passages are vague, taking place in a mythical past, and function as one more commonplace of praise and reward. But in the *praelectio* to the *Odyssey,* something more solid ensues.

Itaque etiam heretici fuere quidam, quos Augustinus Carpocratianos appellat, quorum auctor et princeps Marcella, ture dicatur coluisse Jesum, Paulum, Homerum et Pythagoram; quos scilicet putabant esse homines, sed animam nactos divinarum consciam.[219]

(There were even certain heretics, whom Augustine calls Carpocratians, whose originator and leader was Marcella, and who are said to have worshipped Jesus, Paul, Homer and Pythagoras with incense. These they believed to be men, but men possessing a soul privy to divine things.)

This is a substantially accurate paraphrase of a passage from St. Augustine's *De Haeresibus ad Quodvultdeum.*[220] There is no indication here that Poliziano was interested in the broader doctrines of Gnosticism, so it would be useless to speculate on the influence of such Carpocratian doctrines as metempsychosis, the world's creation by intermediate spirits, or the sect's peculiar antinomianism.[221] What Augustine and Poliziano allude to is the worship of statuettes of deified men. These statuettes could represent Jesus, regarded from an Arian point of view, as well as mortals who had deserved apotheosis by the power of their gnosis. This latter category mixes poets (Homer) and a certain kind of philosopher (Pythagoras) because the Logos does not distinguish among disciplines.[222] It is true that Homer had a privileged status in antiquity; one would be surprised to find Carpocratian statuettes of, say, Anacreon or Ovid.[223] Nevertheless, as I have already claimed, Poliziano's praise of Homer is principally praise of poetry in Homer. If Homer was the supreme poet to the point of being worshipped as a deity, that is because he was an incomparable vessel manifesting the full power of poetry. Poliziano's mention of heretical practice in his panegyric does not, of course, mean that he is advocating anything of the sort. But the exemplum of Homer's immortality is clearly more important than the damnability of the heresy, qui tamen ut error detestabilis atque abominandus piis hominibus est, ita magno sit argumento vulgatae apud omnes opinionis Homericae divinitatis.[224]

(Which, although it is a detestable error abhorrent to pius men, yet let it serve as a great symbol for the universal opinion of Homer's divinity.)

From this error arises truth. The Quattrocento has come full circle from the putative worship of Virgil's statue in Mantua.

LORENZO AND THE POETICS OF PATRONAGE

Given the declaration of such autonomy for poetry, what place could there possibly be for a patron? *Ambra* links the patron to the poet in an intimate exchange, necessary because poetry originates in mortality and the material world (Achilles' grave and Poggio a Caiano). But the autonomy of poetry in *Nutricia* sometimes appears so great as to stand in no need of material support. When poets create society, why beg for a place in society? How, then, can one justify the praise of Lorenzo at the end of this last *Sylva?* Most obviously because he is introduced not as patron, but as poet. This is, of course, consistent with the poem as a whole. In *Ambra* the dialectic between Homer and Achilles and the poet's creation of the cosmos ends up as the dialectic between Poliziano and Lorenzo and the patron's creation of a paradise of *otium.* In *Nutricia* the list of sovereign poets concludes with a poet who is also Poliziano's friend and benefactor.

Of course, it has also become clear in *Nutricia* that poets are rarely independent of their patrons, mortal or divine. This relationship is telescoped in the figure of Lorenzo. In him there appears no tension between the power of poetry and any social power outside it. On the contrary; what has been presented throughout as poetry's social authority and the poet-patron exchange takes shape here as the marriage of poetic and political authority in one person. True to the Horatian topos, Lorenzo dominates both nature and humanity.[225] Both aspects find expression in the pun *Laurens/laurus.* As *dux laureatus,* he protects his city in the shade of his temporal glory:

> Cujus securus ad umbram
> Fulmina bellorum ridens procul aspicit Arnus,
> Maeoniae caput o Laurens.

(730–32)

(Secure in your shade Arno gazes laughing at the distant thunder of wars, o Lorenzo head of Tuscany.)[226]

He is also *poeta laureatus* through a myth of divine poetic endowment similar to the stories Poliziano has already introduced for Branchus, Hesiod, Pindar, and others. In a pastoral setting Lorenzo attracted a nymph with his song. She confirmed his poetic gift with the laurel crown and inspired him with love (the motive of that Laurentian poetry to which Poliziano first refers):

Illa tibi, lauruque tua semperque recenti
Flore comam cingens, pulchrum inspiravit amorem.

(743–44)

(Encircling your hair with your laurel and its brightness always fresh, she breathed into you a beautiful love.)

The inspiration, although less precise physically, also recalls Achilles' endowment of Homer. Through this myth, Lorenzo gains admission to the company of great archaic poets who had erotic commerce with the gods.[227] An allusion to his religious poetry (768–69) makes him exemplify the union of political and cultic function that combines the two currents of poetic paleology. He is privileged above the modern poets mentioned here only summarily: Dante, Petrarca, Boccaccio, and Cavalcanti. Moreover, Poliziano concludes the catalog and sums up these Florentine poets in a tribute to their native city:

Unde tibi immensae veniunt praeconia laudis,
Ingeniis opibusque potens, Florentia mater.

(726–27)

(From whom there comes to you the announcement of immense praise, o Florence our mother, powerful in wit and wealth.)

This, the transition to the passage on Lorenzo that concludes the poem, directs the entire history of poetry toward a paean to contemporary Florence and its ruler. It also makes clear the convertibility of *ingenium* and *opes* that runs through the *Sylvae* and humanist poetics in general.

Lorenzo as laurel is a constant presence in Poliziano's work.[228] Defined as *Laurens/laurus,* he exemplifies the magical or mythical function of the name as principle of individuation.[229] Introduced in *Nutricia* principally as poet, he enjoys the known benefits of the laurel. As patron, he also dispenses those benefits.[230] The shade tree provides an ideal image of free bestowal, where all material calculation disappears and the dematerialization of patronage becomes a second

nature. Lorenzo presides over Poliziano's greatest Italian poem, the
Stanze:

> E tu, ben nato Laur, sotto il cui velo
> Fiorenza lieta in pace si riposa,
> né teme i venti o 'l minacciar del celo
> o Giove irato in vista più crucciosa,
> accogli all'ombra del tuo santo stelo
> la voce umil, tremante e paurosa;
> o causa, o fin di tutte le mie voglie,
> che sol vivon d'odor delle tuo foglie.[231]

(And you, nobly borne Lorenzo, beneath whose protection happy Florence
reposes in peace, and fears neither the winds nor the threatening heavens
nor the angriest frown of enraged Jupiter, receive my voice, humble,
trembling and fearful, into the shade of your holy stem, o beginning and
end of all my desires, which live only from the scent of your leaves.)

The reference to Jupiter's rage may allude to Lorenzo's political suc-
cesses against the hostile pope, Sixtus IV. But it refers primarily to the
recognized property of the laurel (as expressed by Petrarca, for one),
immunity to thunderbolts. That means immunity to time. Not only
does Lorenzo maintain Florence in the peace necessary for art, but
his patronage fosters those works that are proof against time. The immortality of literary works is ever present for Poliziano.[232] He declares
immortalization as the purpose of the *Stanze,* and Lorenzo is the one
who enables the poet to write,

> sì che i gran nomi e i fatti egregi e soli
> fortuna o morte o tempo non involi.[233]

(So that great names and outstanding and unique deeds may not be stolen
away by fortune, death or time.)

The ideal portrait of Lorenzo in *Nutricia,* far from being extraneous
flattery, forms the culmination of the poem. It befits a poem of the
genre *sylva* to declare its debt to the patron's shade. And yet, that
shade also has the effect of setting the poem in opposition to itself. The
essential phrase concerning Lorenzo the patron, *securus ad umbram*
(730), clearly recalls through its cadence and position the famous *lentus in umbra* from Virgil's first Eclogue.[234] Shade can be said to be
"the *sine qua non* of pastoral repose," and thus of literary creation.[235]
As the protection necessary to rural *otium, umbra* also makes possible
the reversion to primitivism that is inherent in pastoral.[236] Anyone

resting in the shade thereby assumes the role of a shepherd in the golden age. However, what is the central myth of *Nutricia* if not a denial of the golden age? The antiprimitivism on which poetic paleology is based would seem to exclude any gesture toward "the good old days." Still, not only Lorenzo's patronage, but also the evocation of his poetic activity unfolds in a setting of just that pastoral regression. Such a setting is fully in keeping, after all, with much of Lorenzo's own poetry.[237]

However, pastoral repose is not the only literary behavior evoked by shade, nor is it the only contribution of shade to literary history. We should recall the primitives called out of their forest dwellings to civilization by Cicero's arch-orator as well as the *silvae* or *silvestris homines* enchanted by Horace's Ur-poet.[238] The forest is the place where the decisive step of human culture was made, where the masters of the eloquent or poetic word bestowed their foundational and enduring gift on bestial humanity. Like Vico's primordial giants, so did the first beneficiaries of literature become civilized when they stopped their wanderings through "la gran selva della terra."[239] So it might be suspected that the generic metaphor of Poliziano's *Sylvae* does not refer primarily to literary activity and literary history as Arcadia. The shade in which poets write is the shade of the *selva* that forms the original situation of poetry. The Florentine professor's exploration of his genre means a return to wandering through the original wood; it means an attempt to renew the power of that original contact between the first barbarism and the first cure for barbarism.[240]

But still: there remains something more for poetry in the forest's shade. *Umbra* evokes not only pastoral repose, not only the obscurity of origins, but also the dead. *Umbrae* populate the underworld in the Latin tradition. Orpheus's descent, which, we recall, resumes the movement of inspiration, takes the poet to the realm of shades.[241] Poliziano's *Sylvae* and *Nutricia,* in particular, seek their inspiration in *otium,* in mythic origins, and among the dead.

The first two kinds of shade and *sylva* help explain the contradiction between primitivism and antiprimitivism in *Nutricia*. Both effect a reversion in time, the first to an Arcadian golden age, the second to primordial barbarism. Both constitute a foundation of poetry, although both cannot be present at the same time unless we admit an amphibolic poetics. The third sort of shade means a different sort of antitemporal (that is, mythical) movement: to the negativity of death that is at the same time the site of immortalizing power.

The pursuit of that complex metaphor helps explain the represented pursuit that ends the poem. Poliziano imagines himself racing his pupil Piero de' Medici through the wood that is *Nutricia*.[242] The pupil/

patron follows close behind Poliziano, who assures him that he will soon leave his teacher far behind. Apart from completely unfounded flattery, what is at issue here? The patron (or the member of the patron's family who is most directly in the humanist's hands) becomes a partner in the exploration of literary history as that primeval forest that provides the locus of poetic paleology. The race makes clear the dynamic emulation informing their exploration of that realm. As Poliziano has done for Lorenzo, he desires to find a place for Piero, not just in the classroom, but as part of the material studied itself. He wants to establish the patron as a literary monument.

The race between poet and patron evidently promises no exit from the forest. The *sylva* in all its senses appears to be their common dwelling place, a dwelling place built (or planted) by the poet. We may recall Cicero's famous metaphor that figures glory itself as a shadow;[243] literary glory would thus be the composite of *otium,* origins, and death enjoyed by those granted existence in the poem. But if the poem is the forest and the patron (Laurus) is the shade tree, who is bestowing upon whom? We find in that confusion of metaphor the complexity of the poet-patron dialectic developed by humanism. As illustrated in the first part of this chapter, the humanist attempts to pull the patron/prince into an exchange relation, making him a benefactor while asserting his own literary dominance. Such interaction becomes second nature in the itinerary of the fourth *Sylva.* We have also seen the elevation of poetry to a supreme category; such an all-encompassing role finds its appropriate image here in the poem as forest that is "la gran selva della terra."

So it can be said that the structure and ideology of *Nutricia* are founded on a triple contradiction, a contradiction representative of the aporias belonging to Quattrocento poetics. The mythical pretense of progress due to Poetry is belied by the immobility of literary history. That pseudo-progress culminates in a figure embodying the virtuous primordiality that has been shown to not exist. And the systematic hymn to poetry's supremacy ends with the poet outstripped, in a race through his native landscape, by the young patron. The contradictory status of Medicean literary practice and patronage, taken as the ideal image of all patronage, constitutes Lorenzo's bequest, both to Poliziano's poem and to posterity.

CODA

Lorenzo died prematurely on 8 April 1492, the anniversary of Petrarca's laurel coronation.[244] Poliziano voices his loss of the ideals embodied by *il Magnifico* in the unique ode "In Laurentiam Medicem."[245] There he effects what can only be considered the destruction of a poetic commonplace. We have already seen how Poliziano uses the topos of the laurel's immunity to lightning. It is explicit in the *Stanze* and underlies the image of Lorenzo as laurel in *Nutricia* and elsewhere.[246] In the ode, however, the laurel lies dead, a victim precisely of lightning and all that means:

> Laurus impetu fulminis
> Illa illa jacet subito,
> Laurus omnium celebris
> Musarum choris,
> Nympharum choris.[247]

(That laurel lies slain by the thunderbolt's attack; that laurel famed among the choruses of all the Muses, famed among the choruses of nymphs.)

Poliziano had a precedent for the laurel's "unnatural" death in a late canzone by Petrarca.[248] In the *Canzone delle visioni* the laurel, as one of the symbols of Laura, is struck down by lightning, thus negating what the poet had asserted in his coronation speech. Lodovico Castelvetro, in his commentary, noted that the unnaturalness of such a demise indicates that Madonna Laura's death was against nature.[249] No doubt; but the death of the laurel results more pertinently from a cosmic failure of patronage. The wrath of the king of the gods has struck down poetry's public honor.[250] The death of Lorenzo and of the Petrarchan laurel as well means that poetry can no longer depend on receiving what is due to it in the proper order of things.[251]

The laurel: "Sub cujus patula coma / Et Phoebi lyra blandius / Et vox dulcius insonat" (16–18) (Beneath whose broad foliage even Apollo's lyre resounds more seductively and his voice more sweetly). *Patula* is the same adjective Virgil applies in the first line of his first *Eclogue* to the archetypal tree of pastoral repose and poetic creation. The Virgilian beech becomes the Medicean laurel in Poliziano's ode, and Poliziano raises the poetic stakes correspondingly as he claims that even Apollo has benefited from Lorenzo's patronage. The laurel's death and the failure of poetry consequent on it reflect the forest exploration of the *Sylvae* a few years earlier. What they amount to is an image of the delegitimation of poetry. The ode on Lorenzo's death makes things plain as the leafless laurel. Or as plain as things can be when based on such contradictions as those that humanism comprises. Deprived of *otium,* deprived of the landscape of its mythical social role, poetry is paradoxically left with one kind of *umbra,* namely, the patron as mortal shade.

As in the case of Petrarca's elegy for King Robert (the *envoi* to the *Africa*), Poliziano's mourning is less personal than symbolic. He regrets, of course, a generous and knowledgeable patron, the dream of all poets. He could say with Petrarca and with the same metaphoric fitness: "Simile ombra mai non si racquista" (such a shade is never found again).[252] But the idealization of Lorenzo goes further, to an image of hyperbolic wholeness and the reconciliation of two parts, *dux* and *poeta,* which had traditionally seemed opposed.[253]

In the aforementioned passage from the ode, he is glimpsed in that characteristic pose of the archaic poet, dancing with the Muses. The time when a poet (better than a philosopher) ruled could indeed seem a golden age.[254] But with the loss of this single example, everything once again is called into doubt. Immunity to time turns out to have been a fantasy. The entire endeavor of immortalization and legitimation that the poet undertakes in the shade of the patron comes into question. Poliziano's attempt to tame both the constitutive violence of poetry and the social conflict it entails runs aground. What can the poet achieve against time and superior powers when his protection forsakes him? For now, nothing.

Nunc muta omnia,
Nunc surda omnia.[255]

(Now all is mute, now all is deaf.)

4

Guillaume Budé

La parole ... est la seule Magie

Wahrlich, ein Ungetüm is die
Macht dieses Lobens und Tadelns.

THE poet is not the only *litteratus* endowed with the power of resurrection. While he naturally hauls needy glory from the tomb as Poliziano's Homer rescues Achilles, the poet may have occasion to benefit in turn from the care of the philologist. We have already seen Salutati express his feeling of responsibility with regard to the *Africa*. Petrarca the cultivator of antiquity is as aware of this function as Petrarca the poet.[1] The author of the preface to the *Raccolta aragonese* repeats the same idea in his praise of Pisistratus. Poliziano the philologist sees himself as Aesculapius, braving the wrath of the gods to bring the ancients back to life.[2] All this suggests that the preeminence of poetry as immortalizer is not based on a radical difference from other literary forms. Its power does does not depend on poetic "creativity" but on the power inherent in the eloquent word, a power only reinforced when submitted to number and measure. The significance of philology in the Renaissance lies, first of all, physically in the discovery and purification of texts that then become available to posterity. But it will come as no surprise to find, in addition, an acute awareness of the word's effective power even in a humanist like Guillaume Budé who, unlike Petrarca and Poliziano, seems at first glance (but only at first glance) to have no poetic alter ego.[3]

Who was Guillaume Budé? Or rather, who is he? Is there any reason to read him after four and a half centuries, or has he found his proper role as a mere name presiding over French humanism?[4] The literary riches of antiquity are published under his protection, but his own works lack critical editions. His statue looks out from the courtyard of the Collège de France,[5] but the only reason to evoke the statue of

191

Virgil in Mantua is for ironic contrast. The fallen status of Renaissance humanism as *nomina nuda* appears embodied in Budé.

The question does not concern Budé's person. He left a substantial correspondence and the public traces one would expect from a member of a prominent family, himself an important figure at court.[6] Budé's European reputation as a humanist rivaled that of Erasmus, with whom he was often paired.[7] Despite his enigmatic style, the man does not seem an enigma and so belies Buffon's equation. But the question concerns the enigma in the work. Budé resembles the Latin Petrarca in remaining a presence in the Renaissance he helped inaugurate, even when his works were subsequently neglected.[8] The traditional image of Budé as founder of French humanism is too simplistic to be maintained and has been modified by critics who stress his French precursors and the influence of Italian humanism.[9] Similarly, we should be suspicious of Budé's self-portrait with its presentation of his heroic erudition acquired alone, himself as the scholar *sui generis*.[10] Nevertheless, Budé does preside over the erudite sixteenth century in France. Then what can it mean to say that the greatest classicist of his time "n'était rien moins que ce qu'il est convenu d'appeler un esprit classique"?[11]

In a humanist as fanatical as Budé (and the adjective does not exaggerate his dedication),[12] the presence of the topos concerning literature's immortalizing power comes as no surprise. The subject of this chapter is how that topos is central to the development of two related themes we have seen adumbrated in Italian humanism: deification of and by the eloquent word and the apologia for political absolutism.

It should soon become clear that Budé thought of himself as a literary artist possessing, or possessed by, poetic inspiration. Although his has traditionally been a name of extra-literary importance, Budé's significance lies very particularly in his literary practice. Before approaching the major themes of this chapter, it will therefore be appropriate to consider some aspects of Budean style. Then the varieties of those major themes will make better sense: mystical philology (*De transitu Hellenismi ad Christianismum*), an ontology (*De studio literarum*), and a sociology (*De Philologia, L'Institution du Prince*) of the eloquent word.

ENCYCLOPEDIC METHOD

In 1513 Nicolas Bérault gave a course in Paris on Poliziano's *Rusticus*. His *praelectio* repeats the Politianesque commonplace of poetry as the foundation of philosophy. He also develops the Platonic theme of the chain of poetic inspiration, which also recurs in Poliziano's work. Bérault emphasizes the idea of reversibility already latent in the chain image: Inspiration is as much effect as reception. The poet both inhales and exhales the divine element: inhales, in the form of inspired afflatus; exhales, in the form of "divine and immortal poems."[13] But such students of poetry as Bérault also have a place in this chain. Inspired by the poets, they serve as intermediaries between these oracles and humanity. Bérault accentuates the fact that the métier of these interpreters (*grammatici,* philologists) is directly bound up in their contact with divinity. "Poetarum interpres et ipsi divino afflati furore mysteria enarrant poetica" (The interpreters of the poets, themselves inspired by a divine madness, expound poetic mysteries).[14] Although the philologists' position may be ontologically inferior to that of the poets, this is neither surprising nor regrettable. Since they are the ones who make the divine word accessible, they thereby put poetic power at the disposal of society.

The more obvious fact that Bérault's course indicates is the importance of Poliziano in early sixteenth-century France. He is the only modern author explicated by Bérault in his series of Parisian courses. Likewise, late in the century, when Justus Lipsius proposes a literary curriculum in his *Epistolica Institutio,* all the suggested authors are ancient save Poliziano, the greatest of the moderns.[15]

In the light of this importance we cannot be surprised by the influence exercised by Poliziano on the greatest French humanist of the day, Guillaume Budé.[16] Budé made two trips to Italy, in 1501 and 1505. When he visited Florence during the latter voyage, he met Poliziano's student, Pietro Crinito (Ricci). Crinito possessed the manuscript of the *Pandects* with Poliziano's annotations that testify to the latter's interest in the textual problems of the great Roman legal corpus.[17] Some of the first fruits of this research are to be found in the *Miscellanea.*[18] Budé consulted Poliziano's manuscript, as he later recalled, although he apparently did not profit much from the barely legible notes.[19] Nevertheless, even apart from the textual usefulness of his manuscript, the example of Poliziano was clearly an impetus to Budé's first major work, the *Annotationes in Pandectas* (1508). A certain nationalism is evident in Budé, manifested as emulation of Italian humanism.[20] Thus, Poliziano's work on the *Pandects* stands in a relationship to the *Annotationes* analogous to the influence of Ermolao Barbaro's *Castigationes Plinianae* on Budé's *De Asse* (1515).[21] The research begun and the problems adumbrated by the Italians (on, respectively, Roman law and ancient numismatics) were brought to their encyclopedic conclusion by Budé.

It is not my intention here to study these two works of Budé. The reason for mentioning them lies not only in the palpable link to Italy, but also in the adjective just used: encyclopedic. This is the word that best characterizes Budé's philological method; as I shall try to show, it is also the foundation of his style. As is known, the concept of *encyclopedia* in the Renaissance originates with Poliziano. In it lies the originality of his philological method. The weakened modern sense of the word may lend itself to some confusion; it is not a question of mere vastness of erudition. The indiscriminate accumulation of references and citations is what Poliziano criticizes in his predecessors, and is, in fact, one of the more obvious shortcomings of Quattrocento scholarship.[22] But in chapter 4 of the *Miscellanea* (first *Centuria*), Poliziano expresses the ideal of total knowledge as the illumination of secrets, as an achieved intimacy.

> Qui poetarum interpretationem suscipit, eum non solum (quod dicitur) ad Aristophanis lucernam, sed etiam ad Cleanthis oportet lucubrasse.

> (Someone who undertakes the interpretation of poets should work not only, as they say, by the lamp of Aristophanes, but also by the lamp of Cleanthes.)[23]

The object of his study is not only poets and philosophers, but also

> quicunque doctrinae illum orbem faciunt, quae vocamus Encyclia. . . . Nec prospiciendae [philosophorum familiae] tantum, verum introspiciendae magis, neque (quod dicitur) ab limine ac vestibulo salutandae, sed arcessendae potius in penetralia, et in intimam familiaritatem.[24]

> (Whoever makes that circle of learning which we call *Encyclia*. Nor are the schools of the philosophers to be merely surveyed, but examined from the inside, nor are they to be, so to speak, greeted from the threshold, but rather summoned in the inmost recesses, and in intimate familiarity.)

The philologist's intimacy means full involvement in what he studies (the difference between *pro-* and *introspiciendae*). Yet this is not an indiscriminate love of antiquity for its own sake. On the contrary: In his notes for the 1480–81 course on Statius, Poliziano claims that controversy, especially controversy with past writers, is essential to *litterati*. By this general rule he justifies his attack on the late Venetian humanist Domizio Calderini. Representing the past as a battlefield where Aristotle attacked Plato, to be attacked in his turn by Theophrastus, or where Homer was criticized by Eratosthenes who was criticized by Strabo, Poliziano gives a rationale for humanist polemics. And his belligerent attitude toward texts and authors is surely not unrelated to the epithet with which he addresses his audience: *commilitones mei.*[25] Here as elsewhere, humanism's bellicose metaphors are evidence not so much of a sublimation of scholars' bloodthirsty urges as of the violently dynamic character of the humanists' métier.

That Budé's encyclopedic method, too, involves conflict with his predecessors is clear enough from *De Asse,* for example, which is not lacking in such marginal glosses as "Ciceronis erratum," "Vallensis erratum," "Nicolai Perotti erratum," or "Omnes recentiores in harum rerum ignorantiam concordes fuerunt" (All modern authors have been in agreement in their ignorance of these matters).[26] Toward antiquity itself, Budé is of two minds. The project of *De Asse* aims to discover the meaning of ancient references to amounts and kinds of money. What he finds from his calculations is that the wealth of the ancients, considered in modern terms, really was fabulous. The Roman empire provides the prime example; Budé returns again and again to its awesome affluence.[27] That such wealth came from conquered tributaries is obvious, but at one point Budé pauses in his exegesis of Roman opulence to consider that fact.

> Equidem (quod ad me attinet) cum haec in hoc opusculum congessi, animo reputarem, ea mihi species urbis Romae animo obversabatur, quasi arcem quantam expilatorum orbis terrarum viderem, et veluti commune gentium omnium cimeliarchium (ut verbo Iustiniani principis utar) id est sanctius conditorium rerum toto orbe eximiarium.

> (For my part, when I considered what I have gathered together in this opuscule, the image of the city of Rome would appear to my mind as if I saw the stronghold of plunderers of the entire world, and as the common *cimeliarchium* [if I may use a term of the emperor Justinian] of all peoples, or, put more virtuously, the tomb [or treasury] of what is remarkable in the whole world.)[28]

He presents Rome as an *arx expilatorum,* a freebooters' stronghold, where wealth is plunder and thus tainted. However, the parallel expression has a different force. The rare word *cimeliarchium* masks the brutal reality with the image of a (legitimate) treasury's precious holdings. The Greek loan-word and its more ambiguous Latin gloss *conditorium* are explicitly both an equivalent and an attenuation of *arx expilatorum (id est sanctius).* Budé's erudite research has elucidated the historical reasons for Roman wealth as well as giving him a precious synonym and the taste for using it. Thus it would be inaccurate to say that in this passage we see the moments of moralist's disapproval and humanist's admiration. Rather, humanism includes both moments.

Budé's double tendency to debunking and admiration works as a scholarly version of the poetic moments of praise and blame. For him, the medium of literature is at once irenic and belligerent, characterized by both continuity and upheaval. The closer one approaches the heart of the matter, the more powerful the contradictions aroused. And those contradictory impulses may regard a glimpsed historical reality, or authors ancient or modern.[29] In the example cited, there is a play between different versions of wealth: booty or treasury? Such a play amounts to an unresolved meditation, in miniature, on the legitimacy of the empire and, by implication, of its famed imperial largesse.

However, we need a better understanding of what Budé means by *encyclopedia.* One strategic introduction of the concept occurs in the digression or epilogue that closes *De Asse.*[30] Speaking of the present day, Budé develops a diatribe against cupidity into an assertion of the superiority of *sapientia.*[31] He calls in the authority of "Solomon" (the author of the biblical *Sapientia,* or Book of Wisdom) in praise of the latter. *Wisdom* 8 particularly develops this praise, from which Budé draws the phrase, first in Greek, then in Latin: "(Sapientia) initiatrix est enim scientiae dei, et inventrix operum eius" (Wisdom initiates into the knowledge of God, and discovers his works) (8.4).[32] There is nothing unusual here, although Budé's interpretation emphasizes the active power of wisdom, despite his assertion of the necessity for a humble expectation of grace. The two aspects that must be balanced are expressed by the Virgilian line describing Fama, which Budé cites: "Ingrediturque solo, et caput inter nubila condit" (She walks upon the earth, and her head disappears among the clouds).[33] This use of both biblical and pagan sources is subsequently compressed in the epithet applied to Solomon: *ille sapientum Plato.*[34] In a similar way, the pursuit of divine wisdom undergoes a sudden transformation into the cultivation of *bonae literae.* Following Solomon's argument, "si . . . cum sapientia omnia bona sibi obvenisse . . . affirmat: quanto magis compendii studium posthabere debemus studio literarum?" (If he assures us that with wisdom all good has come to him, how much the more should we prefer the pursuit of literature to the pursuit of profit?).[35] In this way Budé abruptly introduces literature[36] and equates it with *sapientia.* He does, however, permit the expression of an objection to this equation: What does pagan literature have in common with the pursuit of wisdom, which depends on Christian revelation? Such a view of the ancients' lack of grace considers the cultivation of their literature as a meandering from the path to *sapientia,* which is revealed wisdom. Here is expressed succinctly the tension between pagan antiquity and Christian truth, which runs throughout Budé's works.

In responding to that objection, Budé does not deny the accusation of meandering, and this is where the encyclopedia comes in. If wisdom is something at a great altitude toward which man strives from the ground, the best method resembles the flight of birds, which reach a mountain peak by spiral ascent.

> Ut enim aves in locum arduum subvolaturae, non a solo protinus eum locum rectis lineis petunt, sed volatu verticoso eo commodius evadunt et facilius; sic animus humanus ad contemplationem sapientiae melius per cochleam iustae disciplinae scandere et intelligentius potest.
>
> (285–86)

> (Just as birds, in order to fly up to a lofty place, do not seek that place in a straight line from the ground, but get there more easily and suitably by a spiral flight; so the human mind can ascend better and more intelligently to the contemplation of wisdom through the spiral of true method.)

Iusta disciplina means *encyclopaedia,* as becomes clear when the latter is used in the subsequent assertion that it was the basis of Solomon's wisdom.[37] Budé thus presents the encyclopedic method as a paradox. It is based on *studium,* zeal, but it does not press its ascent to the heights. It keeps its eye on the end, which is divine wisdom, but first wanders through all subordinate disciplines. Even geometrically, there is a striking contrast between the open-ended pluralism of the spiral and the circle's absolutism, inherent in the *orbis doctrinae* (another synonym—or translation—of *encyclopedia*). The encyclopedia is the science of indirection, of the oblique approach.

The true path mapped out in the exegesis of *Sapientia* manifests an aversion to *compendium,* which is first of all "profit," but also, significantly, "a short cut." The encyclopedic method—and Budé's etymological thinking evokes the image of a route behind *methodos* itself—finds itself opposed to both kinds of directness. Neither a crude pursuit of material advantage nor a direct ascent to piety commands the humanist's allegiance.[38]

In this method eloquence holds a privileged place; its place is everywhere. Eloquence infuses the circle of disciplines "quasi in corpore sangui[s]," as blood in the body. That eloquence has the vivifying power of blood is evident from its enduring vitality.

> [Eloquentia] mortuorum apud posteros memoriam in perpetuum renovat, cum in manibus hominum libri eorum semper versentur vivantque, id est ingeniorum morumque simulacra tempore non peritura. (286)

> (Eloquence perpetually renews the memory of the dead among posterity, since their books are always handled by men and live on, as simulacra of minds and mores which will not perish with time.)

In this reference to immortality, the fate in question is that of books, not of the Christian soul. Meandering on the way to salvation is already evident, as eloquence asserts its own eternal life.[39]

ENCYCLOPEDIC STYLE

I have dwelled upon this introduction of the encyclopedia because it gives some idea of the centrality of the concept for Budé. What I now propose is the similarity between the encyclopedic method and Budé's chosen style. Just as the method is oblique by nature, so the style is purposefully enigmatic.

Budé's principal discussion of his style may be found in a letter of 1516 to Erasmus.[40] In this letter he defends himself against a number of criticisms that Erasmus has discreetly offered. To the complaint that he writes obscurely, and for a learned minority of readers, Budé proudly assents. I have written the *De Asse*, he says, "ut a paucis intelligerer," that I might be understood by few (line 125). But that is not all. He desires not to be definitively understood by the few, but understood only in such a way that he may deny their interpretation(s), if necessary: "ita intelligerer ut tamen, si res ita tulisset, in vulgus essem inficiando quod quisque me dixisse pro captu interpretaretur" (126–27). For this reason, Budé accepts Erasmus's characterization of him as an oracle, the Delphic Apollo Loxias, the ambiguous.[41] He adds to this Solomon's words (*Prov.*, 25.2): *doxa theou kruptein logon* (the glory of God is to hide the *logos*). Here we see Budé assuming the role, not of interpreter of oracles, as Bérault saw philologists, but of the oracle itself. This helps explain why Budé makes understanding him so difficult and uncertain. The logos he hides is a divine truth; such truths are by their nature unfit for the eyes of the multitude. We shall see later to what extent *studia humanitatis* are a sort of initiation into mysteries. But there also is a hint that Budé's reticence is a Tacitism. He says, "Sic referre mea id temporis existimabam, ut a paucis intelligerer"; that is, the times made me feel obscurity was in my interest. Before this, Budé declares in Greek (and the very use of Greek is an obfuscation) that he intends his work to remain incomprehensible to those with insufficient education (*tous me akros pepaideumenous*). We might plausibly assume that he is referring not only to the *vulgus*, but above all to the powerful at court. What is it Budé wants to hide? We are not yet in a position to hazard an answer. However, it can be noted that the digressions that abound in *De Asse* are often bitter polemics against such common and dangerous targets as the Sorbonne.

Budé welcomes the epithets *philometaphoros* and *polutropos*, punning epithets of a sort familiar to any reader of Homer. As a lover of metaphor, he is a stylistic Odysseus. To use a metaphor well is, as he says, to use it emphatically, until it has yielded all it can: "cum susceptam metaphoram non ante ponerem quam sententiam coeptam *emphatikos* absoluissem" (291–92). As a consequence, Budé's metaphors grow into conceits. And just as one metaphor may pervade the work, so the language is consistently lofty. Budé agrees with Erasmus that his style is one great single gem rather than punctuated with small individual gems (296–99).[42] As may be inferred, there is nothing pithy about Budé's oracular style. He prides himself on his *copia* and accepts Erasmus's characterization of him as a verbal Lucullus (316–19), the kind of Roman grown rich from Asiatic plunder to which he referred in the passage from *De Asse* cited earlier.

The common ground where obscurity and abundance meet is enthusiasm, or inspiration. In presenting himself as an oracle, Budé naturally dwells on the divine afflatus that determines his style: "Ventis me permitto et quo tulit cunque *enthousiasmos* auferor, quem inhibere incalescentem nequeo" (I entrust myself to the winds and am borne away wherever inspiration carries me; once it gets warmed up I cannot resist it) (184–86). Later, he refers to this force as *pneuma* (192); a Hellenist like Budé could not ignore the theological sense of such a term, particularly in its use here. Budé portrays himself as a sublime writer in precisely the Longinian sense. Indeed, the contrast of Budean and Erasmian style ("ego vim affero et rapio, tu eblandiris et impetras: ego irrumpo, tu irrepis . . . [I use force and snatch away, you coax and entreat; I burst in, you creep in] [210–11]) calls to mind the *Peri hupsous*.[43] Hence, there results the paradox: Budé claims that his style is both deliberate and involuntary. He has decided to present his message enigmatically, but divine furor has equally driven him to express it enigmatically.

Yet another paradox surfaces when Budé pursues his defense to assert that the final section of *De Asse* is not peripheral to the rest of the work. He continues the comparison between himself and Erasmus while using the metaphor of *De Asse* examined earlier. Budé, as a proper encyclopedist, flies indirectly to the heights, in contrast to Erasmus's effortless soaring:

> Tuum est istud, qui per sublimia volare aut raptim aut remisse ita soles ut alas non quatias; nos in scribendi tyrocinio ut columbae ludibundae alis plausitantibus expatiamur.

> (277–79)

> (You are accustomed to fly to lofty heights, hastily or slackly, so that you do not beat your wings; while I move about in the apprenticeship of writing as a playful dove with fluttering wings.)

Here it might seem that Erasmus, not Budé, is the writer of sublime power. It is true that the picture is complicated by effects of modesty and flattery, both part of the attenuation of the two correspondents' mutual criticism.[44] But the paradox lies in Budé's self-image as both driven vessel and circling dove. The distinction he draws in this last passage is between his digressive proceeding through the domains of the encyclopedia and Erasmus's direct treatment of his subject. Only the image may be misleading; far from being antithetical to his sublimity, Budé's encyclopedic meandering is the basis of that sublimity. It affords him copious material in various realms, which when drawn together form Budean metaphor. Moreover, Budé conceives of his digressive style as chiaroscuro. He claims that his digressions play with the main argument of De Asse "ut lumina cum umbris in pictura" (as light with shadow in a painting) (273–74). It is notable that in this simile the digressions (particularly the epilogue) are the light and the treatise's main argument the shadow. Although both aspects are essential, the metaphorical procedure of digression thus receives an ontological superiority. The word Budé applies to the balance of both elements is *contentio* (275): meaning tension, struggle, as well as a labored, formal speech. The artificiality of Budé's style is a product of the elements it holds in tension.

If we compare the letter to Erasmus with Poliziano's statement on style in his letter to Paolo Cortese,[45] the difference between the two humanists is unmistakable. Although they share an opposition to Ciceronianism[46] and both defend their personal styles, Poliziano's style is avowedly self-expression ("me tamen, ut opinor, exprimo"), while Budé seeks to convey something quite different. This difference results at least partly from their conceptions of the encyclopedic method. Poliziano's mature philology aims at penetration and acquaintance with antiquity in all its aspects.[47] In contrast, Budé's metaphor reveals that, although his method seeks to know antiquity in a similarly thorough way,[48] his ultimate goal is transcendent.

It is appropriate to consider here another characteristic of Budé's style. Some of the passages quoted earlier have shown his taste for rare words. *Cimeliarchium* is typical: a Greek word whose introduction in a Latin form is validated by its use once or twice in antiquity. Budé elucidated its meaning and forms in the *Annotationes*[49] before using the term, not quite casually, in the passage from De Asse cited earlier. Sometimes he specifies an unnaturalized loan-word as Greek: "quos Graeci apirocalos vocant" (which the Greeks call *apirocalos*).[50] Elsewhere, a borrowed word may sit in the discourse like an unexplained gem; so *mellodidascalos* in *De Philologia* (47). A reader would have to understand through context or else have read the passage in the

Annotationes where the word is presented as the equivalent of *tiro,* or novice,[51] or else know Greek as well as Budé. Budé regularly draws on his erudite researches for vocabulary that he uses in more "literary" settings.

In addition to such Greek formations, which include compounds,[52] Budé displays a tendency that can be called with some precaution archaizing. That is, a tendency to return to the pristine radical meaning of words or to attempt to do so. For example, in the sentence from *De Philologia* where he uses *mellodidascalos,* he uses as a parallel term of academic standing *bacularios.* Now, it is clear from the context that what Budé means is expressed by the modern French *bachelier,* which derives from the medieval Latin *baccalarius.* The word is probably of Gaulish origin, but Budé has preferred to imagine a "purer" Latin form, *bacularius,* which is related to *baculus,* staff. His choice is not unrelated to the metaphor that Budé has in hand at the moment. He calls students *tyrones,* meaning new soldiers, and their advance through the curriculum is a *tyrocinium,* military march. He pursues the metaphor by considering those who have received an academic degree as possessing a walking stick to help them on their march over the *orbis disciplinae.*

The "archaizing" I mean is thus less the use of archaic forms than a matter of semantics and metaphor. Again in *De Philologia,* Budé complains about the recent neglect of letters and finds a cause for this in "dolo et decuriatione paucorum" (the deceit and divisiveness of a few) (53). *Decuriatio* is found only once in antiquity, with the prosaic meaning "a dividing into *decuriae*" (groups of ten, or, more generally, divisions).[53] Budé uses the word with the clear figurative sense of divisiveness or factiousness. Rather than using another abstraction like *dolus,* he has chosen a term whose literal sense has no relation to contemporary reality but that provides a vivid metaphor.

In a similar case nearby, Budé rails against hypocrites who "fallunt sub integumento frontis vultuumque tectoriis" (deceive beneath the covering of their brow and the plaster of their face) (53). The first term *integumentum* is frequently used figuratively in antiquity,[54] but such a use of *tectorium* is extremely rare. Thus what at first appears as the chiastic balance of two synonymous expressions is really the dramatic movement from a conventional phrase (*integument[um] frontis* is Ciceronian) to a fresh metaphor.[55]

These few examples should be sufficient to suggest the metaphorical nature of Budé's vocabulary. He clearly aims to infuse new life into tired formulas or to invent new ones. Here his anti-Ciceronianism is in action. Moreover, it is hard not to see Budé's stylistic traits as based on a reverence for the word, a reverence that draws the writer deeper into the past in search of a pristine linguistic moment. That is not simply the moment previous to barbaric medieval forms.[56] It is where reality, *res,* found immediate expression in language, through metaphor. *Res* and *verbum* were not yet divorced. It is the moment where commonplaces had not yet become common. It is, in short, an imagined epoch of mythical thought. Cassirer locates the original link between myth and language quite precisely in metaphorical thinking.[57] That is, both myth and metaphorical language posit identity based on similarity, where the boundaries between words and things, thoughts and actions, are fluid. It should thus come as no surprise to find a common movement, by means of metaphor, toward an archaic past in Budé's works. His subjects, whether aiming at a retrieval of the details of ancient civilization (*Annotationes, De Asse*) or a renewal of the former high regard for eloquence (*De studio, De Philologia*), or a call to early Christian piety (*De transitu*), all require as foundation a metaphorical style that aims at an earlier mythical effectiveness. The originality and difficulty of Budé's style are due not to pedantic showiness, but to the peculiar linguistic task he set for himself.[58]

It is a task by no means unique to Budé, although his style absorbs the search into the manner of expression in an unusually concentrated way. What I have referred to in the Italian Quattrocento as poetic paleology continues in full force in the following century north of the Alps. However, in the latter case, the "paleology" might be more accurately characterized as linguistic. For example, in *Nutricia,* Poliziano describes the divine birth and effect of Poetry. Language had already existed (99–100), but had no special importance before its constraint and liberation by poetic power. In general, such a myth contrasts with erudition in the sixteenth century, which seeks the birth of the word itself. This word would possess from the start the effective power that may become more evident in its eloquent, poetic forms. While poetic paleology imagines society as created by poets, the new concern with language as such emphasizes the linguistic genesis of an even vaster reality. The twin aspects of linguistic research in this period can be characterized as "archéologie du langage et alchimie du verbe."[59] C.-G. Dubois's phrase expresses succinctly the belief I have been illustrating in Budé. Why attempt the temporal reversal that seeks the original state of language? Because at that point language had a power it has since lost.

Hence, an extraordinary interest in the divine creation by means of the Logos and the importance of this linguistic intermediary between God and humanity.[60] Hence speculation on the power of Adam's unfallen speech, privileged by its proximity to the divine Word. By his act of naming the animals, Adam united knowledge and possession in an Edenic state confounding *res* and *verbum*.[61] The Last Judgment will retrieve a similar identity; of this point beyond time Guillaume Postel wrote: "Ne se parlera plus par paraboles, mais par les choses mêmes."[62] Hence the resemblance of paleology and eschatology, both outside of historic time; the power language once had it will regain.[63] But traces of unfallen linguistic power were sought in historical languages, too; hence, the Kabbalah's interest. The *Zohar*, for example, stresses the linguistic nature of God's creation more than *Genesis*.[64] Hebrew has a privileged status as the chosen language and possesses unusual effective power and is "de plus grande vertu et efficace," according to Claude Duret.[65] But Hebrew is not the only language studied from such a point of view.[66] The approach to all language at this time is fundamentally mythical.

TRADITIONS OF MYSTICAL PHILOLOGY

Mythical-theological attitudes toward language belong to the vast domain of Renaissance occult and esoteric speculation (and practice), which cannot even be sketched here. However, a selective review of such attitudes in a few exemplary figures may not be out of place.

Marsilio Ficino and Giovanni Pico della Mirandola are seminal for, respectively, a philosophical theory of magic and the Christian interpretation of the Kabbalah. Each in his own way articulates a role for verbal magic.

In the third book of his *De vita,* entitled *De vita coelitus comparanda,* Ficino describes how a healthy way of life may be based on the attraction of favorable spiritual influences from the heavenly bodies. Of the seven ways to benefit from celestial harmony, words and song ("verba, cantus, soni") occupy a central place.[67] Ficino himself played the lyre and sang the Orphic hymns in his Academy, apparently as an application of his theory of natural magic. Moreover, for Ficino it is the words that make music both loftier and more effective.[68]

Although Ficino's musical theory did not have much immediate influence, his conception of the power of words found abundant echoes. Among the nine hundred theses that Pico offered to defend in Rome in 1486, the second of his "Orphic Conclusions" declares that "Nichil efficientius hymnis Orphei in naturali Magia" (nothing in natural magic is more effective than the Orphic hymns) if performed properly.[69] But beyond this role recognized for *prisca poesia,* there is a more momentous assertion in the ninth Magical Conclusion. This conclusion is perhaps the one that caused Pico the most trouble and was one of the thirteen officially condemned. It states: "Nulla est scientia, que nos magis certificet de divinitate Cristi, quam magia et cabala" (there is no kind of knowledge which better assures us of Christ's divinity than magic and the Kabbalah).[70] What forms the point of intersection between the central mystery of Christianity on one hand and magic and the Kabbalah on the other? It is a belief based on the divine efficacy of language and leading to an attitude toward the Logos that can be called mystical philology.[71]

The central text of Renaissance mystical philology is Johann Reuchlin's *De verbo mirifico,* published in 1494. Reuchlin, who had met Ficino and Pico during a voyage to Italy in 1490, cast his work as a dialogue concerning the possibility of true knowledge. This means the possibility of communication between gods and mortals. Communication means language, and so the question concerns those words that can bear to mortals the most divinity and power. What are those words that are *mirifica,* can work wonders? Reuchlin divides the art of wonders into four categories. Three of them are traditional: *physica, astrologia,* and *magia.* The fourth is a novelty. It is *soliloquia,* the science of the miraculous word by which one succeeds in getting what one prays for.[72]

One of the three interlocutors in *De verbo mirifico* is a Jew named Baruchias. He reveals to his companions the marvels of kabbalistic interpretation, culminating in the wonder-working powers of the Tetragrammaton, IHVH, the unpronounceable name of God. Through the four Hebrew letters "God transforms man into himself and allows him to perform whatever he asks in prayer."[73] Reuchlin would later go further in this direction with his *De arte cabalistica* (1517). However, the *verbum mirificum* has undergone a *translatio* from Judaism to Christianity. Although pristine effectiveness belongs to Hebrew alone, the Christian fulfillment of the Old Law has brought with it a linguistic fulfillment of Hebrew word power. The Tetragrammaton becomes the Pentagrammaton by adding the consonant S: IHSVH Christ, the true wonder-working Word. In the last of the dialogue's three books, Capnion (Reuchlin's Hellenized alias) expounds on the supreme power of the Pentagrammaton. It is the Logos in both its aspects, *verbum rationale* and *ratio verbalis,* and to the highest degree.[74] It is, simply, the best magic, as becomes clear from the story of St. John the Evangelist on Patmos, successfully battling hostile magi.[75]

As C. Zika has pointed out, Reuchlin's dialogue is important in the magic debate of his day because he "discards Pico's broader concern for natural magic and limits this magic to the power of words, relating it specifically therefore to Pico's Kabbalistic magic."[76]

A work contemporary with *De verbo mirifico* is Ludovico Lazzarelli's *Crater Hermetis.* Lazzarelli pursues a parallel, if substantially less

Christian, development of Ficinian/Pichian magic.[77] In this dialogue
with King Ferdinand of Aragon, Lazzarelli explains that, "as the mind
of God creates by His Word, so man by his mind and speech can procre-
ate immortal progeny."[78] Human *mens* and *sermo,* as the image of
their divine model, are endowed with immortality. The king, in his
role as neophyte in sacred mysteries, takes the idea of verbal progeny
figuratively to mean the longevity of literary works. However, Lazzarelli
corrects him, claiming a literal and magical effectiveness for the right
words.[79] After a lofty prologue, Lazzarelli sings a *Hymnus divinae
generationis,* where he finally reveals what he means by the "immortal
progeny" that verbal magic can create. What is at issue is the creation
of angels, or demons, in a daring human imitation of God's greatest
attribute.

Mentem propterea persimilem sibi
sermonemque homini iam genitor dedit
ut diis consimilis parturiat deos.[80]

(For this reason the Father gave to man mind and speech just like His own,
so that man, identical to the gods, might himself give birth to gods.)

This remarkable dialogue ends with Lazzarelli's promise to the enthu-
siastic king to instruct him some day in the performance of what he
has described. Here the humanist instruction of the prince has taken
a strange turn and becomes the initiation of a magician. Strange, yet
not too surprising, because the wonder-working word is the basis of
the authority of both humanist-*litteratus* and humanist-*magus.*

Reuchlin exercised a strong influence on another writer about
magic, perhaps the most important one of the sixteenth century. Heinrich Cornelius Agrippa's *De occulta philosophia* is a comprehensive
treatise on magic, which starts out by distributing its three books
among the three worlds (elemental, celestial, and intellectual) and
three sorts of magic (natural, astrological, and ceremonial or religious).[81] Given this structure, the role of verbal magic is particularly
striking. Book 1 ends with several chapters (69–74) about language
and *virtutes verborum.* Agrippa modifies the old maxim about man's
being distinguished from animals by reason, claiming that the distinc-
tively human trait is more precisely linguistic reason, that *ratio* "quae
iuxta vocem in verbis et sermone intelligitur" (which is understood
alongside the voice in words and speech).[82] This inseparability of *ratio*
and *sermo* is, of course, the Greek *logos.* But Agrippa goes further to
examine the phenomenology of speech, claiming that the unique
power of spoken language lies in its ability to communicate from

speaker to listener not only the speaker's interior conception, but also the force of an interior energy.[83] However, not all words provide an equally good medium for that force. The most powerful language is eloquent or poetic, *orationes complexae*. The Orphic Hymns provide an example; Agrippa echoes Pico in declaring "nihil in magia naturali est efficacius."[84] In chapter 72 he brings forth the testimony of ancient (Latin) poets about the power of *carmina*. The examples given, including Virgil, Ovid, Tibullus, and Lucan, show the common fusion of the two senses of *carmen* as verse and magic spell.[85]

What may be obscured in the abundant detail of *De occulta philosophia* is the pursuit of that magical power of words, which leads Agrippa in a direction indicated by Reuchlin. In book 3 Agrippa devotes two chapters (11 and 12) to the names of God and their special power. Whoever uses the right names in the right way "mirifica multa & impetrabit, & efficiet" (will obtain and accomplish many wonderful things).[86] According to kabbalistic tradition, the most effective name is a verbal square producing permutations of the Tetragrammaton. But now that honor belongs to IESU.[87] The Savior works the greatest verbal magic. As F. Yates has recognized, Agrippa's magic "is really a religion . . . and Christian since it accepts the name of Jesus as the chief of the wonder-working Names."[88]

The attribution of divine power to language is not restricted to magical or theological treatises. Even manuals of an apparently more mundane and practical sort may have as a foundation the kind of assumptions we have been considering. A good example is provided by a little-known work of the later sixteenth century, Blaise de Vigenère's *Traicté des chiffres*. As the title indicates, this book is predominantly about secret ciphers. Yet even such an ostensibly practical purpose requires transcendental grounding. Vigenère first establishes a parallel between human language and divine emanation: "Ceste parolle assistee de la raison est en nous, ce qu'en la divinité la premiere emanation eternelle, assavoir le verbe, ou la sapience" (Speech aided by reason is, in us, what the first eternal emanation, namely the Logos or wisdom, is in God).[89] Elsewhere, Vigenère addresses his cryptographic concerns by a more extensive analogy with divinity. Written language is an expression (*bouttehors*) of interior concepts like, respectively, Christ and God the Father. Writing unites in itself the contraries of spirit and materiality just as the Son of God united in himself divinity and flesh. The sense contained in those written signs plays the role of the Holy Spirit.[90] Moreover, not only the emanation of the Trinity, but also the creation of the world has an essentially linguistic structure.[91]

Such logotheology underlies familiar reflections on the relation between action and language, or arms and letters.

Tous leurs beaux faicts d'armes, toutes leurs proüesses & chevaleries fussent bien tost demeurées esteintes & englouties de l'oubliance sans la parole, qui de main en main par une certaine Cabale en transmet successivement la memoire pour durer à perpetuité.[92]

(All their great military deeds, all their knightly prowess would soon have disappeared and been swallowed up by oblivion were it not for speech, which transmits their memory successively from one hand to another by a certain Kabbalah, insuring perpetual duration.)

Perpetuité is, of course, an essential part of the charm of language, both as the immortalization of heroic deeds and as the *in saecula saeculorum* of divinity. In the following passage Vigenère combines both aspects in an image of the classical triumph of language (or, more precisely, of humanity through language):

Et sont ces deux parties en luy [*écriture* and *parole* in man], à guise de deux beaux grands coursiers eslez ou Pegases attelez à un char triomphal; non pour le promener sur la terre, ou le rouller sur la larg'estendu de la marine, comme Neptune fait le sien dans le 13 de l'Iliade; ains pour l'eslever à travers les nues en l'air, au temple de l'immortalité.[93]

(Both these parts [writing and speech] exist in man like two magnificent winged coursers or Pegasuses, harnessed to a triumphal chariot—not in order to carry him upon the earth, or bear him over the wide expanse of the sea, like Neptune in the thirteenth book of the *Iliad,* but to lift him up into the air through the clouds to the temple of immortality.)

It may be objected that a vast difference separates the claims made by a Reuchlin or an Agrippa for the real efficacy of prayer or verbal magic, from the metaphors of a Vigenère, based on perceived analogies. But one of the lessons of the Renaissance occult, as of any mythical thought, concerns the special status of metaphor. As B. Vickers has pointed out, writers on the occult in the Renaissance display an opposition to the classical Aristotelian conception of metaphor.

Given their tendency to treat words as things and essences, to believe in innate notions, to collapse the concept of a linguistic sign, it is not surprising that the occult use of language should also not recognize the distinction between tenor and vehicle.[94]

What this means in practice is that metaphor can lose its conventional docility. The confinement of figurative language to a fictive realm cannot be assumed. In a writer such as Budé, the reader finds tenor and vehicle in a habitually uneasy relationship. His metaphors cannot be reduced to simply illumination or ornamentation. Rather, they voice the pretense of effectiveness born from hypostasis. When we also consider the atavistic movement that Budé shares with contemporary occult discourse, we confront the Vichian theory of metaphor. Budé's erudite Latin enacts Vico's assertion that metaphor embodies a primordial moment of linguistic power.

DE TRANSITU AND THE TWO PHILOLOGIES

Mythical thought about language, such as that just reviewed, is relevant to Guillaume Budé in two ways. First, it sets Budé in context and shows that much of his speculation on language and *bonae literae* is not idiosyncratic. More important, it also suggests a way to reinterpret what has been considered the main crisis of Budé's thought. That "crisis" lies in the tension between Christianity and ancient (pagan) literature. That the tension is real cannot be denied. But that Budé confronted it differently from what has traditionally been thought— this the following considerations may show.

The text that poses the problem most acutely is *De transitu Hellenismi ad Christianismum,* published in 1535. This treatise would seem to recant much of the inspiration of Budé's earlier works, particularly *De Philologia* and *De studio literarum,* both dating from 1532. Those two works, as we shall see, were pleas for the advancement of *bonae literae,* an advocacy that the author pursued untiringly. However, only three years later all seems changed. *De transitu* appears to stress the radical limitations of profane literature (*bonae literae*) and the need for a conversion to Christian devoutness. Certainly, what Budé calls *Hellenismus* is not simply discarded. J. Bohatec has shown how for Budé, *scientia literarum* serves as a propaedeutic to Christian philosophy.[95] Nevertheless, *Hellenismus* is a preliminary stage to be overcome.[96] Budé pursues what seems like a polemic against *Hellenismus* particularly in the last of the treatise's three books. He characterizes ancient philosophy as *hallucinatrix* (246). The bankruptcy of pagan thought lies in its contemplation of death rather than of immortality (251). Such philosopy, which is really a *philomoria,* is entirely inferior to Christian wisdom; we should lose no more time with it. "Non iam in iugis Parnassi nobis cum musis res habenda, non in porticu, non in academia . . . sed in schola evangelii" (We should have nothing more to do on the slopes of Parnassus with the Muses, nor in the Stoa, nor in the Academy . . . but in the school of the Gospel) (231). Although Budé does not propose the most absolute religious objection to ancient culture (not *numquam,* never, but *non iam,* no longer), he seems at first view to abandon what he so vigorously fought for all his life. Is Budé's career, from his first translation of Plutarch (1502) to *De Philologia* (1532), canceled by this ultimate retraction?[97]

A negative answer to this question may begin with the title. M.-M. de la Garanderie has indicated the multiple senses of *De transitu Hellenismi ad Christianismum.*[98] She proposes three possible interpretations, of which the first may seem most natural but is the least defensible grammatically. That is, *transitus Hellenismi* is *transitus ab Hellenismo;* the work would thus be an exhortation to move *ab . . . ad,* to abandon profane letters for sacred.[99] (This is difficult grammatically because an implied *ab* would require the ablative, rather than the genitive *Hellenismi.*) A second interpretation stresses more the *transitus,* the gradual movement from propaedeutic to the real course of study. Third, it is possible to see *transitus* as the action of a menacing Hellenism as paganism invading Christianity. All these interpretations have an element of truth and reflect an aspect of what Budé is about in his treatise. However, I propose a fourth reading of the title. *Transitus* can also mean "transition" in the sense of a passing over or adoption.[100] *Hellenismi* can be an objective genitive; the sense of the whole is then "how Hellenism can be made part of, brought into Christianity." This appropriation is possible because Hellenism and Christianity share the common category of philology.[101]

The fundamental presence of philology is the principal reason *De transitu* does not constitute an about-face for Budé. There are auxiliary reasons. In fact, very little of the treatise directly addresses the conflict between sacred and profane letters. The predominant mode is exhortation to a true Christianity, but what ought to be abandoned is a lukewarmness in faith and an attachment to this world.[102] The polemic is secondarily directed against the excesses of the Reformation and only in the last place against those who do not advance from profane studies to sacred.

Another fact suggests that, even had Budé directed a harsher attack against Hellenism, he would still have at least one foot in that camp. This is because of the way he consistently expresses Christian matters in literary, mythological terms. He refers to Christ as Mercury (136, 147, 235), as Phoebus (144), as *Pythagoras coelestis* (155), as *coelestis Alcides* (165), as *coelestis Prometheus* (166), as Proteus (239).[103] On the other hand, Satan is a *funestus Mercurius* (151), a *Mercurius stygius* (210, 214). Great importance attaches to certain myths read allegorically, particularly those of Homer, whom Budé calls *vir mortalium ingeniosissimus* (206). Thus the Homeric episodes of the Sirens and Circe acquire special significance (205–6, 222), as does, more generally, Odysseus's homeward journey. A term for the spiritually

lukewarm is *Lotophagi* (222). Even in the few places where Budé explicitly attacks Hellenism, he does so with Hellenism's weapons. For
example: we seem to see a blanket condemnation in the statement
"mors est enim non vita . . . Hellenismi sensus" (the sense of Hellenism
is death, not life) (235). But this condemnation subsequently uses the
authority of Plato and his harmony with Christian teaching:

> Quod Plato in universitate, analogiam esse voluit, id est *desmon tou pantos,*
> in Timaeo, hoc idem est Christi charitas sponsalitia, in Ecclesia. (235)

> (What Plato held to be the universal analogy, that is, "the link of everything"
> in his *Timaeus,* this same thing is the love of Christ for his betrothed in
> the Church.)[104]

By themselves, these facts are not conclusive. Even a wholehearted
condemnation of pagan literature (which *De transitu* is not) cannot
entirely dispense with the terms and commonplaces of that literature.[105] And we might be justified in seeing in *coelestis Mercurius*
little more than in Dante's *sommo Giove,* apart from the abundance
of Budé's epithets, if there were nothing else. But, in fact, there is
something else: Both Hellenism and Christianity are considered as
philology. In this light, the identification of Christ with Mercury, the
god of eloquence, is by no means arbitrary.[106]

In the final analysis, the point is not that Christianity must be preferred to Hellenism. That Budé believes this is never in doubt. What is
important is that he subsumes both Hellenism and Christianity under
philology, which is thus revealed as a concept superior to both. Of
course, this implies an idea of philology more comprehensive than is
customary. The expansion, however, makes sense as the culmination
of those lofty claims for the eloquent word already made by other
Renaissance humanists.

Budé spells out his basic position in the preface to *De transitu.*
There are, he says, two philologies: *philologia minor* and *philologia
maior.*[107] The subject of this treatise is the harmonious subordination
of the former (human eloquence, pagan literature, Hellenism) to the
latter (Christian wisdom). How might Christianity be a philology? The
most obvious answer arises from the fact that Christ, the central figure
of Christianity, is the Logos. The customary epithet for him, which
introduces him innumerable times in *De transitu,* is *verbum Dei* or
sermo Dei. Now, the traditional translation of *logos* as *verbum* has
already lost much of the ambiguity of the Greek, as it stresses *oratio*
at the expense of *ratio.* The term *sermo,* which Budé uses at least as
often as *verbum,* pushes the tendency even further. Christ's power
becomes more and more "verbal" and less and less "rational."[108]

A pregnant image for this tendency occurs in the preface. Jesus Christ as *verbum Dei* is a golden chain connecting heaven to earth, a chain that explicitly resembles the one in the *Iliad*.

> Mihi autem videtur catena quaedam aurea verbi divini atque coelestis: argumentosissima serie apta . . . terram et mare . . . in coelum tollere et attrahere: nempe mortales ipsos continentis et insularum incolas. et tollere quidem illos sursum invitos quodammodo et restitanteis, utpote terrae agglutinatos.
>
> (131)

> (Sacred philology seems to me a kind of golden chain of the divine and heavenly word, composed of a most copious series of links, which pulls up into heaven the earth and sea, namely the mortals who inhabit the mainland and islands. It pulls up even those who resist and hold on to the earth.)[109]

The central concern of Christianity for Budé is immortality. The divine word hauls man up to heaven, despite the resistance of his earthly weight. In terms identical to Reuchlin's, Christ is the *verbum mirificum* (164), working his *theurgia mirifica* (166, 168). The word's effective power achieves a literal apotheosis.

> Tanta vis est verbi Dei, tanta facultas, ea facundiae vis latens atque eloquentiae in sermone sapientiae.
>
> (131)

> (So great is the force of God's word, so great is its power, that hidden force of eloquence in the word of wisdom.)

As we see here, the divine *verbum* does not belong to an entirely different order from the human. It is eloquence; eloquence deified.

The divine word bestows humanity's goal, immortality. Such a gift remains impossible for merely human efforts, despite their pretensions. Budé makes it clear that Christ as the Logos fulfills the boast of secular immortalization through eloquence:

> Huius homo philosophiae (sc. Christianae) studiosus, humanum exuperet fastigium, tandemque inter superos divosque allegatur, non hominum quidem ille decreto atque opinione, ut olim divi illi commentitii et poetici, non ut Romani Caesares, aut senatus consultis, aut successorum suorum sanctionibus: sed coelestis ac divinae providentiae placito praerogativo. Haec est illa gratia caelestis, haec benignitas Dei, quae humano generi coeli commercium . . . interventu verbi Dei eiusdemque filii indulsit et largita est.
>
> (141)

(The man who is assiduous in Christian philosophy surpasses the summit of what is human, and is elected at length to the company of the saints and angels. This happens not through the decision and opinion of men, as was the case formerly with those fictitious and poetic gods, nor as Roman emperors were deified by the Senate or by the decree of their successors. It happens rather through the privileged condition of heavenly and divine providence. This is that heavenly grace, this is God's kindness which, through the mediation of the word of God and that of His son, conceded and bestowed upon the human race commerce with heaven.)

Just as Christ in his incarnation unites the human with the divine, so as *sermo* he brings human eloquence to transcend itself and fulfill its boasts of effectiveness. But for this to be possible, human and divine word must have more in common than the bare term, *verbum* or *sermo*. And, in fact, they do. Budé makes explicit the analogy we have already seen in Agrippa and Vigenère: The human mind creates effective language as God begot his Son.

Estque sermo noster, quasi partus quidam mentis nostrae, imagoque ipsius: ut verbum divinum, imago est patris expressissima.

(226)

(Our speech is like an offspring of our mind, and its very image; just as the divine word is the most distinct image of the Father.)[110]

Speech resembles the divine emanation in that it bears with it the power of what engendered it, without diminishing that power.

Sermo etiam humanus, mentis vim et facultatem secum fert, aut similitudine eas refert, cum tamen in mente ut Christus in patre, nihilo minus maneant.

(226–27)

(Human speech bears with it the force and power of the mind, or renders them by analogy; while they nevertheless remain in the mind just as Christ does in His Father.)[111]

In the concept of Hellenism and Christianity as two philologies lies the unity of *De transitu*. It may be true that the sprawling digressiveness of Budé's style obscures the unity. Nevertheless, the digressions and metaphors mostly grow out of that concept. The question underlying the treatise concerns the innocence of philology. Does philology (*minor*) lead to Protestantism or to orthodoxy, or is it rather a neutral tool? Budé's meanderings in the treatise are dialectical twists and turns that address this question. He confronts it by radically broadening the concept of philology, as we have seen. Thus, there is no longer a jump implied from philology into another sphere, religious belief. The entire sphere is philology, and what matters is only the recognition of various levels within that sphere. Hence, it no longer makes sense to ask if the cultivation of literature leads to true or false belief or unbelief. The *object* of one's study makes a difference, as Budé condemns an exclusive attention to profane letters,[112] but the philological discipline itself is already religious contemplation.

Despite its passionate, absolute tone, *De transitu* remains as mercurially ambiguous as Budé's other works. This is due on the one hand to the author's divided sympathies, both on the subject of profane and sacred literature, and concerning the Reformation. Although he ultimately defends orthodoxy and professes a horror of the Reformers' excesses, he obviously finds much that is attractive in Luther.[113] The persecution of dissenters that followed in the wake of the Affaire des Placards could only increase Budé's propensity toward a politic obscurity. On the other hand, his elusiveness is also due to an awareness of the problems that a literary treatment of the ineffable encounters.[114] One of the objectionable traits of Hellenism is its confidence in *facundia,* its inability to admit the insufficiency of language; it thus becomes *vaniloqua* (238). Budé endorses the dictum of Wittgenstein and the mystics, that what we cannot express appropriately we should consign to silence: *contegamus silentii velamento* (224). He stresses, for example, the ineffability of Christ's death.[115] Naturally, divine eloquence does not have the same limitations, but Budé is consistently aware of the insuffiency of his own human eloquence in these matters. Faced with such a problem, Budé uses a literary technique of indirection.

He speaks through a mask, *persona,* which he calls *Aius Loquens.*[116] In Roman history, the name designates a disembodied voice that was once heard to warn against the impending attack of the Gauls. The warning was ignored, Rome defeated, and it was only afterward that the prescient divinity was acknowledged, named, and given a temple.[117] Budé's adoption of this mask has its puzzling aspects. Why would such a nationalist identify with a god opposed to that glorious deed of the ancient Gauls, the conquest of Rome? Evidently, Budé is more interested in the general use of the topos as opposition to barbarism, resembling Valla.[118] As in the letter to Erasmus discussed earlier, Budé presents his discourse as oracular—that is, divinely inspired and so necessarily obscure. He willingly assumes the role of a Cassandra, speaking truths that are not heeded.

But a closer look at the divine persona reveals another aspect. Both elements of the name are based on verbs concerning speech (*aio* and *loquor*).[119] The god's single manifestation was as a disembodied voice in the service of Rome. Aius Loquens is thus the mask of language in its pure state. It is fitting that Budé dons this mask at strategic moments in his effort to reconcile the two philologies.

An examination of the uses of Aius Loquens in *De transitu* shows that the voices that come from the mask are plural and contradictory. Budé first introduces it as something separate from himself, as it refers to the impudence of those (apparently Protestants) who reject the traditional power of councils (152). Likewise, in considering the Affaire des Placards, Budé imagines a Stygian Aius sent by the devil to breath a contagion of impiety on Christians (175). The true believer should be deaf to the rumors produced by Aius, that *autor vanissimus* (186), whose *logodaedalia improba,* or verbal tricks, are contrasted with *facundia iusta* or true eloquence (182). In attributing the mask to his theological opponents, Budé stresses the deceptiveness of its verbalism. It hides the identity of the speaker (that is, the critic), and deploys the treacherous tools of sophism. But as already indicated, Budé, too, finds the mask necessary. To condemn contemporary abuses, the logic of his argument (*scribendi ratio instituta*) compels Budé to put on the mask of Aius or of the related Momus (196). Subsequently, Aius Loquens expresses Budé's repeated condemnations of clerical corruption and his laments for the lost virtue of the early Church (197, 201, 210).

Aius Loquens as the power of language in action is unpredictable, ambiguous, and dangerous. But after all, his ambiguity also characterizes divine truth. "Proteus enim est proprie sermo Dei" (For the word of God especially is a Proteus) (239).[120] The traditional fourfold interpretation of Scripture makes it a doubled *Ianus coelestis* (240), a four-faced guardian of heaven. There is nothing univocal about words or the Word.

De transitu, then, is an exhortation to Christianity as the culmination of philology. Salvation is man's deification by the Verbum (141). We have seen throughout the Italian Quattrocento how often literature's humanizing function becomes a claim of deification. Budé's treatise, which seems to abandon the humanist tradition, is, in fact, a sanctification of it. Yet, even as he sanctifies a mythical conception of language, Budé releases in his metaphor of expression (Aius Loquens) a hint of the dangerous *versatilitas* of poetic language.

DE STUDIO LITERARUM AND THE FOUNDATION OF LITERATURE

For a balanced estimate of Budé, it must be remembered that *De transitu* represents the last period of his thought. Although the treatise is not a palinode to his earlier passions, it is different. For his comtemporaries, Budé was the incomparable Hellenist and advocate of *bonae literae* at the court of François 1er. If *De transitu* is the praise of Christ as the absolutely effective Word, how does the earlier Budé present the secular power of human eloquence?

For that question, the most important texts are the two works published together in 1532, *De studio literarum recte et commode instituendo* and *De Philologia*. Each in its own way makes a case for the centrality of *bonae literae* to the *res publica*. To be sure, human letters cannot be considered in isolation from divine letters. *De studio* in particular has moments that adumbrate *De transitu* from the secular side.[121] *De studio* includes a reminder of the need to advance intellectually and spiritually; if the study of literature is *paedagogos,* sacred philosophy is a *gerontagogos* (29). The deity presiding over eloquence, Mercury, is distinguished in his mortal and in his celestial aspects; the former should yield to the latter (24). Although philology does not have the explicit comprehensiveness it has in *De transitu,* the emphasis placed on the versatility of eloquence (embodied in the figure of Proteus [21]) already points in that direction. The sublimity of the divine word is *flexiloqua,* which means that theologians can use it for good or bad ends. More generally, Budé expresses his confidence that the wrongheaded opinions of antiquity can be abandoned but the scaffolding of eloquence left intact and still used.[122]

De studio proves no exception to Budé's tendency, which is indeed a general tendency of humanism, to discuss language in mythical terms. This involves not simply the use of allegorical figures from classical myth, but the exposition of language (eloquence, poetry) in a cosmic drama. *Nutricia* provides a paradigmatic example. However, in contrast to Poliziano, Budé presents human history not as a progress due to poetry, but as a fall from the primordial unity of *mens* and *sermo,* of *res* and *verbum.* That is, from the unity of *ratio* and *oratio* signified and redeemed by *Logos,* the Son of God (7). It was natural that man should experience this fall from harmony: "Vero loquendi consuetudo, deterior fere tempore fieri solet, et ex patriciis . . . sensim ad plebeios transire" (As a rule, linguistic convention deteriorates with time, and gradually passes from the patricians to the plebeians) (1). But a struggle against the fall has also long been in evidence. Since the Greeks it has been the task of *bonae literae* to permit man to remount the *gradus,* or degrees of nature. The figure of Mercury, qualified as *logios,* presides over this human striving (7). The goal of such an effort, incomplete before the Incarnation, has been ultimately the deification of man through eloquence. That such is the case becomes clear when Budé cites Hermes Trismegistus:

Mentem autem, inquit, et orationem, uni ex omnibus animalibus homini deus ipse largitus est: non minoris utique aestimanda, quam ipsa est immortalitas. Nam quis his convenienter, et ad ea quae decorum est utitur, is nihil ab immortalibus differt.

(8)

(He says: God Himself bestowed mind and speech upon man alone among all the animals; gifts to be valued no less than immortality itself. For he who uses them appropriately, and to the proper ends, differs in nothing from the immortals.)[123]

Although here the deifying power is said to belong to *mens* as well as *oratio,* we must not forget that it is *bonae literae* that must reharmonize the two faculties and so make them effective. Thus Mercury's function as psychopomp takes on a new aspect when he is considered as the god of philology.

The mind restored to its original harmony by *bonae literae* will be superior to time; it will contemplate "praeterita et futura cum instantibus, . . . ex quo fit ut nequeat nec morte, nec adversis rebus opprimi" (the past and future with the present, whence it will come to be immune to death and misfortune) (8). Appropriately, the Muses preside over this realm. Budé interprets the daughters of Mnemosyne and Zeus as a mental faculty that seeks eternity:

Mentis conceptus, aeternarum rerum contemplatores . . . nam Musae dictae sunt quasi indagatrices, utpote per naturae vestigia sensilis atque mathematicae, superna et coelestia indagantes.

(14)

(They are the offspring of the mind, contemplators of eternal things. For they are called Muses, as it were hunters, tracking what is lofty and heavenly in the traces of sensible and mathematical nature.)[124]

Eloquence, which infuses the Muses' domain like blood, serves the strenuous hunt through its immortality: "numquam enim obsolescit ille, nulla vetustate exolescit splendor eloquentiae" (the radiance of eloquence never fades away, never grows old) (13). Inspired by that longing for eternity, the cultivator of the Muses is perpetually unquiet.[125]

Such a cultivator is a Hercules.[126] In the myth, Hercules was incited to his labors by Eurystheus. Budé gives a double interpretation of the figure of Eurystheus. On the one hand, he is internal, figuring the natural desire for glory that drives one to do great deeds (20). Such an *intestinus Eurystheus* is identical with the love of literature.[127] On the other hand, Budé does not forget the one to whom the treatise is directed, nor its opening words which establish the subject. "Honos alit artes."[128] Despite all their native power, *bonae literae* require nourishment. Such nourishment can only come from a patron; in this case, from the king, to whom Budé has long presented his plea for literature in the *res publica*. Hence, the other Eurystheus is external, namely, a prince who supports and inspires the work of humanists.

Inherent in the concept of liberal arts (*liberales, ingenuae*) is their opposition to those arts that aim at material gain (*quaestuariae*). Like his fellow humanists, Budé desires a Mercury without *merx;* that is, the public function of eloquence without the form of commerce. In this, Budé follows the main development of Italian humanism since the mid-Quattrocento. Expressed by such writers as Pontano and Budé's contemporary Agostino Nifo in his *De Divitiis* (1531), the main idea is that "the only inoffensive wealth is that which is not infected by the sweat of work for profit."[129] But the uncomfortable truth remains that, although the liberal arts aim at the supersensible, they are required to subsist in the material world. Because they do not submit to the marketplace as do law and medicine, they are bound more closely to the political realm. The Renaissance prince feigns a distance from bourgeois life, as he works to seem motivated by arbitrary munificence rather than commercial calculation. The more independent the prince, the purer appears the support he can lend letters. That is, the more absolute the prince, the more attractive his patronage.

It is no accident that the initial declaration "Honos alit artes" is followed by the passage cited earlier on the mythical fall of language. Nor are the terms describing that decadence ill-chosen: "ex patriciis . . . sensim ad plebeios transire" (1). The negative *transitus* that set the humanist his task was a social process in an imagined prehistory. As for both Vico and the tradition of poetic paleology, class conflicts underlay the development of language in a mythical past. As Budé elaborates his work of linguistic and spiritual redemption, it becomes clear that the movement to reascend the current of time to a pristine past also has a sociopolitical aspect. The primordial unity of *res* and *verbum* is matched by a similar unity of authority; the desired return goes from the many to the few to the undisputed power of one.

As Budé approaches the end of *De studio,* he states his often repeated preference for absolute monarchy. An important element of this theme, also often repeated, as we shall see, is the idea that political absolutism is only tempered by the prince's subjection to letters. He can do as he pleases but will want to maintain a good name among posterity—a realm under the dominion of literature.

Reges enim et monarchae, tametsi legibus soluti sunt, nec civili tenentur actione, honoraria tamen ipsi in iudicium famae vocari possunt, atque etiam periclitari.

(29)

(Kings and monarchs, even though they are not bound by law, and cannot be held by any civil suit, yet by the praetorian suit [sc. of literature] can they be called before the judgment of fame, and even brought to trial.)[130]

DE PHILOLOGIA 1: SERVICE AND LITERARY PURSUITS

The gaze at the public realm with which *De studio* concludes fittingly sets the stage for the dialogue *De Philologia*. The most general theme of this latter work is the life of philology or *bonae literae* in society. *De Philologia* is dedicated to the sons of François 1er, Henri and Charles, but the work is obviously directed to the king. I say obviously because the interlocutors in the dialogue are Budé and François himself. This fact introduces us to something characteristically bizarre about the work. The dialogue is, of course, in Latin. The king himself had little Latin; he did not read Latin works, let alone speak the language.[131] So on the one hand, Budé portrays François speaking a language he could not speak, while on the other hand, he thereby directs to the king a plea, which the king could not read, for classical literature which he also could not read. There is no indication that a translation of *De Philologia* was ever written;[132] to profit from the treatise, François would depend on an extemporaneous translation.[133] That is, to gain access to the work, the king would require the services of those humanists whose case the work argues. In the dialogue the king speaks a Latin as elegant as Budé's and shows a comparable culture. He speaks as an intellectual equal of the great humanist, without losing any of his royal dignity. Budé has thus created a portrait of the ideal prince/ patron: The ruler has become an eloquent philosopher. But for the real François 1er to enter this enchanted garden and contemplate himself, he must request the key from the custodian humanist. I am aware of no indication that he ever did so.

The dialogue treats the place of literature in the *res publica*. It develops as a dialectical *Pro Archia*. Yet not in the sense that one character (Budé) simply pleads for letters and the other (François) opposes him. Both interlocutors are conscious of assuming roles in the discussion. At one point François declares that he will change from being a passive *auditor* to a *perconctator* who may dispute with Budé (44). In a somewhat different manner, Budé puts in his own mouth the words of those opponents of *bonae literae* with whom he carries on a polemic throughout the treatise. Thus he refers to himself as Epimetheus and to Philologia as a Pandora who has loosed innumerable evils on the world. The king is surprised by this about-face but already has an inkling of the truth ("si tamen ex animi tui sententia, non aliquorum tantum loqueris" [if you are speaking your own mind, and not someone else's] [66]). Budé later admits that he was indeed only speaking through a hostile persona.[134]

Although the king occasionally plays the part of a skeptic, it is by no means his only role. Budé focuses his hopes for the reward of *bonae literae* on a promise that François made in the past. That was the promise to found an institution where the classical languages would be cultivated; an institution that ultimately became the Collège de France.[135] Budé's effort is not so much to win over the king as to recall to him the past enthusiasm in which he freely vowed his support to humanism. Budé must construct a panegyric that works as evocation of a past moment. Operating in the temporal dimension of gift bestowal, that panegyric seeks to realize the process begun by the initial promise. We can understand the dialogue form as a verbal manifestation of exchange structure. Their praise and qualification, doubt and defense are voiced by both interlocutors in verbal exchange.

Budé begins the dialogue by expressing the fear that he may seem to be devoted to the cultivation of *sapientia* unwedded to *prudentia*.[136] That is, that he has pursued his dedication to literature at the expense of neglecting a wise way of life. In this manner the scene is set for assertions that *sapientia* does indeed have its place in the world. The equation between *bonae literae* and *sapientia*, familiar from *De Asse*, is explicit from the start; the latter term is defined as "artium liberalium consummata cognitio" (perfect knowledge of the liberal arts) (33). Within the general movement toward vindicating a place for literature in the *res publica*, Budé introduces relevant bits of his own story. He recalls how after a wasted youth he threw himself with fervor into the acquisition of erudition and the bitter opposition this aroused in his father. The elder Budé had hoped to see his son pursue (with moderation) the lucrative career of law and instead saw him dedicated to an indefinite period of unremunerative study (35–36).[137] In the present, Budé sees *bonae literae* menaced from both sides. On the one hand, he disapproves of those who use their eloquence for unlicensed invective and ignore the ancient equation of *vir eloquens* and *vir bonus* (45). On the other hand, the barbarous Latin used in courts by those hostile to humanistic learning appalls Budé (63). As in *De studio* (17–19), Budé argues against both the abusers of pure form and those who would throw out the baby Eloquence with the bathwater of paganism.

But the most important opposition develops between the man of letters and the prince. At issue are power and need and the ability to bestow. Letters obviously need the prince/patron, in that a material existence is necessary. It is also true that the prince's approval is required to assure the humanist of the value of his endeavor (35). The initial question in the dialogue, concerning the relationship of *sapientia* and *prudentia,* requires the prince as guarantor of a place in the *res publica.* Thus Budé praises François for giving Greek letters a *civitas* in France (58). In another system of metaphors, he conceives the role of the prince as an adornment and endowment of the personified Philologia. Erotic metaphors concerning philology play an important role in this dialogue and elsewhere.[138] Budé portrays himself as a wooer of Philologia who has loved her desperately (*perdite,* 35) and sung serenades at her door (65). Eventually, he wed her, destitute though she was materially, for the sake of her grace and beauty. But now the king's promise in favor of *bonae literae* is a rich dowry that makes the bride all the more attractive (51). Newly enriched Philologia will have many new suitors, but Budé claims that he is not bothered by these rivals for her favors. He rejoices that she has become *communis* (51), and *morigera,* compliant to all comers (65). The link is clear between the *versatilitas* of eloquence and the promiscuity of Philologia.[139]

But to return to the king's role. He is both endower of nubile Philologia and godfather of infant letters, owing them support. François accepts the role of godfather because he has assisted Budé in christening the subject of their conversation, *bonae literae* (41). The need of literature for royal patronage is clear; the act of naming brings with it a material commitment. Equally clear, what Budé desires for literature is not simply material gain in the most direct sense. The entry of humanistic letters into the *res publica* will take the form of appointments of humanists to remunerative offices. As Budé says outright: We seek not gold and gems but *honoraria* (87).

Prince and letters mutually depend on each other. To isolate one side of the dialectic in *De Philologia* is artificial, but Budé aims primarily to show the prince's need for literature. To do so, needless to say, he does not proceed in a straight line. The argument that literature is indispensable advances in reaction to the king's objections. For example: At one point early in the dialogue, François protests against the vast claims (*venditatio*) Budé has been making for his subject. The identification of humanistic letters with *sapientia* makes them a supreme category and boundless,

quae nullis finibus ius suum cognitionemque suam terminarit quae velut
quaedam artium regina praepotens, vectigales caeteras artes sibi, et tanquam clientulas in fide sua semper esse dictitet.

(42)

(Which would bound its own law and knowledge with no limits, which like
some sovereign queen of the arts would claim the other arts as tributaries
and petty clients in allegiance to her.)

What the king articulates here is not merely the rise of poetry and
eloquence to a place of supremacy among the disciplines. The terms
used represent *bonae literae* as literally autonomous (its law, *ius
suum,* knows no bounds), as a powerful monarch dominating her clients. The king is somewhat disturbed by this rival authority, confined
though it may be to the realm of metaphor. He warns Budé with some
emphasis ("Vide igitur, vide inquam Budaee, ne" [So watch out, Budé,
I'm telling you]) to make sure that such boasts for literature do not
turn out to be vain, *vaniloquentia* (42).

Such doubts provide an invitation to panegyric. Budé does not retreat from the claims made and appeals to antiquity for support. He
does not wonder that the king should be suspicious, considering the
matter from the point of view of the present and recent past. "At vero
nos eloquentiae studium ... finibus antiquis complecti instituimus"
(However, we are establishing the pursuit of eloquence by encircling
it within its ancient limits) (42). The all-embracing domain formerly
held by eloquence was broken up by subsequent compartmentaliza-
tion, just as an empire dissolves, divided among the conqueror's epi-
gones. That original unity was the *orbis disciplinaris* that the
encyclopedic approach aims to recapture. It was, in fact, the unity
of *mens* and *sermo,* whose divorce was the primordial starting point
described in *De studio.* Literary study aims to repair that original sin;
it is "corruptae humanitatis elaborata quaedam reconcinnatio" (a thorough refurbishing of corrupt humanity) (57). The fall of eloquence
was thus ontological and academic as well as social. Budé returns to
the image used by the king in stressing the difference between then
and now:

Nam cum olim rerumpublicarum magnorumque imperiorum domina fuit
ipsa et gubernatrix eloquentia, nunc vero a gubernaculis reiecta sit.

(43)

(While formerly eloquence was ruler and pilot of republics and mighty em-
pires, now she has been dismissed from the helm of the ship of state.)

Given its former preemininence in the *res publica,* what real contribution did eloquence make then that it could make now? Budé enumerates a few of its powers: Eloquence can equally well extinguish
sedition or inflame men to battle; it is more useful than fire and water
to the *res publica.* But at the head of its attributes lies its immortalizing power.

> Age, quid si etiam reges et principes viros, egregie de patria singulisque
> meritos, immortalitate donare sola potest, atque inter divos propemodum
> coelitesque referre? quo nihil amplius in rebus humanis exoptatiusque
> censetur.
>
> (44)

> (Now, what if eloquence alone can bestow immortality upon kings and lead-
> ing citizens, who deserve the highest reward from the state and from indi-
> viduals, and just about place them among the gods and the other inhabitants
> of heaven? There is considered to be nothing greater or more desirable than
> this in human affairs.)

By this point the courtly audience to the dialogue is laughing at what
it takes to be Budé's hyperbole. The king notices and asks Budé, perhaps ironically, if eloquence may be related to Aesculapius in their
common ability to raise the dead. Budé assents to this mythological
parallel and proposes in addition the figures of Mercury and Hecate,
both *herebo coeloque potente*[*s*] (powerful over heaven and hell). In
the case of Mercury this is more than a mere analogy. The ancients,
and first of all Homer, signified eloquence by his figure. We recall the
importance of Mercury in *De transitu* and *De studio,* where he embodies respectively the saving power of the sacred and the secular word.[140]
Here he is set historically, albeit vaguely, in society; the psychopomp
is the indispensable functionary of the *res publica.*

Budé's declaration that Mercury conducts souls to either Erebus
or Heaven indicates the double power of eloquence in panegyric and
invective. The king is disturbed by this amphibole, this ability to "coelum ac terras ... miscere ... et summa imis aequare" (mix heaven
and earth and put the highest on a level with the lowest) (44). If the
plea concerns a social function for eloquence, then this *versatilitas*
must appear anarchic. In particular, François complains about the too-
numerous eloquent men at present who abuse their talent in blaming
rather than in praising. As previously indicated, Budé responds by
assuring the king of the identity of *eloquens* and *bonus*—which here
means obscuring the invective side. A defense of the usefulness of
invective would be possible; we have seen it sketched by Italian humanists. But to attain his end, Budé wants to convince the king that

bonae literae are not subversive. For this reason, he points the immortalizing power of letters solely toward heaven.

The "national interest" of the matter becomes clearer with a concrete example of royal rancor against literary blame. The king himself reintroduces the theme of glorification, recognizing the power of the nation (*natio*) of writers to save great deeds from oblivion. That François has in mind the *res gestae* of the French monarchy is shown by what follows in the same breath. He regrets that his ancestors the ancient Gauls did not commit their (undoubtedly glorious) deeds to writing.

> Quod utinam nobis contigisset, ut tam accurati scriptores mediocris notae, in veris laudibus maiorum nostrorum extitissent memoriae mandandis, quam nobilis ille Romanarum rerum scriptor Livius.
>
> (49)

> (I wish that it had befallen us to have as meticulous writers of some quality, in order to consign to memory the true praise of our ancestors, as that noble writer of Roman deeds, Livy.)

The interest in ancient Gaul is widespread in sixteenth-century France.[141] From Lemaire's *Illustrations de Gaule et Singularitez de Troye* to Ronsard's *Franciade* and beyond, there is a passion to establish a prestigious origin for French history and royalty. Within this movement, the lament for an absence of literary monuments to the Gauls is a commonplace.[142] However, the mention of Livy here leads to a brief tirade against the Latin writer who defamed the Gauls (themselves defenseless without letters) in his history. Livy's invective constitutes a hostile act against the French monarchy. Similarly, Budé sees the capital crime of *lèse-majesté* in the more recent neglect of learning that deprived France of her past. The impoverishment resulting from either foreign invective or native indifference finds an appropriate image in the desiccated laurel (49).

The assertion that literature's civic service lies in its glorifying power turns up once more toward the end of book 2. This time it is Budé who voices the complaint that past French glories lie buried in silence through a lack of writers, "silentio sepulta ob scriptorum inopia" (87). Again Budé declares that rescue from such burial is the highest human achievement; the elegance, dignity, and majesty of liberal studies

> regum gentiumque nomen et gloriam illustrant, et memoriae commendant in perpetuum: quo honorificentius nihil esse, nihil magis expetendum in rebus humanis potest.
>
> (86)

(They give lustre and glory to the name of kings and peoples, and consign
them to memory forever. Nothing in human affairs can be more honorable,
nothing to be more sought than this.)

When, as mentioned earlier, Budé considers recent lack of support
for letters as treason, he is referring to the defect of patronage in
Charles VIII and particularly Louis XII. What this means is that he
surreptitiously presents *bonae literae* as somehow superior to the
monarch, since harming them constitutes *lèse-majesté,* even when the
culprit is the monarch himself. In what has developed into a rivalry
between literature and the prince, Budé's argument is double-edged.
He wants to show the power of literature to return it to the *res publica.*
But in representing that power as unbounded, his metaphors menace
the stability of the *res publica*—at least under a prince aiming at
absolutism, such as François 1er. Hence, Budé reminds the king of the
support he can find in letters, how their glorifying power has traditionally increased the ruler's prestige and power. Yet enthusiasm and his
manner of expression—that is, his metaphors—repeatedly arouse the
king's suspicions.[143]

François is clearly entertained by Budé's fanaticism and virtuousity.
Himself inclined to libertinism, the king shows indulgence toward the
humanist's private affair with Philologia. In the social realm, however,
he remains more hesitant. Near the end of book 1, Budé expresses his
desire to see the cultivators of *bonae literae* find employment in the
judiciary and the governmental bureaucracy. In this way eloquence
will ascend in the class structure (represented in ancient Roman
terms). But, says Budé,

Nec nobis . . . aut primam aut secundam classem petimus . . . sed ut iustae,
germanae, humanissimaeque doctrinae . . . autoritatem, in omni parte rei-
publicae fundatam velis et stabilitam, atque ita per omnia membra fusam,
ut sanguis et succus civilis corporis.

(59)

(We do not seek for ourselves either the first class or the second class, but
rather that you found and establish the authority of just, authentic and
most humane doctrine in every part of the state, infused in every member
like the blood and sap of the civil body.)

It is no accident that Budé uses the same image of blood here for *bonae
literae* in society and in the epilogue of *De Asse* for eloquence in the
encyclopedia. The king makes explicit this connection between the
domination of academic categories and that of society. "Ut ea facultas,
quae orbi disciplinarum oram circunfusam cingit et cludit, etiam ad

centrum ex omni parte ipsius circuli tendat" (As that faculty, which encircles and encloses the circumference of the round of disciplines, it also tends to the center from every part of the circle). He realizes that the claims for eloquence cannot be moderate. Once public language is submitted to its power, it cannot remain a mere guide or limit but penetrates *etiam ad centrum.* The restoration proposed in *De studio* of "original" power relations among social classes reveals here that literature is not merely a means to that end. For this reason, the king understands that Budé's apparent modesty ("Nec ... aut primam aut secundam classem petimus") is really an ambition that aims at absolutism.

> Profecto, Rex inquit, Budaee, non primum aut secundum locum tuae Philo-
> logiae, ut dixisti, petis; sed summum, imum, et medium flagitas subsellium
> in consessu reipublicae.
>
> (59)

> (Certainly, as you said, you are not seeking the first or second place for your
> Philologia, but the highest, the lowest and the middle seat in the assembly
> of the state.)

This, the king declares, constitutes an obstacle that may prove difficult to dispose of. Until this point, his objections have been devices to incite Budé to greater eloquence. But the present problem is more serious. He says:

> Velim igitur ut quod Philologorum ordini petis, ... id commode quoque
> fieri posse doceas: ac si factum fuerit, id e republica futurum existimatio-
> neque nostra atque regali.
>
> (59)

> (I would like you to show that what you seek for the class of philologists
> may feasibly be done, and if it were done, that it would be in accordance
> with the state and our royal estimation.)

Existimatio is the key word here. On the one hand, it is our judgment; the king wants to be sure that the followers of Philology would not usurp his authority in the *res publica.* On the other hand, it is our royal good name; he must be convinced that *bonae literae* can be used for his own prestige, to consolidate royal, not literary absolutism.[144]

The issue, which has been touched on through the first book of *De Philologia,* here becomes explicit. Budé recognizes that the point is critical ("in ipso pene cardine causae in quo summa quaestio caputque vertebatur" [at the very hinge of the case, as it were, on which the main point turned] [59]) and trembles with anxiety for a response to the objection. But just as the king has expressed his misgivings, a courtier enters and interrupts the dialogue, François is called away to other business, and Budé is left to brood over an answer and hope for an opportunity to deliver it. At this point, book 1 ends, thus emphasizing the centrality of this question: literature as support or threat to absolutism.

DE PHILOLOGIA 2: THE LITERARY HUNT

When another occasion for conversation presents itself, how does Budé, at the beginning of book 2, address the king's objection? Obliquely, to be sure. His first words ("ut sermoni tuo nunc respondeam" [that I may reply to what you said] [60]) claim to pursue the king's challenge, but this promise is not borne out immediately. He does indeed consider what happens to humanists once admitted from exile into the res publica, but for him the change is wholly positive. The more letters are favored, the better. Budé compares humanists to gems, which "ad solem flagrare solent," shine with their full potential in the sunlight of a patron's favor. They are not like bats or the glow of decayed wood, thriving at night but paling at the approach of dawn (61). That is to say that Budé claims to see no incongruity in the establishment of humanists in the res publica; they lose nothing by their elevation in affluence and public opinion, and the state can only gain by having its offices filled by literate men.[145] The cultivators of those arts that are not venal nevertheless become themselves precious objects.

This postponement of the main issue is not unrelated to the obvious center of interest in book 2. At the king's request, Budé extemporizes a short treatise on hunting. What place does it have in the dialogue? It is explicitly a *tour de force* of Latin. It is meant to show that even such a specialized vernacular terminology as that of the hunt can be rendered in a lively Latin. In this way Budé pursues his argument that humanistic learning (that is, good Latin) would not be out of place in civic office. He implicitly answers the king's musing whether Latin is fit only for conversation with the shades of Roman antiquity (69). In contrast to Dante, who claims in *De vulgari eloquentia* to be hunting a desired literary vernacular, Budé aims to track down the humanists' artificial tongue.[146] However, this episode is not only a linguistic, but also a metaphorical *tour de force*. The spectacle of the hunt unfolds as an allegorical play of themes developed elsewhere in the dialogue.

Before the king's request that Budé translate a French hunt into

Latin, Budé introduces the metaphor as he describes his amorous pursuit of Philologia. He ends up calling her *fera*, a wild beast, qualifying her as *fugax, fallax, lubrica,* and comparing his studious pursuit to hunting dogs' pursuit of deer (66). The hunt is one of the king's great passions, so he is delighted by this new metaphor. He refers to Budé's recently published *Commentarii linguae graecae* (1529) as a mapping of Philologia's windings through the forest, which helps assure her ultimate capture. He then speaks of the similarity of this pursuit to his own, real hunts. But as the two interlocutors develop metaphorical parallels, differences also become evident. The desire that Budé's image reveals is one of cornering and taming Philologia. It concerns sexual possession, as, for example, the ambiguous adjective *lubrica* suggests. For François, on the other hand, it is a matter of killing the captured game. But, in fact, the royal hunt, as Budé soon describes it, means more than the king's recreation. The terms in which it is represented make it an allegory of statecraft. The *concilium venaticum* that precedes the hunt has the marks of a council of state with its rational strategic planning (68). The chief huntsman bears the fasces of command (77). The signs of war are evident enough, as in the battle trumpets (*buccina*) that arouse the dogs ("tanquam bellicum canitur" [70]), which are themselves described in military terms (77). There is also an explicit and repeated legal metaphor in which an escaped deer is arraigned for its deceit and executed if caught.[147] The hunt is a miniature showing the king's exercise of his executive, military, and judicial powers.

The hunt unfolds under the sign of Diana, and in contrast to Minerva, who presides over *bonae literae.* Budé's express intention is to discover what compatibility there may be between the two goddesses and their realms.[148] In its most general form, this is the question concerning the appropriateness of eloquence for public affairs. The king reveals his doubts when he claims the superiority of his Diana to Budé's Minerva, based on the greater certainty of the former. If both philology and the hunt are a pursuit, the essential faculty for both is the *vis inveniendi,* the inventive faculty or ability to find. Budé himself expresses the wish that this *vis inveniendi* were as sure in men as it is in hunting dogs (67).[149] But in this comparison, eloquence is not simply weaker; it also suffers from its characteristic *versatilitas.* Despite the difficulties of deerhunting, the king seems to regard it as essentially unambiguous. The deer is always there, and only a good nose is required to overcome the deviousness of its flight. Moreover, just what culminates the hunt is quite clear: the animal's death. The pursuit of Philologia remains far murkier, both as to what attainment might mean and as to the meanderings to trace in following her. Translated prosaically: In statecraft, there may be great deviousness and indirection of means, but for François 1er the end, power, is not problematic. On thinks of his obsession with his claims in Italy, the rivalry with Charles V throughout his career, or more generally his dogged aggrandizement of absolutism. But for a humanist, and particularly one like Budé, the pursuit of eloquence in the modern world is inevitably caught up in reflection. He must justify his hunt, but things are further complicated by the ambiguity of this philological hunt itself. The figure of Philologia, combining the beloved pursued amorously and the tracked beast, combines the twin aspects of violence and love inherent in humanistic use of the past. The humanist's métier is by nature mercurial, both because of the faculty used and because of the domain explored. Human invention suffers by comparison to hounds' noses because it confronts signs far more ambiguous.

However, that constitutes only one side of the coin. Budé describes the hunt not only as an image of the exercise of political power, but also as a sort of writing. First, the king asserts that he hunts not so much for the kill as for the aesthetic "pleasure of eyes and ears" ("voluptas aurium et oculorum") (75). Budé repeatedly refers to the hunt as a drama, which begins as comedy and ends as tragedy (80), and which obtains an ovation at its conclusion (73). The twists and turns of pursuit are strophes and antistrophes (69).[150] And to switch genres, François compares Budé with Homer and the hunt he has created to the *Iliad* (80). Budé calls the dog pack *Flaccorum gens,* which alludes to the hounds' floppy ears, but also makes them the kin of a poet by giving them the cognomen of Horace (Q. Horatius Flaccus) (78).

But the hunt is also writing in a more purely semiotic sense that derives from the conceit of the hounds' *vis inveniendi.* The deer, showing the same *versatilitas* as Philologia, is said to write its trail: *circumscripserit* (78).[151] The dogs must be able to read this trail. They must also be on guard against the other common meaning of *circumscribo,* to deceive or defraud.[152] In the indirectness of the deer's style lies its fraudulence. In fact, however, there is a double signification and a double hermeneutic, since the voice (*sermo*) of his dogs is a sign the hunter must be able to read, and the hunters themselves *circumscribunt* (70). But unlike the deer, the hounds are not *vaniloqui* (79–80). The deer writes, is interpreted by the hounds, which give voice, and their voice is, in turn, interpreted by the hunter. The dogs prove their skill in *inventio* by uncovering the traces (*vestigia*) of the deer (84). In them alone is *inventio* both hermeneutic and creative. Could we say that in this the hunting dogs provide an ideal image of the humanist writer? They pursue treacherous ambiguity and strive to render it univocal. They put their inventive skill at the service of the hunter, who is the king himself. In the same way, throughout his career and particularly in this dialogue, Budé reduces his richly complex love for philology to a few seductive formulas for the king's service. In the hunt as described by Budé, the final ideal is a silent pursuit, where the complications of language are abandoned. Or rather, the canine imitation of human eloquence gives way to a system of mute, unambiguous signs. At a point where the deer's trace is especially hard to follow, the hunters release the prize dog, described as *harpocrates* (after the Egyptian god of silence),[153]

> qui quasi quidam antistes Dianae, non voce, sed caudae verberatu atque murmure et gannitu dare responsa solet: non flexiloqua, non ambigua, omnique vestigiali argumento indicioque certiora.
>
> (79)

> (Which, like a priest of Diana, is accustomed to give responses not with its voice, but with the wagging of its tail, with whines and growls—responses which are not ambiguous, more certain than any [narrative] trace and sign.)

The hunt for univocal signification thus becomes a pursuit of nonvocal signification. This elevation of mute language anticipates Vico's historical linguistics. Vico claims that the language of the first period, the age of the gods, was a system of mute signs.[154] It was sacred and superior to the later heroic and human languages. In this light, we can better see the regressive movement of Budé's hunt. The superiority of force over culture, of Diana over Minerva, is attained through the imagined infancy of humanity, in a landscape that looks suspiciously like Vico's primordial *selva*.[155] The authority attributed to the hunter, the prince, consists in the renewal of that foundational power that Vico's giants exercised unfettered. It may thus seem that the humanist in his inventive role renounces eloquence to promote the atavistic legitimation of political power. However, the distinctive difference between humanist and hound is that Budé cannot fall silent. He maintains a tension between the true breadth of his work and his attempts to make it serviceable to political power. The hunting dogs represent a palinode to Budé's rich polysemy. But of course the palinode is only one voice among the many orchestrated by his master hand.

The hunt episode is thus at the same time a triumph of Latin and an allegory of the difficulties of literature in proximity to power—difficulties that can lead the humanist to evoke a utopian dream of unambiguous signification. In the context of the dialogue, both aspects function strategically in urging the monarch to fulfill his promise to *bonae literae*. After praising Budé's performance, the king declares that he will undertake a complementary movement. As Budé put on the persona of the hunt, so François will put on the persona of Philologia (80, 84). He speaks of being adopted into the humanist *familia* (83). As a new-made servant of eloquence and honorary *literatus,* the king cannot decline to raise letters in the *res publica.*

While the king voluntarily lowers himself to the level of a *familiaris,* Budé raises him to be a peer of the god Apollo. Through his patronage, François would be able to create great poets and orators, just as the deity did in antiquity.[156] He marvels at the largesse by which Budé has made him a *numen,* endowed him "mirifica illa . . . facultate" (with that wonder-working faculty).[157] In this bestowal, he says, Budé has exhibited a magnificence not regal but divine.[158] It is thus the generosity of the humanist's eloquence that has made possible the patronage he awaits from the king.

There is a reversal of patronage of another sort when the *numen* presiding over the last part of *De Philologia* turns out to be Minerva, who takes over from the huntress Diana. Beyond the traditional metaphorical connections between Pallas and eloquence (her birth, the effect of her aegis, and so on), the important point concerns her pervasiveness. Like the *orbicularis doctrina,* she presides over every people and imperium (89). Budé's explication of this is even aided by another of those objections with which the king momentarily stumps him. François recalls that Pallas is also the goddess of weaving, and thus has her plebeian side. Budé denies that this fact demeans her. On the contrary; it is an allegory of her patronage of eloquence. The art of weaving (*exordiendi et contexendi*) is a figure of the oratorical art; but not of this art alone. "Tametsi oratoriae dico? quid si etiam imperatoriae? quid si regiae?" (Did I say of the orator's art? Why not of the general's art? Or of the king's?) (90). The thread of an argument, context, exordium; metaphor admits manual labor to wherever the effective use of language is important. However, a new questioner objects that the figure of Homer's Penelope, with her deceitful weaving and unweaving, seems to signify the ultimate futility of eloquent *versatilitas.* Budé replies sharply that the deception was only aimed at Penelope's suitors and served her faithfulness to her long-absent husband. He insists that, in the end, the amphibolic nature of eloquence is not relativistic.

Budé attempts to conjure away the contradiction in his use of the figures of Pallas and Penelope. In this final movement of *De Philologia,* we find again the relation between language, truth, and social class introduced in *De studio.* It would seem that one of two things has to be true: either the art of weaving patronized by Pallas is purposive manual labor, or if, in the hands of Penelope, weaving can be nonpurposive, then that fact would indicate the art's versatility and potential deceptiveness. If purposive, then plebeian, like the *artes quaestuariae;* if non-purposive, then promiscuous and deceptive. Since weaving serves as a figure for eloquence, no wonder Budé wants to keep it pure from both contraries. Eloquence, like a noble lady's domestic craft, must avoid the opposite taints of commercial labor and amoral gaming. More generally, faithful Penelope and promiscuous Philologia illustrate the irreconcilable tensions of the humanist's task.

The king was provoked to smile by Budé's exclamation on the power of Pallas's art ("Quid si etiam imperatoriae?"). When Budé wishes subsequently to return to a more elaborate interpretation of Penelope, he asks the royal permission.[159] The king again smiles his assent. In the assurance of these smiles, we glimpse the dialogues's final innocuousness. Royal power is cheerful in its solidity, confident that nothing from the world of metaphor can threaten it. In the end, it remains unclear whether Budé has convinced the king of the real usefulness of *bonae literae* or has merely staged a successful *divertissement.* As if invited to act his part in a court pageant, François has entered eagerly the figurative world prepared for him and has applauded Budé's erudite virtuousity of metaphor. Both interlocutors are aware that something concrete is also at issue here. Both would like this concrete element to be delimited. King and humanist undoubtedly agree that well-educated men should receive employment in the state. In the end, Budé believes he has achieved his purpose when François declares that he will admit Minerva into his kingdom.[160] But the unsubmissive element of humanism insistently makes its presence felt. It pervades Budé's style, with its riot of metaphor and conceit. That style manifests the necessary hubris of claims for the power of *bonae literae.* A threat to political authority has flashed here and there in the dialogue; the king was startled by it on occasion, but was soon reassured as he recalled its metaphorical nature. So that he can listen to a final expression of the immortalization topos without demurral.

Eloquentia vero, . . . nunquam satis laudata, Minervae quidem ipsa alumna et discipula sola omnium artium res astruere satis potest et evertere . . . Tametsi quid si etiam passim mortuos excitare, sermonemque ita iis tribuere, ut audientes vivos se audire et superstites atque spirantes putent? . . . Quid si plus quam Aesculapius ipse deus [pollet] . . . ?

(92)

(Eloquence, never sufficiently praised, protégée and pupil of Minerva, is alone able to build up and tear down the subject matter of all the arts. Yet what if eloquence can even arouse the dead, and give them speech, so that those who listen to them think they are hearing the living, the surviving, the breathing? What if it can do more than the god Aesculapius himself?)

The king renews his promise, and a flood of courtiers and petitioners arises to end the dialogue.[161] After their brief literary cohabitation, the monarch departs to resume his royal business, while the humanist returns home to his study. There he broods over his recent words and is filled with a not wholly assured hope, that Philologia may receive her endowment and rise "e sordibus inopiae, e nominis obscuritate, in lautas vitae conditiones splendidasque" (from the squalor of poverty, from obscurity of name, into a sumptuous and shining way of life) (95).

After Budé's self-fashioning, in the form of the arch-humanist, after his dialogic fashioning of the ideal royal patron, there remains a question mark regarding the fate of their common child, or prey.

L'INSTITUTION DU PRINCE: LANGUAGES OF PRAISE OLD AND NEW

To move from De transitu to De studio to De Philologia and finally to L'Institution du Prince is not simply to imitate the humanist movement backward in time.[162] It is also to leave behind a style of bewildering richness in favor of a bald, almost banal directness. This has partly to do with the choice of language. L'Institution du Prince is the only work in French by Budé, who differs from Petrarca and Poliziano, both of whom took some pains to master their vernacular poetic idiom. Even apart from the fact that his work is in prose, Budé behaves as if he were less at home than the Italians in his native language. One might even wonder if native is the right word, although French was the first language he knew. Of his three languages, Budé admits that he has less practice and less confidence in his French than in Latin and Greek (26v). The effect this linguistic choice has on the style of L'Institution du Prince is an impoverishment. The thick texture, the virtuosity of metaphors of the Latin treatises seem to have disappeared. In fact, Budé's vernacular appears as an attempt to realize the ideal of unambiguous service to royalty that he figured in the hunt of De Philologia.

Of course, the impoverishment is also due to the genre chosen. L'Institution du Prince comprises, in addition to a dedication and an introduction, a series of vignettes and apophthegms illustrating the right behavior of monarchs. These individual elements are for the most part quite brief and contain only the essential. If Budé's digressive tendency finds a footing here, it is only in the combination of the elements; one classical reminiscence produces another in an association of parables for the prince. Budé's manner of proceeding is understandable given the purpose of *L'Institution du Prince*. Unlike his other works, which were intended for a learned audience (though they might be dedicated to the king), this one is aimed expressly at François. It is written in a language he could read and is composed with an eye to his tastes and limitations. Moreover, Budé made no effort to publish the treatise; it appeared after his death, in several reworked versions. It poses as a "chamber-treatise," the contact of humanist and prince at its most private and intimate.

Despite the characteristics that make *L'Institution du Prince* unique among Budé's works, it pursues the concerns he expressed throughout his career. Chronologically, it follows the specialized treatises, the *Annotationes* and *De Asse*, but precedes the more speculative works of the 1530s (*De studio, De Philologia, De transitu*). As an earlier, perhaps cruder presentation of themes we have seen wrapped in metaphor in the later works, it may serve as a useful recapitulation of Budé's significance to this study. It also provides an appropriate conclusion to a topological study because it is a tissue of topoi. Rarely do we find commonplaces at work in a manner so pure. What are those recurrent concerns that the topoi of *L'Institution* represent with such clarity? The literary support of absolutism; the deification of the eloquent word; and, as synthesis of these, the plea for the place of literature based on its bestowal of glorification in the *res publica*.

It should first be made clear how much Budé is an advocate of absolutism. My concern here is not to examine François 1er's own ambitions and actions toward consolidating his personal power and weakening parliamentary and provincial checks on that power. That tendency is well attested.[163] What is more relevant is that the period's greatest advocate of humanism is also the most extreme advocate of unfettered absolutism. Budé's thought on the latter is best expressed by C. Bontems, the most acute of the few critics of *L'Institution du Prince*:

> Budé se présente ... comme un farouche partisan du pouvoir absolu. ... Tout est mis en oeuvre pour garantir au Prince un pouvoir sans limites, même Dieu est repoussé au loin, laissé sans grande influence. ... Rien n'est épargné pour assurer un souverain incontesté à la France, nul ne doit lui résister, nul ne peut lui disputer, ni mettre en cause son pouvoir. ... Aucun auteur jusqu'alors n'avait osé aller aussi loin dans la voie de l'absolutisme, et on peut se demander si d'autres l'osèrent par la suite.[164]

The question we must ask concerns the relationship between Budé's advocacy of *bonae literae* and absolutism.

Let this question be held in suspension until it becomes clear that the faith in the deified word is also an important element of *L'Institution*. This prosaic treatise seems worlds away from the rhapsodic theology of *De transitu*. Yet both works have an identical dedicatory formula, this distich:

Verbi certa fides ut mundo augustior esset,
    Principe Francisco nobilitata fuit.[165]

(A certain faith in the Word was ennobled by our leader François, that it might be more venerable in the world [or than the world].)

In the context of *De transitu*, the *Verbum* is clearly religious; particularly since the formula follows a description of the penitential procession François led to purify the faith after the Affaire des Placards. In the almost wholly secular setting of *L'Institution*, the lines commemorate the king more as *père des lettres*. Nevertheless, the theological sense is already present, just as the secular element has by no means evaporated from *De transitu*.

An interesting detail also turns up in the ornamentation of the dedicatory page of *L'Institution* (2r). The text is surrounded by illuminated squares that portray the royal fleur-de-lys, alternating with other flowers and a dragon. Across three of the squares containing fleurs-de-lys we read: "e caelo / descendit / GNOTHISEAUTON" (he [she, it] descended from heaven / know thyself). Juvenal's line, with the Delphic maxim given in Greek characters, may become, in this context, an allusion to the descent of Christ the Verbum from heaven to earth to save humanity.[166]

Moreover, Budé translates and endorses a verse from *Proverbs* (25.2) concerning the duty of kings: "la gloire de dieu est en celant et occultant la parole, et la gloire des roys est en investigant la parolle et enquerant le mot" (32v–33r).[167] According to his interpretation, it befits a king to inquire into Sapience and through her to know divine truth. This is a text that had a certain popularity among kabbalistic writers of the sixteenth century, a fact that gives a greater weight to the philological task of kings than may at first appear.[168] Although *L'Institution du Prince* does not reach the level of explicit logolatry found in Budé's later works, we see, nevertheless, the usual humanist pattern: Promotion of *bonae literae* brings with it a mythical ontology or theology of the word.[169]

Eloquence makes a twofold promise to the prince: prudence in this life, and glorious survival after death. Prudence is the faculty, essential to the prince, which will improve on acquaintance with letters. In this way the ruler will become wise and the Platonic utopia be realized (115v). Yet for all his emphasis that prudence is the wisdom that masters worldly things (as distinct from *sapience,* contemplation of the immutable [117v]),[170] Budé delivers almost nothing in the way of concrete instruction. The contrast with Erasmus's contemporary *Institutio principis Christiani* is striking. Both treatises are full of classical exempla, but while Erasmus's work provides precepts for the well-rounded prince, illustrated by the exempla, the main body of Budé's work contains nothing but exempla. And insofar as a lesson can be drawn from the French work, it tells nothing about the ruler's education, nor what sort of policies he should initiate for foreign peace, domestic well-being, and so on. The message to the prince comprises essentially endorsement of his absolutism and encouragement to cultivate *bonae literae.*

Budé's picture of the ideal ruler portrays an absolute autocrat, whose exercise of power is limited only by his own virtue. But not quite; there is one exception to the prince's freedom from external restraints. Again and again Budé introduces princes who were obsessed with the reputation they would have for posterity. The wise ruler does not misuse his power, because he wants to be remembered as a wise ruler. There exists an even surer way than personal virtue to shine on in the future, and that is the unique service that men of letters fulfill. Again and again in the exempla, those past princes have found balm for their obsession in the immortalizing power of those who write their praises. Literary power alone remains exempt from the prince's domination.

The immortalization topos in *L'Institution* consistently informs Budé's treatment of his favorite princes. The rulers to whom he returns repeatedly as implicit models for the French king are Philip of Macedon, his son Alexander the Great, Julius Caesar, and Augustus Caesar.[171] Both Philip and Alexander are embodiments of an insatiable thirst for glory. Their efforts to quench this thirst take two forms: unbounded military conquest and cultivation of letters to immortalize their name. That cultivation is not only positive patronage; it also means exempting letters from the fortunes of war, as when Philip had the opportunity to destroy Athens but refused out of consideration for the city "ou estoit la source de science et eloquence, laquelle a la puissance de donner gloire et renommee perpetuelle aux roys conquerans" (where was the source of knowledge and eloquence, which has the power to give perpetual glory and renown to conquering monarchs) (53v).[172] On the positive side, Philip, who "aymoit la gloire sur toutes choses" (who loved glory above everything), engaged Aristotle as his son's tutor in the hope that through the philosopher's *doctrine,* Alexander and his realm would be talked about in ages to come (52v). That

Alexander learned his lesson is shown by his statement that he was as indebted to his teacher as to his father. "Le feu roy mon pere (disoit-il) est cause de ce que je viz, mais mon precepteur est cause que je vivray par honneur et mourray en gloire" (the late King my father, he would say, is the reason I am alive, but my teacher is the reason that I will live through honor and will die in glory) (115r-v).

Budé's displays his admiration for the power of Alexander most strikingly when he imagines the latter's military victories and literary glory as the complementary forces of thunderbolt and lightning. Alexander was

> quasi comme une fouldre courant depuis la Grece jusques en Inde, abatant et ravissant tout devant soy et a dextre et a senestre sans que riens luy peust resister, mais toutesfoys sa gloire resplendissant par les escriptures, est comme l'escler espartissant qui tousjours se renouvelle et redouble quant on list les histoires faisans mention de lui.

> (100v–101r)

> (like a thunderbolt running from Greece all the way to India, hurling down and sweeping away everything before it, right and left, without anything resisting it. Yet his glory, shining through written texts, is like lightning as it spreads out, which always is renewed and redoubled when we read the histories mentioning him.)[173]

By distinguishing the twin aspects of a single atmospheric phenomenon, Budé represents an essential division of labor. Conquest is admirable and irresistible through its destructive force (*abatant, ravissant*). The movement of literary glory, although tending to a similar universality (*espartissant*), has principally a signifying and aesthetic function (*resplendissant*). But what it signifies and reveals as beautiful is precisely that military devastation. Budé anticipates the Vichian representation of lightning as *Ursprache* but goes beyond Vico in his use of the metaphor by emphasizing literary glory's collaboration in destruction, or triumph. Alexander manifests his recognition of that alliance through patronage of men of letters.

Budé pursues the rapprochement of poetry with military conquest when he stresses Alexander's knowledge as a patron. Like Augustus after him, Alexander refused to let himself be memorialized by any but the most talented (17r-v).[174] This fact explains his wish that he had a poet like Homer. Inevitably, Budé produces the scene of Alexander at Achilles' tomb, following Cicero's account (16r-v).[175]

Julius Caesar, too, was a connoisseur of eloquence, as is clear from his appreciation of Cicero's art (21v), as well as *assoiffé* of glory (68r). The death of the Roman Republic was apparently more than compensated by the literary life that imperial patronage bred. Budé dwells on the size of Virgil's pension from Augustus as well as Octavia's lavishness on hearing the lines from the *Aeneid* on her late son Marcellus. Not to mention the eponymous significance of Maecenas: "Et dit-on aujour-duy que par faulte de mecenates il n'est plus de Virgiles ne de Horaces, non est-il de Tulles ou Quintilians par faulte d'entretenement" (and they say nowadays that through lack of Maecenases there are no longer Virgils and Horaces; nor are there Ciceros or Quintilians, through lack of patronage) (19r-v). (The presence on this list of Cicero, a republican who notoriously did not manage to benefit from imperial largesse, appears an ironic oversight.)[176]

Naturally, Budé directs his anecdotal exploration of antiquity toward a contemporary and French application. As in *De Philologia,* he reminds the king of the obscurity that has covered early Gallic glories not committed to literature.[177] If François pays attention to these lessons—which are both the great deeds and sayings of the ancients, and the fact that they must be entrusted to patronized letters—the glory that will redound to him will be both immediate and posthumous. Budé tells him: You will be enabled to "grant honneur acquerir en vostre vie par toute la crestienté, et si loing que la renommée de France s'estend, et apres la mort delaisser de vostre nom memoire immortelle" (acquire great honor during your life, throughout the Christian world and as far as French glory extends, and after your death leave behind immortal memory of your name) (15v). In his role as patron, the king will be in some measure deified, as he creates poets and orators and dispenses inspiration like the Muses.[178]

This verbal portrayal of a *rex Musagetes* echoes *De Philologia,* as does an element of the illuminated manuscript. The first folio (1v) shows the king on his throne with the present book in hand, which he has apparently just received from its author. To his left Budé kneels, gestures, and speaks to him. To the king's right stands the figure of Philologia, now endowed (in contrast to a previous illumination) with gold medallions. She holds in one hand a falcon and a leash with a hunting dog in the other. Over a dozen years before *De Philologia,* royal support for humanistic learning is already intimately connected with that metaphor for royal imperium, the hunt. Whether or not Budé had anything to do with the illumination, it provides a pregnant image for the continuity of his concerns.[179]

But it is the gesture of bestowal that dominates that liminal image and establishes the central metaphor of *L'Institution du Prince.* The metaphor of gift exchange comes into play in three stages. First, the dedication to the king that follows the illumination almost immediately cites and translates *Proverbs* 18.16 to the effect that a gift is a man's best access to princes.[180] With this foundation upon Scripture's absolute wisdom, Budé next establishes the necessity of unequal exchange and the obligation to receive as well as to give. The Persian king Artaxerxes understood that royal magnificence consists of not only abundant bestowal, but just as much the acceptance of well-meant presents, no matter how small.[181] The final step is to dematerialize that principle of unequal exchange by establishing a precedent for the use of honor as a gift. Such a precedent is supplied by the anecdote of the Corinthian ambassadors' bestowal of citizenship on the world conqueror Alexander. The honor, which had previously been offered only to Hercules, must have satisfied Alexander's well-known taste for mythical legitimation.[182] Once Budé has justified his literary offering and represented the king's acceptance (portrayed in the illumination) as royal citizenship in the republic of letters, the way lies clear for the ordinary commerce between prince and humanist that runs through the treatise.[183]

As he repeatedly reminds the king of great rulers' generosity to men of letters, Budé draws explicitly on his work in *De Asse* to translate amounts of ancient largesse into modern French currency.[184] This display of a price tag may be meant to show François how far modern patronage falls short of ancient models.[185] But the materialization and specification of what princes owe to writers also moves, significantly, in a direction opposite to the principle of dematerialization that legitimizes the gift of literature. Budé's metaphors represent literature as a mythical force, like the lightning accompanying Alexander's conquests. Literary activity moves back beyond its classical exemplars to an ever murkier realm of effectiveness. In contrast, the models of correct princely behavior are updated by the rational calculation that makes antiquity understandable in modern economic categories. Thus Budé's "entrepreneurial spirit" is only half the truth about the movement in history that he effects in *L'Institution*.[186]

Scripture, Greece, and Rome provide the sources of Budé's vignettes. The structure of *L'Institution du Prince* groups the vignettes roughly thus: Scripture-Greece-Rome-Greece-Scripture.[187] Thus, the example of Rome sits at the center of the work. The establishment of the empire is a historical realization of Budé's ideal, both as the consolidation of absolutism and as the cause of incomparable patronage. The empire of Philip and Alexander (Greek figures that elicit even more of Budé's admiration) is less exemplary only because of its greater ephemerality.

The centrality of Rome does not result only from the author's personal preference. The Roman tradition is the principal source of absolutist thought in the sixteenth century. With the revived study of Roman law came a keener perception of what universal authority meant.[188] Budé himself, in his *Annotationes,* made an early and magisterial contribution in that line. As already suggested, he went further than most of his contemporaries in drawing the parallel Roman emperor-French king, with the concomitant emphasis on the king's power, autonomy, and near-godlike status. In *L'Institution du Prince,* Budé declares the prince not subject to the laws of his kingdom and answerable only to divine law (7v–8r). He already commented at some length in the *Annotationes* the text *princeps legibus solutus est.* There he considered the king "quasi deu[s] . . . inter homines" (like a god among men). And yet one difference remains between kings and gods that, as we have already seen, subjects the monarch to the power of literature. Kings are "humani Ioves . . . sed qui tamen hominum more emoriantur" (human Jupiters, who however die according to the custom of men).[189] Even the most daring elevation of royal autonomy reminds the prince that he is mortal and so in need of literary immortality. Moreover, if we consider how gift exchange underlies the development of Roman law, we find the fundamental humanistic gesture of bestowal present from the very beginning of Budé's project and intimately tied to his political vision.[190]

Budé had some company in his political thought, but the way in which he outstripped his contemporaries is instructive.[191] Claude de Seyssel, for example, published his *La Monarchie de France* in 1519. Dedicated to François 1er, to whom *L'Institution du Prince* was presented in the same year, Seyssel's treatise is notable for the checks it proposes to monarchy. Religion, justice, and *police* (customary law) prevent the king's power from being absolute, although he submits to these checks voluntarily and for his greater glory.[192] What makes Budé so different? I would suggest that the difference results from his humanism. Immersed in the Roman legal corpus read as the codification of imperial glory, Budé was relatively uninterested in the more limited autonomy of medieval kingship. He was drawn like his fellow humanists to a point of early, unsurpassed power.[193] If for Budé justice and *police* are essentially concepts inherited from Roman law, that leaves religion as the only possible brake on absolutism. And we have seen to what extent Budé's Christian piety is a worship of sacred philology. If religious power lies in a transcendent verbal effectiveness, religion is already an ally of secular absolute power.

Moreover, Budé's contribution to royal power was more than metaphorical. He held the office of *maître des requêtes,* which means that he helped supervise every level of the judicial system. The *maîtres des requêtes* were key functionaries in the move toward increasing centralization and extended legal rights for the monarchy.[194] More than most writers, Budé was a part of the machinery of domination.

François 1er learned part of Budé's lesson, insofar as he needed any instruction in the focusing of all authority in himself. However, the Latin language was not to be part of that lesson, nor of that authority. Indispensable though it was for the full force of Budé's argument, Latin must have seemed too unreliable for loyal service. The age of Budé's humanism is also the age of the vernacular's triumph.

In 1539, François promulgated the ordinance of Villers-Cotterets. Its most momentous provision commanded that the official language of the judicial system should henceforth be French. If we are to believe a theory proposed by F. Brunot, Villers-Cotterets was a political act and a moment in the king's consolidation of his power. In a prophetic manner, Claude de Seyssel exhorted Louis XII in the dedication of his translation of the historian Justin.

> Qu'ont fait le peuple et les princes romains quand ils tenoient la monarchie du monde et qu'ils taschoyent a la perpetuer et rendre eternelle? Ils n'ont trouue autre moyen plus certain ne plus seur que de magnifier, enrichir et sublimer leur langue latine, qui, du commencement de leur empire, estoit bien maigre et bien rude, et après, de la communiquer aux païs et prouinces et peuples par eux conquis, ensemble leurs lois Romaines couchees en icelle.[195]

> (What did the Roman people and their rulers do when they held sovereignty over the world and tried to perpetuate that sovereignty and make it eternal? They found no more certain means than aggrandizing, enriching and elevating their Latin language which, at the beginning of their domination, was quite meager and crude, and then communicating it to the lands and provinces and peoples conquered by them, together with their Roman laws couched in that language.)

If, as Seyssel recommends, the king is to imitate the ancient "illustres conquereurs," his course of action should be clear. Language, the master of eternity, opens the way to enduring temporal power. But it must be the conqueror's own language.

Whether or not such a motive underlies Villers-Cotterets, the reason for preferring French over Latin is explicit. One of the articles of the ordinance deplores the obscurity available in Latin and commands the use of French "afin ... qu'il n'y ait ne puisse auoir aucune ambiguïté ou incertitude, ne lieu à demander interpretation" (so that ... there may be no room for any ambiguity or uncertainty, nor any need for interpretation).[196] Although specifically applying only to the judicial realm, the provision is emblematic, both of the royal appropriation of language and of the humanist's ultimate superfluousness. To appropriate the authority and immortalizing power of eloquence, yet be able to leave aside the dangers of its ambiguities: Such is the dream of nascent French absolutism, as embodied by François in the works of Budé.

With the rise of the vernacular, in France as elsewhere, came cultural independence from Italy, as Italy itself fell under foreign domination. There also developed a very gradual and limited liberation from the topical tradition conveyed in the classical languages. With the beginnings of a more recognizably modern world, with the consolidation of centralized authority in various parts of Europe, a new dialectic was developing between new languages and new structures of power. Naturally, French (for example) did not remain long at the level of bald anecdote and eager service found in *L'Institution du Prince*. Boasts from the humanist tradition, with some of the same troubling undertones, are abundantly expressed in French throughout the sixteenth century.[197] Words that claim to be more than words, those new words inherit many of the contradictions of their "dead" ancestors.

Epilogue

From antiquity through the Renaissance, the topos of literary glorification makes a plea for the rapprochement of poet and patron. That rapprochement is taken to mean the poet's admission to the center of the *res publica*. The history of the topos is the history of that utopian dream; its pathos lies in the tension between such visions and the fact that they have not been realized.

The rise of the vernaculars encourages a glimpse forward in time, where the topos appears to have not lost its centrality. However, it reveals its radical amphibole by turning in the opposite direction. Precisely because of the power he claims, the poet embraces exile and opposition to the status quo.

Ugo Foscolo's *Dei Sepolcri,* written in 1806, develops a meditation on the kinship between sepulchers and poetry. Appealing to the humanist tradition of poetic paleology and Vico, he finds the civilizing function of poetry in its dialogue with the dead. As the poem approaches its conclusion, Foscolo introduces the figure of Cassandra, who foresees and laments the fall of Troy. She invokes the trees in whose shadow she stands and prays for poetic memory as compensation for the disaster of history. She introduces the figure of Homer, imagined in a reversal of the anecdote of Alexander at Achilles's tomb, in a posture that typifies poetic activity.

>   Un dì vedrete
> mendico un cieco errar sotto le vostre
> antichissime ombre, e brancolando
> penetrar negli avelli, e abbraciar l'urne,
> e interrogarle. Gemeranno gli antri
> secreti, e tutta narrerà la tomba
> Ilio raso due volte e due risorto
> splendidamente su le mute vie
> per far più bello l'ultimo trofeo
> ai fatati Pelidi. Il sacro vate,
> placando quelle afflitte alme col canto,
> i prenci argivi eternerà per quante
> abbraccia terre il gran padre Oceàno.
> E tu onore di pianti, Ettore, avrai

ove fia santo e lagrimato il sangue
per la patria versato, e finché il Sole
risplenderà su le sciagure umane.[1]

(One day you will see a blind beggar wander in your ancient shade, and
groping penetrate the tombs, and embrace the urns, and question them.
The secret recesses will groan, the entire tomb will narrate Ilium razed
twice, rebuilt twice splendidly on the silent site, in order to magnify the
final trophy of the fated sons of Peleus. The sacred poet, placating those
suffering souls with his song, will immortalize the Argive princes throughout all the lands embraced by Father Ocean. And you, Hector, will have the
honor of tears, wherever blood shed for the homeland may be holy and
mourned, and as long as the Sun shines upon human disasters.)

Notes

INTRODUCTION

Friedrich Hölderlin, "Brot und Wein" (*Gedichte Hyperion* [Munich: W. Goldmann Verlag, 1981], 96).

1. *Iliad* 6.357–58. Text: Homer, *Opera,* ed. David B. Monro and Thomas W. Allen, 5 vols. (Oxford: Oxford University Press, 1917–20, 1946). Unless otherwise indicated, all translations are my own. Cf. *Odyssey,* 8.579–80; and Jasper Griffin, *Homer on Life and Death* (Oxford: Oxford University Press, 1980), 98.

2. Cf. Ovid, *Tristia,* 4.3.75: "Hectora quis nosset, si felix Troia fuisset?"

3. *Odyssey,* 24.60–61.

4. Ibid., 1.347–48.

5. Cf. Thamyris in *Iliad,* 2.594–600; Homeric *Hymn to Apollo,* 172; Thucydides, 3.104. For the blindness of Homer, with an attempt to derive the poet's name from his infirmity, see Giambattista Vico, *Principj di Scienza nuova,* in *Opere,* ed. Fausto Nicolini (Milan: Ricciardi, 1953) sections 869–71.

6. *Odyssey,* 8.63.

7. Ibid., 22.344–49. However, we should not underestimate the complexity of the scene and Phemius's compromised situation; Odysseus does not answer the poet directly but spares him together with the herald Medon. See Siegfried Besslich, *Schweigen-Verschweigen-Übergehen: Die Darstellung des Unausgesprochenen in der Odyssee* (Heidelberg: C. Winter, 1966), 101–4.

8. *Odyssey,* 8.479. Cf. 8.472, 13.28. On the importance of the etymology of the poets' names, see Werner Jaeger, *Paideia: The Ideals of Greek Culture,* trans. Gilbert Highet (New York: Oxford University Press, 1945), 40; Gregory Nagy, *The Best of the Achaeans: Concepts of the Hero in Archaic Greek Poetry* (Baltimore: Johns Hopkins University Press, 1979), 17.

9. See *Odyssey,* 1.246, 9.24, and elsewhere.

10. Sonnet "A Zacinto," vv. 12–13. Text: Ugo Foscolo, *Opere,* ed. Franco Gavazzeni, 2 vols. (Milan: Ricciardi, 1974–81), 1:237.

11. *Dei Sepolcri,* 226–34. Text: Foscolo, *Opere,* vol. 1.

12. Certainly, examples are neither innocent nor transparent (see John D. Lyons, *Exemplum: The Rhetoric of Example in Early Modern France and Italy* [Princeton: Princeton University Press, 1989] passim). I have chosen these introductory ones to emphasize certain aspects of the topos and to give an impression of both its span and its historical fragmentation.

Topoi, and this one in particular, by their nature lend themselves to exemplification. If we accept the definition of example/exemplum as "a dependent statement qualifying a more general and independent statement by naming a member of the class established by the general statement" (Lyons, x), we will find that one of the qualities characterizing this topos is its excess (one of the characteristics of an example, according to Lyons). To use the example of Alexander's comment at Achilles' grave that will turn up repeatedly in this study: the "general class" to which it most obviously refers is the usefulness of poets to conquerors. However, when we read the anecdote in context, its "excess" may also suggest another general class: namely, death as the ultimate locus for the contradictions of the poet-patron relation. Hence generally the supreme importance of context for the discovery of that excess.

13. Sappho, fr. 211 in *Lyrica graeca selecta,* ed. D. L. Page (Oxford: Oxford University Press, 1973).

14. Theognis, 1.237–46. Text: *Iambi et Elegi Graeci,* ed. M. L. West, 2 vols (Oxford: Oxford University Press, 1989), vol. 1.

15. Theocritus, 16.48–59. Text: *Bucolici Graeci,* ed. A. S. F. Gow (Oxford: Oxford University Press, 1952).

16. Propertius, *Carmina* 3.2.17–26 (ed. E. A. Barber [Oxford: Oxford University Press, 1960]).

17. Benedetto Accolti, *Dialogus de praestantia virorum sui aevi* (Parma, 1689), 1.

18. Matteo Bandello, *Le Novelle* 1.46, ed. Francesco Flora (Milan: Mondadori, 1934), 553. This popular anecdote is also told by Clément Marot, *Epistre* "Bien doy louer la divine puissance"; Agrippa D'Aubigné, *Lettres touchant quelques poincts de diverses sciences,* no. 11 (*Oeuvres complètes,* ed. Henri Weber et al. [Paris: Gallimard, 1969], 859); Etienne Pasquier, *Recherches de la France,* 6. 16; George Puttenham, *The Arte of English Poesie,* 1.8; and Robert Burton, *The Anatomy of Melancholy,* part. 3, sect. 1, mem. 2, subs. 3, who gives François de Belleforest as his source.

19. Denys Lambin, *Oratio de laudibus litterarum . . .* (Paris, 1564), A2v.

20. Ludovico Ariosto, *Orlando Furioso,* 35.22. Text: ed. Marcello Turchi, 2 vols. (Milan: Garzanti, 1974).

21. Ronsard, *Oeuvres complètes,* ed. Jean Céard et al., 2 vols. (Paris: Gallimard, 1993–94), 2:683–84.

22. Ernst Robert Curtius, *European Literature and the Latin Middle Ages,* trans. Willard R. Trask (Princeton: Princeton University Press, 1973), 70, 82; as well as Curtius, "Begriff einer historischen Topik," *Toposforschung,* ed. Max L. Baeumer (Darmstadt: Wissenschaftliche Buchgesellschaft, 1973), 1–18. The semantic shift effected by Curtius has not, of course, gone uncriticized; see Peter Jehn, ed., *Toposforschung: eine Dokumentation* (Frankfurt: Athenäum, 1972), particularly the introduction by Jehn (VII–LXIV), and Edgar Mertner, "Topos und Commonplace" (20–68).

23. Curtius, *European Literature . . . ,* viii, 391–97.

24. For important critiques, see Leo Spitzer, review of *Europäische Literatur . . . ,* by Curtius, *American Journal of Philology* 70 (1949): 425–31; María Rosa Lida de Malkiel, "Perduración de la literatura antigua en Occidente," *Romance Philology* 5 (1951–52): 99–131; Alexander Gelley, "Ernst Robert Curtius: Topology and Critical Method," *Modern Language Notes* 81 (1966): 579–94; Arthur R. Evans Jr., "Ernst Robert Curtius," in *On Four Modern Humanists,* ed. Evans (Princeton: Princeton University Press, 1970), 140–43; Rolf J. Goebel, "Curtius, Gadamer, Adorno: Probleme literarischer Tradition," *Monatshefte* 78 (1986): 151–66.

25. *Institutio Oratoria* 5.10.20.

26. Walter Benjamin, *The Origins of German Tragic Drama,* trans. John Osborne (London: Verso, 1977), 48. Cf. 29.

27. See Giovanni Pozzi, "Temi, *topoi,* stereotipi," in *Letteratura italiana,* ed. Alberto Asor Rosa, *Volume terzo: Le forme del testo:* 1. *Teoria e poesia* (Turin: Einaudi, 1984), 391–436.

28. As will be seen, the claim to glorify tends to become confounded with the claim to immortalize. Strictly speaking, the two are different, but in practice immortalization is figured as not simply perpetual existence but rather a heightened duration in the state of glory.

29. Ernst Cassirer, *Language and Myth,* trans. Susanne K. Langer (New York: Dover, 1953), 44–45.

30. Cassirer, *The Philosophy of Symbolic Forms,* trans. Ralph Manheim, 3 vols. (New Haven: Yale University Press, 1955), 2:58.

31. Cassirer, *The Philosophy of Symbolic Forms,* 2:40.

32. Citations: Cassirer, *Language and Myth,* 83; Marcel Mauss, *Théorie de la magie* in his *Sociologie et anthropologie* (Paris: PUF, 1966), 50.

33. Jean Yoyotte, "La pensée préphilosophique en Egypte," *Histoire de la philosophie,* ed. Brice Parain, 3 vols. (Paris: Gallimard, 1969), 1:7. Cf. Alexandre Moret, *Mystères égyptiens* (1913; reprint, Brionne, France: Gérard Monfort/Imago Mundi, 1983), 103–39.

34. Moret, *Mystères égyptiens,* 117.

35. Anita Seppilli, *Poesia e magia* (Turin: Einaudi, 1971), 17.

36. Mircea Eliade, *Le sacré et le profane* (Paris: Gallimard, 1965), 67; Paul Garelli, "La pensée préphilosophique en Mésopotamie," *Histoire de la philosophie,* 1:24.

37. Yoyotte, *Histoire de la philosophie,* 15, 18.

38. Cited in Cassirer, *Language and Myth,* 48.

39. Christian Jacq, *Egyptian Magic,* trans. Janet M. Davis (Warminster, UK: Aris & Phillips, 1985), 49.

40. See Seppilli, *Poesia e magia,* 26, 73 ff.

41. Jacq, *Egyptian Magic,* 49; Seppilli, *Poesia e magia,* 25.

42. See Seppilli, ibid., 167–68.

43. Cf. Daniel Lawrence O'Keefe, *Stolen Lightning: The Social Theory of Magic* (New York: Vintage, 1982), 53–54, who, following Anders Jeffner (*The Study of Religious Language*), proposes a typology of magical speech acts. For O'Keefe, performative sentences are only one sort of magical utterence (albeit the "most typical"), but a closer look at the examples he gives reveals the performative nature of the others as well.

44. See, for example, Yrjö Hirn, *The Origins of Art* (London: Macmillan, 1900), 278–97; Sigmund Freud, *Totem and Taboo,* trans. James Strachey (New York: Norton, 1950), 113; and Arnold Hauser, *The Social History of Art,* trans. Stanley Godman, 4 vols. (New York: Vintage, 1951), 1:3–11. However, cf. Theodor W. Adorno, *Aesthetic Theory,* trans. C. Lenhardt (London: Routledge & Kegan Paul, 1984), 447–55 (original text, *Ästhetische Theorie* [Frankfurt: Suhrkamp, 1970], 480–90).

45. See Seppilli, *Poesia e magia,* 188 ff.

46. Horace, *Epodes,* 17.4–5.

47. Ovid, *Ex Ponto,* 4.8.55.

48. See Georges Mounin, *Histoire de la linguistique des origines au XXe siècle* (Paris: PUF, 1967), 18. However, for the renewed legitimacy of glottogenetics or the study of the origin(s) of language, see Marcel Danesi, *Vico, Metaphor, and the Origin of Language* (Bloomington: Indiana University Press, 1993), and the references there.

49. Thomas M. Greene, *Poésie et magie* (Paris: Julliard, 1991), 18. I cite these admirable lectures as confirmation of some of my own conclusions, reached independently.

50. *Language and Myth,* 97–98.

51. Michel de Montaigne, *Oeuvres complètes,* ed. Albert Thibaudet and Maurice Rat (Paris: Gallimard, 1962), 601 (*Essais* 2.16: "De la gloire").

52. See Seppilli, *Poesia e magia,* 208.

53. Vico, *Scienza nuova,* sec. 404.

54. Ibid., sec. 429. See Gianfranco Castelli, "Myth and Language in Vico," trans. Margaret Brose, *Giambattista Vico's Science of Humanity,* ed. Giorgio Tagliacozzo and Donald Phillip Verene (Baltimore: Johns Hopkins University Press, 1976), 49.

55. Vico, secs. 375, 410.

56. Ibid., secs. 377–83, 404–5. Especially sec. 383:

Tal generazione della poesia ci è finalmente confermata da questa sua eterna propietà: che la di lei propia materia è l'impossibile credibile, quanto egli è impossibile ch'i corpi sieno menti (e fu creduto che'l cielo tonante si fusse Giove); onde i poeti non altrove maggiormente si esercitano che nel cantare le maraviglie fatte dalle maghe per opera d'incantesimi: lo che è da rifondersi in un senso nascosto c'hanno le nazioni dell'onnipotenza di Dio.

57. On Vico and Cassirer, see Cassirer, "Descartes, Leibniz, and Vico," in his *Symbol, Myth, and Culture: Essays and Lectures 1935–1945,* ed. Donald Phillip Verene (New Haven: Yale University Press, 1979), 95–107; Enzo Paci, "Vico and Cassirer," *Giambattista Vico: An International Symposium,* ed. Giorgio Tagliacozzo and Hayden V. White (Baltimore: Johns Hopkins University Press, 1969), 457–73; and Donald Phillip Verene, "Vico's Science of Imaginative Universals and the Philosophy of Symbolic Forms," in Tagliacozzo and Verene, *Vico's Science of Humanity,* 295–317 (especially 311–17). On Vico and humanism, see Eugenio Garin, "Vico and the Heritage of Renaissance Thought," *Vico: Past and Present,* ed. Giorgio Tagliacozzo (Atlantic Highlands, N.J.: Humanities Press, 1981), 99–116; and various works by Ernesto Grassi, particularly *Rhetoric as Philosophy: The Humanist Tradition* (University Park: Penn State University Press, 1980), 35–67, and *Vico and Humanism: Essays on Vico, Heidegger, and Rhetoric* (New York: Peter Lang, 1990).

58. Adorno, *Aesthetic Theory,* 202 (original: 210).

59. Adorno, *Aesthetic Theory,* 201 (original: 209).

60. Marcel Mauss, *Essai sur le don,* in *Sociologie et Anthropologie,* 145–279. Geographical and temporal extension of gift-exchange system: 227, 272 and passim; place in economic development: 227, 265–73; the three obligations: 161–64, 205–14; bestowal as power: 249, 269–70; gift giving, friendship and war: 278; potlatch: 151–53.

Of the abundant and growing literature on the gift that takes Mauss as its point of departure, the most important theoretical works include: Claude Lévi-Strauss, "Introduction à l'oeuvre de Marcel Mauss," in Mauss, *Sociologie et Anthropologie,* xxiv-lii; Georges Bataille, *La Part maudite précédé de La notion de dépense* (Paris: Minuit, 1967), particularly 100–15; Lévi-Strauss, *Les Structures élémentaires de la parenté* (Paris: Mouton, 1967), 61–79; Pierre Bourdieu, *Esquisse d'une théorie de la pratique précédé de trois études d'ethnologie kabyle* (Geneva: Droz, 1972), 221–43, 261–67; Marshall Sahlins, *Stone Age Economics* (Chicago: Aldine-Atherton, 1972), 149–82; Jacques Derrida,

Donner le temps: 1. *La fausse monnaie* (Paris: Galilée, 1991); Jacques T. Godbout and Alain Caillé, *L'Esprit du don* (Paris: Editions de la Découverte, 1992).

61. See chapter 1, below. In addition, see the latter part of Seppilli, *Poesia e magia,* on Greek literature; Mauss, *Essai sur le don,* 229–39, 250–55 for the Roman and Germanic tradition; Emile Benveniste, "Don et échange dans le vocabulaire indo-européen," *Problèmes de linguistique général* (Paris: Gallimard, 1966), 315–26; Benveniste, *Le vocabulaire des institutions indo-européennes,* 2 vols. (Paris: Minuit, 1969), 1:65–86; Paul Veyne, *Le Pain et le cirque* (Paris: Editions du Seuil, 1976).

62. Adorno, *Aesthetic Theory,* 468. It may be worthwhile to cite the original (506): "Allein durch den Fetischismus, die Verblendung des Kunstwerks gegenüber der Realität, deren Stück es selber ist, transzendiert das Werk den Bann des Realitätsprinzips als ein Geistiges."

63. On the work of art as a monad, see particularly Adorno, *Aesthetic Theory,* 7, 126–27, 257–60, 335–36 (original: 15–16, 132–33, 268–70, 350–51), who has a debt to Benjamin (*The Origins of German Tragic Drama,* 48).

64. Mauss, *Essai sur le don,* 273–76.

65. Cassirer, *Language and Myth,* 99. Cf. *The Philosophy of Symbolic Forms,* 2:260–61. Cassirer has been criticized for such a view by Hans Blumenberg, *Work on Myth,* trans. Robert M. Wallace (Cambridge: MIT Press, 1985), 168.

66. See notably Lévi-Strauss, *La Pensée sauvage* (Paris: Plon, 1962). For a succinct critique of Cassirer's theory of language and magic, see Stanley Jeyaraja Tambiah, "The Magical Power of Words," *Culture, Thought, and Social Action: An Anthropological Perspective* (Cambridge: Harvard University Press, 1985), 33–34.

67. For the Jungian basis of Curtius's historical topics, see *European Literature . . . ,* 82, 101, 122–23. Cf. Lévi-Strauss, "Introduction à l'oeuvre de Marcel Mauss," xxxii on the important difference between Mauss and Jung.

68. See, for example, Wilton Sterling Dillon, "Giving, Receiving and Repaying: An Examination of the Ideas of Marcel Mauss in the Context of International Technical Assistance" (Ph.D. diss., Columbia University, 1961); C. A. Gregory, *Gifts and Commodities* (London: Academic Press, 1982); David Cheal, *The Gift Economy* (London: Routledge, 1988); Caroline Humphrey and Stephen Hugh-Jones, eds., *Barter, Exchange, and Value: An Anthropological Approach* (Cambridge: Cambridge University Press, 1992); Godbout and Caillé, *L'Esprit du don.*

69. Ludwig Wittgenstein, *Remarks on Frazer's* Golden Bough, ed. Rush Rhees, trans. A. C. Miles (Retford, Nottinghamshire, UK: Brynmill, 1979), 10.

70. See Adorno, *Aesthetic Theory,* 320–21 (original: 334–35): Art is social because it is opposed to society; it can only be oppositional when it is autonomous; art was not autonomous before the bourgeois era.

71. However, the topos is not uncommon in the Middle Ages. See Curtius, *European Literature,* 476–77; María Rosa Lida de Malkiel, *La Idea de la Fama en la Edad Media Castellana* (México: Fondo de Cultura Económica, 1952), 99–294; Achatz Freiherr von Müller, *Gloria bona fama bonorum: Studien zur sittlichen Bedeutung des Ruhmes in der frühchristlichen und mittelalterlichen Welt* (Husum: Matthiesen Verlag, 1977).

72. As a foundation, I adopt P. O. Kristeller's definition of a humanist as one whose profession lay in the *studia humanitatis,* "namely grammar, rhetoric, history, poetry, and moral philosophy," as found mainly in the texts of

Latin and Greek antiquity (Kristeller, "The Humanist Movement," *Renaissance Thought: The Classic, Scholastic and Humanist Strains* [New York: Harper, 1961], 10).

73. See, for example, Peter Burke, *The Renaissance Sense of the Past* (London: Edward Arnold, 1969); Ricardo J. Quinones, *The Renaissance Discovery of Time* (Cambridge: Harvard University Press, 1972).

74. See, for example, David Quint, *Origin and Originality in Renaissance Literature: Versions of the Source* (New Haven: Yale University Press, 1983).

75. See Giuseppe Toffanin, *Storia dell'umanesimo,* 4 vols. (Bologna: Zanichelli, 1964), 3:85 ff.

76. Cf. Jacques Derrida, "Freud et la scène de l'écriture," *L'écriture et la différence* (Paris: Seuil, 1967), 293–340.

77. I attach Cassirer's name to this conceptual network for the sake of convenience, without necessarily identifying him with all the anthropological aspects considered under its heading (and, of course, without considering him as a "proponent" of mythical thought).

78. Adorno, *Aesthetic Theory,* 416: "Immanent critique . . . traces the truth content of canonical works back to their inner breaks [*Brüchigkeit*]" (original: 444).

79. Adorno, *Aesthetic Theory,* 77–78 (original: 84). Cf. 194 ("Wanting to immortalize the transitory—life—art in fact kills it") and 267 (original: 202, 278).

CHAPTER 1. ANTIQUITY

Marguerite Yourcenar, *Mémoires d'Hadrien* (*Oeuvres romanesques* [Paris: Gallimard, 1982], 449).

Philippe Jaccottet, *La Semaison.*

1. See Griffin, *Homer on Life and Death,* 95; Gregory Nagy, *Comparative Studies in Greek and Indic Meter* (Cambridge: Harvard University Press, 1974), passim; Nagy, *The Best of the Achaeans,* 187 ff.; Rüdiger Schmitt, *Dichtung und Dichtersprache in indogermanischer Zeit* (Wiesbaden: Harrassowitz, 1967), 64–70.

2. Schmitt, ibid., 306.

3. Schmitt, ibid., 70, 86, 101. For the extra-Indo-European tradition, see Marcello Durante, *Sulla preistoria della tradizione poetica greca,* parte seconda: *Risultanze della comparazione indoeuropea* (Roma: Edizioni dell'Ateneo, 1976), 179–84.

4. See Durante, 179. Cf. Cassirer, *The Philosophy of Symbolic Forms,* 2:105: "The true character of mythical being is first revealed when it appears as the being of origins."

5. See for example *Iliad,* 12.381–83 and 447–49.

6. For example, *Iliad,* 1.260–72.

7. Richard John Cunliffe, *A Lexicon of the Homeric Dialect* (1924; reprint, Norman: University of Oklahoma Press, 1963), s.v. *kleos.* For detailed studies of the terminology of glory in Greek literature, and particularly in Homer, see Gerhard Steinkopf, *Untersuchungen zur Geschichte des Ruhmes bei den Griechen* (Halle: Konrad Triltsch, 1937); and Max Greindl, *Kleos kudos euxos time phatis doxa: Eine bedeutungsgeschichtliche Untersuchung des epischen und lyrischen Sprachgebrauches* (Munich, 1938).

8. See Julius Pokorny, *Indogermanisches etymologisches Wörterbuch*, 2 vols. (Bern: Francke Verlag, 1959), 1:605–6. *Kleos* derives from the medium of its communication, the verb *kleio* or *kleo*, just as Latin *fama* is related to *for*, ultimately, to Greek *pheme*.

9. *Iliad* 2.485–86. Cf. Ugo Foscolo's version in the *Grazie* (1.155–59):

> ... e noi
> quaggiù fra le terrene ombre vaganti
> dalla fama udiam timido avviso.
> Abbellitela or voi, Grazie, che siete
> presenti a tutto, e Dee tutto sapete.

Text: *Opere*, ed. Gavazzeni, vol. 1. And Poliziano's translation (his *Iliad* 2.490–91) that, incidentally, owes its last verse to *Aeneid* 7.646: " . . . vos omnia mente tenetis; / Ad nos vix tenuis famae perlabitur aura." Text: Poliziano, *Prose volgari inedite e poesie latine e greche edite e inedite*, ed. Isidoro Del Lungo (Florence: Barbèra, 1867).

10. E. R. Dodds, *The Greeks and the Irrational* (Berkeley: University of California Press, 1951), 81.

11. Vico, *Scienza nuova*, sec. 905.

12. *Theogony*, 27–28. Text: *Opera*, ed. Friedrich Solmsen, R. Merkelbach and M. L. West (Oxford: Oxford University Press, 1990).

13. *Theogony*, 32–33.

14. In this light, it is significant that the Muses' activity closely echoes the poet's, both as regards the verb (*kleioimi* [32], *kleiousin* [44]) and subject matter (future, past, and eternal for the poet [32–33]; present, future, and past for the Muses [38]).

15. Archilochus, fr. 1 (West, ed., *Iambi et Elegi Graeci*); Theognis 250 (cf. 1057); Solon, fr. 13.51 (*Iambi et Elegi Graeci*); Alcman, fr. 19 b (Page, ed., *Lyrica Graeca Selecta*); Anacreon, fr. 2.3 (*Iambi et Elegi Graeci*); Bacchylides 13.222–23, 19.3–4 and fr. dub. 55 (and cf. 3.3 and 5.4) (Bacchylides, *Carmina cum fragmentis*, ed. B. Snell and H. Maehler [Leipzig: Teubner, 1970]). For the formula's continued existence in Latin poetry (as *Musarum munera* or *dona*, or something similar), see Catullus 68.10, Tibullus 1.4.62, Horace, *Epistulae* 2.1.243.

16. *Hymn to Hermes* 442 (*doron agauon*) and 462 (*aglaa dora*), in Homer, *Opera*, ed. Thomas W. Allen, vol. 5 (Oxford: Oxford University Press, 1946).

17. *Hymn to Hermes*, 477.

18. The mediated nature of divine self-possession becomes even more accentuated when we consider that Hermes refers to Apollo's qualities as *aglaa dora* bestowed upon him by Zeus (470). The character of Hermes as a god of bestowal is expressed by the epithet *dotor eaon* (*Odyssey* 8.335; shorter Homeric *Hymn to Hermes* 12)

19. *Hymn to Hermes* 516.

20. See M. I. Finley, *The World of Odysseus* (New York: Viking, 1978), 64–68, 95–100, 120–23; Anthony Snodgrass, *Archaic Greece* (London: Dent, 1980), 132; Christoph Ulf, *Die homerische Gesellschaft* (Munich: C. H. Beck, 1990), 191–212. Still in the fifth century, Herodotus (1.69–70) portrays diplomacy between the Spartans and Croesus based on gift exchange.

For the Greek vocabulary of gifts in an Indo-European context, see Benveniste, *Problèmes de linguistique générale*, 315–26, and *Le vocabulaire des institutions indo-européennes*, 1:65–79.

21. *Works and Days,* 354.

22. Finley, *The World of Odysseus,* 145.

23. *Iliad* 1.213, 230; 9.155, 164, 297, 602, 604; 19.3; 22.341; 24.76, 119, 147, 176, 196, 447, 458. Of course, *dora* are also central to the relation between humanity and the gods, whether in the form of sacrificial gifts (*Iliad* 1.390; 6.293; 8.203; 20.299; 24.68, 425) or, in the other direction, as the good or bad destinies granted to mortals (*Iliad* 24.528), personal qualities or talents (3.54, 64–65), or the divine gift of sleep (the formula found at *Iliad* 7.482 and 9.713, as well as *Odyssey* 16.481 and 19.427)

24. In the former case, the term is *apoina* (*Iliad* 1.13, 20, 23); in the latter, as already indicated, we find the repeated use of *dora.* We might go even further, and recognize the principal causes of the Trojan war in (1) Paris's abuse of the gift-based relationship of host and guest (see Proclus's summary of the cyclic epic *Cypria* [Homer, *Opera,* 5:103], which has Paris treated as *xenos* by Menelaus, but corrupting Helen with gifts); and (2) the refusal of King Laomedon to compensate Poseidon and Apollo for their labor in constructing Troy (at *Iliad* 21.445 and 450 the term is *misthos*). Cf. Horace, *Carm.* 3.3.21–22 on Laomedon's denial of *merces* to the builders of Troy.

25. If we set aside the amateur poet Achilles (9.189); 18.604, rejected by the modern editors, which adds an *aoidos* to the figures on Achilles' shield (but cf. 18.569–71); and 24.720–21, referring to the "leaders of the dirge" (*aoidous / threnon exarchous*) for Hector.

26. *Iliad* 2.594–600. If we take *peron* (599) to refer to blindness, the contrast with Demodocus becomes all the more striking; Demodocus was maimed (blinded) by the Muses but also endowed with poetic talent (*Odyssey* 8.63–64). Cf. Pindar, *Paean,* 7b on the blindness of the human mind without the Muses.

27. The expression *aoiden / thespesien aphelonto* (599–600) recalls the god-given origin of the gift.

28. Odysseus becomes a Homeric rhapsode as he supplements the *Iliad*'s account of the Trojan War, reporting to Achilles within his narrative the deeds of Achilles' son (11.506–37). Moreover, "Alcinous praises Odysseus the storyteller in much the same terms that Odysseus had praised Demodocus" (8.487–98) (Alfred Heubeck on 11.368–69, in *A Commentary on Homer's Odyssey,* vol. 2 [Oxford: Oxford University Press, 1989]).

29. However, it is true that the Phaeacians committed themselves to transporting Odysseus even before he told his story.

30. Max Horkheimer and Theodor W. Adorno, *Dialectic of Enlightenment,* trans. John Cumming (New York: Continuum, 1972), 59, 63, 64. For the Cyclopes as representatives of a primitive state of society, see Plato, *Laws,* 680 b, adduced by Vico, *Scienza nuova,* sec. 2; as well as Finley, *The World of Odysseus,* 101.

31. Horkheimer and Adorno, *Dialectic,* 61.

32. Ibid., 78.

33. *Odyssey,* 10.221.

34. *Odyssey,* 12.44, 183, 198. They promise a poem on the Trojan War; a material to which Odysseus is susceptible, as in the case of Demodocus's poem. The Sirens' boast of knowledge (*idmen d'hossa genetai epi chthoni pouluboteire* [191]) recalls the Muses as characterized by both Homer (*Iliad* 2.485–86) and Hesiod (*Theogony,* 27–28).

35. *Odyssey,* 22.376.

36. He is first named by his neighbors reacting to his cries of rage (9.403)

(apart from an early mention by Zeus [1.70]), and only later by the poet, that is, by Odysseus the narrator.

37. Citation, 9.504. See Heubeck's commentary on 9.500–5: "By identifying himself Odysseus exposes himself to the curse which follows (528–35); we have here the ancient belief that knowledge of a man's name bestows some kind of magical power over him." See also Calvin S. Brown, "Odysseus and Polyphemus: The Name and the Curse," *Comparative Literature* 18 (1966): 193–202.

38. On this episode and particularly Polyphemus's curse, see also Denys Page, *The Homeric Odyssey* (Oxford: Oxford University Press, 1955), 1–20; A. J. Podlecki, "Guest-Gifts and Nobodies in *Odyssey* 9," *Phoenix* 15 (1961): 125–33; and Giacomo Bona, *Studi sull'Odisseia* (Turin: G. Giappichelli, 1966), 35–51.

39. 9.224–30; 259–71, with a high concentration of *xeinos* and its derivatives at 267–71.

40. 9.369–70. Cf. 20.293–98, where the suitor Ctesippus makes the same ironic use of the language of guest gifts before throwing a cow's hoof at Odysseus disguised as a beggar.

41. See Horkheimer and Adorno, *Dialectic,* 58–60, on this episode.

42. Which is not to claim that Odysseus's performances are limited to the period of his wandering. After his homecoming, at the moment of supreme suspense, he strings his great bow as a musician would tune his lyre (21.406–8). He grimly pursues the conceit as he promises the suitors appropriate after-dinner entertainment with "singing [or dancing] and the lyre" (21.430).

As Joseph Russo points out in his commentary on 19.203, Odysseus is characterized there in terms echoing Hesiod's Muses in the *Theogony,* 27.

43. Gregory Nagy, "Early Greek views of poets and poetry," *The Cambridge History of Literary Criticism,* vol. 1, *Classical Criticism,* ed. George A. Kennedy (Cambridge: Cambridge University Press, 1989), 9.

44. *Odyssey,* 11.488–503.

45. See Erwin Rohde, *Psyche: The Cult of Souls and Belief in Immortality Among the Greeks,* trans. W. B. Hillis (London: Routledge & Kegan Paul, 1925), 3–54; and Jan Bremmer, *The Early Greek Concept of the Soul* (Princeton: Princeton University Press, 1983), passim. On Pindar and the soul, see Rohde, *Psyche,* 414–21; and Hugh Lloyd-Jones, "Pindar and the After-Life," *Pindare: Huit exposés suivis de discussions,* ed. André Hurst (Geneva: Fondation Hardt, 1985), 245–79, with important comments on the relationship between patronage and "sincerity" of doctrine.

46. Pindar, *Isthmian* 3.19 (text: Pindar, *Carmina cum fragmentis,* ed. C. M. Bowra [Oxford: Oxford University Press, 1947]). I have benefited throughout from the translation by Frank J. Nisetich (*Pindar's Victory Songs* [Baltimore: Johns Hopkins University Press, 1980]).

47. *Isthmian* 8.64. Cf. Nagy, *The Best of the Achaeans,* 176–77, as well as his *Pindar's Homer: The Lyric Possession of an Epic Past* (Baltimore: Johns Hopkins University Press, 1990), 204–6.

48. See Hermann Fränkel, *Early Greek Poetry and Philosophy,* trans. Moses Hadas and James Willis (Oxford: Blackwell, 1975), 434.

49. Jacqueline Duchemin, *Pindare: Poète et prophète* (Paris: Les Belles lettres, 1955), 269–334.

50. Concerning the later (Roman) survival of this tradition, see the works of Franz Cumont: "Un sarcophage d'enfant trouvé à Beyrouth," *Syria* 10

(1929): 217–37; *Lux Perpetua* (Paris: Geuthner, 1949), 324; and particularly *Recherches sur le symbolisme funéraire des Romains* (Paris: Geuthner, 1942), 253–87. Also Curtius, *European Literature,* 234–35; and Henri–Irénée Marrou, *Mousikos aner: Etudes sur les Scènes de la Vie Intellectuelle figurant sur les Monuments Funéraires Romains* (Grenoble: Allier, 1937), 34–36, 231–57. In these cases, the Muses represent the immortalizing power of culture in general (what Marrou terms *mousike*) rather than strictly of poetry. Concerning the Renaissance cult of glory as expressed in funerary monuments, see André Chastel, *Art et humanisme à Florence au temps de Laurent le Magnifique* (Paris: PUF, 1982), 350 ff.

51. For example, the parallel clauses in the first strophe of *Olympian* 2 set the victor Theron beside Hercules and Zeus. Indeed, the question the poet asks his poem ("What god, what hero, what man shall we sing?" [2]) shows the mobility he can effect among the realms of being. Imitated by Horace, *Carm.* 1.12.1–3.

52. Duchemin, 298 ("Just as a metaphor, in contrast to a simile, omits the distinction between the two terms, so does the myth inserted without visible articulation, simply by juxtaposition, suggest an assimilation of the present-day hero to the hero of the myth.")

53. Frazer, *The Golden Bough,* 1:55–174; Freud, *Totem and Taboo,* 101–2. Cf. Roman Jakobson, "Two Aspects of Language and Two Types of Aphasic Disturbance," in his *Language in Literature* (Cambridge: Harvard University Press, 1987), 113.

54. Notably by Hubert and Mauss, *Esquisse d'une théorie générale de la magie,* 91–95.

55. For Pindar's frequent use of chiaroscuro, see Gilbert Norwood, *Pindar* (Berkeley: University of California Press, 1945), 86 ff.

56. Leslie Kurke, *The Traffic in Praise: Pindar and the Poetics of Social Economy* (Ithaca: Cornell University Press, 1991). Mauss is particularly important for pp. 85–107; the author also makes use of Finley's work on the *Odyssey* (not to mention other significant studies of the gift such as those of Lévi-Strauss, Bourdieu, and Sahlins).

57. "Just as when a man, taking with his rich hand a golden goblet foaming within with the dew of the vine, the best of his possessions, bestows it on his young son-in-law, toasting him from one home to another for the sake of the feast, honoring his family relationship, and among those present makes him enviable for a harmonious marriage;

"so do I, sending to the prize-winners liquid nectar, the Muses' gift, sweet fruit of my mind, make the gods propitious toward the victors at Olympia and Pitho. He is wealthy, whom good reputation surrounds." (*Olympian,* 7.1–10)

58. On the latter point—the role of *hedna* or marriage gifts—see notably Kurke, *The Traffic in Praise,* 118–25, with references (119) to various recent discussions of this passage.

59. On the semantic shift of *misthos* itself, from honorific compensation to artisan's wages, see Benveniste, *Le vocabulaire des institutions indo-européennes,* 1:163 ff.; Nagy, "Early Greek views of poets and poetry," 19–20.

60. Cf. Leonard Woodbury, "Pindar and the mercenary muse: *Isthmian* 2.1–13," *Transactions of the American Philological Association* 99 (1968): 527–42.

61. *Isthmian* 2.6 and 48. See the interpretation by Kurke, *The Traffic in Praise,* 240–56.

62. "Yet payment with interest is able to remove sharp reproach. Now see how the running wave washes over the tumbling pebble, how we pay for gratitude with public praise." (*Olympian* 10.9–12)

63. Cf. D. S. Carne-Ross, *Pindar* (New Haven: Yale University Press, 1985), 11 on "this *don gratuit,* this supererogatory largesse" of Pindar's victory odes.

64. Jaeger, *Paideia,* 1:207; and Kurke, *The Traffic in Praise,* 3, with a note including references and a caveat on the generalization.

65. *Olympian* 1 and *Pythian* 1–3 for Hieron, *Olympian* 2 and 3 for Theron; not to mention their allies (for example, *Olympian* 6 for Hieron's friend Hagesias). See generally Nagy, *Pindar's Homer,* 274–313.

66. Jaeger, *Paideia,* 1:231.

67. For the poet as *Mousaon therapon,* see *Theogony* 100, Homeric *Hymn to Selene* 20, *Margites* fr. 1, Theognis 769. Cf. Archilochus fr. 1, where the poet refers to himself as *therapon Enyalioio* (that is, of Ares), as well as *Mouseon eraton doron epistamenos.*

68. *Paean,* 5. 45.

69. In the victory odes *therapon* is associated with hospitable Corinth (*Olympian* 13.3). Hence, Pindar claims that the city he praises observes the norms inherited from the heroic world. It is not irrelevant here to note the semantic shift of *therapon* in its literal sense, from an attendant who serves freely, as in Homer, to something like a slave by the later fifth century (Herodotus and Thucydides).

70. *Nemean,* 10.82–88.

71. *Nemean,* 10.89–90.

72. Glory as the shadow of virtue: *Tusculanae Disputationes* 1.45.109. Cf. *De officiis* 1.19.65: "Vera autem et sapiens animi magnitudo honestum illud, quod maxime natura sequitur, in factis positum, non in gloria iudicat principemque se esse mavult quam videri" (text: ed. C. Atzert [Leipzig: Teubner, 1958]). For one example of the influence of the *Somnium Scipionis* (book 6 of *De re publica*), see chapter 2, below, on book 2 of Petrarca's *Africa.*

73. Of course, Cicero was himself also a poet who thought highly of his poetic accomplishments.

74. *In Catilinam* 4.11.23: "Pro his igitur omnibus rebus . . . nihil a vobis nisi huius temporis totiusque mei consulatus memoriam postulo" (text: ed. P. Reis [Leipzig: Teubner, 1933]). Cf. *Pro Archia,* 11.28.

75. *Ad Familiares,* 5.12.1 (text: ed. W. S. Watt [Oxford: Oxford University Press, 1982]). Not content with posthumous fame, Cicero wants to enjoy glory during his lifetime ("Neque enim me solum commemoratio posteritatis ac spes quaedam immortalitatis rapit sed etiam illa cupiditas, ut vel auctoritate testimonii tui vel indicio benevolentiae vel suavitate ingenii vivi perfruamur" [sec. 1; cf. sec. 9]).

76. There is also a subsequent declaration of the superiority of books to plastic arts in the matter of glorification: "Unus enim Xenophontis libellus in eo rege [Agesilaus] laudando facile omnis imagines omnium statuasque superavit" (sec. 7). Cf. *Pro Archia,* 12.30.

77. "ut mihi non solum praeconium quod, cum in Sigeum venisset, Alexander ab Homero Achilli tributum esse dixit, sed etiam grave testimonium impertitum clari hominis magnique videatur" (sec. 7).

78. See *Ep. ad Atticum,* 1.19.10.

79. Text: ed. P. Reis (Leipzig: Teubner, 1933). Parenthetical references are to chapter and section.

80. Harold C. Gotoff, *Cicero's Elegant Style: An Analysis of the* Pro Archia (Urbana: University of Illinois Press, 1979), 81.

81. For the *Pro Archia* as a *Pro Cicerone,* see Félix Gafflot's introduction to his edition of the oration (Paris: Les Belles Lettres, 1938).

82. "Fructum a me repetere prope suo iure debet" (1.1).

83. "Quod quasi deorum aliquo dono atque munere commendati nobis esse videantur [poetae]" (8.18). In a departure from the Greek tradition, poets themselves rather than poetry are the divine gift.

84. Carus fuit Africano superiori noster Ennius, itaque etiam in sepulcro Scipionum putatur is esse constitutus ex marmore; at iis laudibus certe non solum ipse, qui laudatur, sed etiam populi Romani nomen ornatur.

(9.22)

85. See on Petrarca in chapter 2.

86. "Ergo illum, qui haec fecerat, Rudinum hominem maiores nostri in civitatem receperunt; nos hunc Heracliensem multis civitatibus expetitum, in hac autem legibus constitutum, de nostra civitate eiciamus?" (10.22)

87. Of course, since Archias wrote in Greek, the "Roman literature" referred to here is of a particularly cosmopolitan sort. The greater universality of Greek constitutes another argument in the poet's favor ("quod Graeca leguntur in omnibus fere gentibus, Latina suis finibus, exiguis sane, continentur" [10.23]). The same argument would apply soon enough to Latin when its frontiers became less *exigui.*

88. Cicero probably used a lost literary source. That the other ancient versions, in Plutarch (*Life of Alexander* 15.8 [672c]) and Arrian (*Anabasis of Alexander* 1.12.1–5) contain details not found in Cicero's account suggests a tradition.

89. For a similar paradigmatic use of the pluperfect subjunctive, cf. Seneca, *Epistulae ad Lucilium* 21: "quis Idomenea nosset nisi Epicurus illum litteris suis incidisset?" (Text: ed. L. D. Reynolds, 2 vols. [Oxford: Oxford University Press, 1965], vol. 1.

90. Hauser, *The Social History of Art,* 1:117.

91. See Simone Weil, "L'*Iliade,* ou le poème de la force," in her *La source grecque* (Paris: Gallimard, 1953), 11–42.

92. Tenney Frank, *Roman Imperialism* (New York: Macmillan, 1929), 324.

93. For Cicero's personal ambitions with regard to Pompey, see the curious letter *Fam.* 5.7, written to the *imperator* in the same year as his defense of Archias. Cicero expresses the wish that he may play the proverbial friend Laelius to Pompey's Scipio.

94. "Iam me vobis, iudices, indicabo et de meo quodam amore gloriae nimis acri fortasse, verum tamen honesto, vobis confitebor" (11.28); "trahimur omnes studio laudis, et optimus quisque maxime gloria ducitur" (11.26).

95. Quas res nos in consulatu nostro vobiscum simul pro salute huius [urbis] atque imperi et pro vita civium proque universa re publica gessimus, attigit hic versibus atque inchoavit. (11.28)

96. *Ep. ad Atticum,* 1.16.15.

97. Theodor W. Adorno, *Minima Moralia,* trans. E. F. N. Jephcott (London: Verso, 1978), 190. The citation is from *Carmina* 3.1.1.

98. Curtius, *European Literature,* 66.

99. For examples of poetic topoi subsequently taken up by orators, see Theodore Burgess, "Epideictic Literature," *The University of Chicago Studies*

in Classical Philology 3 (1902): 115, 129, 146–47, 166–80; and Curtius, *European Literature,* 82.

100. *Carm.,* 3.30.13–14.

101. Eduard Fraenkel, *Horace* (Oxford: Oxford University Press, 1957), 30.

102. Ibid., 41

103. Ibid., 41.

104. On Augustan classicism as "chiusura sociale," or the exclusion of lower-class concerns such as daily reality, see Antonio La Penna, *Orazio e l'ideologia del principato* (Turin: Einaudi, 1963), 183–87.

105. *Carm.,* 4.9.7. For Alcaeus's oppositional poetry, see C. M. Bowra, *Greek Lyric Poetry from Alcman to Simonides* (Oxford: Oxford University Press, 1961), 135.

106. For an important analysis of the Roman odes, see La Penna, *Orazio,* 13–124.

107. Clifford Herschel Moore, ed., *Horace: The Odes, Epodes and Carmen Saeculare* (New York: American Book Co., 1902), 389.

108. All Horatian textual references are to his *Opera,* ed. D. R. Shackleton Bailey (Stuttgart: Teubner, 1985).

109. For the interplay of poet's and choral voice in Pindar, see Carne-Ross, *Pindar,* 19–21.

110. See Ronald Syme, *The Roman Revolution* (Oxford: Oxford University Press, 1962), 444.

111. *Ars poetica (Epistulae* 2.3), 391–99. Cf. *Carm.,* 1.12.7–12 for Orpheus's power, *Carm.,* 3.11.2 for Amphion's.

112. Cf. *Carm.,* 1.10, addressed to Mercury as god of verbal power, "qui feros cultus hominum recentum / voce formasti" (2–3).

113. The *Lex Julia de maritandis ordinibus* and the *Lex Julia de adulteriis* were both passed in 18 B.C. (see Syme, *The Roman Revolution,* 443). The *Ars poetica* belongs to about the same period.

114. "Sic honor et nomen divinis vatibus atque / carminibus venit" (*Ars poetica,* 400–1). See chapter 3, below, on poetic paleology.

115. See J. K. Newman, *The Concept of Vates in Augustan Poetry* (Brussels: Latomus, 1967); in particular (for *vates* in the *Ars poetica*), 75–81. Although *vates* does not occur in the *Carmen Saeculare,* it does conclude the ode that reads like a prelude to the longer poem (*Carm.* 4.6.44).

116. *Aeneid,* 1.7. For the image of the wall, central to Roman destiny in Virgil's epic, see also *Aeneid,* 1.259, 164. For the political nature of Amphion's performance, see Ernesto Grassi, *Rhetoric as Philosophy: The Humanist Tradition* (University Park: Penn State University Press, 1980), 75. Vico (*Scienza nuova,* sec. 81 and 734) interprets the stones moved by Amphion as *balordi plebei,* thus giving the poet a role in class conflict.

117. *Epistulae,* 2.1.124.

118. *Epistulae,* 2.1.126–38.

119. "Patronus si clienti fraudem fecerit, sacer esto," cited by La Penna, *Orazio,* 44. Cf. *Carm.,* 2.18.23–26.

120. For poetry as *opes,* see *Epistulae,* 1.3.16.

121. Acro: "Quam pretiosum sit carmen, ostendere, non quo pretium speraret"; Porphyrio: "Id est, ostendere, quam pretiosum munus carmen" (*Acronis et Porphyrionis commentarii in Q. Horatium Flaccum,* ed. F. Hauthal, 2 vols. [1864; reprint, Amsterdam: P. Schippers, 1966], 1:410–11).

122. Cf. Valerius Maximus 3.8.1; and chapter 2, below, on Petrarca's *Africa.*

123. See Pindar's use of *misthos* and *kerdos: Pythian* 11.41, *Nemean* 7.63, *Isthmian* 1.51.

124. Horace does use *divites insulas* again in *Epode* 16.42. It is also true that the adjective *fortunatus* itself can mean "wealthy."

125. Understanding *potens* as referring to *princeps* rather than to Daunus.

126. Cf. Janice M. Benario, "Book 4 of Horace's *Odes:* Augustan Propaganda," *Transactions and Proceedings of the American Philological Association* 91 (1960): 352: odes 7, 8, and 9 of book 4 "stress the stability of the immortality of poetry in the midst of a changing life, just as the Augustan regime brought an end to some of the unrest in the Roman world."

127. Cf. Vico's parallel between Pindar and Horace with regard to their position in a period of opulence in the development of Greece (Pindar "ne'tempi della virtù pomposa") and Rome (Horace "a' tempi più sfoggiosi") (*Scienza nuova*, sec. 909).

128. Cf. the understandably less influential Satire, 1.3.107–8: "nam fuit ante Helenam cunnus taeterrima belli / causa . . . "

129. For *illacrimabiles,* cf. the conclusion of Foscolo's sonnet "A Zacinto," cited above: "a noi prescrisse / il fato illacrimata sepoltura."

130. Cf. Sallust, *Catilina* 1.3 (ed. A. Kurfess [Leipzig: Teubner, 1954]), broadening the field to historical writing:

Atheniensium res gestae, sicuti ego aestumo, satis amplae magnificaeque fuere, verum aliquanto minores quam fama feruntur. Sed quia provenere ibi scriptorum magna ingenia, per terrarum orbem Atheniensium facta pro maxumis celebrantur. Ita eorum qui fecere virtus tanta habetur, quantum eam verbis potuere extollere praeclara ingenia.

And Pindar, *Nemean,* 7.20–21: "I imagine that the praise of Odysseus became greater than what he suffered, because of sweet-voiced Homer."

131. Velleius Paterculus, *Historia Romana,* 2.97 (text: ed. Karl Halm [Leipzig: Teubner, 1876]). Cf. Velleius, 11.102; Pliny, *Naturalis Historiae,* 9.35 (58); Tacitus, *Annales* 3.48; and Syme, *The Roman Revolution,* 428–29. Cf. *Carm.* 2.2.1–4 in praise of C. Sallustius Crispus, contradicted at least partially by Tacitus, *Annales,* 3.30.

132. Cf. *Carm.,* 3.16, where the poet condemns what is represented by the equivalent expressions *pretium, aurum, lucrum, munera, pecunia,* before assuring Maecenas: "nec, si plura velim, tu dare deneges" (38).

133. See Peter White, "*Amicitia* and the Profession of Poetry in Early Imperial Rome," *Journal of Roman Studies* 68 (1978): 74–92; Matthew Santirocco, "Poet and Patron in Ancient Rome," *Book Forum* 6 (1982): 57.

134. James Zetzel, "The Poetics of Patronage in the Late First Century B.C.," *Literary and Artistic Patronage in Ancient Rome,* ed. Barbara K. Gold (Austin: University of Texas Press, 1982), 101.

For the Roman tradition of clientage, see Vico, *Scienza nuova*, secs. 106, 260–63, 629, 1062, 1068; and particularly 556 on the common origin of *clientes* and *cluere*. As so often, Vico's etymological fantasy holds an element of truth.

135. White, "*Amicitia,*" 80.

136. Like Latin *hospes* and its Romance derivatives (*hôte, ospite, huésped,* etc.)

137. See, for example, *Pythian,* 4.22, 35, 129.

138. *Ep.,* 2.1. See in particular the repeated emphasis on *munus, donum*

and so on, in the last part of the poem as well as the use of *praeceptis ... amicis* in the passage cited earlier. Although P. White (*"Amicitia,"* 74) declines to consider imperial patronage in his analysis of *amicitia,* that special kind of patronage does appear to be an outside limit of the more general pattern.

139. *Carm.,* 1.26.1. Cf. as mentioned above the Greek expression for the poet, *Mouson therapon,* meaning someone who actually works for his superiors.

140. Only in *Carm.,* 3.13 and 3.25.

141. One exception: Douglas J. Stewart, "The Poet as Bird in Aristophanes and Horace," *Classical Journal* 62 (1967): 357–61.

142. See Herbert Musurillo, "The Poet's Apotheosis: Horace, *Odes* 1.1," *Transactions and Proceedings of the American Philological Association* 93 (1962): 230–39.

143. This contrasts with *Carm.* 2.17.2–3: "Nec dis amicum est nec mihi te prius / obire, Maecenas."

144. In Cicero's *Tusculanae Disputationes,* 1.15.34 and 1.49.117:

> Nemo me lacrumis decoret, ne funere fletu
> Faxit. cur? volito vivus per ora virum.

(See chapter 2, below.)

145. Maecenas is invoked at the beginning of each of Horace's collections: in the first ode, the first epode, the first satire, and the first epistle (see Zetzel, "The Poetics," 94).

146. See Kenneth J. Reckford, "Horace and Maecenas," *Transactions and Proceedings of the American Philological Association* 90 (1959): 204; Matthew Santirocco, *Unity and Design in Horace's* Odes (Chapel Hill: University of North Carolina Press, 1986), 154 ff.

147. Steele Commager, *The Odes of Horace: A Critical Study* (New Haven: Yale University Press, 1962), 315.

148. N. E. Collinge, *The Structure of Horace's Odes* (London: Oxford University Press, 1961), 69. Cf. Commager, *The Odes,* 314.

149. For the imagery, cf. Simonides, fr. 531 (*Lyrica Graeca Selecta,* ed. Page); and Pindar, *Pythian,* 6.10–14.

150. *Aeneid,* 9.446–9; *Tristia,* 3.7.50–52.

151. See Michael C. J. Putnam, "Horace C. 3.30: The Lyricist as Hero," *Ramus* 2 (1973): 10.

152. In contrast to Pindar's *thesauros* (*Pythian* 6.8), which is only a treasury.

153. As also in Propertius's boast (3.2.18), cited above in the introduction. Cf. Martial 1.1.

154. Hence, a richer meaning to "non omnis moriar." Cf. *Carm.,* 2.6.23–24 for the association between *favilla* and *vates.*

155. See G. W. F. Hegel, *Phänomenologie des Geistes* (Frankfurt: Suhrkamp, 1973), 508–9; *Vorlesungen über die Ästhetik,* 3 vols. (Frankfurt: Suhrkamp, 1970), 1:458–60, 2:290–96. Cf. J. Derrida, "Le puits et la pyramide: Introduction à la sémiologie de Hegel," *Marges de la philosophie* (Paris: Minuit, 1972), 79–127.

156. Cf. the invocation of Melpomene in a poem of mourning, Horace's *lugubris cantus* for Quintilius Varus (*Carm.,* 1.24.2–3).

157. *Metamorphoses* 15.871 ff. Text: ed. W. S. Anderson (Leipzig: Teubner, 1977).

158. In Horace, *non . . . non . . . aut,* and here a fourfold *nec.* There is also the shared adjective *edax* and the verb *exegi.* For *tempus edax,* cf. *Ex Ponto* 4.10.7. For the special sense of *exegi* in Horace's poem (which also exists in Ovid's), see Putnam, "Horace, C. 3.30," 2.

159. Cf. *Amores,* 1.15.42: "Vivam, parsque mei multa superstes erit" (*Amores, Medicamina faciei femineae, Ars amatoria, Remedia amoris,* ed. E. J. Kenney [Oxford: Oxford University Press, 1965]); *Tristia* 3.7.50: "me tamen extincto fama superstes erit" (*Tristia, Ibis, Ex Ponto, Halieutica,* ed. S. G. Owen [Oxford: Oxford University Press, 1915]); and Martial 10.2: "meliore tui parte superstes eris" (*Epigrammata,* ed. W. M. Lindsay [Oxford: Oxford University Press, 1929]).

160. What information exists, mostly from Ovid's own works (and thus to be used with extreme caution) is summarized and weighed by John C. Thibault, *The Mystery of Ovid's Exile* (Berkeley: University of California Press, 1964). According to Hermann Fränkel (*Ovid: A Poet Between Two Worlds* [Berkeley: University of California Press, 1945], 111–12) and others, the charge against Ovid was *maiestas,* or the crime of *lèse majesté.* Ironically, Ovid before exile named *maiestas* (here, majestic dignity) as something owed to poets and formerly given to them: "sanctaque maiestas et erat venerabile nomen / vatibus, et largae saepe dabantur opes" (*Ars amatoria* 3.407–8); after his banishment, he uses the term to refer to the honor of the gods, which is a product of poetry: "tantaque maiestas ore canentis eget" (*Ex Ponto* 4.8.56; see below).

161. *Tristia,* 1.1.72. For *fulmen* and *ira caeli* as divine punishment for vice, cf. *Metamorphoses,* 14.471.

162. *Carm.,* 1.12.59–60: "tu parum castis inimica mittes / fulmina lucis"; *Carm.,* 1.34 (where the identification with Augustus remains only implicit).

163. *Tristia,* 2.207.

164. See the apposition in this poem of *crimina* with *carmen* (207), with *damnatas . . . Musas* (3), with *libros* (61).

165. *Tristia,* 4.9.12. Ovid claims that he was condemned not as *exul* but as *relegatus,* meaning someone banished without loss of property or civil rights (*Tristia,* 5.2.57 ff. and 5.11). The terminology fluctuates, however, as elsewhere the poet refers to himself as *exul* and his situation as *exilium* (for example, *Ex Ponto,* 1.1.61 and 65).

166. *Tristia,* 3.14.46, 5.5.6, 5.12.57. The complaint of the threat posed to Latin by barbarian tongues turns up again in the exiled Seneca (*Consolatio ad Polybium* 18). However, Ovid also claims to have written a poem, in "Gothic" (*Getico sermone*), in praise of Augustus and his family (*Ex Ponto,* 4.13.17–23).

167. *Tristia,* 4.1.43–48.

168. Ibid., 4.10.117–18 and 5.1.33--34. Cf. *Tristia,* 4.1.17–18 for an interpretation of Orpheus's song as self-consolation in his bereavement.

169. Ibid., 4.10.119–20.

170. Ibid., 4.10.129–30.

171. *Ex Ponto,* 4.16.2–3. The poet also directs the topos to his faithful wife (*Tristia,* 5.14.5–6: "dumque legar, mecum pariter tua fama legetur, / nec potes in maestos omnis abire rogos"). Cf. *Ex Ponto,* 3.2.31–32: "corpora debentur maestis exsanguia bustis: / effugiunt structos nomen honorque rogos."

172. *Amores,* 1.15.7–8. For analogies between *Tristia,* 4.10, *Amores,* 1.15 and Propertius, 4.1 concerning the conflict between *labor* and *otium,* see B. R. Fredericks, "*Tristia* 4.10: Poet's Autobiography and Poetic Autobiography," *Transactions of the American Philological Association* 106 (1976): 148.

173. *Amores,* 1.15.33.

174. *Tristia,* 3.7.47–48.

175. Nec tibi de Pario statuam, Germanice, templum
    marmore: carpsit opes illa ruina meas.
 templa domus facient vobis urbesque beatae.
 Naso suis opibus, carmine gratus erit.

(Ex Ponto, 4.8.31–34)

Parenthetical line references are to this poem.

176. For the superiority of the poetic gift, cf. *Tristia,* 5.14.13–14: "perpetui fructum donavi nominis idque, / quo dare nil potui munere maius, habes."

177. Throughout the poems of exile, Ovid refers very often to Augustus as Jupiter or *numen;* for example, *Tristia,* 3.8.13, 3.11.62, 4.3.69, 4.4.20, 4.8.50, 4.9.14, 5.2.45–46, 5.3.46, 5.4.17, 5.10.52, 5.11.20; *Ex Ponto,* 1.2.126, 1.4.44, 1.7.50, 1.10.42, 2.1.47, 2.2.41 and 109, 3.1.97 and 163, 4.6.10, 4.9.108 and 133, 4.13.26. For these poems as the culmination of "an Augustan poetic mystique of ruler worship," see Gordon Williams, *Change and Decline: Roman Literature in the Early Empire* (Berkeley: University of California Press, 1978), 97.

178. Like *pretium,* the use of the necessarily polyvalent word *res* here defies translation: It combines the economic senses of "wealth," "business matter," with legal "case" and literary "subject matter" under the broader and vaguer term I have chosen to render it.

179. Notice again, as in the *legar* of *Metamorphoses,* 15.878, the emphasis on written culture in *scripta.*

180. See *Ex Ponto,* 2.2.116 ("qui fulmineo saepe sine igne tonat"), suggesting a situation akin to that of Vico's primitive giants (*Scienza nuova,* sec. 379), grateful to the celestial power which has frightened without destroying them.

181. See *Ex Ponto,* 2.1.

182. See *Tristia,* 3.3.77–78 ("maiora libelli / et diuturna magis sunt monimenta mihi"), where he also (81–82) requests posthumous tribute (*feralia munera*) at his grave. We are encouraged to see behind *expers sepulcri* (*Ex Ponto,* 4.8.47) the opposite, *expertus sepulcri;* both equally true of Ovidian poetry.

183. Insofar as one period or individual can represent that gradual process. See earlier on Horace.

CHAPTER 2. PETRARCA

Wallace Stevens, "To an Old Philosopher in Rome" (*The Collected Poems of Wallace Stevens* [New York: Knopf, 1978], 508).

1. Cf. Quinones, *The Renaissance Discovery of Time,* 106: "Time is directly and explicitly active as one of the great forces behind most, if not all, of his interests," although Quinones pursues the analysis of that force differently from me.

2. Cited by Cassirer, *The Philosophy of Symbolic Forms,* 2:111, referring to the present of magic.

3. Francesco Petrarca, *Le Familiari,* ed. Vittorio Rossi and Umberto Bosco, 4 vols. (Florence: Sansoni, 1933–42).

4. For Petrarca's literary friendship with those long dead, see *Fam.,* 15.3, and Adelia Noferi, *L'esperienza poetica del Petrarca* (Florence: Le Monnier, 1962), 99–100. On his friendship with Cicero, see Maristella Lorch, "Petrarch,

Cicero, and the Classical Pagan Tradition," in *Renaissance Humanism: Foundations, Forms, and Legacy,* ed. Albert Rabil, Jr., 3 vols. (Philadelphia: University of Pennsylvania Press, 1988), 1:71–94.

Cf. his repeated invocation of each of a series of great Roman heroes in *Fam.,* 23.1: "Utinam viveres, tecum loquerer." Which desire will become an ideal of humanistic pedagogy; cf. Ermolao Barbaro's *prolusione* to his course in Padua on Aristotle: "ut cum ipso vivo et praesente loqui videamur" (cited in Eugenio Garin, *L'umanesimo italiano* [Rome: Laterza, 1990], 21).

5. Cf. *De remediis utriusque fortunae,* 1.44 (*Opera,* 3 vols. [1554; reprint, Ridgewood, N.J.: Gregg Press, 1965], 1:57): writing is excusable "si ut obliviscaris temporum praeteritique memoria praesens taedium effugias."

6. Enrico Carrara, "L'Epistola 'Posteritati'," *Studi petrarcheschi ed altri scritti* (Turin: Bottega d'Erasmo, 1959), 52 ff.

7. Francesco Petrarca, *Prose,* ed. G. Martellotti, P. G. Ricci, E. Carrara, E. Bianchi (Milan: Ricciardi, 1955), 2. Cf. *Fam.,* 23.18.4, also referring to posterity, "ad quos nescio an vestigium aliquod mei nominis sit venturum."

8. For this symmetrical relation, cf. *De vita solitaria,* 1.6 (*Opere latine,* ed. Antonietta Bufano, 2 vols. [Turin: UTET, 1975], 1:334): "Legere quod scripserunt primi, scribere quod legant ultimi, et beneficii literarum a maioribus accepti, qua in illos non possumus, in posteros saltem gratum ac memorem animum habere...", *Fam.,* 15.3.11 ("preteritorum memor ventura delibero"); and *Fam.,* 19.3.13, where Petrarca recommends that the Emperor Charles earn inclusion in *De viris illustribus,* "ut cum veteres legeris, tu legaris a posteris."

9. *Fam.,* 24.6.

10. "Incubui unice, inter multa, ad notitiam vetustatis, quoniam michi semper etas ista displicuit" (*Ep. posteritati,* in *Prose,* 2). *Triumphus Cupidinis* (1.17) refers to "lo secol noioso in ch' i' mi trovo." "Hic sum, et mallem etate qualibet natus esse" (*De vita solitaria,* 1.8). And, more radically: "sic in rebus humanis, semper odiosius quod est. quando et praeteritum quoque dum aderat odiosum fuit, futurumque cum venerit odiosum erit. sola rerum vel memoria vel expectatio dulcis est" (*Seniles,* 3.9 [*Opera,* 2:863]). Cf. the famous passage in *Rerum memorandarum libri* (1.19) on Petrarca's position in time between two peoples.

11. "Ita enim ferme quisque loquitur, ut impellit non veritas sed voluptas" (*Prose,* 2).

12. Petrarca, *De viris illustribus,* ed. Guido Martellotti (Florence: Sansoni, 1964). Cf. *Sen.* 16.4 (*Opera,* 2:1055) on the (literary) presence of absent friends in memory: "Neque tantum eos qui procul absunt, sed eos quoque, qui penitus abierunt, iamque exiguum in cinerem versi sunt, vos adestis, vivunt illi."

13. B. Zumbini, "L'Africa," *Studi sul Petrarca* (Florence: Le Monnier, 1895), 158–59.

14. At least since Landino in the late fifteenth century. See Cristoforo Landino, *Scritti critici e teorici,* ed. Roberto Cardini, 2 vols. (Rome: Bulzoni, 1974), 1:xxviii.

15. "He says not what wells up from within him, but what can be rendered in such a form or according to such a model" (Francesco De Sanctis, *Storia della letteratura italiana,* 2 vols. [Bari: Laterza, 1949], 1:262). Cf. 1:358; and De Sanctis, *Saggio critico sul Petrarca,* ed. Ettore Bonora (Milan: Marzorati, 1971), 61–62: "E impossibile scrivere letterariamente in una lingua morta"... "Le parole latine giacciono senz'anima." Cf. also Eduard Norden, *Die antike*

Kunstprosa, 2 vols. (Stuttgart: Teubner, 1958), 2:773: "Durch den Human-
ismus die lateinische Sprache zu Grabe getragen wurde" (although he praises
Petrarca's Latin style).

16. "It became a sort of sacred language, sacred in a secular or laic sense,
surrounded by love and reverence" (Benedetto Croce, "La poesia latina," *Poesia
popolare e poesia d'arte: Studi sulla poesia italiana dal Tre al Cinquecento*
[Bari: Laterza, 1933], 443). Cf. A. Carlini, *Studio su "L'Africa" di Francesco
Petrarca* (Florence: Le Monnier, 1902), 191: Latin was "come dice il Settem-
brini, la voce de' padri che dal sepolcro chiamava i contemporanei a grandi
imprese."

17. See Cassirer, *The Philosophy of Symbolic Forms,* 2:104–40.

18. Cassirer, *The Philosophy of Symbolic Forms,* 2:111. Cf. his *An Essay
on Man* (New Haven: Yale University Press, 1944), 83; Eliade, *Le Sacré et le
profane,* 60–98 ("*le Temps sacré est par sa nature réversible*" [60; emphasis
in original]); Eliade, *Aspects du mythe* (Paris: Gallimard, 1963), 98–118.

19. Cassirer, *The Philosophy of Symbolic Forms,* 2:105. Blumenberg
(*Work on Myth,* 160), however, disagrees, properly emphasizing the importance
of what happens to myths.

20. See, for example, Eliade, *Aspects du mythe,* 28: "En effet, connaître
l'origine d'un objet, d'un animal, d'une plante, etc., équivaut à acquérir sur eux
un pouvoir magique"; and 35–55 (chap. 2: "Prestige magique des «origines»").

21. Cassirer, *The Philosophy of Symbolic Forms,* 2:119: "In the concrete
mythical-religious consciousness of time there always lives a specific dynamic
of feeling—a varying intensity with which the I devotes itself to the present,
past, or future and so places them in a definite relation of affinity to or dependence on one another." Cf. Lévy-Bruhl, *La Mentalité primitive,* 89–91.

22. Cassirer, *The Philosophy of Symbolic Forms,* 2:45.

23. On the date, see E. H. Wilkins, "The Coronation of Petrarch," *The Making of the "Canzoniere" and other Petrarchan Studies* (Rome: Edizioni di
storia e letteratura, 1951), 9–69. For some doubts about the traditional identification of the coronation with Easter Sunday (8 April), see Carlo Godi, "La
'Collatio laureationis' del Petrarca," *Italia medioevale e umanistica* 13
(1970): 1–7.

24. Likewise his inspiration for the *Africa* (see *Ep. Posteritati* [*Prose,* 12])
and the setting of the *Trionfi* (see *Triumphus Cupidinis* 1.1–6). On Laura and
the laurel, see, for example, Aldo S. Bernardo, *Petrarch, Scipio and the "Africa": The Birth of Humanism's Dream* (Baltimore: Johns Hopkins University
Press, 1962) 47–71; Gordon Braden, "Love and Fame: The Petrarchan Career,"
Pragmatism's Freud: The Moral Disposition of Psychoanalysis, ed. Joseph H.
Smith and William Kerrigan (Baltimore: Johns Hopkins University Press,
1986), 126–58; and Sara Sturm-Maddox, *Petrarch's Laurels* (University Park:
Penn State University Press, 1992), passim. For the promise of victory over
time common to Laura and laurel, see Quinones, *The Renaissance Discovery
of Time,* 123.

25. See generally, J. B. Trapp, "The Poet Laureate: Rome, *Renovatio* and
Translatio Imperii" and Janet Smarr, "Petrarch: A Vergil Without a Rome,"
both in *Rome in the Renaissance: The City and the Myth,* ed. P. A. Ramsey
(Binghamton, N.Y.: Medieval & Renaissance Texts & Studies, 1982), 93–130
and 133–40.

26. See Wilkins, "The Coronation of Petrarch," drawing mainly on the poet's
correspondence.

27. Wilkins, "The Coronation of Petrarch," 56; Wilkins, *Life of Petrarch* (Chicago: University of Chicago Press, 1961), 28.

28. This oration is one of the few works that Petrarca did not later revise (see Hans Baron, *From Petrarch to Leonardo Bruni: Studies in Humanistic and Political Literature* [Chicago: University of Chicago Press, 1968], 15).

29. Text of *Privilegium* in Petrarca, *Opera* (1554), 3:1254–56. (There is now an edition of the *Privilegium,* which I have not been able to consult, by D. Mertens in *Litterae Medii Aevi. Festschrift für Johannes Autenrieth . . . ,* ed. M. Borgolte and H. Spilling [Sigmaringen: J. Thorbecke, 1988].) Text of *Collatio* in Godi, 13–27 (references here by section number).

30. *Opera,* 3:1256. One is reminded of the popular approval that bestowed citizenship on Theophanes of Mytilene, described in *Pro Archia,* 10.24.

31. The present subject is poets and historians, "quorum industria ac labore tam sibi ipsis, quam aliis claris viris, quos dignabantur nobilitare carminibus nominis immortalitas querabatur" (1254).

32. The expression recurs in the *Collatio* (section 11), where Petrarca dwells at greater length on the significance of the laurel. On the laurel's immunity to lightning, cf. Columella, *De re rustica,* 8.5.12; Pliny, *Naturalis Historia,* 2.56.146; Isidore, *Etymologiae,* 17.7.2; Servius on *Aeneid,* 1.394; Suetonius, *De vita Caesarum,* 3.69, who reports that Tiberius used to wear a laurel crown in stormy weather; and *Canzoniere,* 29.48. But cf. also the end of the following chapter.

33. Such a claim neglects Albertino Mussato's coronation in Padua in 1315, albeit with ivy and myrtle rather than with laurel (see Giorgio Petrocchi, "Cultura e poesia del Trecento," in *Storia della letteratura italiana,* ed. Emilio Cecchi and Natalino Sapegno, vol. 2, *Il Trecento* [Milan: Garzanti, 1987], 580), and although Mussato's coronation was apparently an academic affair (see Werner Suerbaum, "Poeta laureatus et triumphans: Die Dichterkrönung Petrarcas und sein Ennius-Bild," *Poetica* 5 (1972): 297). For other examples of poetic coronation, see Trapp, 97 ff.

34. *Pro Archia* 8.18. Petrarca ends his citation with an omission of the elements (*quasi, aliquo*) that attenuate the representation of poetry as a divine gift: the Ciceronian "quod quasi deorum aliquo dono atque munere commendati nobis esse videantur [poetae]" becomes Petrarca's "quod deorum munere nobis commendati esse videantur" (2). The future laureate discovered Cicero's oration in 1333.

35. The present is contrasted with a past, Augustan Rome, for example, where poets received their due: "Fuit enim quoddam tempus, fuit etas quedam felicior poetis quando in honore maximo habebantur" (4). Juvenal is cited: "Tunc par ingenio pretium" (*Satire* 7.96) (4). For an account of mountain climbing (in particular, the ascent of Mt. Ventoux) as the pursuit of literary glory, see Lyell Asher, "Petrarch at the Peak of Fame," *PMLA* 108 (1993): 1050–63.

36. "ex tribus quoque radicibus exoritur [affectus iste animi], quarum prima est honor rei publice, secunda decor proprie glorie, tertia calcar aliene industrie" (5).

37. *Aeneid,* 6.823. *Inmensa cupido:* see Giovanni Gentile, "La Filosofia del Petrarca," *Studi sul Rinascimento* (Florence: Sansoni, 1936), 9 ("La gloria infatti fu forse il suo ideale più sinceramente e profondamente coltivato e servito"); Georg Voigt, *Il Risorgimento dell'antichità classica, ovvero il primo secolo dell' umanesimo,* trans. D. Valbusa, 2 vols. (Florence: Sansoni, 1888–

1890), 1:124, on Petrarca's "sete morbosa ed inestinguibile di gloria." In a manuscript of Cicero, Petrarca annotated every mention of glory (see Giuseppe Billanovich, "Petrarca e Cicerone," *Miscellanea Giovanni Mercati,* 6 vols. [Città del Vaticano: Biblioteca Apostolica Vaticana, 1946], 4:91).

38. *Metamorphoses,* 15.871–72, *Thebaid,* 12.810–12 and 10.445–46, *Aeneid,* 9.446–49, *Bellum civile,* 9.985–86.

39. *Carm.,* 4.9.25–28.

40. Claudian, *De consulatu Stilichonis* 3, praef. 5–6.

41. See Godi's notes (section 11) for references to many of the ancient and medieval sources and analogues for the laurel's properties.

42. *Canzoniere,* 161. Cf. *Ep. met.,* 2.10: "Sunt laurea certa Poëtis / Caesaribusque simul parque est ea gloria utrisque" (*Opera,* 3:1350); *Fam.,* 12.15; and Statius, *Achilleid,* 1.15–16 (referring to the Emperor Domitian): "cui geminae florent vatumque ducumque / certatim laurus," which Petrarca cites here (*Collatio* 11).

43. See in particular *Collatio,* sec. 9; cf. below on book 9 of the *Africa.*

44. *Prose,* 16.

45. Wilkins, "The Coronation of Petrarch," 68–69.

46. See *Fam.,* 4.6. In *Bucolicum Carmen* 10, entitled *Laurea occidens,* the poet portrays himself as obtaining the laurel crown, aided by "Argus" (King Robert) (372 ff.).

47. Carlini, *Studio su "L'Africa,"* 52. Pietro Fedele has called the *Privilegium laureae* "l'atto di nascita dell'Umanesimo" (cited by Carlo Calcaterra, "Sub lauro mea," *Nella selva del Petrarca* [Bologna: Licinio Cappelli, 1942], 104).

48. *Secretum,* 3 (*Prose,* 158).

49. Anonimo Romano, *Cronica. Vita di Cola di Rienzo,* ed. Ettore Mazzali (Milan: Rizzoli, 1991), 190: "Tutta dìe se speculava nelli intagli de marmo li quali iaccio intorno a Roma. Non era aitri che esso, che sapessi leiere li antiqui pataffii." Cf. Ugo Dotti, *Vita di Petrarca* (Bari: Laterza, 1987), 109.

50. Anonimo Romano, *Cronica,* 217: "Tutta Roma staieva leta, rideva, pareva tornare alli anni megliori passati." Cf. Giovanni Villani on Cola: "Volea riformare tutta Italia all'ubedienza di Roma al modo antico" (cited by Denys Hay, *The Italian Renaissance in its Historical Background* [Cambridge: Cambridge University Press, 1968], 97).

51. *Sine nomine,* 4 (text in Paul Piur, *Petrarcas 'Buch ohne Namen' und die päpstliche Kurie* [Halle: Max Niemeyer, 1925], 183): "Ad aurei seculi initium via est." Cf. *Fam.,* 18.1; and *Invectiva contra eum qui maledixit Italie* (*Opere latine,* 2:1170–72).

52. *Fam.,* 11.17.1. Cf. the conclusion of the *Hortatoria* to Cola (*Ep. variae* 48, in Petrarca, *Lettere disperse: Varie e miscellanee,* ed. Alessandro Pancheri [Parma: Fondazione Pietro Bembo-U. Guanda, 1994], 74–76).

53. *Fam.,* 7.7.6. Cf. Smarr in *Rome in the Renaissance,* 134.

54. *Sine nomine,* 7 (Piur, 191).

55. *Fam.,* 13.6.22 ff. Petrarca thus blocks a tendency sketched in his writings to and about Cola; namely, the tendency to make the relationship between poet and "patron" reversible, as when the poet represents the latter as a poet and himself as a man of action (cf. Petrarca's abortive trip to Italy during the Tribune's crisis).

56. See Vico, *Scienza nuova,* sec. 699, 786, 819. Nicholas Mann (*Petrarch*

[Oxford: Oxford University Press, 1984], 36) has noted the resemblance of Cola to Mussolini.

57. *Hortatoria* (*Lettere disperse,* 42); *Fam.,* 11.16.9; *Fam.,* 11.17.3. Cf. *Africa,* 2.305–7.

58. *Fam.,* 13.6.

59. See E. H. Wilkins, *Petrarch's Eight Years in Milan* (Cambridge, Mass.: The Medieval Academy of America, 1958), 3–15; and generally Francesco Novati, *Il Petrarca ed i Visconti* (Milan: Cogliati, 1904).

60. See Novati, 16 ff.; Wilkins, *Petrarch's Eight Years,* 10.

61. Giovanni Boccaccio, *Opere in versi, Corbaccio, Trattatello in laude di Dante, Prose latine, Epistole,* ed. Pier Giorgio Ricci (Milan: Ricciardi, 1965), 1100–10.

62. *Fam.,* 16.12. Cf. Petrarca's explanation of why the Pope (Gregory XI) has summoned him: "ut mei praesentia suam curiam honestet" (*Sen.,* 15.2 [*Opera,* 2:1031]).

63. *Fam.,* 16.11

64. Cf. Ugo Dotti, *Petrarca a Milano* (Milan: Ceschina, 1972), 62–63. (This volume also includes the relevant documents.)

65. Petrarca's language shows the influence of Seneca's *Epistula 1 ad Lucilium;* cf. *De brevitate vitae* by the same.

66. *Invectiva* . . . , in *Prose,* 700, as well as *Opere latine,* 2:1012 (like all passages cited here).

67. Although that is the sense of another self-defense in *Sen.,* 6.2 (written after Petrarca's departure from Milan).

68. *Fam.,* 7.15 and *Ep. met.,* 3.6 (in *Rime, Trionfi e poesie latine*). *Ep. met.,* 2.11, although its heading gives Luchino Visconti's name and it has a subject similar to 3.6, was sent not to him but to Giovanni da Parma (see E. H. Wilkins, *The "Epistolae Metricae" of Petrarch* [Rome: Edizioni di storia e letteratura, 1956], 20, following Arnaldo Foresti, *Annedoti della vita di Francesco Petrarca*).

69. *Ep. met.,* 3.6.27 (*Aeneid,* 6.853).

70. "Et nimirum quis est hominum, nisi sit idem prorsus agresti duritie, qui etsi non valde literis delectetur, clarum saltem non cupiat nomen, quod profecto, sicut sine virtute non queritur, sic sine literis non servatur?" (*Fam.,* 7.15.10)

71. Wilkins, *The "Epistolae metricae" of Petrarch,* 29–30. The first letter replies to an attack made in the name of Petrarca's friend Lancilotto Anguissola. Some time afterward the poet discovered the true identity of his opponent (although he had already suspected the fraudulent use of his friend's name), and the second letter reflects that knowledge.

72. Cf. *De sui ipsius et multorum ignorantia,* near end (*Opere latine,* 2:1148).

73. See *Sen.,* 15.14 (*Opera,* 2:1043): "Soleo enim eorum contra quos loquar nominibus abstinere, ne vel famae, vel infamiae illis sim." Cf. Arnaud Tripet. *Pétrarque ou la connaissance de soi* (Geneva: Droz, 1967), 52 ff., 130.

74. See *Invectiva contra quendam magni status hominem* (*Opere latine,* 2:1018).

75. I cite *Ep. met.,* 2.10 from *Opera* 3:1350–52, although with orthographical changes (*ae* to *e, mihi* and *nihil* to *michi* and *nichil,* etc.), according to the principles of the Edizione nazionale, and occasionally modified punctua-

tion. Giorgio Ronconi analyzes this poem in his *Le origini delle dispute umanistiche sulla poesia* (*Mussato e Petrarca*) (Rome: Bulzoni, 1976), 65–82.

76. "Sunt laurea certa Poëtis / Cesaribusque simul parque est ea gloria utrisque" (20–21).

77.   Decuitne per urbes
Circumferre nova viridantia tempora fronde?
Testarique greges hominum populique favorem
Infami captare via? laudarier olim
A paucis propositum. (41–45)

78. Cf. Thomas M. Greene, *The Light in Troy: Imitation and Discovery in Renaissance Poetry* (New Haven: Yale University Press, 1982), 101: "Petrarch grew up without strong attachments [to class, place, community] . . . , without a ceremonial identity, and his bookish genius transformed a dislocation in space into a dislocation in time."

79. Line 175 in *Opera* reads "Et memorum secreta placent" that might permit an interesting interpretation, but I have followed Ronconi (74) in preferring the *facilior lectio*. These lines owe something to Horace, *Epistulae*, 2.2.77–80.

80. To the general assertion of poetic service, Petrarca adds concrete examples: the primordial mythical poets (Orpheus, Amphion, Linus, and Musaeus [230–31]), and the near-mythical figure of Homer. (He has already introduced the theme of *poetae-theologi* from Aristotle [*Metaphysics*, 1.3.6 (983 b)]: "Nonne Deum primos olim quesisse Poëtas / Inquit Aristoteles?" [188–89].) Petrarca praises Homer's *copia*, and marvels, as he does also in the *Africa* (9.200–2), that a blind man should have such creative power (235 ff.).

81. Although Petrarca wrote the separate parts of the *Invective contra medicum* during his last two years in Provence (1352–1353), he unified, published, and revised the work during his Milanese years (see *Prose*, 1172).

82. *Invective contra medicum* 4 (*Opere latine*, 2:972); *Invectiva contra quendam* . . . (*Opere latine*, 2:1018).

83. For a contrary opinion, however, see Calcaterra, "Sub lauro mea."

84. Wilkins, "The Coronation of Petrarch," 29–35.

85. *Prose*, 12–16.

86. Pier Paolo Vergerio in his *Vita* of Petrarca says that the poet was crowned for the *Africa*, Eclogues and *De vita solitaria*. But this is impossible, since the latter two works were begun in 1346. See Carlini, *Studio sull' "L'Africa,"* 51, and Wilkins, *Life of Petrarch*, 54, 57.

87. These are by no means the only contemporary texts in praise of the *Africa* or that encourage its publication. See Petrarca, *L'Africa*, ed. Nicola Festa (Florence: Sansoni, 1926), xxxv ff.; Arnaldo Foresti, *Aneddoti della vita di Francesco Petrarca* (Padua: Antenore, 1977), 466 ff.; also Giuseppe Piazza, *Il poema dell'umanesimo: Studio critico sull'"Africa" di Francesco Petrarca* (Rome: La vita letteraria, 1906), 21, who mentions a certain Domenico di Silvestro "che scrive in versi che se l'*Africa* dev'esser pubblicata dopo la morte del Poeta, muoia pure subito il Petrarca!"

88. *Seniles*, 2.1.

89. Coluccio Salutati, *Epistolario*, ed. Francesco Novati, 4 vols. (Rome: Forzani, 1891–1905), 1:229–41. Parenthetical references are to page and line (line numbering is not cumulative, but begins again with each page).

90. Giovanni Boccaccio, *Opere latine minori*, ed. Aldo Francesco Massèra (Bari: Laterza, 1928), 100–5. Parenthetical line references are to this edition.

The attribution to Boccaccio has been questioned by Corradini in his edition of the *Africa* (Padua, 1874), 97–98, and Festa in his edition, xlii–xliii. For Boccaccio's acquaintance with the epic, see Festa's edition, xxxix.

91. Salutati, *Metra* . . . , 240.14: "Sola tibi clarum quod prebuit Africa nomen"; 240.25: "Eternum tibi sola dabit tamen Africa nomen." Cf. his *Epistolario*, 2.8 (vol. 1, pp. 72 ff.), a letter of 1369 to Petrarca; Boccaccio, *Versus* . . . 39–40, cited below. And cf. the letter (of 1396) from Pasquino Capelli, chancellor of Giangaleazzo Visconti, to Petrarca's son-in-law Francescuolo da Brossano about the recent edition of the *Africa*, "cuius maxime gracia et poeticam lauream meruit et in eternum mansurum est poete nomen merito consecutum" (cited in Vincenzo Fera, *Antichi editori e lettori dell'*Africa [Messina: Centro di studi umanistici, 1984], 87).

92. In *Sen.*, 13.3, Petrarca himself mentions the ancient debate over Homer's birthplace while referring to his own birth in Arezzo.

93. Cf. Boccaccio's *De vita et moribus domini Francisci Petracchi de Florentia*, where the crowning of Petrarca is explicitly the cause of a return to the golden age: "puto . . . felicia tempora ac regna saturnia rediisse" (*Opere latine minori*, 241). Here, too, the *Africa* is declared Petrarca's principal work (243).

94. *Epistolario* 4.5 (vol. 1, p. 251). Cf. 7.11 (vol. 2, pp. 289 ff.) and 8.7 (vol. 2, p. 392).

95. For Petrarca the celebrator of Scipio as successor to Homer the celebrator of Achilles and Virgil the celebrator of Aeneas, see Boccaccio, *Genealogie deorum gentilium* 6.53.

96. For the date of the first edition, see Fera, *Antichi editori e lettori* . . . , 86.

97. Carlini, *Studio sull' "Africa"*, 28.

98. Niccoli speaks in Leonardo Bruni's *Dialogus ad Petrum Paulum Histrum* (1401), followed by this passage: "Vide quantum inter hunc (sc. Petrarca) et Maronem nostrum intersit: ille homines obscuros carmine suo illustravit; hic Africanum, hominem clarissimum, quantum in se fuit, obscuravit" (*Prosatori latini del Quattrocento*, ed. Eugenio Garin [Milan: Ricciardi, 1952], 72). Cf. Antonio Beccadelli's letter of 1428 to Cambio Zambeccari, where Beccadelli both recognizes the power of the *Africa* to perpetuate King Robert's name and issues a harsh judgment on Petrarca the poet: "Quis Robertum regem cognosceret, nisi et a Petrarcha nescio quo non quidem poeta sed poetarum simia versibus celebratus sit . . . ?" (L. Barozzi and Remigio Sabbadini, *Studi sul Panormita e sul Valla* [Florence: Le Monnier, 1891], 36). Other fifteenth-century writers who recognize King Robert's debt to Petrarca include Poggio Bracciolini in his *De avaricia* (*Prosatori latini del Quattrocento*, 268), and Flavio Biondo in his *Italia Illustrata* (see Jacob Burckhardt, *The Civilization of the Renaissance in Italy*, trans. S. G. C. Middlemore, 2 vols. [New York: Harper & Rowe, 1958], 1:152 n.

Petrarca's early biographer Sicco Polenton (1437) admits the prevalent stylistic objection (*Scriptorum illustrium latinae linguae libri XVIII*, ed. B. L. Ullman [Rome: American Academy in Rome, 1928], 139): "Gratus tamen illorum gustui non solet esse qui sunt adeo delicati ut nihil omni parte non perfectum laudent."

99. See, for example, Antonio Enzo Quaglio, *Francesco Petrarca* (Milan: Garzanti, 1967), 82.

100. For the "passionate inception," at Vaucluse in 1338 or 1339, see *Fam.*, 8.3.11: "*Africam* meam cepi, tanto impetu tantoque nisu animi, ut nunc limam

per eadem referens vestigia, ipse meam audaciam et magna operis fundamenta quodammodo perhorrescam." For the other period of intensive work, at Selvapiana in 1341, see *Posteritati* (*Prose*, 16): "Ad intermissam *Africam* stilum verti, et fervore animi ... excitato, ... tanto ardore opus illud non magno in tempore ad exitum deduxi, ut ipse quoque nunc stupeam."

101. Edward Gibbon, *The History of the Decline and Fall of the Roman Empire*, 3 vols. (New York: Modern Library, n.d.), 3:823. Cf. Henri de Ziegler's defense of the poem: "Elle ne fut pas le rêve d'un cuistre" (*Pétrarque* [Neuchâtel: La Baconnière, n.d. (1940?)], 70).

102. For a study of the *Africa* as an epideictic poem, from a different point of view (the influence of the *Aeneid* and the praise of virtue), see Craig Kallendorf, *In Praise of Aeneas: Virgil and Epideictic Rhetoric in the Early Italian Renaissance* (Hanover, N.H.: University Press of New England, 1989), 19–57.

103. Petrarca possessed a manuscript of Homer in Greek, but knew him in translation: "Virum michi pande" (Pierre de Nolhac, *Pétrarque et l'humanisme*, 2 vols. [Paris: Champion, 1907], 1:103, 2:156 ff.).

104. All citations of the poem are from Francesco Petrarca, *L'Africa*, ed. Nicola Festa (Florence: Sansoni, 1926). This edition is not wholly satisfactory. See the following important critiques: Adolfo Gandiglio, in *Giornale storico della letteratura italiana* 90 (1927): 289–308; Eduard Fraenkel, in *Gnomon* 3 (1927): 485–94; Giuseppe Billanovich, *Petrarca letterato*: 1. *Lo Scrittoio del Petrarca* (Rome: Edizioni di Storia e letteratura, 1947) 365 n. This last concludes: "L'edizione dell'*Africa* è da rifare, o piuttosto da fare." Vincenzo Fera is currently preparing a new edition, which is eagerly awaited.

105. Apart from the special case of the late *De gestis Cesaris*.

106. The subtitle of Aldo Bernardo's *Petrarch, Scipio and the "Africa"* (Baltimore: Johns Hopkins University Press, 1962), still the best book on the subject.

107. *Et michi* may owe something to Statius, *Achilleid* 1.3–4, which refers to Homer's previous poetic treatment of Achilles (see Giuseppe Velli, "Il proemio dell'*Africa*," *Petrarca e Boccaccio: Tradizione Memoria Scrittura* [Padua: Antenore, 1979], 47).

108. *Fam.*, 10.4.20.

109. Francesco Petrarca, *Rime, Trionfi e Poesie latine*, ed. F. Neri, G. Martellotti, E. Bianchi, N. Sapegno (Milan: Ricciardi, 1951), 816.

110. *Familiares*, 10.4.34: "Et Ennium de eo multa scripsisse non sit dubium 'rudi et impolito' ut Valerius ait, 'stilo', cultior tamen de illius rebus liber metricus non apparet." The Valerius referred to is Valerius Maximus, *Factorum et dictorum memorabilium libri* 8.14.1. Petrarca did not know Silius Italicus's *Punica*.

111. For the uniqueness of this privilege, see 1.438–41; 2.2–3.

112. The virtuous nature of Roman conquest becomes particularly clear in book 7, with the confrontation between Scipio and Hannibal (178–448) and the celestial debate, judged by God, of figures representing Carthage and Rome (506–728).

For a more systematic moral interpretation of the poem, see Richard Seagraves, "The Moral Virtues and Petrarch's 'Africa,'" *Acta Conventus Neo-Latini Turonensis*, 2 vols. (Paris: J. Vrin, 1980), 1:93–107.

113. In book 3 of the *Secretum* (*Prose*, 202–4), Augustinus cites several similar passages (*Africa*, 2.361–63, 431–32, 455–57, 464–65) in his attack on Franciscus's love of literary glory. Among other Petrarchan passages, cf. *De*

remediis, 1.44, 92, 117. The famous soliloquy of the dying Mago (*Africa,* 6.889–913) shares the "Ecclesiastes" tone of Publius Cornelius's speech.

114. See, for example, Umberto Bosco, *Francesco Petrarca* (Bari: Laterza, 1961), 83 ff.

115. See first of all *De remediis,* 1.9, "De eloquentia": "Magnum . . . instrumentum gloriae, sed anceps, cuspide gemina." Another neat example is in the letter to M. Varro, where at one point Petrarca exclaims "Sed, o incredibilis fame vis, vivit nomen sepultis operibus." But soon afterward he looks at Varro's lost works in another light (as in *De remediis,* 1.44): "Sciebas peritura dum scriberes: mortali enim ingenio nichil efficitur immortale" (*Fam.,* 24.6.5 and 9)—words that he could address to himself as well as to Varro.

116. For example, 1.225, 459, 584.

117. See Enrico Fenzi, "Dall'"Africa' al 'Secretum': Nuove ipotesi sul 'Sogno di Scipione' e sulla composizione del poema," *Il Petrarca ad Arquà. Atti del Convegno di studi nel VI centenario (1374–1974),* ed. Giuseppe Billanovich and Giuseppe Frasso (Padua: Antenore, 1975), 88.

118. *Fam.,* 1.2.

119. *Fam.,* 24.1.27. There follows, however, a *nisi:* unless, by exercising *virtus,* we lay the way to true, eternal life.

120. *Fam.,* 13.7. Cf. *Rerum memorandarum libri* 3.93.41 ff. on the "insanabile . . . scribendi cachetes" (i.e., *cacoethes;* citing Juvenal, 7.51–52).

121. *Fam.,* 21.12.

122. From Montaigne, *Essais,* 1.20; and Cicero, *Tusculanae Disputationes,* 1.30.74 with a *translatio* from philosophizing to writing. Petrarca thought of "dying reading like Ptolemy (*Sen.,* 1.5), or dying writing like Plato (*Sen.,* 15.6)" (N. Mann, *Petrarch,* 22).

123. See Aldo Scaglione, "Petrarca 1974: A Sketch for a Portrait," *Francis Petrarch, Six Centuries Later: A Symposium,* ed. Aldo Scaglione (Chapel Hill: Dept. of Romance Languages, University of North Carolina, Newberry Library, 1975), 7: Petrarca's search embodies, "to put it with Freud, the principle that the psyche ignores the rule of non-contradiction."

124. Cf. *Rerum memorandarum libri,* 1.19.

125. Cf. *Africa,* 2.433–34, and *Triumphus temporis,* 88–93. Petrarca expresses the hierarchy of temporal endurance thus in his letter to Luchino Visconti, discussed above (*Fam.,* 7.15.10): "Fluxa est hominum memoria, picture labiles, caduce statue, interque mortalium inventa nichil literis stabilius."

126. *Triumphus eternitatis,* 67–68 (text in *Rime, Trionfi e Poesie latine*). Cf. *Sen.,* 3.9 (*Opera,* 2:863), following the passage quoted in note 10, above: "ò iucunda semperque eadem coelestis habitatio, ubi nec praeteritum aliquid nec futurum, sed praesentia cuncta sunt." For the continuity of the theme in humanism, cf. Michele Marullo's hymn *Aeternitati* (*Hymni naturales* 1.5): "amfractus aevi varios venturaque lapsis / intermixta legens praesenti inclusa fideli, / diversosque dies obtutu colligis uno" (*Poeti latini del Quattrocento,* ed. Francesco Arnaldi et al. [Milan: Ricciardi, 1964]).

127. Cf. K. Heitmann, *Fortuna und Virtus,* 249–50 (cited by Baron, *From Petrarch to Leonardo Bruni,* 12), who claims that the contradictory elements of Petrarca's moral philosophy "sich beständig selbst aufheben."

128. See Hans-Georg Gadamer, *Truth and Method,* tr. Garrett Barden and John Cumming (New York: Crossroad, 1975), 325–41; and Otto Pöggeler, "Dichtungstheorie und Toposforschung," *Toposforschung,* ed. Max L. Baeumer (Darmstadt: Wissenschaftliche Buchgesellschaft, 1973), 93–107.

129. Nicola Festa, *Saggio sull' "Africa" del Petrarca* (Palermo: Sandron, 1926), 71. Cf. Bernardo, *Petrarch, Scipio,* 121 (that, according to Macrobius, Cicero's *Somnium* embraces the whole of philosophy).

130. Preface to *L'Africa,* ed. Festa, lxv ff.; Festa, *Saggio sull' "Africa",* 94–109.

131. *Prose,* 22.

132. See 9.393–97. In *De viris illustribus* (*Vita Scipionis* 10.80) Petrarca claims explicitly that Scipio's victory over Carthage opened the door to all later Roman victories.

133. *Aeneid,* 8.348.

134. See Guido Martellotti and Pietro Paolo Trompeo, "Cartaginesi a Roma," in Martellotti, *Scritti petrarcheschi* (Padua: Antenore, 1983), 27–43.

135. Unlike the poet's belief that he was delivering his coronation oration in the same senatorial palace where Cicero had spoken before Caesar (it was really built in the twelfth century: *Collatio,* 7 (Godi, 19); cf. Wilkins, "The Coronation of Petrarch," 62.

136. "The activity of memory and imagination intensifies; the spirit feels itself close to contact with the infinite, and contemplates human affairs from a marvelous height" (Festa, *Saggio sull' "Africa,"* 79).

137. *De Consulatu Stilichonis* 3, praefatio (cited above).

138. This bit of modesty derives from Valerius Maximus, 8.14.1

139. *Tristia,* 2.424. Cf. Valerius Maximus, 8.14.1

140. Werner Suerbaum, "Ennius bei Petrarca: Betrachtungen zu literarischen Ennius-Bildern," *Ennius: Sept exposés suivis de discussions* (Geneva, 1971), 310; Nolhac, 1:193.

141. Suerbaum, "Ennius bei Petrarca," 293.

142. Ennius's modesty may also be a *captatio benevolentiae* similar to Lelius's manner of prefacing his praise of Scipio (4.34–45). Cf. *De viris illustribus* (*Vita Scipionis,* 11.13): Scipio deserved a better poet, "sed sic est: preterita ac futura optari possunt sed presentibus uti oportet," where we notice the central role of time in the problem of praise.

143. Bernardo, *Petrarch, Scipio and the "Africa,"* 47.

144. The source is the previously cited passage by Claudian. Cf. later the Fifth Eclogue of Battista Spagnoli (Mantuanus): "Heroica facta / Qui faciunt reges heroica carmina laudant" (cited by Wilfred P. Mustard, "Petrarch's *Africa,"* *American Journal of Philology* 42 (1921): 120).

145. The conversation with Scipio also resembles Petrarca's conversation/ examination with King Robert in Naples before his laureate crowning (see Martellotti, "Stella difforme," *Scritti petrarcheschi,* 413).

146. And a poet who invents everything is a liar (103–5; cf. *Collatio,* 9).

147. "Partemque diei / Et partes pelagi minuens" (130–31).

148. The moment is reminiscent of the dramatic hush that awaits the story told by Aeneas in Dido's palace (*Aeneid,* 2.1).

149. "I have never been able to penetrate without a shiver these gates, of ivory or of horn, which separate us from the invisible world" (Gérard de Nerval, *Aurélia,* in *Oeuvres,* 2 vols. [Paris: Gallimard, 1966], 1:359).

150. Sigmund Freud, "'The Antithetical Sense of Primal Words'," trans. M. N. Searl, in *Character and Culture,* ed. Philip Rieff (New York: Collier-Macmillan, 1963), 44–50; and *Introductory Lectures on Psychoanalysis,* trans. James Strachey (New York: Liveright-Norton, 1977), 178–80. Freud uses the work of Karl Abel as his point of departure. Cf. Lévy-Bruhl (*La Mentalité primitive,*

99) on the absurdity of dreams: "Dans la mentalité primitive, le principe de contradiction n'exerce pas le même empire sur les liaisons de représentations que sur celles des nôtres." Suzanne K. Langer draws an explicit parallel between Freudian dream theory and Cassirer's mythical thought ("On Cassirer's Theory of Language and Myth," in *The Philosophy of Ernst Cassirer,* ed. Schilpp, 395 ff.). Mauss too (*Essai sur le don,* 193), although for different reasons, has mentioned languages where antithetical operations are expressed by the same word.

151. For the regression in dreams to prehistory both individual (i.e., early childhood) and phylogenetic (i.e., archaic culture) see Freud, Lecture 13 ("The Archaic Features and Infantilism of Dreams"), *Introductory Lectures on Psychoanalysis,* 199–212; and *The Interpretation of Dreams,* trans. James Strachey, 2 vols. (London: The Hogarth Press, 1953), 2:548–49.

152. Benveniste, "Remarques sur la fonction du langage dans la découverte freudienne," *Problèmes de linguistique générale,* 75–87. Jacques Lacan has suggested, without pursuing the matter explicitly, that the question introduced by Freud should remain open ("Séminaire sur *la Lettre volée," Écrits* [Paris: Seuil, 1966], 22 n.).

153. M. Tullius Cicero, *De re publica* 6.10, ed. K. Ziegler (Leipzig: Teubner, 1964). Cf. Petrarca, *Historia Iulii Caesaris,* chap. 2 (ed. C. E. Chr. Schneider [Leipzig, 1827], 4); Vitruvius, *De Architectura,* 9 praef. 16, cited by Giuseppe Velli, "La memoria poetica del Petrarca," *Petrarca e Boccaccio,* 19; and Fronto, cited by Renato Reggiani, *I Proemi degli Annales di Ennio: Programma letterario e polemica* (Rome: Edizioni dell'Ateneo e Bizzarri, 1979), 29: "Magistra Homeri Calliope, magister Enni Homerus et Somnus." See also W. R. Hardie, "The Dream of Ennius," *Classical Quarterly* 7 (1913): 188–95.

154. "Precipue illustres calamo florente poetas / Admisi atque ima cordis sub parte locavi" (142–43).

155. Petrarca contemplated replacing *recessit* with *abscessit,* which would strengthen the contrast between sleep and waking (Fera, *La revisione petrarchesca . . .,* 439).

156. Macrobius, *Commentarii in Somnium Scipionis,* 1.3.

157. *Rerum memorandarum libri,* 4.40. Cf. *Fam.,* 5.7, *De remediis,* 1.112.

158. However, in a marginal note where the lacuna starts at 9.215, Petrarca wrote "hic somnium interiectum debet esse" (Fera, *La revisione petrarchesca . . . ,* 433).

159. For the poet's contradictory attitude regarding dreams, see Antonio Belloni, "Il Petrarca e i sogni," *Padova in onore di Francesco Petrarca MCMIV, II: Miscellanea di studi critici e ricerche erudite* (Padua: Società cooperativa tipografica, 1909), 31–46.

160. Cf. *Aeneid,* 6.700–2, *Purgatorio,* 2.80–81; as well as *Iliad,* 23.99–101 and *Odyssey,* 11.204–8.

161. Cf. *Fam.,* 24.12.42 (to Homer): "Multa dixi quasi ad presentem; sed iam ab illa vehementissima imaginatione rediens, quam longe absis intelligo. . . ."

162. For example, Antonio Belloni, "L'Africa del Petrarca," *Il poema epico e mitologico (Storia di generi letterari italiani)* (Milan: Vallardi, n.d.), 83; Carlini, *Studio su "L'Africa,"* 36–37; Ettore Paratore, "L'Elaborazione padovana dell' *Africa,"* in *Petrarca, Venezia e il Veneto,* ed. Giorgio Padoan (Florence: Olschki, 1976), 80–81.

163. "Prosiluit dextramque dedit" (67) (Petrarca, *Laurea Occidens: Bucolicum Carmen X,* ed. Guido Martellotti [Rome: Edizioni di Storia e Letteratura,

1968]). What begins as a geographical flight from one poet to another settles down in a limbo of poets reminiscent of Dante's (*Inferno* 4).

164. Unless otherwise indicated, all references to the *Annales* are to *The Annals of Q. Ennius,* ed. Otto Skutsch (Oxford: Oxford University Press, 1985).

165. For Petrarca's acquaintance with the individual authors, see de Nolhac, *Pétrarque et l'humanisme.*

166. Donatus's commentary to Terence's *Andria,* 429, *Phormio,* 74, *Adelphi,* 106.

167. Lucilius, 1189; Horace, *Epistula,* 2.1.50.

168. Lactantius Placidus, *Commentarii in Statii Thebaida et Commentarius in Achilleida,* ed. Richard Jahnke (Leipzig: Teubner, 1898), on *Thebaid,* 3.483 ff.

169. Ennius, ed. Skutsch, 164 n.; Skutsch, *Studia Enniana* (London: Athlone, 1968), 152 ff.; Suerbaum, *Untersuchungen zur Selbstdarstellung älterer römischer Dichter* (Hildesheim: Olm, 1968), 318–19.

170. See *De remediis,* 1.62 (*Opera,* 1:70); and Augustine, *De civitate Dei,* 21.4.

171. Suerbaum, *Untersuchungen . . . ,* 111.

172. With regard to Pythagoras, it is worth mentioning, as Rohde (*Psyche,* 598–601) points out, that the traditions of his previous lives included a descent to Hades.

173. Cicero, *Tusculanae Disputationes,* 1.15.34; 1.49.117. Petrarca echoes these lines in *Epistola metrica,* 1.13.10, *Fam.,* 1.9.1, and *Sen.,* 9.2, although he may have been inspired by Virgil's imitation in *Georgics,* 3.9 (which he cites in *Sen.,* 16.6). In his letter to Homer (*Fam.,* 24.12.37), Petrarca revises Ennius's last line, modifying *ora* with *docta* to better express his elitist sense of glory (cf. *Ep. met.,* 3.17.15, *Fam.,* 10.6.1, *Sen.,* 15.6, and *Africa,* 2.410–11). And in a letter after Petrarca's death, Lombardo della Seta anticipates editorial correction of the *Africa* "ut unici vatis laurea totum per orbem volitet ac per ora docta virum" (cited in Fera, *Antichi editori e lettori . . . ,* 33, 83). These latter passages are perhaps modeled on Cicero's epitaph: "Vivus in aeternum docta per ora volat." (See Velli, "Il proemio dell' «Africa»," *Petrarca e Boccaccio,* 53–54 n.)

Cf. Petrarca's *Testamentum* 5: "Quod nemo me fleat, nemo mihi lacrimas, sed pro me Christo preces et qui potest Christi pauperibus caritatem pro me orare monitis porrigat; hoc mihi prodesse poterit, fletus autem et defunctis inutilis et flentibus est damnosus" (*Petrarch's Testament,* ed. and trans. Theodor E. Mommsen [Ithaca: Cornell University Press, 1957]).

For continuation of the tradition, cf. Poliziano, *Ambra,* 478, his *Epigrammata latina* 89 and 90 ("In Joctum pictorem"), and *Ep.,* 10.7 (*Opera* [1553], 143); Sperone Speroni, *Dialogo delle lingue* (*Trattatisti del Cinquecento,* ed. Mario Pozzi, vol. 1 [Milan: Ricciardi, 1978], 616); Joachim Du Bellay, *La deffence et illustration de la langue françoyse,* 2.3; Torquato Tasso, *Discorsi dell'arte poetica* (Tasso, *Prose,* ed. Ettore Mazzali [Milan: Ricciardi, 1959], 372), and *Discorsi del poema eroico* (*Prose,* 573).

174. The only ancient precedent for poetic metempsychosis, also involving Homer's soul, is suggested by an epitaph for Stesichorus (seventh to sixth century B.C.) by Antipatros of Sidon (second century B.C.). See Suerbaum, *Untersuchungen . . . ,* 83, 88; and Harald Fuchs, "Zu den Annalen des Ennius," *Museum helveticum,* 12 (1955): 201–2.

For a later extension of the genealogy, see Ronsard's ode "A Joachim Du Bellai Angevin" (*Oeuvres complètes,* 1:984):

> Si ce qu'a dit Pythagore
> Pour vrai l'on veut estimer,
> L'ame de Petrarque encore
> T'est venue r'animer:
> L'experience est pour moi,
> Veu que ses vers Tuscans tu ne leus onques,
> Et tu écris ainsi comme lui, donques
> Le même esprit est en toi.

Cf. Ronsard's ode to Amadis Jamyn (*Oeuvres complètes,* 2:1134–36): Homer reborn as his translator Jamyn (!); and, more generally, Du Bellay's Ode 13 "A Heroet" of his *Vers liriques* (*Oeuvres poétiques,* ed. Henri Chamard [Paris: Cornély, 1912], 3:136).

175. *De viris illustribus* is mentioned as another project to glorify Rome and Scipio (257–60), but it is clearly secondary to the *Africa.*

176. Cf. *Fam.,* 18.2.10 where Petrarca thanks Nicola Sygeros for a manuscript of Homer that he cannot read but cherishes all the same: "Homerus tuus apud me mutus, imo vero ego apud illum surdus sum. Gaudeo tamen vel aspectu solo et saepe illum amplexus et suspirans dico: 'O magne vir, quam cupide te audirem! . . .'" He ends the letter with a wish that his own fame may extend to the East: "ut quod romanus cesar amplectitur, constantinopolitanus non fastidiat imperator" (18.2.14).

177. Piazza, *Il Poema dell' umanesimo,* 72; Zumbini, *"L'Africa",* 160.

178. Book 9 is clearly posterior, probably far posterior, to the 1341 coronation (see Martellotti, "Sulla composizione del *De viris* e dell'*Africa* del Petrarca," *Scritti petrarcheschi,* 19 ff.). Here is Petrarca's first-person introduction of himself into the poem:

> Ipse ego ter centum labentibus ordine lustris
> Dumosam tentare viam et vestigia rara
> Viribus imparibus fidens utcumque peregi,
> Frondibus atque loco simul et cognomine claro
> Heroum veterum tanto imitatus honores,
> Irrita ne Grai fierent presagia vatis.

(404–9)

(I myself, with fifteen hundred years passing by, succeeded as best I could in following the thorny way and rare traces, trusting in my unequal powers. And I imitated those honors with the leaves, in the same place and with the illustrious name of ancient heroes, lest the prophecy of the Greek poet should be unfulfilled.)

Fera (*La revisione petrarchesca* . . . , 452–53) suggests *utrumque* (both *via* and *vestigia*) rather than *utcumque* for line 406, thus stressing the magnitude of the poet's achievement rather than a sign of modesty. Line 409 asserts, with a characteristically circular inspiration, the poet's desire not to belie what he has made Homer predict for him.

179. Naturally, combinations of the two cases are possible; the patron may be portrayed as promising but not ideal. See the first part of the next chapter for some illustration.

180. For the importance of Apollo to Petrarca generally, see Marjorie O'Rourke Boyle, *Petrarch's Genius: Pentimento and Prophecy* (Berkeley: University of California Press, 1991), 11–43, and 37 on the *Africa* in particular.

181. This detail was probably inspired by Horace, *Carm.*, 4.8.18–19.

182. Ennius's triumph is not historical. For the idea, Petrarca is again indebted to the previously cited passage from Claudian. See Suerbaum, "Ennius bei Petrarca," 315–16.

183. Fera, *La revisione petrarchesca* . . . , 451–52.

184. Homer is an honorary Latin poet, having apparently learned the language as he waited to be reborn as Ennius.

185. See 9.416–17. In *De viris illustribus* (*Vita Scipionis* 12.45), Petrarca cites Scipio's epitaph at Liternus, addressed to Rome: "Ingrata patria, ne ossa quidem mea habes." Petrarca admires this verbal revenge of the hero's ashes against the city he defended from becoming ashes:

> Ac nescio an nulla unquam maior ultio cuiusquam fuerit iniuriae; cetere enim transierunt, vox hec autem, tunc saxis insculpta nunc libris, dum memoria erit ulla romani nominis nunquam silebitur, magnificentiusque se paucis literis ultus est, quam si vastatis finibus romanis urbem ipsam armatis legionibus obsedisset

(12.46).

186. As Silius Italicus does (*Punica*, 17.625–54).

187. Zumbini, *"L'Africa,"* 76 ff., Piazza, *Il Poema dell'umanesimo*, 69. Cf. Croce's judgment that contemporary hopes that saw in Robert a possible unifier and protector of Italy turned out to be "utterly fantastic" (Benedetto Croce, *History of the Kingdom of Naples*, trans. Frances Frenaye [Chicago: University of Chicago Press, 1970], 51).

188. *Ep. met.*, 2.8; *Fam.*, 5.1; *Bucolicum Carmen*, 2.

189. See *Rerum memorandarum libri*, 1.37: Robert cultivated literature "ut ingenia seculi sui complecteretur benignitate regia."

190. See Bernardo, *Petrarch, Scipio and the "Africa"*, 162. In addition to the texts that Bernardo cites, cf. *Rerum memorandarum libri*, 3.96.3. Billanovich's critical text (Florence: Sansoni, 1945) has: "ut *Africam* sibi [sc. to King Robert] Scipiadamque nostrum dicaremus." But the 1554 Basel text gives: "ut Africam sibi Scipioni denique nostro dicaremus." Whatever the editor's reasons for his reading, the characterization of Robert as a *Scipio noster* (1554 edition) seems more satisfying than a second title for the poem (critical edition).

191. *Fam.*, 4.3.13.

192. *Laurea occidens*, 288 ff. Cf. *Fam.*, 1.2 and 4.7 for the parallel Robert-Augustus, and see above on *Ep. met.*, 2.10.

193. See Jacques Le Goff, *Les intellectuels au Moyen Age* (Paris: Editions du Seuil, 1985), 142 ff., 180 ff.

194. Cf. Boccaccio on Petrarca: *De vita et moribus domini Francesci Petracchi* (*Opere latine minori*, 238–44).

195. See Ruggiero Romano, "L'Italia nella crisi del secolo XIV," *Tra due crisi: L'Italia del Rinascimento* (Turin: Einaudi, 1971), 13–34.

196. Romano, 29–30.

197. See *Fam.*, 10.1, 19.3, 23.21, and especially 18.1.

198. Croce, *History of the Kingdom of Naples*, 52.

199. *Scienza nuova*, sec. 272, 414.

200. *Scienza nuova*, sec. 273–79.

201. See *Fam.*, 11.3.2, concerning the death of another patron, Jacopo da Carrara.

202. *Consummata* is puzzling, as is the expression *ad exitum deduxi* in the *Epistola posteritati* (*Prose*, 16), in light of the poem's manifestly unfinished form as we possess it. A possible explanation is that the *Africa* reached the end that Petrarca desired for it and that he considered the remaining necessary work (filling in the lacunae, completing verses, checking metrical correctness) as mere polishing. However, Petrarca contemplated replacing *consummata* with either *festinata* or *exhausta* (Fera, *La revisione petrarchesca* . . . , 454). For a different view, see David Groves, "Petrarch's Inability to Complete the *Africa*," *Parergon* 12 (1975): 11–19.

203. See Enrico Carrara, "Sulla soglia dell'«Africa»," *Studi petrarcheschi ed altri scritti* (Turin: Bottega d'Erasmo, 1959), 127–28.

204. Cf. Thomas M. Greene, "Petrarch *Viator*," *The Vulnerable Text: Essays on Renaissance Literature* (New York: Columbia University Press, 1986), 44–45.

205. Cf. *Canzoniere*, 333, "Ite, rime dolenti, al duro sasso" (Laura's tomb).

206. "Nos, nisi fallor, amat" (439).

207.

> Poterunt discussis forte tenebris
> Ad purum priscumque iubar remeare nepotes.
> Tunc Elicona nova revirentem stirpe videbis,
> Tunc lauros frondere sacras; tunc alta resurgent
> Ingenia atque animi dociles, quibus ardor honesti
> Pyeridum studii veterem geminabit amorem. (456–61)

For the seminal importance of Petrarca's historical periodization culminating in the future Golden Age, see Theodor E. Mommsen, "Petrarch's Conception of the 'Dark Ages,'" *Speculum* 17 (1942): 241.

208. Fera, *La revisione petrarchesca* . . . , 439.

209. "Affirmation does not surround the status quo with a halo [*in Gloriolen*]. What it does is resist death, the *telos* of all domination, and in so doing it allies itself with what is" (Adorno, *Aesthetic Theory*, 357 [original: 374]).

210. At the end of the translation of the *Iliad* that he used, Petrarca summarized the Homeric poem thus: "opus humanum ab ira ceptum ac superbia in gemitum desinit ac sepulcrum" (De Nolhac, *Pétrarque et l'humanisme*, 2:183).

In a marginal note on the manuscript of the *Epistola Posteritati*, Petrarca wrote of the *Africa*: "Raro unquam pater aliquis tam moestus filium unicum in rogum misit, ut ego librum illum quem multo labori mihi genueram" (P. P. Vergerio, *Petrarchae Vita*, in Angelo Solerti, ed., *Le Vite di Dante, Petrarca e Boccaccio scritte fino al secolo decimosesto* [Milan: Vallardi, n.d.], 300, where Petrarca is apparently referring to his imitation of Virgil's desire that the incomplete *Aeneid* should be burned).

And in an epistolary tribute to King Robert, Petrarca compares their friendship with that of Ennius and Scipio. What he writes of the latter couple can also be said of the former. Both Ennius and Petrarca are "Et vitae mortisque comes, custosque sepulchri" (*Ep. met.*, 2.9 [*Opera*, 3:1350], following Valerius Maximus, 8.14.1. Cf. Foscolo's formula for the Muses, *custodi de' sepolcri* [*Dei Sepolcri*, v. 230]).

Even the poetic triumph in Rome in 1341 resembles the *Africa* in this as in so many other ways. In explaining his preference of Rome for the laureate ceremony, Petrarca pictures himself there, "super cineribus antiquorum vatum" (*Fam.*, 4.6.5). As in the *Familiares* to ancient authors, intimacy with literary tradition is a sojourn in the graveyard or catacombs.

If the tomb is the place of the great poem's accomplishment, we may see another meaning behind the obvious one when in a sonnet (*Canzoniere*, 291) Petrarca mourns the loss of his *dolce alloro* and realizes that to rejoin it or her, he must die: "se 'l vo' riveder, conven ch'io mora."

Giuseppe Mazzotta recognizes that the question "at the center ... of his historical and poetic thinking" concerns "the relationship between history and death" (*The Worlds of Petrarch* [Durham: Duke University Press, 1993], 125).

211. See, for example, *Africa*, 9.414, 483; *Historia Iulii Caesaris*, cap. 26; *Ep. met.*, 2.10.286–87; *Ep. Posteritati* (*Prose*, 16).

CHAPTER 3. THE QUATTROCENTO AND POLIZIANO

Thomas Gray, "Elegy Written in a Country Church-Yard," (Thomas Gray and William Collins, *Poetical Works*, ed. Roger Lonsdale [Oxford: Oxford University Press, 1977], 36).

1. Giovanni Boccaccio, *Opere in versi, Corbaccio, Trattatello in laude di Dante, Prose latine, Epistole*, ed. Pier Giorgio Ricci (Milan: Ricciardi, 1965), 1054. The other citations in this paragraph are from the same page. Cf. Petrarca's version of the conversation in *Rerum memorandarum libri*, 1.37.12–13.

2. Cf. Roberto Weiss, "Il Petrarca e i Malatesta," *Il Primo secolo dell'umanesimo* (Rome: Storia e letteratura, 1949), 77–79.

3. *Canzoniere*, 104 (text in *Rime, Trionfi e Poesie latine*). The boast that literature has greater durability than the products of plastic arts is a common one. For examples in antiquity (Catullus 68, Propertius 3.2), besides Horace's *Exegi monumentum* and Cicero (*Ad Fam.*, 5.12.7, *Pro Archia*, 12.30), see Suerbaum, *Untersuchungen* ... , 193–95; see also Seneca, *Consolatio ad Polybium*, 18; among later examples: Petrarca, *Fam.*, 7.15.10; P. P. Vergerio, *De ingenuis moribus* ... , in Eugenio Garin, *Educazione umanistica in Italia* (Bari: Laterza, 1975), 91–92; Poliziano, *Epistolae*, 9.1 (*Opera* [1553], 117). Cf. for a late example this passage from the German Baroque (preface to Jakob Ayrer's *Dramen*) cited by Benjamin (*The Origins* ... , 141): "nichts Tauerhaffters vnd vnsterblichers ist, als eben die Bücher."

4. See Voigt, *Il Risorgimento* ... , 1:572–74 (but cf. the *Giunte e correzioni* to Voigt by Giuseppe Zippel [Florence: Sansoni, 1897], 40); Jacob Burckhardt, *The Civilization of the Renaissance in Italy*, tr. S. G. C. Middlemore (New York: Harper and Row, 1958), 1:155–56; Salutati, *Epistolario*, 3:285–308; Vladimiro Zabughin, *Virgilio nel Rinascimento italiano da Dante a Torquato Tasso* (Bologna: Zanichelli, 1921), 1:113; Pier Paolo Vergerio, *Epistolario*, ed. Leonardo Smith (Rome: Istituto storico italiano per il Medio Evo, 1934), 189–202; Alan Fisher, "Three Meditations on the Destruction of Vergil's Statue: The Early Humanist Theory of Poetry," *Renaissance Quarterly* 40 (1987): 607–35.

5. There is a third, anonymous letter of 25 October in the same year, relatively unimportant for my purposes. For the text, see D. J. B. Robey, "Virgil's

Statue at Mantua and the Defense of Poetry," *Rinascimento* Ser. 2,9 (1969): 183–203.

6. See Zabughin, 1:109 ff.

7. Vergerio, *Epistolario* (parenthetical page references are to this edition). Vergerio dramatizes the danger his invective confronts with the comment "non esse quidem tutum in eos scribere qui possunt proscribere" (it is not safe to write against those who can proscribe) (199). This is an imitation of the maxim with which Asinius Pollio explained his decision not to respond to a satire against him by Augustus: "non est enim facile in eum scribere qui potest proscribere" (Macrobius, *Saturnalia,* 2.4.21). Petrarca also imitated it in a letter to Luchino Visconti (*Familiares,* 7.15.7), as did Valla in his *De falso credita et ementita Constantini donatione* (1.1).

8. Cf. the discussion above of Petrarca's metrical epistle to Brizio Visconti.

9. Vergerio ranks Virgil above Homer (196).

10. Cf. Salutati, *Epistolario,* 3.18 (vol. 1, pp. 198 ff.), where he makes the same comparison with regard to Petrarca's literary executors, who he fears may burn the *Africa.* The ancient arsonist's name was Herastratos, but he is purposefully left anonymous by both Vergerio and Salutati, as if to thwart his ambition. See Valerius Maximus, 8.14. ext. 5, who also declines to name the culprit.

11. There follow varied examples of literary commemoration: of great men like Alexander and Ulysses, of places like Troy and Pharsalia, and even Rome. The urgency of Vergerio's anaphora ("quis Romulus fuerit . . . quis Numa, quis Tullus uterque, quis Ancus, etc." [192]) unites the satisfaction of erudition (the result of literature) to the dismal catalog of loss (without the aid of literature). For the same sort of anaphora in a similar context, cf. (1) Petrarca, *Ep. met.,* 2.10.193–97, cited above; (2) Francesco da Fiano, *Contra oblocutores et detractores poetarum,* ed. Igino Tau, *Archivio italiano per la storia della pietà* 4 (1965): cap. 39:

Que hodie gestorum Achyllis apud Troiam, que Ulixee peregrinationis, que Enee, que Turni et, ut reliquos sileam carminibus poetarum omni vivaces evo, que Edippi et natorum natarumque ac coniugis Iocaste memoria, nisi eos Homerus, illos Virgilius, hos vero Statius et Tragicus Seneca rutilantis et generosi stili fulgoribus illustrassent?

and (3) Bartolommeo della Fonte, *De Poetice,* 1.1 (in Charles Trinkaus, "The Unknown Quattrocento Poetics of Bartolommeo della Fonte," *Studies in the Renaissance* 13 (1966): 40–122:

Quae vero deorum, quae heroum, quae regum, quae ducum clarissimorum, quae gentium, quae urbium, quae rerum antiquissimarum esset memoria, nisi fuissent carmina poetarum?

The commonplace *Ubi essent,* as it were.

12. Petrarca was occasionally fond of the expression *nomina nuda;* see, for example, *Sen.,* 5.6, 11.4, 11.6, 12.1 (*Opera,* 2:890, 978, 980, 993). Cf. Bernard de Cluny, *De contemptu mundi,* cited in Lida de Malkiel, *La Idea de la Fama,* 108; a poem of the same name by Roger de Caen, cited by Lida de Malkiel, 109; and the final sentence of Umberto Eco, *Il nome della rosa* (borrowed from Bernard de Cluny).

13. Cf. Boccaccio, *Trattatello in laude di Dante,* in *Opere in versi . . . ,* 600.

14. In his *De viris illustribus,* Bartolomeo Fazio claimed that Malatesta

restored Virgil's statue, concerned to save his reputation from Vergerio's invective, thus showing the power of the literary word. This is, however, contradicted by other accounts. See Voigt, *Il Risorgimento,* 1:574.

15. Salutati, *Epistolario,* book 10, epistle 16 (vol. 3, pp. 285–308). Parenthetical page references are to this edition and volume.

16. See the comment of the editor Novati (286 n.)

17. Hans Baron has seen in this letter a crucial moment in the evolution of Salutati's thought on poetry (*The Crisis of the Early Italian Renaissance* [Princeton: Princeton University Press, 1966], 298).

18. Cf. Vergerio, 195.

19. *Poetics,* 4.8; Averroes's Paraphrase of the *Poetics,* 2.217B. Cf. Salutati, *De laboribus Herculis,* 1.13: "Omne itaque poema et omnis oratio poetica aut est vituperatio aut laudatio" (text: ed. B. L. Ullman [Zürich: Artemis, 1951]); as well as *Epistolario,* 10.6

20. The idea is at least latent in antiquity. See O. B. Hardison Jr., *The Enduring Monument: A Study of the Idea of Praise in Renaissance Literary Theory and Practice* (Chapel Hill: University of North Carolina Press, 1962), 31; and Burgess, 94–95. Cf. Petrarca's *Senile,* 14.1 to Francesco da Carrara (*Opera,* 1:419), where he claims that the praise of princes spurs them to virtue.

21. *Epistolario,* 12.18 (vol. 3, pp. 534–38).

22. See, for example, Voigt, *Il Risorgimento* 2:353–61; John Addington Symonds, *Renaissance in Italy: The Revival of Learning* (London: Smith and Elder, 1882), 510 ff.; Giuseppe Toffanin, *Machiavelli e il "Tacitismo"* (Padua: Draghi, 1921), 73–76; Vittorio Rossi, *Storia letteraria d'Italia: Il Quattrocento* (Milan: Vallardi, 1973), 43–44.

23. Symonds, *Renaissance in Italy,* 513.

24. Boccaccio in the passage cited above (*Opere in versi . . . ,* 1054) also uses the term *preci*[*um*].

25. Cf. *Pro Archia,* 8.18.

26. Cf. the reciprocity demanded in such a construction as this: "aut magis duces indigne ferent hunc honorem vatibus reddi, qui honorem et memoriam ex vatibus habent?" (197)

27. "Impudent moral flexibility and presumptuous fakery" (Rossi, *Il Quattrocento,* 38). Cf. J. E. Sandys, *A History of Classical Scholarship,* 3 vols. (New York: Hafner, 1958), 2:56: "He combined the accomplishments of a scholar with the insidiousness and the brutality of a brigand." See, however, the reevaluation by Diana Robin, "A Reassessment of the Character of Francesco Filelfo (1398–1481)," *Renaissance Quarterly* 36 (1983): 202–24; and more generally her *Filelfo in Milan: Writings 1451–1477* (Princeton: Princeton University Press, 1991).

28. See Rossi, *Il Quattrocento,* 42; Voigt, *Il Risorgimento* 1:524–30.

29. See Eugenio Garin, "La letteratura degli umanisti," in *Storia della Letteratura Italiana,* ed. Emilio Cecchi and Natalino Sapegno, vol. 3, *Il Quattrocento e l'Ariosto* (Milan: Garzanti, 1988), 123. Voigt (*Il Risorgimento,* 2:355) mentions the irony that the *Sforziade* has never even been printed. For a summary of the epic, see Antonio Belloni, *Il poema epico e mitologico* (Milan: Vallardi, n.d.), 100–2. Book 3, at least, is printed as an appendix to Robin, *Filelfo in Milan* (177–96).

30. *Cent-dix lettres de François Filelfe,* ed. Emile Legrand (Paris: Legoux, 1892), 334 ff. Parenthetical page references are to this edition.

31. See Mauss, *Essai sur le don,* 169. Cf. Poliziano's epigram to the Cardinal

of San Sisto (Xistus): "Verba dedi Xisto; decet haec dare dona poetam; / Aera decet Xistum reddere" (*Prose volgari inedite e poesie latine e greche edite e inedite di Angelo Ambrogini Poliziano,* ed. Isidoro Del Lungo [Florence: Barbèra, 1867], 111). There is also, it should be added, a Biblical and medieval background: "Date, et dabitur vobis" (*Luke* 6.38; cf. *Carmina Burana* 1).

32. See Mauss, *Essai sur le don,* 269–70: "Donner, c'est manifester sa supériorité, être plus haut, *magister;* accepter sans rendre ou sans rendre plus, c'est se subordonner, devenir client et serviteur, devenir petit, choir plus bas (*minister*)." And 249: "Le donataire se met dans la dépendance du donateur."

33. See Mauss, *Essai sur le don,* 200–4.

34. "Honos alit artes"—Cicero, *Tusculanae Disputationes,* 1.2.4.

35. From Beccadelli's *Carmina varia,* in *Poeti latini del Quattrocento,* ed. and trans. Francesco Arnaldi et al. (Milan: Ricciardi, 1964), 26.

36. *Poeti latini del Quattrocento,* 28.

37. For an interesting change of role, cf. the poem addressed by Enea Silvio Piccolomini to Charles VII of France (*Poeti latini del Quattrocento,* 136–38). In it, the future Pius II uses the various boasts of poetic immortalization (including multiple references to poetry as *munus*) to recommend poets as a necessity for the prince. Among the contemporary poets recommended by name is Beccadelli.

Cf. also the letter (*Ep.,* 9.1) with which Poliziano dedicates *Nutricia* to Matthias Corvinus, as a gift, he claims: "Nec autem vendito ista tibi" (*Opera* [Basel, 1553], 118).

In the lines cited in the introduction, Theognis boasts of his ability to bestow immortality upon Cyrnus. But he then abruptly ends the passage with a reproach for an unfair return: "But I meet with little respect from you; as if I were a little boy, you deceive me with words" (*logois m'apatais*) (253–54).

38. Antonio Beccadelli, *Epistolarum libri V* (Venice, 1553), 1v–2v. The subsequent citation is from 1v of this edition. For the date (1429), see Alberto Tenenti, *Il Senso della morte e l'amore della vita nel Rinascimento (Francia e Italia)* (Turin: Einaudi, 1957), 23. For the relationship between Beccadelli and Visconti, see Voigt, 1:481–82, 510.

39. Visconti's response (in same edition, 3r–3v) is of some interest. He attributes Beccadelli's excessive praise to the tendency that makes a friend or lover exaggerate the qualities of the beloved. He admits his desire to see his deeds immortalized but appeals to "omnipotentem et immortalem Deum" to permit the poet's Muses to achieve this (3v).

Cf. Beccadelli's letter of May 1428 to Cambio Zambeccari, and the letter of April 1429 by Bartolomeo Capra recommending Beccadelli to the Viscontean secretaries (in L. Barozzi and Remigio Sabbadini, *Studi sul Panormita e sul Valla* [Florence: Le Monnier, 1891] 36–37, 41–42). In both letters, assurances of the immortalizing power of literature alternate with the evocation of gift exchange (for example: "Gratae quidem ac memores sunt [musae] et, quod saepe dicimus, beneficia perire non sinunt" [37]; "hic divinus homo [Beccadelli] . . . vos simul cum Principe nostro divinitatis hoc est immortalitatis participes faciet. Credite mihi: fortunati ambo, si quid carmina sua possunt [echoing *Aeneid* 9.446]. Quid enim pulchrius quid homine dignius, quam afficere donis, praemiis ornare virtutes . . ." [42]).

Antonio Beccadelli was crowned poet laureate by the Emperor Sigismund in Parma in 1432.

40. Erasmus, *Opus Epistolarum,* ed. P. S. Allen (Oxford: Oxford University

Press, 1906), 1:239–41. The letter, written in autumn 1499, is numbered 104. Among examples boasting the superiority of literary rewards to material ones, see Basinio da Parma, *Cyris,* 6.15–16: "Divitiae pereunt et opes labuntur inanes; / vivit in aeternum gloria carminibus" (*Poeti latini del Quattrocento,* 220). The influence of Horace's *Carm.,* 4.8 is pervasive.

41. See Symonds, *Renaissance in Italy,* 512; and Rinaldo Rinaldi, *Umanesimo e Rinascimento* (in *Storia della civiltà letteraria italiana,* ed. Giorgio Bárberi Squarotti), 2 vols. (Turin: UTET, 1990–94), 1:260 for the general shift in Quattrocento historiography toward encomiastic biography. And cf. Petrarca's famous exclamation: "Quid est enim aliud omnis historia, quam romana laus?" (*Invectiva contra eum qui maledixit Italie* [*Opere latine,* 2:1198–1200]).

42. Guarino Veronese, *Epistolario,* ed. Remigio Sabbadini, 3 vols. (Venice: Ferrari, 1915–19), 2:458–65 (letter 796). Parenthetical page references are to this edition.

43. For a similar portrait of the ideal historian, cf. Lorenzo Valla, *Gesta Ferdinandi Regis Aragonum,* ed. Ottavio Besomi (Padua: Antenore, 1973), 8.

44. On the etymological significance of *hospes* and its relevance to archaic relations of exchange, see Benveniste, *Le vocabulaire des institutions indo-européennes,* 1:87–101. The historian as *hospes* inhabits a world like Homer's, where guest-gifts are of central importance. Throughout this passage, Guarino is imitating Lucian's *Quomodo historia scribenda sit* (cited by Gérard Defaux, *Marot, Rabelais, Montaigne: l'écriture comme présence* (Paris: Slatkine, 1987), 149 n.)

45. According to Guarino, the historian should be free from hate, love, and pity. It is true, on the other hand, that humanists more generally show (apart from their observable literary hatreds) the ideal of love as one of the central characteristics of their office. We have seen the importance of this for Petrarca; it is somewhat different in the Quattrocento. We shall see how the philologist's love, true to his name, is directed not so much to great men of the past or present, as to the eloquent Word itself.

46. Cf. Aristotle, *Poetics,* 9.1–3

47. Poggio Bracciolini, *Opera* (Basel, 1538), 49. All references to Poggio are from this edition.

48. For an analogous condemnation of *otium,* cf. Pindar, *Olympian,* 1.82–84. Of course, elsewhere (for example, in the letter to Leonello d'Este discussed below) *otium* is the element necessary to letters.

49. See Cicero, *Tusculanae Disputationes,* 1.10.22; Poliziano, *Miscellanea* (*centuria prima*) 1; Budé, *De Asse* 12–16 (*Opera omnia* [1557], vol. 2); and, comprehensively, Eugenio Garin, "*Endelecheia* e *Entelecheia* nelle discussioni umanistiche," *Atene e Roma,* Serie III-Anno V (1937): 177–87.

50. However, for an opposite view of this relationship, cf. Poggio's letters to Scipione of Ferrara (especially p. 365) and to Francesco Barbaro (365 ff.) arguing Scipio's superiority to Caesar: the death of republican liberty at the hands of the lawless conqueror caused the death of great Latin literature.

51. Poggio also has *confirmatio* rather than *conformatio.*

52. Cicero, *Pro Archia,* ed. P. Reis (Leipzig: Teubner, 1933), xix, 172.

53. More generally on *ratio-oratio* as a "jeu de mots plein de sens," see Jean-Claude Margolin, *L'humanisme en Europe au temps de la Renaissance* (Paris: PUF, 1981), 96; also, Giovanni Gioviano Pontano, *De sermone,* ed. S. Lupi and A. Risicato (Lucania: Thesaurus Mundi, 1954), 1.

54. Cf. Mauss, *Essai sur le don*, 200: "C'est à qui sera le plus riche et aussi le plus follement dépensier. Le principe de l'antagonisme et de la rivalité fonde tout."

55. Etienne Gilson, "Le message de l'Humanisme," *Culture et politique en France à l'époque de l'Humanisme et de la Renaissance*, ed. Franco Simone (Turin: Accademia delle Scienze, 1974), 3–9. Cf. Marc Fumaroli, *L'Age de l'éloquence* (Paris: Droz, 1980), 41.

56. See Concetta Carestia Greenfield, *Humanist and Scholastic Poetics: 1250–1500* (Lewisburg, Penn.: Bucknell University Press, 1981), 22.

57. For the later history of "The Classification of Poetics Among the Sciences," see chapter 1 of Bernard Weinberg, *A History of Literary Criticism in the Italian Renaissance*, 2 vols. (Chicago: University of Chicago Press, 1961), 1:1–37.

58. Petrarca, *Opere latine*, 2:898 (=*Prose*, 654–56). Cf. the late *Sen.*, 15.11. Budé retells the same anecdote in *L'Institution du Prince* (40r–v).

59. Cf. Cristoforo Landino, *Proemio al commento dantesco:*

La poesia non essere alcuna di quelle arti le quali gl'antichi per la eccellenzia di quelle nominorono liberali . . . ma è una certa cosa molto più divina che le liberali discipline, la quale quelle tutte abbracciando, conlegata con diffiniti numeri e circunscritta con distinti piedi e di vari lumi e flori ornata, quantunque mai gl'uomini hanno fatto, quantunque hanno conosciuto, quantunque hanno contemplato con maravigliosi figmenti adorna e in altre spezie traduce. . . .

(Landino, *Scritti critici e teorici*, 1:141). And cf. Aldo S. Bernardo's interpretation of Laura in the *Trionfi* as a figure of Philologia, and of her triumph as a "reductio omnium artium ad Philologiam" ("Petrarch, Dante, and the Medieval Tradition," *Renaissance Humanism: Foundations, Forms, and Legacy*, ed. Albert Rabil, Jr., 3 vols. [Philadelphia: University of Pennsylvania Press, 1988], 1:130).

60. Coluccio Salutati, *De laboribus Herculis*, ed. B. L. Ullman (Zürich: Artemis, 1951). Parenthetical references to book, chapter, and section are to this edition.

61. *Epistolario*, 10.22 (vol. 3, p. 320).

62. *Epistolario*, 12.3 (vol. 3, p. 454): "Verborum et rerum cuncta pertractat per omniaque dominatur et currit."

63. For example, Alain de Lille's *Anticlaudianus*, Ristoro d'Arezzo's *Composizione del mondo*, Dante's *Convivio*.

64. *Convivio*, 2.13–14. Dante's criterion for assigning a discipline to a planet is usually based on the planet's perceived nature. Salutati depends on etymology and the character of the presiding deity; that is, poetic fictions.

65. Cf. Greenfield, *Humanist and Scholastic Poetics*, 136–40. Salutati's exposition of meter's metaphysical value helps explain the superiority of poetry to prose—notably, to rhetoric (*De laboribus*, 1.11; however, just the opposite judgment turns up in *Epistolario*, 4.20 [vol. 1, p. 338]).

66. Albertino Mussato, in the early Trecento, already defended the putative divine nature of poetry by identifying it with theology, at the summit of the system of learning. At the same time, he called poetry divine for its eternal glory:

Utque viget Laurus semper, nec fronde caduca
Carpitur, aeternum sic habet illa decus.

Inde est, ut Vates cingantur tempora Lauro
Pergat ad aeternos ut sua fama dies.

(Cited by Giuseppe Saitta, *Il Pensiero italiano nell'Umanesimo e nel Rinascimento* [Florence: Sansoni, 1961], 1:9). Generally on Mussato's defense of poetry, see Ronconi, *Le origini,* 17–59.

67. See Cesare Vasoli, "L'estetica dell'Umanesimo e del Rinascimento," *Problemi ed orientamenti critici di lingua e di letteratura italiana,* vol. 5: *Momenti e problemi di storia dell'estetica,* parte prima: *Dall'antichità classica al barocco* (Milan: Marzorati, 1959), 333. However, as we have seen above, Salutati himself occasionally moves beyond the allegorical defense of poetry.

68. Fiano, *Contra oblocutores,* cap. 40. It should be noted that this passage, like the entire treatise, appeals to the dedicatee Cosimo Migliorati, Cardinal of Bologna. There ensues an exhortation to "colere et . . . venerari poetas."

69. See Pontano's dialogue *Actius,* in *I Dialoghi,* ed. Carmelo Previtera (Florence: Sansoni, 1943), 238 ("ut omne dicendi genus a poetica emanaverit") (cf. Greenfield, *Humanist and Scholastic Poetics,* 277). Likewise Bartolommeo della Fonte, *De Poetice ad Laurentium Medicem libri III : Praefatio;* 1.1; 1.5 (see below). Related to this view of poetry's generative power is the idea, to be examined below, that poetry is at the origin of civilization.

70. Vittore Branca, *Poliziano e l'umanesimo della parola* (Turin: Einaudi, 1983), 3–36. Cf. Poliziano, *Rime,* ed. Daniela Delcorno Branca (Florence: Accademia della Crusca, 1986), 148–49 and the references there.

71. As Branca admits (*Poliziano,* 12).

72. However, the chronology of the *Rime* is highly uncertain. Ida Maïer (*Ange Politien: La formation d'un poète humaniste [1469–1480]* [Geneva: Droz, 1966], 247) situates them between 1473 and 1480, while V. Branca (5) believes that some can be attributed to the 1480s and 1490s.

73. Too much should not be made of this last opposition, which is only relative. Poliziano continued to prepare courses on the poets at the time of his death. See Branca, *Poliziano,* 86.

74. See *Oratio super Fabio Quintiliano et Statii Sylvis* (*praelectio* for academic year 1480–81) in *Opera* (1553), 492–98 (= *Prosatori latini del Quattrocento,* 870–84). There is also a poem called *Sylva in Scabiem,* but it is of a different sort altogether and belongs to Poliziano's youth (see Maïer, *Ange Politien,* 191–202).

75. On the distinction between *praelectio* (introduction to an individual teacher's course) and *prolusio* (to all the courses of a *studio*), see Remigio Sabbadini, *Il Metodo degli umanisti* (Florence: Le Monnier, 1920), 35, who admits that the distinction is not rigorously observed.

76. Among many examples, see Fiano, *Contra oblocutores,* cap. 35.

77. Sabbadini, *Il Metodo* . . ., 35.

78. All line references to the four *Sylvae* are to Angelo Poliziano, *Le Selve e la Strega,* ed. Isidoro Del Lungo (Florence: Sansoni, 1925). There is a partial, contemporary commentary to *Ambra*: Alessandro Perosa, *Un commento inedito all' «Ambra» del Poliziano* (Rome: Bulzoni, 1994). See also Giuseppina Boccuto's commentary on *Nutricia* (Perugia: Galeno, 1990). For important source notes on *Ambra* (and *Manto* too), see Elisabeth Klecker, *Dichtung über Dichtung* (Vienna: Verlag der österreichischen Akademie der Wissenschaften, 1994), 21–123.

79. Likewise in Poliziano's prose *Oratio in expositione Homeri* (*Opera*, 477).

80. The other sense "nourishment" is also relevant. It is an interesting aspect of Poliziano's encyclopedic use of culture that he probably borrowed this term, here applied to poetry, from the legal context of the *Pandects* (*Dig.*, 50.13.1).

In two of his Greek epigrams, Poliziano refers to two of his teachers, Joannes Argyropoulos and Demetrius Chalcondyles, as nurses (*tithenoi*) (epigrams 11 and 17, *Prose volgari inedite* . . ., 184, 190).

In his letter to Homer (*Fam.*, 24.12.5), Petrarca calls Homer one of his *nutritores.*

81. "Spicea si Cereris templo suspensa corona / Donum erat agricolae quondam . . . " (1–2), and line 7, above.

82. Stat vetus . . . lex . . . [q]uae . . .
longum . . . pia mercede laborem
Pensat, et emeritis cumulat compendia curis. (1–8)

The same emphasis is also evident in the change of title to *Nutricia* from the original *Nutrix,* (see Poliziano's dedication of the poem to Antoniotto Gentile, in *Prose volgari inedite* . . . , 370).

83. For the date, see Maïer, *Ange Politien,* 227.

84. In favor of Lorenzo's authorship is Attilio Simioni, the editor of Lorenzo's *Opere,* 2 vols. ([Bari: Laterza, 1939], 2:344, 353); followed by Claudio Varese, ed., *Prosatori volgari del Quattrocento* (Milan: Ricciardi, 1955), 982. In favor of Poliziano: Juliana M. S. Cotton, "Per l'attribuzione al Poliziano dell'Epistola a don Federigo d'Aragona," *Giornale storico della letteratura italiana* 106 (1935): 282–85 (who refers to Michele Barbi's treatment of the question in *Studi sul Canzoniere di Dante* [1915], 222–23); Rossi, *Il Quattrocento,* 331, 381 n.; Mario Santoro, "Poliziano o il Magnifico," *Giornale italiano di filologia* (1948) 139 ff. (reprinted in his *Note umanistiche* [Naples: Liguori, 1970), 79–99); Maïer, *Ange Politien,* 226 ff.; Emilio Bigi, "Il Poliziano critico," *La cultura del Poliziano e altri studi umanistici* (Pisa: Nistri-Lischi, 1967), 117–19; David Thompson and Alan F. Nagel, eds. and trans., *The Three Crowns of Florence: Humanist Assessments of Dante, Petrarca and Boccaccio* (New York: Harper & Row, 1972), 105 n.; Gianfranco Contini, *Letteratura italiana del Quattrocento* (Florence: Sansoni, 1976), 129; Francesco Tateo, *Lorenzo de' Medici e Angelo Poliziano* (Rome: Laterza, 1990), 36, 104.

85. "The letter to Federico of Aragon, written under the auspices and in the name of Lorenzo the Magnificent, is surely a faithful expression of the tasts and aspirations of his circle" (Maïer, *Ange Politien,* 236).

86. All page references to this letter are to Lorenzo de' Medici, *Opere,* ed. Attilio Simioni, 2 vols. (Bari: Laterza, 1939), 1:3–8.

87. Likewise (although with the focus narrowed to eloquent men) in Poliziano's *Oratio super Fabio Quintiliano et Statii Sylvis* (*Prosatori latini del Quattrocento,* 884 = *Opera,* 496): "Quid ego nunc iam inde usque ab heroicis temporibus posita facundiae summa praemia, maximos oratoribus honores habitos, maxima commoda publicis rebus per homines eloquentissimos importata commemorem?"

88. *Tusculanae disputationes,* 1.2.4.

89. Can it be a coincidence that, according to Mauss, "«Potlatch» veut dire essentiellement «nourrir», «consommer»" (Mauss, *Essai sur le don,* 152)?

90. Cf. Benedetto Varchi's dedication to Cosimo de' Medici of his *Storia*

fiorentina, which also quotes Petrarca's lines in evoking the scene (text in Eugenio Garin, *Il Rinascimento Italiano* [Bologna: Cappelli, 1980], 189). Spenser, too, was influenced by the Petrarchan version of the anecdote: *The Ruines of Time* 433–34; cf. E. K.'s commentary to *The Shepheardes Calender,* "October" 65.

91. Cf. *Oratio in expositione Homeri* (*Opera,* 486).

92. Cf. Ennius's triumph "sub tanto auctore" (Scipio) in the *Africa* (9.402). For the root meaning of *auctoritas* ("ce don réservé à peu d'hommes de faire surgir quelque chose et—à la lettre—de produire à l'existence"), see Benveniste, *Le vocabulaire des institutions indo-européennes,* 2:151.

93. The *Raccolta aragonese* has a pedagogical intent comparable to that of the *Sylvae:* it will educate Federico about Italian poetry.

94. For *carmina=munera,* cf. Elegy, 6.31–32 (*Prose volgari inedite . . . ,* 238).

95. Poliziano speaks "de Homero vate, doctrinarum omnium, atque ingeniorum autore, et principe" (*Oratio . . . ,* in *Opera,* 477). Cf. Vico, *Scienza nuova,* sec. 899–901.

96. "Neque ullum unque extitisse ingenium Homerico maius, neque opus aliquod extare humanum, quod sit Homericae poesi anteferendum" (*Opera,* 478).

97. "In qua [sc. philosophia] nulla est ferme nobilior posterorum sententia, aut opinio celebrata, cuius non in poeta Homero originem agnoscamus" (*Opera,* 479). For example, he anticipates Thales in making water (Okeanos) the origin of all things.

98. Cf. the verses, influenced like Poliziano by the pseudo-Plutarchan *De Homero,* with which Carlo Marsuppini dedicated his translation of book 1 of the *Iliad* to Pope Nicholas V:

> Ac velut Oceano dicuntur flumina labi
> Cunctas per terras uno decurrere ab ortu,
> Sic uno sacri vates nascuntur Homero,
> Ora rigant illo, pater est atque omnibus idem.

(Cited by Sabbadini, *Il Metodo degli umanisti,* 51. Cf. Georg Finsler, *Homer in der Neuzeit von Dante bis Goethe* [1912; reprint, Hildesheim: G. Olms, 1973], 24 ff.)

99. See his letter to Paolo Cortese in *Opera,* 113–14 (= *Prosatori latini del Quattrocento,* 902–4).

100. "Longis siquidem obsita saeclis / Fama tacet, centumque deae premit ora vetustas" (33–34).

101. Florence, 1488, edited by Poliziano's teacher Demetrius Chalcondyles.

102. In 1485–86 Poliziano only taught the *Iliad* (in addition to Juvenal), so the myth predominantly addresses that poem. However, *Ambra* also later introduces and resumes the *Odyssey,* so the *praelectio* serves both epics.

103. The subsequent description of how Thetis immediately repairs her beauty and becomes sociable (180–201) emphasizes the consolatory power of the divine gift.

104. He also has the power, similar to Jupiter's promise to Thetis, of placating what would otherwise be everlasting sorrow: "Ipsa etiam lachrymas sipyleia fundere cautes [Niobe] / Destitit audito" (223–24).

105. See Giuseppe Toffanin, "L'Omero del Poliziano," *La Rinascita* 4 (1941): 550.

106. Cf. Poliziano's letter to Jacopo Antiquario (*Opera*, 40–41), "del dovere di non rispettare i morti," as Eugenio Garin summarizes it in "L'Ambiente del Poliziano," *La cultura filosofica del Rinascimento* (Florence: Sansoni, 1979), 342. There, the context is philology. Cf. also Greene, *The Light in Troy*, 39: creative imitation involves "a civilized violence, a loving sacrilege."

107. "et longa rursum Hectora vulnerat umbra" (278).

108. *Iliad*, 18.483–85; *Ambra*, 279–81.

109. Poliziano echoes this in his narration of the blinding of Tiresias by Pallas in Callimachus' Hymn 5, which he translated in 1489 (*Miscellanea*, 1.80; *Prose volgari inedite* . . . , 535; cf. *Nutricia* 236–37). Tiresias was punished for seeing the goddess nude. Poliziano may also have been influenced by the legend of the blinding of Stesichorus, according to which the poet's maltreated subject, Helen, avenged herself on him until he composed a palinode (see Plato, *Phaedrus*, 243a–b; Isocrates, *Helen*, 64; Horace, *Epodes*, 17.42–44; *Nutricia*, 599–600); and by the blinding of Thamyras (at least in *Nutricia* 330 he specifies the poet's punishment for competing with the Muses as blinding and deprival of the poetic gift; see *Iliad*, 2.594–600 [discussed above] and Poliziano's translation [*Prose volgari inedite* . . . , 451], and Statius, *Thebaid*, 4.182–86).

110. See, for example, Cassirer, *Language and Myth*, 47, 49.

111. Cf. *Manto*, 50–51 and 313–14, where the Muse Calliope and the nymph Manto grant Virgil inspiration and the laurel crown with a somewhat gentler kiss. On the crucial role of the kiss in establishing the various intimate relations of Greek culture (of love, divinity, hospitality, and hierarchy), see Benveniste, *Le vocabulaire des institutions indo-européennes*, 1:344–45.

112. Mauss, *Essai sur le don*, 153.

113. The synopses of the two epics are not without interest, although a thorough examination here would lead too far afield. One characteristic that deserves at least passing notice is how Poliziano makes Homer's composition of his poem's plot become the poet's participation in the action itself. For example (regarding the duel between Menelaus and Paris):

> Ipsos icto mox foedere amantes
> Committit, victumque rapit phryga nubibus atris,
> Victorem Atriden nec opino vulnerat arcu.

(323–25)

Cf. 367–68. This procedure is related to a certain sort of metalepsis, following Fontanier's definition: "ce tour . . . par lequel, dans la chaleur de l'enthousiasme ou du sentiment, on abandonne tout-à-coup le rôle de narrateur pour celui de maître ou d'arbitre souverain, en sorte que, au lieu de raconter simplement une chose qui se fait ou qui est faite, on commande, on ordonne qu'elle se fasse" (Pierre Fontanier, *Les Figures du Discours* [Paris: Flammarion, 1977], 129).

114. For the ancient tradition of Homer's apotheosis, see Franz Cumont, *Recherches sur le symbolisme funéraire des Romains* (Paris: Geuthner, 1942), 7–8.

115. Cf. the wandering poet's *inoffensos* . . . *gressus* (292).

116. Cf. 29–30. The picture recalls the beginning of *De rerum natura*, book 2.

117. "Sive beati / Te decor eloquii seu rerum pondera tangunt" (481–2).

118. Cf. *Manto*, 351–67 (on Virgil).

119. Alexander and Ptolemy divide between them the moments of violence and aggrandizement present in Achilles: Ptolemy killed Homer's violent critic Zoilus, while Alexander stored the Homeric poems in a precious casket (584–87).

120. See *Ambra,* 291, 307, 329, 342, 412, 416.

121. Poliziano evidently felt the influence of Statius's *Silvae* 1.3 (*Villa Tiburtina Manilii Vopisci*) and 2.2 (*Villa Surrentina Pollii Felicis*), both descriptions of the country villas of literary patrons.

122. Lorenzo too wrote an *Ambra,* an etiological poem on Poggio a Caiano (as he also wrote two *Selve*).

123. Cf. *Epigrammata latina* 99 and 100 ("In fontem Laurentii Medicis Ambram," *Prose volgari inedite . . .* , 162).

124. In his Elegy 12, "Ad Laurentiam Medicem iuniorem," Poliziano refers to *omnifera . . . Ambra* (*Prose volgari inedite . . .* , 253).

125. The catalog of all the arts and sciences deriving from Homer, which closes the part of *Ambra* devoted to his praise (up to 589), is strengthened by the anaphora of personal pronouns (*huius, huic, hunc, hoc*) referring to the poet. In the declension of the pronoun, we may see something of the grammarian's elementary exercises beneath his present lofty flight.

126. Elsewhere, the praise of Lorenzo with which Poliziano follows a narration of his death (*Ep.,* 4.2 [*Opera,* 49]) emphasizes first of all his magnificence as seeker and purchaser of classical texts. (Admittedly, the fact that Lorenzo was also a poet complicates the matter. Cf. on *Nutricia,* below.)

127. I refer only to the overall movement; the survey of ancient poetry is organized not chronologically but (mostly) by genre.

128. The same holds true for the second *Sylva, Rusticus.*

129. See generally Arthur O. Lovejoy and George Boas, *Primitivism and Related Ideas in Antiquity* (1935; reprint, New York: Octagon Books, 1965). See also Erwin Panofsky, "The Early History of Man in Two Cycles of Paintings by Piero di Cosimo," in *Studies in Iconology* (New York: Icon-Harper & Row, 1972), 40–42 (who, however, misinterprets Lovejoy's and Boas's use of the terms "hard" and "soft" primitivism on their pp. 10–11).

130. For a different approach to some of the same material, see Charles Trinkaus, *In Our Image and Likeness,* 2 vols. (London: Constable, 1970), 2:683–721; and Curtius, *European Literature,* 214–27.

131. Herodotus, 2.53.

132. *Frogs,* 1030–36.

133. On the three functions, see Benveniste, *Le vocabulaire des institutions indo-européennes,* 1:279–92; and the work of Georges Dumézil, for example *Mythe et épopée,* vol. 1: *L'idéologie des trois fonctions dans les épopées des peuples indo-européens* (Paris: Gallimard, 1968).

134. *De Oratore,* 1.8 (text: ed. A. S. Wilkins [Oxford: Oxford University Press, 1902]). Cf. Isocrates, *Nicocles* (*The Cyprians*) 6; Quintilian, *Institutio Oratoria,* 2.16.9; and Cicero, *De Inventione,* 1.2 (text: ed. E. Stroebel [Stuttgart: Teubner, 1977]):

Quidam magnus . . . vir et sapiens . . . dispersos homines in agros et in tectis silvestribus abditos ratione quadam conpulit unum in locum et congregavit et eos in unam quamque rem inducens utilem atque honestam primo propter insolentiam reclamantes, deinde propter rationem atque orationem studiosius audientes ex feris et inmanibus mites reddidit et mansuetos. ac mihi quidem hoc nec tacita videtur nec

inops dicendi sapientia perficere potuisse, ut homines a consuetudine subito convert-
eret et ad diversas rationes vitae traduceret.

In the Quattrocento, cf. Cristoforo Landino's version in his *Prolusione petrarchesca* (*Scritti critici*, 1:39):

> La eloquenzia poté da principio gl'uomini, e' quali a guisa di fiere sanza constumi,
> sanza leggi e' boschi e le spilonche abitavono, in uno ceto e congregazione ragunare,
> e, ragunati, alle leggi e al giusto vivere sottomettergli;

as well as Bartolommeo della Fonte, *Oratio in laudem oratoriae facultatis,*
cited by Attilio Bettinzoli, *A proposito delle* Sylvae *di Angelo Poliziano: ques-
tioni di poetica* (Venice: Istituto Veneto di Scienze, Lettere ed Arti, 1990), 68 n.

135. *De Oratore*, 1.16: "Est enim finitimus oratori poeta."

136. *Ars poetica*, 391–401.

137. Cf. *Satires*, 1.3.99–106. Among other ancient references, see Strabo,
Geography, 1.2.3 ff.; Plutarch, *On the Pythian Oracle*, 18 and *On the Procre-
ation of the Soul*, 33; Lactantius, *Institutiones divinae*, 5.5; Augustine, *De
civitate Dei*, 18.14.

138. *Etymologiae*, 8.7 (text: ed. W. M. Lindsay, 2 vols. [Oxford: Oxford University Press, 1911], vol. 1). It is not clear whether Isidore is only quoting Suetonius for these three sentences (which is what Lindsay indicates) or for the
entirety of chapter 7. For the latter opinion, see Augusto Rostagni, "Il proemio
di Svetonio «De poetis»," *Mélanges Marouzeau* (Paris: Les Belles Lettres,
1948), 509–23.

139. De Nolhac, 2:209–10; B. L. Ullman, "Petrarch's Favorite Books," *Studies in the Italian Renaissance* (Rome: Edizioni di storia e letteratura, 1955),
130–31.

140.

> Cum olim rudes homines, sed noscendi veri praecipueque vestigande divinitatis stu-
> dio—quod naturaliter inest homini—flagrantes, cogitare coepissent esse superiorem
> aliquam potestatem per quam mortalia regerentur, dignum rati sunt illam omni plus-
> quam humano obsequio et cultu augustiore venerari. Itaque et edes amplissimas
> meditati sunt, que templa dixerunt, et ministros sacros quos sacerdotes dici placuit,
> et magnificas statuas et vasa aurea et marmoreas mensas et purpureos amictus; ac ne
> mutus honos fieret, visum est et verbis altisonis divinitatem placare et procul ab omni
> plebeio ac publico loquendi stilo sacras superis inferre blanditias, numeris insuper
> adhibitis quibus et amenitas inesset et tedia pellerentur. Id sane non vulgari forma
> sed artificiosa quadam et exquisita et nova fieri oportuit, que quoniam greco sermone
> "poetes" dicta est, eos quoque qui hac utebantur, poetas dixerunt. (*Fam.*, 10.4.3–4)

Cf. *Fam.*, 3.22; *Invective contra medicum* 3 (*Opere latine*, 2:920); *Ep. met.*,
2.10.188 ff.

141. See Mauss, *Essai sur le don*, 164–69.

142. *Opere in versi* ... , 950–52 ("Et quoniam appareret incongruum non
aliter quam si cum villico, aut servulo, seu contubernali amico loquereris
divinitatem alloqui, voluere prudentiores ut exquisitus loquendi modus inve-
niretur, quem excogitandum sacerdotibus conmisere") and 614 ("Si vollono
che, di lungi da ogni plebeio o publico stilo di parlare, si trovassero parole
degne di ragionare dinanzi alla divinità").

143. *Opere in versi* ... , 952 ("Ut amplioris essent autoritatis, ... volentes
ob hoc ne talium veneranda maiestas ob nimiam vulgi notitiam in contemptus

precipitium efferetur") and 614 ("Acciò che queste parole paressero avere più d'efficacia, vollero che fossero sotto legge di certi numeri composte").

144. *Metaphysics,* 1.2.9 (982 b). Cf. Plato, *Theaetetus,* 155 d; and Poliziano, *Lamia (Opera,* 461): "Siquidem, ut Aristoteles ait. etiam philosophus natura philomythos, id est, fabulae studiosus est. Fabula enim admiratione constat, admiratio philosophos peperit."

145. *Thebaid,* 3.661 (for Petrarca, see De Nolhac, *Pétrarque et l'humanisme,* 1:202). Cf. Vico, *Scienza nuova,* sec. 191.

146. Boccaccio, *Opere in versi . . .,* 614.

147. *Opere in versi . . . ,* 614, continuing the passage cited above: "parole degne di ragionare dinanzi alla divinità, nelle quali le si porgessero sacrate lusinghe."

148. Boccaccio uses the expression "alle loro necessità rendere propizia [la potenza divina]," as well as the richly troubling verb *umiliare.*

149. For an anthropological view of the distinctive character of magical language as removed from ordinary language, see Bronislaw Malinowski, *Coral Gardens and their Magic,* 2 vols. (New York: American Book Company, 1935), 2:223–25.

150. Beccadelli, *Epistolarum libri V,* 2r: "Poëtae primum ex hominibus Deos introduxisse proditum est." Cf. what follows: "Magnam mehercule, et admirabilem poëtarum vim, siquidem homines humo factos, modo velint, coelo pene dixerim donant, tum posteros illustrant, et exemplo maiorum incendunt ad immortalitatem, et ut mortui etiam prosint, efficiunt."

151. Salutati, *De laboribus Herculis,* 1.2 and 2.1; *Epistolario,* 10.6 (vol. 3, p. 226). Pontano, *I Dialoghi,* 239: "[Poetica] quae princeps de Deo et disseruit et eius laudes cecinit, instituitque sacra." And what follows: "Haec e terris piorum animos in coelum devexit, impiorum detrusit in Tartara. . . . Tu e silvis homines eruisti atque e speluncis."

152. *Prosatori latini del Quattrocento,* 594. Cf. the beginning of *Ambra,* as cited earlier.

153. *Disputationes Camaldulenses* 1 (*Prosatori latini del Quattrocento,* 782), *Prolusione petrarchesca (Scritti critici e teorici,* 1:39), *Proemio al commento dantesco (Scritti critici e teorici,* 1:145).

Cf. the Florentine *prolusio* (1421) of Andrea Benzi (Ugo da Siena) in Karl Müllner, ed., *Reden und Briefe italienischer Humanisten* (1899; reprint, Munich: W. Fink, 1970), 110–11. The praise of rhetoric as one of the liberal arts utilizes the Ciceronian topos: "[rhetorica] vagos dissipatosque homines ab ferina atque agresti vita ad humanum cultum civilemque deduxit"; but subsequently praises the immortalizing power of eloquence in terms that echo the poet's defense in *Pro Archia,* 6.14: "hac una maximarum rerum memoria tenetur clarissimorumque virorum nomen immortalitati commendatur, quae nisi ab oratoribus mandata fuissent litteris, haud dubie in tenebris iacuissent" (*ab oratoribus* is Benzi's addition).

154. For the date, see Charles Trinkaus, "The Unknown Quattrocento Poetics of Bartolommeo della Fonte," *Studies in the Renaissance* 13 (1966): 45. Trinkaus gives the text of the treatise on pp. 95–122.

155. Trinkaus, "The Unknown Quattrocento Poetics . . . ," 97.

156. Cf. Manlio Pastore Stocchi, "Il pensiero politico degli umanisti," *Storia delle idee politiche economiche e sociali,* ed. Luigi Firpo, vol. 3 (Turin: UTET, 1987), 24.

157. See Vico, *Scienza nuova,* secs. 721, 724, 734. For significant examples

of poetic paleology between the Quattrocento and Vico, see Ariosto's Satire 6, and Ronsard's Ode "A Michel de L'Hospital" 527–68.

158. See Vico, *Scienza nuova*, sec. 367:

> Dobbiamo ... dar incominciamento alla sapienza poetica da una rozza lor metafisica [of the *poeti teologi*], dalla quale, come da un tronco, si diramino per un ramo la logica, la morale, l'iconomica e la politica, tutte poetiche; e per un altro ramo, tutte eziandio poetiche, la fisica, la qual sia stata madre della loro cosmografia, e quindi dell'astronomia, che ne dia accertate le due sue figliuole, che sono cronologia e geografia.

Cf. secs. 199 and 381.

159. Vico, *Scienza nuova*, secs. 199 and 250.

160. Ibid., secs. 18 and 555.

161. Ibid., secs. 523 and 694.

162. Ibid., sec. 782.

163. Ibid., secs. 517–18. For an important later text, which both carries on the tradition of poetic paleology and absorbs the Vichian influence, see Ugo Foscolo, "Dell'origine e dell'ufficio della letteratura," *Opere*, ed. Gavazzeni, 2:1285–1325.

164. Cf. Anthony Grafton and Lisa Jardine, *From Humanism to the Humanities: Education and the Liberal Arts in Fifteenth- and Sixteenth-Century Europe* (Cambridge, Mass.: Harvard University Press, 1986).

165. In the tradition of poetic paleology, Poliziano preserves some of the Ciceronian uncertainty about what powers are to be attributed to rhetoric and what to poetry. In his *Oratio super Fabio Quintiliano et Statii Sylvis* (1480), Poliziano delivers a panegyric of rhetoric, including its civic powers: "Haec igitur una res [sc. eloquentia] et dispersos primum homines in una moenia congregavit, et dissidentes inter se conciliavit, et legibus moribusque omnique denique humano cultu civilique coniunxit" (*Opera*, 496 = *Prosatori latini del Quattrocento*, 882). However, if this echoes the passage from *De oratore* just cited, in his *Panepistemon* (1490) Poliziano also cites Cicero's judgment from the same work that "finitimus oratori poeta est" (*Opera*, 473; cf. Salutati, *De laboribus Herculis, prohemium* to book 2).

For the systematic preeminence that Poliziano attributes to poetry, see Ida Maïer, "Un inédit de Politien: la classification des «Arts»," *Bibliothèque d'Humanisme et Renaissance* 22 (1960): 338–55 (= Poliziano, *Opera omnia*, ed. Maïer, 3:191–208). Cf. Perrine Galand, introduction to Poliziano, *Les Silves* (Paris: Les Belles Lettres, 1987), 42 ff. According to Poliziano's *Panepistemon* and *De laudibus artium liberalium,* poetry possesses a supremacy both transcendent and primordial: It both founds and surpasses all other disciplines. But cf. the important dissent in interpreting *Panepistemon* expressed by Mario Martelli, "La politica culturale dell'ultimo Lorenzo," *Il Ponte* 36 (1980): 1062–64; and Bettinzoli, *A proposito delle* Sylvae, 81–83.

166. For the importance of *furor* in *Nutricia* (and in *Ambra* as well), see Bettinzoli, *A proposito delle* Sylvae, 27–33.

167. Cf. Poggio's condemnation, cited above, of the principle of inertia by which everyone remains "suo quisque contentus."

168. *De rerum natura*, 5.973–81.

169. Poliziano follows Manilius, *Astronomica*, 1.66–72 and Statius, *Thebaid*, 4.282–84.

170. When Vico imagines primitive humanity, he characterizes their state

with a similar formula, *ignoranza di cagioni* (*Scienza nuova*, sec. 375). However, for Vico it is that very ignorance that underlies the supreme poetry they possessed, while for Poliziano poetry acts as the negation of the primitive mind.

171. *De rerum natura*, 5.1026.

172. Ibid., 5.1028–29.

173. Ibid., 5.1444–45.

174. I refer to Poetry majuscule as the actor in this story; poetry minuscule is used in the more general sense. Obviously, a sharp distinction is not always possible. The movement of divine descent to rescue savage humanity is reminiscent of what takes place on an individual scale in the *Stanze*: Love's civilizing effect on Giuliano (see Tateo, *Lorenzo de' Medici e Angelo Poliziano*, 152).

175.   . . . Quod mentis acumine totum
      Naturae lustraret opus, causasque latenteis
      Eliceret rerum, et summum deprenderet aevi
      Artificem nutu terras maria astra regentem;
      Quod fretum ratione animi substerneret uni
      Cuncta sibi, ac vindex pecudum domitorque ferarum
      Posset ab ignavo senium defendere mundo. (36–42)

176. Cf. Ovid, *Fasti*, 1.306.

177. See Vico, *Scienza nuova*, sec. 375. Hence the possibility of more interpretations than the alternatives posed by Alain Michel with regard to line 95: "S'agit-il d'un socratisme lié à la civilisation de la parole ou d'une prise de conscience quasi-chrétienne, qui révèle à l'homme sa culpabilité?" ("La parole et la beauté chez Ange Politien," *Validità perenne dell'umanesimo*, ed. Giovannangiola Tarugi [Florence: Olschki, 1986], 201–2)

178. The origin of culture as escape from *ennui*: just as God sent Poetry to humanity because he was weary or disgusted (*pertaesus* [67]) with their state, so man leaves his primitive way of life because *pertaesus* (98). Paolo Paolini distinguishes two moments of Poetry's effect: *pars destruens* and *pars construens*, corresponding respectively to a passive and an active humanity ("Sul tema dell'incivilimento attraverso la poesia nei «Nutricia» del Poliziano e in altri autori" (*Italianistica* 12 [1983]: 227)).

179. Note Poliziano's use of the term for a sharply studded curb (*lupatus*) in this image. The acquiescence of the vanquished (bowing to the yoke) is a common element in the humanist ideology of Roman imperialism. One is reminded, for example, of Valla's preface to his *Elegantiae linguae latinae*, which imagines the Latin language as an imperial force parallel to Roman military power (*Prosatori latini del Quattrocento*, 594–96; cf. Flavio Biondo, proem to *Roma triumphans*, in Francesco Tateo, *La «letteratura umanistica»* [Palermo: Palumbo, 1989], 151). Linguistic empire is superior to the other kind, both because it lasts (literary monuments outlast military ones) and because it is willingly embraced by the conquered peoples.

180. Cf. Vico, *Scienze nuova*, sec. 340 for the way in which "modo e misura" (here, *numer*[*i*] and *mod*[*i*] [78]) act upon the original human passions.

181. Nunc age, qui tanto sacer hic furor incitet oestro
      Corda virûm, quam multiplices ferat enthea partus
      Mens alto cognata polo, qui praemia doctae
      Frontis apollineas ausi sibi nectere lauros
      Inclyta perpetuis mandarunt nomina saeclis,
      Expediam. (139–44)

182. In addition, a theological aspect of the simile is noted by the commentators (Kohlbürger and Sanchez, cited by Del Lungo): there are verbal parallels to a traditional simile of the Virgin Mary's conception: the conception of the Logos.

183. *Ambra,* 284–85.

184. Although the personal subject is *Deus,* this must be understood not as Jupiter, but as the *numen* Poetry (176).

185. *Phaedrus* 244 a (*theia . . . dosei*). See Dodds, *The Greeks and the Irrational,* 64.

186. Michel Foucault, *Histoire de la folie à l'âge classique* (Paris: Gallimard, 1972), 111.

187. There remains the final Foucauldian twist, in which unreason as complete negativity finds a renascence in such artistic heroes as Van Gogh, Nietzsche, and Artaud.

188. Notably Plato, *Ion,* 534, *Phaedrus,* 244–45; Cicero, *De divinatione,* 1.31.66–1.32.70, 1.36.80–1.37.81; Plutarch, *De defectu oraculorum,* 437–38.

189. The mortal direction of the passage is accentuated by the echo in 166–67 of Turnus's death in the last verse of the *Aeneid:* "sociumque hominem indignatus [Deus], ad imas / Cunctantem absterret latebras." Only, of course, here it is the slayer rather than the slain who is *indignatus.*

190. Hence a movement away from Ficinian culture. Mario Martelli has argued that such is the overall movement of the Laurentian circle ("La politica culturale dell'ultimo Lorenzo," 923–50, 1040–69).

Nevertheless, Ficino's *Platonica Theologia de immortalitate animorum* (ed. Raymond Marcel, 3 vols. [Paris: Les Belles Lettres, 1964]) is not irrelevant to the humanistic currents discussed here. In particular, among the proofs of the soul's immortality, Ficino proposes (1) the *natural* appetite for self-deification ("Totus . . . animae nostrae conatus est, ut deus efficiatur" [book 14, chap. 1]), 2) the ambition of human industry that competes with the gods ("Caelesti virtute ascendit caelum atque metitur. Supercaelesti mente transcendit caelum" [13.3]), 3) the innate desire to dominate ("Superare autem obnixe qualibet in re contendit" [14.4]), 4) "Quod homo affectat ubique esse atque item esse semper" (14.5), which includes the desire for the immortality of fame. What is missing here is the central function of poetry, even though Ficino considers language (*sermo*) "infinitorum inventorum praeco et nuntius infinitus" (13.3). Cf. Trinkhaus, *In Our Image and Likeness,* 2:461–504.

191. Inde sacrosanctas modulati carmine leges,
    Multisonum fecêre nomon: nec vulnera tantum
    Saeva, sed et caecos vincebant carmine morbos:
    Sacrifici quondam nec dis ignara poetae
    Nomina: quin magicas arcano murmure linguas
    In varios duxere modos. (278–83)

192. The language is similar: "Dulci leo carmine captus / Submittit cervice jubas" (124–25); cf. 118–19.

193. Orpheus's traditional role as originator of pederasty points in the same direction; it is not mentioned here (where that distinction belongs to Thamyras [332]), but has a prominent place in Poliziano's *Fabula di Orfeo.*

194. *Manto, praefatio,* 13–28. Cf. *Rusticus* 4–6, where Poliziano begins by acknowledging a gift from Tityrus (Virgil), the rustic pipe that will enable him to praise pastoral poetry in this *praelectio.*

195. *Morgante* 28.146 (ed. George B. Weston, 2 vols. [Bari: Laterza, 1930]).

Cf. Poliziano's *Epigramma latinum* 23, praising a certain improvisor named Antonio: "Antonius Orpheo / Hoc differt: homines hic trahit, ille feras" (*Prose volgari inedite* . . . , 121).

196. *Prose volgari inedite* . . . , 432, 434. While the first passage cited above clearly refers to Lorenzo as poet as distinct from his role as patron, the conclusion of the dedication (including the second passage cited) mixes the two roles, and, with the term *dux* and the subsequent request for protection against Zoiluses, may place more emphasis on Lorenzo the patron.

197. *Georgics*, 4.519–20 (Orpheus "inrita Ditis / dona querens"); *Metamorphoses*, 10.37 (Orpheus appeals: "pro munere poscimus usum"), 10.52 (he fears "inrita dona futura"), 10.74 (finally, "sine munere sedit"). Cf. Seneca, *Hercules Oetaeus* 1088 ("cantus praemia perdidit"). Generally on Orpheus in all these works, see Charles Segal, *Orpheus: The Myth of the Poet* (Baltimore: Johns Hopkins University Press, 1989).

When in the *Fabula di Orfeo* (v. 220) Orpheus says to Pluto and Proserpina: "i' non vel chieggio in don, quest'è prestanza" (Poliziano, *Stanze Orfeo Rime*, ed. Davide Puccini [Milan: Garzanti, 1992]), he is not denying the structure of bestowal; on the contrary, he is only emphasizing its reciprocal nature (*prestanza* as Maussian *prestation*). In the same poem, Orpheus refers later to the "commerzio . . . co' mie' sermoni" (275).

198. Maurice Blanchot, "Le regard d'Orphée," *L'espace littéraire* (Paris: Gallimard, 1955), 227–34.

199. Cf. *Fabula di Orfeo* (v. 252), where Orpheus exclaims upon losing Eurydice again: "O mie furore!"

200. Similarly in *Georgics*, 4.523–27; *Metamorphoses*, 11.50–53; Statius, *Silvae*, 2.7.98–99.

201. Following Macrobius (*Saturnalia*, 4.4.12), Poliziano noted in his commentary to the *Georgics* (4.525) the pathetic effect of Virgil's repeated *Eurydicen* (see Poliziano, *Commento inedito alle Georgiche di Virgilio*, ed. Livia Castano Musicò [Florence: Olschki, 1990], 223). Petrarca, too (*Triumphus Cupidinis*, 4.15), follows the tradition of Orpheus's posthumous poetizing: "Con la lingua già fredda anco la chiama."

For the head of Orpheus in plastic art, see José Doerig, "La tête qui chante," *Orphisme et Orphée en l'honneur de Jean Rudhardt*, ed. Philippe Borgeaud (Geneva: Droz, 1991), 61–64.

202. Cf. the three great Greek tragedians, each of whom is mentioned only through an account of his death (666–69).

203. Significantly, Orpheus's statue acts as a silent oracle upon the passage of Alexander the Great: "Quin et, pellaei quondam praesaga triumphi, / Delicuit sudore sacro libethris imago" (315–16). His lyre ascends to the heavens where, as a constellation, it exercises the same power over stars that it did formerly over earthly nature (313–14).

204. "L'Ambiente del Poliziano," 339. Cf. Garin, *Ritratti di umanisti* (Florence: Sansoni, 1967), 136 ff.

205. However, if we remember that Pico's *Oratio* is a prologue to his 900 *Conclusiones*, where verbal magic (Kabbalah, Hermeticism) plays a crucial role (see the following chapter), Adam and Orpheus may not seem so far apart after all.

206. As a matter of fact, the *Sylvae* themselves, as texts delivered from a professorial chair at the Florentine Studio, embody the degree to which Poliziano has "made it." See Bettinzoli, *A proposito delle* Sylvae, 43.

207. Vico, *Scienza nuova,* sec. 912.

208. Cf. the elegy *De Ovidii exilio et morte (Prose volgari inedite* . . . , 255–56), which was apparently a *praelectio* to Poliziano's course on Ovid in 1493–94.

209. Or another of the Muses. See *Paulys Real-Encyclopädie der classischen Altertumswissenschaft,* ed. Georg Wissowa and Wilhelm Kroll (Stuttgart: Metzler, 1927), vol. 13: col. 716. The story is found in Apollodorus (2.4.9), who calls Linus the brother of Orpheus; and in Diodorus Siculus (3.67), who makes him the teacher of Orpheus as well as Hercules.

210. Apollodorus says that Hercules struck Linus because the latter had already struck him with the lyre; while Diodorus has Hercules beaten for incompetence in his lesson.

211. See *Odyssey,* 22.330–80.

212. For example, Giordano Bruno's *Candelaio,* Giambattista Della Porta's *La Fantesca.* Montaigne alludes to the convention at the beginning of "Du pedantisme" (Montaigne, *Oeuvres complètes,* 132).

213. See Pausanias, 9.23.

214. See Norwood, *Pindar,* 65: "Between the gods and the nobles of his own day he [Pindar] observes differences great, indeed, but less than they have ever been in the view of any other civilized man."

215. Cf. *Nutricia,* 637 where Poliziano follows an epigram from the Greek Anthology (1.67.11) in showing Sappho become the tenth Muse. (Poliziano cites the epigram in his *Enarratio in Sapphus epistolam,* ed. Elisabetta Lazzeri [Florence: Sansoni, 1971], 5.)

216. See Tzvetan Todorov, "Histoire de la littérature," in Oswald Ducrot and Tzvetan Todorov, *Dictionnaire encyclopédique des sciences du langage* (Paris: Seuil, 1972), 191–92.

217. Text in Léon Dorez, "L'Hellénisme d'Ange Politien," *Mélanges d'archéologie et d'histoire* 15 (1895): 25–28.

218. "omnis effinxisse rerum omnium voces, ab uno illo et celeberrimam quanque philosophi sectam defluxisse et poetas omnis emanasse, etc." (Dorez, 26).

219. Dorez, "L'Hellénisme d'Ange Politien," 26. Cf. Silius Italicus, *Punica,* 13.784–89, where Scipio Africanus, who has descended alive to the underworld, sees Homer and exclaims his admiration:

> "qui vultus! quam, si Stygia non esset in umbra,
> dixissem facile esse deum!" "non falleris," inquit
> docta comes Triviae [a Sibyl], "meruit deus esse videri,
> et fuit in tanto non parvum pectore numen.
> carmine complexus terram, mare, sidera, manes
> et cantu Musas et Phoebum aequavit honore. . . . "

Text: ed. J. D. Duff, 2 vols. (Cambridge, Mass.: Loeb, 1934).

220. *Patrologiae cursus completus, series latina,* ed. J.-P. Migne (Paris, 1886), vol. 42: col. 27. However, Marcellina (not Marcella) was only a member of the sect, which was founded by Carpocrates. She was in Rome in the mid-second century.

221. See Irenaeus, *Adversus haereses,* 1.25; *Dictionnaire de Théologie Catholique,* ed. A. Vacant et al. (Paris: Letouzey et Ané, 1923–50), 2:1800; *Enciclopedia cattolica* (Città del Vaticano, 1949), 3:929–30.

222. Irenaeus (1.25) mentions Plato and Aristotle as well as Pythagoras. Cf. Cumont, *Recherches sur le symbolisme funéraire des Romains,* 263–64.

223. For the ancient tradition, in literature (Philo Judaeus, Heraclitus the Stoic) and art, concerning the apotheosis of Homer, see Cumont, *Recherches . . . ,* 7–8.

224. Dorez, "L'Hellénisme d'Ange Politien," 26.

225. Cf. *Epigramma latinum* 17, where Lorenzo is credited with the construction of the body politic, figured as a human body.

226. *Maeonia* refers to Lydia in Asia Minor, both the land of Homer and where the Etruscans allegedly originated. Hence, *Maeonius* or *Maeonides* is elsewhere an epithet for Homer (*Nutricia* 343, 455). See, for example, Horace, *Carm.,* 4.9.5; Petrarca, *Africa* 9.66; *Ambra,* 12; Poliziano's elegy to Bartolommeo della Fonte, lines 135 and 164 (della Fonte, *Carmina,* ed. J. Fógel and L. Juhász [Leipzig: Teubner, 1932]; reprinted in Poliziano, *Opera omnia,* ed. Maïer, 3:171–72); and his dedication to Lorenzo of book 2 of his Latin *Iliad,* line 4, where both senses are probably present.

227. This passage recalls young Homer's divine companions in *Ambra* (225–32). Cf. the ambiguity of *Maeonia/Maeonius,* above (*Nutricia,* 732).

228. The image of his shade is also present in Ficino, Naldo Naldi, Bernardo Bellincioni and others (see André Rochon, "A l'ombre du laurier," *Florence au temps de Laurent le Magnifique* [Paris: Hachette, 1965], 167). Lorenzo's own *Altercazione* (or *De summo Bono* [1.13]) represents him as reposing "là dove un verde lauro faceva ombra" (text: Lorenzo de' Medici, *Tutte le Opere,* ed. Paolo Orvieto, 2 vols. [Rome: Salerno, 1992], 2:927).

Poliziano extended the metaphor to other patrons. See his letter to Pope Innocent VIII (*Ep.,* 8.4 [*Opera,* 105]): "Spero autem fore, ut quam diu sub umbra tui numinis recubuero. . . . "

For the broader tradition of the shade of patronage, see Annabel Patterson, *Pastoral and Ideology: Virgil to Valéry* (Berkeley: University of California Press, 1987), 49–57, 84; more generally on poetic landscapes, including shade, see Curtius, *European Literature,* 183–202.

229. See Cassirer, *Language and Myth,* 51, *The Philosophy of Symbolic Forms,* 2:40–41.

230. This latter aspect is developed elsewhere. See, for example, *Miscellaneorum centuria prima, praefatio* (*Opera,* 216): "Sicuti sub Aiacis clypeo Teucer Homericus, ita nos utique sub umbra tui nominis latitantes, centuriatim dabimus in barbaros impressionem."

231. *Stanze cominciate per la giostra del magnifico Giuliano di Piero de' Medici,* stanza 4 (text: Poliziano, *Stanze Orfeo Rime,* ed. Puccini).

232. For examples from Poliziano's correspondence, see: *Ep.,* 4.10 (*Opera,* 57) to Giovanni Gozzo (Ioanni Gottio Ragusino) with thanks for the immortality bestowed on him by the dedication of a collection of poetry ("Equidem gratias tibi ago immortaleis, utpote quem tuis illustrando carminibus immortalitate donaveris"); *Ep.,* 12.5 (*Opera,* 167), where he likewise thanks Pico for immortalizing him by the dedication of *De ente et uno:* "Arsi pene semper, nimis improbe forsitan, sed arsi tamen semper studio famae perpetuae" (with an echo of the epithet *improbus* which describes both Homer at Achilles' tomb in *Ambra* [266], and Poliziano himself in *Nutricia* [25]); and *Ep.,* 10.1 (*Opera,* 136–38) to King John of Portugal, which includes Alexander at Achilles' tomb. In the *Stanze,* see 1.1; 2.12, 15, 32, and 40–43.

233. *Stanze,* stanza 1.

234. "Tu, Tityre, lentus in umbra / formosam resonare doces Amaryllida silvas" (*Eclogues,* 1.4.). For the same position and relation to literary production, cf. Martial 9.84.3: "haec ego Pieria ludebam tutus in umbra"; and (for the same position and withdrawl from active life) Statius, *Silvae* 5.2.104: "tacita studiorum occultus in umbra. . . . " Poliziano uses *silvae* and *umbracula* in *Manto* (112, 128, 132) to evoke Virgil's pastoral poetry.

235. Peter L. Smith, *"Lentus in umbra:* A Symbolic Pattern in Vergil's *Eclogues," Phoenix* 19 (1965): 298. See also Michael C. J. Putnam, "Virgil's First Eclogue: Poetics of Enclosure," *Ancient Pastoral:* Ramus *Essays on Greek and Roman Pastoral Poetry* (Berwick, Australia: Aureal Publications, 1975), 81–104. Cf. Curtius, *European Literature,* 187, on poetry under trees.

236. See Smith, *"Lentus in umbra,"* 301. Cf. the repeated emphasis on shade in Ennius's vision of Petrarca, at a supreme moment of temporal reversal (*Africa* 9.274–78).

237. For a representative example, see the sonnet "Cerchi chi vuol le pompe e gli alti onori" in the *Comento de' miei sonetti* (*Tutte le Opere,* 1:455), where the poet professes to abandon civic ennuis in favor of *ombrose selve* (which expression, as editor Orvieto points out, echoes Petrarca's *Canzoniere,* 162.7). As Domenico De Robertis comments: "immagine, la «selva», della storia poetica di Lorenzo" ("L'esperienza poetica del Quattrocento," in Cecchi and Sapegno, 3:524).

238. See *De Inventione,* 1.2, cited earlier, *Carm.,* 1.12.8 and *Ars Poetica,* 391. Cf. Pontano, *Actius* (*Dialoghi,* 239), also cited earlier.

239. Vico, *Scienza nuova,* sec. 388. On Vico's forest, see Robert Pogue Harrison, *Forests: The Shadow of Civilization* (Chicago: University of Chicago Press, 1992), 3–13.

240. The exercise of philology and thus of pedagogy is itself a wandering in the forest. See *Ep.,* 12.1 (*Opera,* 165) to Pico: "Non mediocres enim tenebrae in sylva, ubi haec captanda."

241. Cf. the epithet for Cerberus, *umbrarum custos* (*Nutricia* 127), charmed by the Orphic spell.

242. Meque per aoniae sequitur compendia sylvae
    Ereptans avide montem, jamque instat anhelo.
    It jam pene prior. Sic, o, sic pergat! et ipsum
    Me superet majore gradu, longeque relinquat
    Protinus! et dulci potius plaudatur alumno,
    Bisque mei victore illo celebrentur honores! (785–90)

The use of *compendia* as both "short cut" and "summary" here at the end of the poem, echoing its use at the beginning (8) as "profit," makes all the clearer the poem's incorporation of exchange structure.

243. *Tusculanae Disputationes,* 1.45.109: "nihil habet in se gloria cur expetatur, tamen virtutem tamquam umbra sequitur." On the other hand, Cicero asserts later in the same work that true glory is not *adumbrata* ("est enim gloria solida quaedam res et expressa, non adumbrata" [3.2.3]).

244. For an influential interpretation of Lorenzo's death as the end of the good times in Italy, see Francesco Guicciardini, *Storia d'Italia,* ed. Ettore Mazzali, 3 vols. (Milan: Garzanti, 1988), 1:4–9. For the historical myth of Lorenzo as presiding over a golden age, see André Chastel, "La légende médicéenne," *Revue d'histoire moderne et contemporaine* 6 (1959): 161–80 (= Chastel, *Art et humanisme,* 11–27); Felix Gilbert, *Machiavelli and Guicciardini: Politics and History in Sixteenth Century Florence* (New York: Norton, 1984),

105–22; and Melissa Meriam Bullard, "The magnificent Lorenzo de' Medici: between myth and history," *Politics and Culture in Early Modern Europe: Essays in Honor of H. G. Koenigsberger,* ed. Phyllis Mack and Margaret C. Jacob (Cambridge: Cambridge University Press, 1987), 25–58.

245. On the unusual metrical form of this ode, resembling that of the chorus of classical tragedy, see Ugo Enrico Paoli, "La trenodia del Poliziano «In Laurentiam Medicum» [sic]," *Studi italiani di filologia classica,* n.s. 16 (1939): 165–76.

246. And cf. *Nutricia* 132–38 for the ability of poetry to placate Jupiter's thunderbolts.

247. *Prose volgari inedite* . . . , 275. All citations from this poem are on the same page. John Sparrow has mentioned Eduard Fraenkel's suggestion of *impete* rather than *impetu* (Sparrow, "Latin Verse of the High Renaissance," *Italian Renaissance Studies: A Tribute to the late Cecilia M. Ady,* ed. E. F. Jacob [New York: Barnes & Noble, 1960], 404–5; as well as Sparrow and Alessandro Perosa, eds., *Renaissance Latin Verse: An Anthology* [Chapel Hill: University of North Carolina Press, 1979], 140).

Cf. Filelfo's *Satire* 4.9.97 ff., where he prays that God may blast his enemy, Lorenzo's grandfather Cosimo, with a thunderbolt (*Poeti latini del Quattrocento,* 46).

248. *Canzoniere,* 323.25–36. Poliziano may have been influenced by Propertius, 2.28.36: "iacet exstincto laurus adusta foco" (where, however, the laurel, like *carmen* [line 35], has been an element in a magical rite). Cf. also Lorenzo's own *Canzoniere,* 14, where the poet imagines himself as laurel dying for want of his beloved's favor (figured as Apollo's rays).

249. Castelvetro cited by Michele Feo, "Il sogno di Cerere e la morte del lauro petrarchesco," *Il Petrarca ad Arquà,* 143.

250. On the other hand, Petrarca denies (*Fam.,* 15.9) that lightning striking the Roman Tarpeian Rock is proof of God's wrath against that place.

251. One can only speculate where such a twist to the myth would lead Vico. Considering the foundational role of thunderbolts for poetry (and, consequently, for religion and politics etc.), Vico would confront the impasse of poetry destroyed by its very origin, of the cosmic gesture as both bestowal of sublime style and negation of the right to exist. (See *Scienza nuova* sec. 377–83, introduction above, and the discussion of poetry as lightning for the conqueror in Budé's *L'Institution du Prince,* below).

252. *Canzoniere,* 323.36. Cf. sonnet 269, which mourns the death of both the laurel and the patron (Giovanni Colonna), "che facean ombra al mio stanco pensero." Cf. also Greene, *The Light in Troy,* 134 on the poet as lover of shadows.

253. Poliziano's translation of *Iliad* 2–5 is followed by a final formula naming the dedicatee Lorenzo, "du[x] et auctor . . . ingenui laboris" (*Prose volgari inedite* . . . , 523).

254. This helps us understand the motto Lorenzo wore for a tournament in 1469: "le temps revient."

255. Cf. *Ep.,* 4.2 (*Opera,* 46): "Illo [sc. Lorenzo] igitur nunc extincto, qui fuerat unicus autor eruditi laboris, videlicet ardor etiam scribendi noster extinctus est, omnisque prope veterum studiorum alacritas elanguit."

However: an ancient tradition sketched by Rohde (*Psyche,* 581–82) turns us once again in a contrary direction. "In many legends death by *lightning* makes the victim holy and raises him to godlike (everlasting) life. . . . The body of the person struck by lightning remains uncorruptible" (581; emphasis in original).

CHAPTER 4. GUILLAUME BUDÉ

Pierre de Ronsard, Elegy 21 ("La Promesse") (*Oeuvres complètes,* 2:391).

Friedrich Nietzsche, *Also sprach Zarathustra,* erster Teil, "Von tausend und einem Ziele" (*Werke,* ed. Karl Schlechta, 5 vols. [Frankfurt: Ullstein, 1984], 2:597).

1. See Greene, *The Light in Troy,* 81–103.

2. *Miscellaneorum centuria secunda,* cap. 1. In *Ep.,* 6.11 (*Opera,* 83) he refers to Ficino as *Platonis Aesculapiu[s].* Cf. below on Budé's *De Philologia* (92). For other examples of the humanist as Aesculapius (Petrarca, *Fam.,* 24.7; Boccaccio, *Genealogie,* 1.9), see Paul Colilli, "Scipio's Triumphal Ascent in the *Africa,*" in *Petrarch's* Triumphs: *Allegory and Spectacle,* ed. Konrad Eisenbichler and Amilcare A. Iannucci (Toronto: Dovehouse Editions, 1990), 150, 157–58.

3. In the prefatory letter for his *Commentarii linguae latinae* (1536), addressed to Budé, Etienne Dolet claims that reference books, which must be taken up again and again, possess an immortality naturally superior to works of fiction (*ficta orationum argumenta*) (in *Prosateurs latins en France au XVIe siècle,* ed. and trans. Stephen Bamforth et al. [Paris: Presses de l'Université de Paris, 1987], 250–52). In a letter to Poliziano, Macario Mutio assures the author of the *Miscellanea* immortality from his elucidation of classical writers in that work (Poliziano, *Ep.,* 7.1 [*Opera,* 87]).

Something similar holds true for literary historians, for example Estienne Pasquier. In *Les Recherches de la France* (Paris: Laurens Sonnius, 1621), 594, he boasts: "Si les Poëtes par leurs livres font revivre ceux qui sont morts, j'auray par un privilege special de ma plume, donné la vie à nostre Poësie, recitant son origine, ancienneté & progrez" (bk. 7, chap. 1).

Hence a tradition that produces literature professors as "salaried, middle-class shamans" (Stephen Greenblatt, *Shakespearean Negotiations* [Berkeley-Los Angeles: University of California Press, 1988], 1).

4. The question asked by Lucien Febvre is still valid today: "C'est un fort grand nom sans doute, dans l'histoire de l'humanisme français que celui de Guillaume Budé; mais, à vrai dire, est-ce autre chose qu'un nom?" ("Guillaume Budé et les origines de l'humanisme français à propos d'ouvrages récents," *Revue de Synthèse historique* [1907]: 1).

5. Erasmus claimed to wish that golden statues of Budé (*holochrusoi*) were raised all over France (*Opus Epistolarum,* ep. 531, l. 55). Cf. *De Philologia,* where Budé has his interlocutor François 1er imagine philologists as erectors of golden and silver statues in public places (Budé, *Opera omnia,* 4 vols. [Basel, 1557], 1:52).

6. Most informative on Budé's life and times are Eugène de Budé, *Vie de Guillaume Budé: Fondateur du Collège de France (1467-1540)* (1884; reprint, Geneva: Slatkine, 1969); Louis Delaruelle, *Guillaume Budé: les origines, les débuts, les idées maîtresses* (Paris: Champion, 1907); Augustin Renaudet, *Préréforme et humanisme à Paris pendant les premières guerres d'Italie* (Paris, 1953); Madeleine Foisil, "Guillaume Budé (1467–1540)," in Roland Mousnier et al., *Le Conseil du Roi de Louis XII à la Révolution* (Paris: PUF, 1970),

277–92; David O. McNeil, *Guillaume Budé and Humanism in the Reign of Francis I* (Geneva: Droz, 1975); Marie-Madeleine de la Garanderie, *Christianisme et lettres profanes: Essai sur l'Humanisme français (1515–1535) et sur la pensée de Guillaume Budé* (Paris: Champion, 1995).

7. See, for example, Luis Vives, *De conscribendis epistolis,* and Christophe de Longueil, letter of 29 January 1519 to Jacques Lucas, both cited in *La Correspondance d'Erasme et de Guillaume Budé,* trans. Marie-Madeleine de la Garanderie (Paris: Vrin, 1967), 49, 274–75, respectively; as well as Cuthbert Tunstall's letter to Budé in Erasmus, *Opus Epistolarum,* 2:538–42 (ep. 571).

8. Orest Ranum refers to Budé as "the Petrarch of France" (*Artisans of Glory: Writers and Historical Thought in Seventeenth-Century France* [Chapel Hill: University of North Carolina Press, 1980], 36).

9. See, for example, Renaudet, and such works of Franco Simone as *La Coscienza della Rinascita negli umanisti francesi* (Rome: Edizioni di storia e letteratura, 1949), or "Une entreprise oubliée des humanistes français: De la prise de conscience historique du renouveau culturel à la naissance de la première histoire littéraire," in *Humanism in France at the end of the Middle Ages and in the early Renaissance,* ed. A. H. T. Levi (New York: Barnes & Noble, 1970), 106–31.

10. See his letter to Cuthbert Tunstall in Budé, *Opera,* 1:356–64 (*Ep.* 5.1) (= Erasmus, *Opus Epistolarum,* 2:560–75 [*Ep.* 583]); *De Philologia* (*Opera,* 1:60); more generally on Budé's education, Delaruelle, *Guillaume Budé,* 67–76.

11. "Was anything but what is conventionally called a classical spirit" (Marie-Madeleine de la Garanderie, "L'Harmonie secrète du 'De Asse,'" *Bulletin de l'Association Guillaume Budé* 27 [1968]: 485).

12. See *Ep.* 5.3 (*Opera,* 1:368): "hoc insano literarum amore captus sum." Cf. Louis Le Roy, *Vita Budaei* (init.), in vol. 1 of Budé's *Opera.*

13. De la Garanderie, *Christianisme et lettres profanes,* 56.

14. De la Garanderie, 56.

15. See Morris R. Croll, "Juste Lipse et le mouvement anticicéronien," *Style, Rhetoric and Rhythm* (Princeton: Princeton University Press, 1966), 24–25.

16. Bérault was a friend and correspondent of Budé. See de la Garanderie, *Christianisme . . . ,* 47–68; and Budé's epistles to him in *Opera omnia,* vol. 1.

17. See Delaruelle, *Guillaume Budé,* 103 ff.; Donald R. Kelley, *Foundations of Modern Historical Scholarship: Language, Law, and History in the French Renaissance* (New York: Columbia University Press, 1970), 46–50, 68; Branca, *Poliziano e l'umanesimo della parola,* 182–92.

18. For example, *Miscellaneorum centuria prima,* capp. 41, 77, 78, 82, 84, 93, 95; *Miscellaneorum centuria secunda,* capp. 8, 20, 56, and especially 44; cf. his *Ep.* 5.9 (*Opera,* 69–72). See also Anthony Grafton, "Quattrocento Humanism and Classical Scholarship," in *Renaissance Humanism,* ed. Rabil, 3:39–40.

19. *Annotationes in Pandectas* (*Opera,* 3:67).

20. See Budé's criticism of Poliziano in *De Asse* (*Opera,* 2:13, 196–97). He finds fault with Valla too (*Opera,* 2:224), although he also praises him (2:213), applying to him the same epithet, *Hercules Alexicacus,* which he applies elsewhere (2:301) to Christ.

21. See Erasmus's *Ep.* 531, lines 47 ff.: "Videmus egregios illos heroas et

omnium consensu prorsus inimitabliles, Hermolaum Barbarum et Angelum Politianum, . . . longe abs te superatos" (*Opus Epistolarum*, 2:460).

22. See Branca, *Poliziano*, 194; and Grafton, "Quattrocento Humanism and Classical Scholarship," *Renaissance Humanism*, 3:32–54.

23. Cf. Varro, *De lingua Latina*, 5.

24. Poliziano, *Opera*, 229.

25. See Branca, *Poliziano*, 167; Poliziano's letter to Jacopo Antiquario mentioned above; and, for the classical tradition of a battle with predecessors, Pliny, *Epist.*, 7.9

26. In his preface to the 1557 edition of Budé's *Opera* (vol. 1), Coelius Secundus Curio expresses thus the autodidact Budé's conquest of ancient literature: "Suo Marte sine praeceptore et duce, una pertinaci fretus diligentia, ut cum ipsis linguarum autoribus certaret" (first page of the unpaginated preface). Also, in a more general sense, three pages later: "Non sine sudore quidem et pulvere, sed sine sanguine sunt Musarum certamina: et quos litterae dissociavere, eaedem saepe reconciliant," and what follows. On the Renaissance (largely Italian) current of ancient numismatics which *De Asse* crowned, see Roberto Weiss, *The Renaissance Discovery of Classical Antiquity* (Oxford: Blackwell, 1973), 167–79, 206–7.

27. For example, *Opera*, 2:73, 145, 270.

28. *Opera*, 2:65. Cf. Delaruelle, *Guillaume Budé*, 146; and Gilbert Gadoffre, "Guillaume Budé e la storia di Roma," trans. Franca Bevilacqua Caldari, *Studi Romani* 35 (1987): 271–72.

29. For an example of Budé's ambivalence toward an ancient author (Pliny), see *De Asse* (*Opera*, 2:9).

30. For other Budean references, see Delaruelle, *Guillaume Budé*, 120; and Maurice Lebel, "Le concept de l'encyclopaedia dans l'oeuvre de Guillaume Budé," *Acta Conventus Neo-latini torontonensis* (Binghamton, N.Y.: Medieval & Renaissance Texts & Studies, 1991), 3–24. For the classical tradition, see Henri–Irénée Marrou, *Saint Augustin et la fin de la culture antique* (Paris: Boccard, 1958), 215 ff.

31. According to de la Garanderie, the conflict between cupidity and wisdom is the theme that unifies *De Asse* ("L'Harmonie secrète du 'De Asse'"). Cf. the letter to Erasmus discussed below (*Ep.* 493, lines 260 ff.).

32. In the Greek, Budé reads *heuretis,* that is, *inventrix,* rather than the Septuagint *haeretis,* that is, *electrix.*

33. *Aeneid,* 4.177.

34. Cf. Budé, *De transitu hellenismi ad Christianismum,* in *Opera,* 1:171, where St. Paul is called *Theosophorum Plato.*

35. *Opera,* 2:284. All parenthetical page references to *De Asse* are to this volume.

36. As de la Garanderie notes (*Christianisme et lettres profanes,* 291.)

37. Budé is probably referring to the enumeration in *Wisdom* 7.16–21.

38. Cf. in contrast Poliziano's use of *compendia* in *Nutricia,* 785, as noted in the previous chapter.

39. Cf. Petrarca's account of the circuitous route he took in climbing Mt. Ventoux, in contrast to his brother (*Fam.,* 4.1). It is worth noting that the epilogue to *De Asse* concludes with hopes for the advancement of letters as news arrives of the death of Louis XII and the accession of François 1er. *De Asse* ends when Budé ends a dialogue on this subject between himself and his friend François Deloynes, with an evocation of Alexander at Achilles' tomb

and a hope for the immortality of his own work: "Eam autem disputationem nostram simul animi causa huic operi attexendam esse dixi, simul ut monumentum esset aeternum (ut spero) amicitiae nostrae" (315).

40. Text in *Opus Epistolarum Des. Erasmi Roterodami,* letter 493 (2:390–405 = Budé, *Opera,* 1:368–75 [*Ep.* 5.3]), replying to Erasmus's letter 480. All parenthetical line references are to this edition. I have, however, benefited from the French translations, with notes (*La Correspondance d'Erasme,* trans. Marcel A. Nauwelaerts [Brussells: University Press, 1974], 2:512–28; and *La Correspondance d'Erasme et de Guillaume Budé,* trans. Marie-Madeleine de la Garanderie [Paris: Vrin, 1967], 81–96).

41. For the significance of Apollo Loxias in Rabelais's *Tiers Livre* (chap. 19) and Montaigne's "De l'expérience," see Terence Cave, *The Cornucopian Text: Problems of Writing in the French Renaissance* (Oxford: Oxford University Press, 1979), 318.

42. "[Les métaphores] ne sont pas cousues au discours, elles sont le discours même; elles en soutiennent la dialectique" (de la Garanderie, *Christianisme et lettres profanes,* 265). Cf. Louis Le Roy, on the ninth page of his (unpaginated) *Vita Budaei* in Budé's *Opera,* vol. 1:

> Metaphoris dicebant nimium delectari, que magnum ornamentum orationi adferunt: sed ut virtutibus vitia proxima sunt, sic in his obscuritatem esse fugiendam, tanquam stellis quibusdam notare et illuminare orationem: sed si crebriores fuerint, ea fieri quae dicuntur aenigmata.

43. Cf. Nicolas Bourbon, "De Budaeo et Erasmo" (*Nugae* [1538], 107): "Scis quid ab Hollando Francus Budaeus Erasmo / Differat? Hic dictis allicit, ille rapit." On Budé's sublime style, see de la Garanderie, "La fascination du sublime. Réflexions sur la rhétorique de Guillaume Budé," *Bulletin de l'Association Guillaume Budé* (1992): 62–72.

44. Cf. Erasmus's *Ep.* 480 for similar precautions, which run throughout their correspondence.

45. *Prosatori latini del Quattrocento,* 902–4; (= Poliziano, *Opera,* 113–14 [*Ep.* 8.16]).

46. For Budé's attitude toward Ciceronianism, see de la Garanderie, *Christianisme et lettres profanes,* 98–99 (for example, *Commentarii linguae graecae* [*Opera,* 4: col. 1422]).

47. See Branca, *Poliziano,* 83.

48. Both humanists share a recognition of the need to exceed the limits of purely literary study. Compare Poliziano, cited above: "non solum . . . ad Aristophanis lucernam, sed etiam ad Cleanthis oportet lucubrasse," and Budé: "opus est . . . ut ex universa lectione, non ex singulis modo orbis partibus . . . existat illa sapientia" (*De Philologia* [*Opera,* 1:43]).

49. *Opera,* 3:340.

50. *De Philologia* (*Opera,* 1:46). All parenthetical page references to *De Philologia, De studio literarum* and *De transitu* are to this volume. Cf. *De Asse* (*Opera,* 2:33), where *apirocalia* (Greek *apeirokalia*) is glossed as *ignorantia;* as well as *Commentarii linguae graecae* (*Opera,* 4: coll. 907, 1015); and Poliziano, *Miscellaneorum centuria secunda* 29.3 and 52.27. Aristotle (*Nicomachean Ethics* 4.2.4) uses *apeirokalia* as the opposite of *megaloprepeia,* or magnificence.

51. *Opera,* 3:351.

52. See de la Garanderie, *Christianisme et lettres profanes,* 269–71. Mau-

rice Lebel's edition and translation of *De transitu* (Sherbrooke, Quebec: Editions Paulines, 1973) includes an index of neologisms, mostly Grecisms.

53. Cicero, *Pro Plancio,* 18.45 (although the context concerns wrongdoing). Elsewhere in *De Philologia* (65) Budé uses a form of the verb *decurio* with a similar sense.

54. And cf. *De Philologia,* 45.

55. See Cicero, *In Pisonem,* 12 for "nequitiam frontis involutam integumentis." Budé uses *mentis tectoria* and *tectoria linguae* (the latter expression repeats Persius 5.25) in the same way in *De transitu Hellenismi ad Christianismum* (158). For more on Budé's style, see de la Garanderie, *Christianisme et lettres profanes,* 259–71; and Douglas F. S. Thomson, "On the Latin Style of Some French Humanists," *Crossroads and Perspectives: French Literature of the Renaissance. Studies in honour of Victor E. Graham,* ed. Catherine M. Grisé and C. D. E. Tolton (Geneva: Droz, 1986), 84–90.

56. Budé does not hesitate to use postclassical forms; see the index of these in Lebel's edition of *De transitu.*

57. Cassirer, *Language and Myth,* 84.

58. See Coelius Secundus Curio, imitating Cicero (*De Oratore* 3.8): "Novam quandam rationem attulit orationis ... et dicendi genus induxit singulare" (Budé, *Opera* vol. 1, fourth page of preface). Also Fumaroli, *L'Age de l'éloquence,* 664 on Budé's task: "Racheter la 'corruption de l'éloquence' en remontant vers la densité première, quasi prophétique, du verbe archaïque." And Le Roy: "Omnia quae suscepit clarissimis dicendi luminibus ornat, et facit ampliora, novata plurima venuste, prisca et vetera in usum scite revocata" (ninth page of *Vita Budaei*).

59. Claude-Gilbert Dubois, *Mythe et langage au seizième siècle* (Bordeaux: Ducros, 1970), 20. And see generally the exceedingly rich study by Marie-Luce Demonet, *Les Voix du signe* (Paris: H. Champion, 1992).

60. See, for example, Petrus Galatinus, *Opus de Arcanis Catholicae Veritatis* (Basel, 1550), book 3. This work was composed in 1516 and first published in 1518 (François Secret, *Les Kabbalistes Chrétiens de la Renaissance* [Neuilly-sur-Seine: Arma Artis, 1985], 102).

61. See Dubois, *Mythe et langage,* 46.

62. Cited by Dubois, 39.

63. "Une caractéristique de la langue idéale—qui se confond avec la langue originelle—est précisément cette adéquation du mot et de la chose. Il n'y a pas de différence entre le dénominatif et l'objet dénommé, si bien que le nom est porteur d'être" (Dubois, 39).

64. See, for example, *Zohar: The Book of Splendor. Basic Readings from the Kabbalah,* ed. Gershom Scholem (New York: Schocken, 1949), 27; cf. Scholem, *Kabbalah* (New York: Meridian-Penguin, 1978), 99, 137–38, 169–77.

65. Claude Duret, *Thresor de l'histoire des langues de cest univers contenant les origines, beautés, perfections, decadences, mutations, changemens, conversions et ruines des langues* (1613; reprint, Geneva: Slatkine, 1972), 25. Despite its late date, this treatise is typical of sixteenth-century speculation and amounts to a "bibliographia kabbalistica" (Secret, *Les Kabbalistes Chrétiens,* 17, 341).

66. See, for example, Jan Van Gorp, *Hermathena* and *Hieroglyphica* (Antwerp, 1580), who claims that the primordial language was *lingua Cimbrica.*

67. Ficino, *De vita,* 3.21. Text: *Three Books on Life,* ed. and trans. Carol V.

Kaske and John R. Clark (Binghamton, N.Y.: Medieval & Renaissance Texts & Studies, 1989).

68. See D. P. Walker, *Spiritual and Demonic Magic from Ficino to Campanella* (Notre Dame: University of Notre Dame Press, 1975), 22. On Ficino's Orphic hymns, see his letter to Cosimo de' Medici cited in Arnaldo Della Torre, *Storia dell'Accademia platonica di Firenze* (Florence: G. Carnesecchi, 1902), 537–38; cf. 789 ff. For Ficino in the role of Orpheus, calling back to life Eurydice, that is, the *Platonica sapientia,* see Poliziano's *Miscellaneorum centuria prima* (*Opera,* 310); Poliziano's elegy to Bartolommeo della Fonte, line 183 (Poliziano, *Opera omnia,* ed. Maïer, 3:172); and August Buck, *Der Orpheus-Mythos in der italienischen Renaissance* (Krefeld, Germany: Scherpe, 1961), 21–22. However, for the evolution of Poliziano's attitude toward the Orphic Ficino, see Vittore Branca, "Tra Ficino 'Orfeo ispirato' e Poliziano 'Ercole ironico'," in *Filologia e forme letterarie. Studi offerti a Francesco della Corte,* 5 vols. [Urbino: Università degli studi di Urbino/Edizioni Quattro Venti, 1987], 5:445–59). Generally on Ficino and Orpheus, see John Warden, "Orpheus and Ficino," in Warden, ed., *Orpheus: The Metamorphoses of a Myth* (Toronto: University of Toronto Press, 1982), 85–110, with other references.

69. Giovanni Pico della Mirandola, *Conclusiones,* ed. Bohdan Kieszkowski (Geneva: Droz, 1973), 80.

70. Pico, *Conclusiones,* 79.

71. The term was apparently coined, although with a somewhat more limited meaning, by Charles Zika, "Reuchlin's *De Verbo Mirifico* and the Magic Debate of the Late Fifteenth Century," *Journal of the Warburg and Courtauld Institutes* 39 (1976): 132.

72. Zika, 117.

73. Ibid., 127.

74. Ibid., 130.

75. Ibid., 133.

76. Ibid., 136.

77. However, there was an accentuation of the Christian element between the manuscript and the first printed edition (ed. Lefèvre d'Etaples, 1505). See Claudio Moreschini, *Dall'*Asclepius *al* Crater Hermetis. *Studi sull'ermetismo latino tardo-antico e rinascimentale* (Pisa: Giardini, 1985), 206–7. This volume includes an edition of the *Crater Hermetis* on pp. 221–65.

78. Walker, *Spiritual and Demonic Magic,* 67.

79. *Crater Hermetis* 25 (Moreschini, *Dall'* Asclepius *al* Crater Hermetis, 254).

80. *Crater Hermetis* 27 (Moreschini, 258).

81. A first version dates from around 1510, but the treatise was not published in its revised form until 1533.

82. Heinrich Cornelius Agrippa von Nettesheim, *Opera,* 2 vols. (n.d. [1600?]; reprint, Hildesheim: Olm, 1970), 1:139.

83. "Sunt itaque verba aptissimum medium inter loquentem & audientem deferentia secum non tantum conceptum, sed & virtutem loquentis energia quadam transfundentes in audientes & suscipientes, tanta saepe potentia, ut non immutent solummodo audientes, sed etiam alia quaedam corpora & res inanimatas" (Agrippa, *Opera,* 1:139). Agrippa owes something here to Ficino, *De vita* 3.21.

84. Agrippa, 1:143.

85. Agrippa adds: "Omnes praeterea poetae canunt, & philosophi non neg-

ant, posse carminibus miranda multa effici, ut pelli segetes, cogi fulmina, vel imperari, curari morbos, & eiusmodi" (1:145).

86. Agrippa, 1:337.

87. Ibid., 1:343.

88. Frances A. Yates, *The Occult Philosophy in the Elizabethan Age* (London: Routledge & Kegan Paul, 1979), 46. Cf. her *Giordano Bruno and the Hermetic Tradition* (New York: Vintage-Random House, 1969), 137–41.

89. Blaise de Vigenère, *Traicté des chiffres, ou secretes manieres d'escrire* (Paris: Abel L'Angelier, 1586), 2v.

90. Car l'escriture est un certain bouttehors des conceptions de nostre ame, qui se vont incorporer en des notes, marques, & signes sensibles, pour se manifester taisiblement des uns aux autres: & est ceste conception de pensee, comme un symbole de Dieu le PERE; les marques & notes, du FILS incarné; & le sens contenu là dessous, du SAINCT ESPRIT: si que tout ainsi qu'il faut que l'escriture tienne du corps & de l'esprit, qui sont les deux extremes d'icelle; aussi le corps & la deité deux extremes, se vindrent assembler au CHRIST pour en faire une moienne disposition & mediateur, entre Dieu son pere, & ses confreres par adoption. (Vigenère, *Traicté des chiffres,* 130r–v)

91. A cela correspond encore la facture du monde, que Dieu souverain . . . , tenant en cest endroit lieu de notre conception interieure, boutta hors comme une escriture formee du ciel & des corps luisants qui y sont, & de la terre avec ce qui s'y produit, & en l'eau, tout cela tenant lieu de lettres; & ce qui en resulte à la gloire du Createur, est le sens contenu soubs ce beau chiffre universel. (Vigenère, 130v)

92. Vigenère, 31r. He continues: "mais plus encore sans l'escriture, qui faict assez mieux sans comparaison ce devoir que la parole," showing here as well as elsewhere (2v, 130r–v) a decided preference for the written over the spoken word.

93. Vigenère, 31r. Claude Duret, who was a cousin of Vigenère, abundantly plagiarized the *Traicté* in his own *Thresor des langues* (see Secret, *Les Kabbalistes Chrétiens,* 341). Duret's thefts include the passage just cited (Duret, *Thresor,* 21), and the previously cited passage on the "parole assistee de la raison" as divine emanation (Duret, 19). He also owes a good deal to Vigenère on the Trinity (see note 90) but modifies his source to reflect his own profound interest in the Kabbalah: Duret conceives of the physical enunciation of language

à l'exemple du grand et premier exemplaire, lequel en sa propre essence et substance qui sont en luy une mesme chose, estant renclos dans son Ensoph, ou infinitude hors du monde sensible, s'y vient a espandre par ses sephirots ou emanations, comme les clairs rayons du Soleil à travers un gros amas de nuées, et produire au dessous de luy des effects conceus en sa premiere idee ou image, qui est le verbe et le fils, la forme des formes, et l'ame de tout l'univers. (Duret, 27; cf. 31.)

Duret also shares Vigenère's relative valuation of writing and speech (Duret, 21, 22, 29, 34 ff.).

94. Brian Vickers, "Analogy versus identity: the rejection of occult symbolism, 1580–1680," *Occult and scientific mentalities in the Renaissance,* ed. Vickers (Cambridge: Cambridge University Press, 1984), 117.

95. Josef Bohatec, *Budé und Calvin: Studien zu Gedankenwelt des französischen Frühhumanismus* (Graz: Böhlaus, 1950), especially 23–31.

96. See Bohatec, *Budé und Calvin,* 82–89.

97. *De transitu* was Budé's last work before his death in 1540.

98. *Christianisme et lettres profanes,* 357–59.

99. On p. 138 we find the phrase "de hellenismo transeundum . . . ad Christianismum." Petrarca (*Fam.,* 12.3.18) refers to grammar and the other liberal arts as only a *transitus* to greater things.

100. As, for example, Aulus Gellius uses it (*Noctes Atticae* 5.19.8).

101. Other more specialized meanings of *transitus* are not irrelevant here. The term can mean a musical interval (Quintilian, *Institutio Oratoria* 8.6.38, 12.10.68) or a grammatical inflexion (Varro, *De Lingua Latina* 9.109, 10.28, 10.52) and so points to a whole—scale or paradigm—greater than the individual notes or inflected forms.

102. That Hellenism is not necessarily allied with lukewarmness is shown by the citation of pagan authors against the latter (for example, 138–39).

103. Cf. *De Asse:* "Mercurius est Christus" (*Opera,* 2:292), "Christus verus Hercules" (301, 308).

104. Cf. 239, where Christ is introduced as the herald (*pronunciator*) that antiquity lacked; but he is introduced by the term of those who lacked him (*ut prisci loquebantur*).

105. Cf. for example Giovanni Dominici's *Lucula noctis,* to which Salutati was preparing a reply at the time of his death.

106. The identification with Phoebus and Hercules can be similarly explained. For Hercules as a symbol of eloquence, see M. R. Jung, *Hercule dans la littérature française du XVIe siècle: de l'Hercule courtois à l'Hercule baroque* (Geneva: Droz, 1966), 73–93; and Robert E. Hallowell, "L'Hercule gallique: expression et image politique," *Lumières de la Pléiade* (Paris: Vrin, 1966), 243–53. On Mercury, see generally the collective volume *Mercure à la Renaissance,* ed. M.-M. de la Garanderie (Poitiers: P. Oudin, 1988).

107. Cf. Coelius Secundus Curio's exclamation concerning Budé's *copia:* "Quam enim philosophiae partem, quam philologiae divinae humanaeque in eius scriptis immortalibus desiderabis?" (*Opera,* vol. 1, first page of preface).

108. Budé was influenced by Valla's *Adnotationes in novum Testamentum* on the translation of *logos* (see *Annotationes in Pandectas* [*Opera,* 3:56–57]). He may well have also been influenced by Erasmus's *Annotationes in Novum Testamentum,* which from its second edition in 1519 declared a preference for *sermo* rather than the Vulgate *verbum* as a translation of *logos* at the beginning of St. John's Gospel. By the last edition, in 1535 (the year *De transitu* appeared), Erasmus had amplified the point considerably. See *Erasmus' Annotations on the New Testament: The Gospels,* ed. Anne Reeve (London: Duckworth, 1986), 218–21; C. A. L. Jarrott, "Erasmus' *In Principio Erat Sermo:* A Controversial Translation," *Studies in Philology* 61 (1964): 35–40; and Marjorie O'Rourke Boyle, *Erasmus on Language and Method in Theology* (Toronto: University of Toronto Press, 1977), 3–31.

109. Cf. 235, where the divine chain is somewhat different: "Verbum dei, mundi et naturae vinculum esse, atque retinaculum."

110. Cf. R. R. Bolgar, "Humanism as a Value System: with Reference to Budé and Vivès," *Humanism in France . . . ,* ed. Levi, 204–5.

111. *Similitudo* also means simile and so reminds us of the metaphorical nature of language human and divine.

112. Hellenism is condemnable only if "hanc tute institeris cum illa [Christian philosophy] contendere" (148).

113. For example, 173, 181–82.

114. Budé praises the obscurity of Biblical language (140).

115. Which death is "beneficium humana oratione nequaquam enarrabile" (232).

116. He may be following the precept of Aristotle (*Rhetoric* 3.17.16 [1418 b 23]) that an orator should let invective be spoken by a different character. See Bruno Gentili, *Poesia e pubblica nella Grecia antica: Da Omero al V secolo* (Bari: Laterza, 1984), 145 ff.

117. See Cicero, *De Divinatione* 1.45.101, 2.32.69; Varro apud Aulus Gellius, *Noctes Atticae* 16.17; Livy 5.32, 5.50; Plutarch, *De fortuna Romanorum*, which Budé translated (*Opera*, 1:488); and Diderot's article *Aius-Locutius* in the *Encyclopédie*.

118. Preface to the *Elegantiae* (*Prosatori latini del Quattrocento*, 598–600).

119. On the relation of the verb *aio* to authoritative verbal *prodigia*, see Benveniste, *Le vocabulaire des institutions indo-européennes*, 2:260–63.

120. For the same equation, cf. Erasmus's *Ratio verae theologiae*, cited by Cave, *The Cornucopian Text*, 110 n.

121. Starting from the fact that both works are dedicated to François 1er.

122. "Proinde antiquitatis sententias relinquendas esse nobis repudiandasque censeo. . . . Forma autem utendum illorum et materia orationis, qua nihil est flexibilius et sequacius" (21).

123. The source is *Corpus Hermeticum* 9.1. Cf. on the same page Budé's citation of *Corpus Hermeticum* 2.17: "Beatus deus animam in corpore, mentem in anima, in mente verbum pronunciavit: deum autem horum patrem esse affirmavit." This is echoed in Pico della Mirandola's third Hermetic *Conclusio*: "Anima in corpore, mens in anima, in mente verbum, tum horum pater Deus."

124. For the hunt metaphor, see below on book 2 of *De Philologia*.

125. "Nam animus philosophus, celer, impiger, inquies, actuosus, in nulla re acquiescere potest, extraquam cum totus est in contemplatione rerum sempiternarum . . . " (17).

126. "Tales ferme Hercules sunt . . . aut Heraclidae certe hodie, eius philosophiae alumni quam antiqui Graeci eruditionem circularem apellaverunt" (3) (*eruditionem circularem* meaning, of course, the encyclopedia). Cf. *De Philologia* (64) for the labor of cleaning verbal Augean stables. But in the latter work (94) princes too can be Hercules.

127. *Intestinus Eurystheus*, that is, "literarum amor flagrantissimus, cupiditasque honestissima constituendae maestatis eloquentiae" (19).

128. Cicero, *Tusculanae disputationes*, 1.2 and Erasmus, *Adagia* 792. Seneca (*Epistulae ad Lucilium*, 102.16) cites an *antiquus poeta* to the effect that "laus alit artis." For this humanistic commonplace, see, for example, Salutati, *Epistolario*, 2.7 and 9.9; Preface to the *Raccolta aragonese* (Lorenzo de' Medici, *Opere*, ed. Simioni, 1:3), as discussed above.

129. Hans Baron, "Civic Wealth and the New Values of the Renaissance: The Spirit of the Quattrocento," *In Search of Florentine Civic Humanism: Essays on the Transition from Medieval to Modern Thought*, 2 vols. (Princeton: Princeton University Press, 1988), 1:243. The terms used by Nifo, cited by Baron, are: "Qui pro laboribus mercedem accipit, mercenarius est et sordidus et vilis et servilis."

130. There is a typically Budean pun here: the term *honoraria actio* refers

literally to a higher court under Roman law than that appropriate to a mere civil suit (*civilis actio*), but the adjective also contains *honor*, which is the basis of literary power. In *De Philologia* (41) François 1er refers to his obligation to aid *bonae literae* as *honoraria actio*.

131. See de la Garanderie, *Christianisme et lettres profanes*, 221; R. J. Knecht, *Francis I* (Cambridge: Cambridge University Press, 1982), 4.

132. Louis Le Roy did translate the hunt episode from book 2 (pp. 67–81) and dedicate it to Charles IX in about 1572 (*Traitté de la Vénerie*, ed. Henri Chevreul [Paris, 1861]). But during Budé's or François's lifetime there was no translation or version of *De Philologia* on the model of the French epitome of *De Asse* (1522) or the translation of the dedicatory letter in Greek to the *Commentarii linguae graecae*, addressed to the king (see de la Garanderie, *Christianisme et lettres profanes*, 232–33).

133. As, for example, when Budé impressed the king by translating, on the spot, a Greek letter from Lascaris (*Opera*, 1:422–3; Louis Delaruelle, *Répertoire analytique et chronologique de la correspondance de Guillaume Budé* [Toulouse, 1907], 156).

134. At more than one point the king wonders if Budé is speaking for himself ("si ex animi sententia loqueris" [87]). Cf. above on Aius Loquens in *De transitu*. On *De Philologia* as a dramatic dialogue, see de la Garanderie, "Un Vrai Dialogue: Le *De Philologia* de Guillaume Budé," *Acta Conventus Neo-Latini Guelpherbytani* (Binghamton, N.Y.: Medieval & Renaissance Texts & Studies, 1988), 491–501.

135. See Abel Lefranc, *Histoire du Collège de France* (Paris: Hachette, 1893), 39 ff.

136. On the relation between *sapientia* and *prudentia* in this work, see Eugene F. Rice, Jr., *The Renaissance Idea of Wisdom* (Cambridge, Mass.: Harvard University Press, 1958), 150–52.

137. The passage recalls the reproaches young Ovid heard from his father; for example: "'studium quid inutile temptas? / Maeonides nullas ipse reliquit opes'" (*Tristia* 4.10.21–22).

138. In his letters, Budé refers to Philologia as his *contubernalis* (for example, *Ep.* 5.11 [*Opera*, 1:384]). Cf. *Ep.* 1.5 (*Opera*, 1:247), where he alludes to his real wife's jealousy: "quae meam Philologiam velut suam pellicem sibi praeferri dolebat et fremebat." In *De transitu* (130) he describes *philologia minor* as promiscuous and venal. Cf. below on the hunt in book 2 of *De Philologia*.

139. For an example of how far Budé's metaphors may go, see the passage where he blandly confesses to pedophilia: "clancularius tum eram amator impuberis adhuc Philologiae, et pene etiam infantis" (53).

The description of newly endowed and adorned Philologia also recalls a passage in *De studio* (2–3) that tells the parable of Hercules at the crossroads, sollicited by Felicitas (Inertia) and Virtus. It is to the former that Philologia bears a resemblance.

140. However, in *De transitu* there is both a *coelestis* and a *funestus Mercurius*.

141. See Franco Simone, "Une entreprise oubliée des humanistes français: De la prise de conscience historique du renouveau culturel à la naissance de la première histoire littéraire," *Humanism in France . . .*, ed. Levi, 106–31; and Claude-Gilbert Dubois, *Celtes et Gaulois au XVIe siècle: Le développement littéraire d'un mythe nationaliste* (Paris: Vrin, 1972).

142. For example: (1) Robert Gaguin, letter to Ambroise de Cambrai (20 June 1479), concerning both ancient and recent history:

> Mirere desidiam . . . ne dicam ignorantiam nostratium scriptorum quibus ad res gloria dignissimas animus non incalescit patrie calamitates complorare, seque saltim tollere ex obscuro, dum principis gesta litteris illustrare possunt, and so forth.

(*Roberti Gaguini epistole et orationes,* ed. Louis Thuasne, 2 vols. [Paris: Bouillon, 1904], 1:280).

(2) Joachim Du Bellay, *La Deffence et illustration de la langue françoyse* 1.2.

(3) Jean Bodin, *Oratio de instituenda in republica juventute ad senatum populumque Tolosatem* (1559), speaking of

> reconditam Druidûm ac Samotheorum Celtopaediam, qua nihil est antiquis celebratum illustrius . . . neque vero dubium est, quin si literis suas cogitationes illi mandarent, magnam sui admirationem essent excitaturi; sed in eo Chaldaeos, Aegyptios, et Gymnosophistas maluerunt quam Grecos imitari.

(*Oeuvres philosophiques de Jean Bodin,* ed. Pierre Mesnard [Paris: PUF, 1951], 10).

(4) Estienne Pasquier, *Recherches de la France* (Paris: Laurens Sonnius, 1621) 1.1: "Du tort que les anciens Gaulois, et ceux qui leur succederent se feirent, pour estre peu soucieux de recommander par escrits leur Vertu à la posterité." However, this seems to be contradicted by the late addition of the chapter 9.1: "Que la Gaule . . . de toute ancienneté a esté studieuse des bonnes lettres."

On the other hand, cf. the title of a work by Jean Picard (1556): *De Prisca Celtopaedia libri quinque, quibus admiranda priscorum Gallorum doctrina et eruditio ostenditur, necnon literas prius in Gallia fuisse, quam vel in Grecia vel in Italia: simulque Graecos nedum Latinos scientiam priscis Gallis (quos vel ab ipso Noachi tempore Graece philosophatos constat) habuisse* (cited by Simone, "Une entreprise oubliée des humanistes français . . . ," 118).

143. Those suspicions concern the absoluteness of philology's claims in the personal realm as well as in society. The king warns Budé against the danger in his amorous embrace of Philologia: "Vide vero, inquit, Budaee, ne complexu quodam hederaceo ista tua Philologia te semel complexa sit" (51), and develops the metaphor, which Budé does not dispute: ivy embraces a tree in such a way that the tree is strangled by that parasite, but also suffers if deprived of the ivy.

144. Significantly, the word *existimatio* recurs at the beginning and at the end of book 2 (61, 94). Cf. its use at 45, 49, 64; as well as *De transitu,* 159.

145. "Neque enim aeque doctrina facunda esse potest in toga et in purpura. Neque tam in plano, quam e loco superiore" (61).

146. For the metaphor of hunting, see *De vulgari eloquentia* 1.11.1, 1.14.1, 1.15.8, 1.16.1, 2.6.3, and so forth.

147. "Id est ferme e perinde, ac si iurisconsultorum verbo dicerem, cervum requirendum adnotare, ut delatum ac reum doli mali, buccinaeque praeconio pervulgare furtum sui fecisse" (79). "Ad locum supplicii cervum ipsum quasi reum peractum damnatumque deduxerimus" (80).

148. François says, "Scire enim avemus an Minerva et Diana colloquia serere inter se consentanea didicerent" (69).

149. Cf. 84–85.

150. Similarly, the birds involved in falconry are tragic actors that, "tanquam in theatro commissi, spectaculum suae necis praebere adigantur aucupantium oculis" (75).

151. Cf. *De Philologia,* 55. The deer is compared to Proteus (73), a figure that also represents eloquence (*De studio,* 21) as well as *sermo Dei* (*De transitu,* 239).

152. Cf. 46, as well as *Commentarii linguae graecae* (*Opera,* 4: col. 1019), *De Asse* (*Opera,* 2:13), and *De transitu,* 167. But Budé is also fond of the less common meaning, to cancel or omit (*Forensia* [*Opera,* 3:8, 33, 80], *Commentarii linguae graecae* [*Opera,* 4: col. 992] and *De transitu* [177] as well as a second time in *De Philologia* [46]). Finally, there is this passage from *De Philologia* (48) that is illuminated by all the meanings in a reference to the *circularis disciplina* or encyclopedia, "quae omneis alias complectitur, atque intra suum orbem coercet, quae suis finibus singulas quasi architectonico iure circumscribit" (cf. *De transitu,* 157).

153. For an exhaustive esoteric interpretation of the figure of Harpocrates, see Jan Van Gorp, *Hieroglyphica* (Antwerp, 1580), 48–81. See also Poliziano, *Miscellaneorum centuria prima,* cap. 83. The Carpocratian sect of Gnostics apparently owe their name to Harpocrates (see *Enciclopedia cattolica* [Città del Vaticano, 1949], s.v. Carpocrate e Carpocraziani). Elsewhere in *De Philologia* Budé refers to the dogs as *generis harpocratici* (70) and gives them the epithets *echemythos* and *Pythagoreos* (67). He claims that the hunters too communicate best in silence: "Non contemnenda autem pars pronunciationis atque renunciationis, in nutibus, in vultibus, in gestibus . . . eminet" (72).

154. Vico, *Scienza nuova,* sec. 434. Cf. sec. 401 for the kinship between *mutus* and *mythos.*

155. See Vico, *Scienza nuova,* sec. 369, and the latter part of the discussion of *Nutricia,* above.

156. Cf. *L'Institution du Prince,* 5r. All page references to this work regard Bibliothèque de l'Arsenal MS 5103.

157. Note the vocabulary of Reuchlin and Agrippa (see above).

158. "Omnem haud dubie regiam munificentiam serasti, divinam etiam beneficentiam aequasti" (82).

159. "Nihil mei iudicii esse intelligo, nisi eadem tua maiestas me iudicem esse iubeat" (92).

160. "Atqui, Rex inquit, Budaee vestram iam inde Palladem tantarum rerum praesidem ac magistram, libens credo fecero ut in regiam admittendam, non modo in curiam censeam: idque additamento et elogio autoritatis meae regiaeque confirmem. . . . Post haec regis verba, cum ego quasi voti compos victorque propositi, ab omnibus plausum non mediocrem expectarem . . . " (90–91).

161. The interruption of the dialogue's suspended time, which ends both books 1 and 2, recalls the flurry of military activity that arouses the dreamers in books 2 and 9 of Petrarca's *Africa.*

162. Delaruelle (*Guillaume Budé . . . ,* 201) and Claude Bontems ("*L'Institution du Prince* de Guillaume Budé," in *Le Prince dans la France des XVIe et XVIIe siècles* [Paris: PUF, 1965], 5) agree in assigning the work to early 1519. The Arsenal MS is untitled; I follow Bontems in calling it *L'Institution du Prince,* rather than Delaruelle's awkward *Recueil d'apophtegmes offerts à François 1er*—without, however, confounding the Arsenal MS with any of the three 1547 printed editions entitled *L'Institution du Prince* which, as Delaruelle has shown (231–45) do not faithfully reflect Budé's work.

Guy Gueudet has taken issue with Delaruelle's interpretation of the manuscript tradition and argued that one printed edition at least (Paris: Jean Foucher, 1547) is as authentic as MS 5103 ("Guillaume Budé, parrain d'«encyclopédie» ou le vrai texte de l'*Institution du Prince*," *Le Génie de la forme*: *Mélanges de langue et littérature offerts à Jean Mourot* [Nancy: Presses universitaires de Nancy, 1982], 87–96). In any case, the overall character of the two texts is not essentially different; as Gueudet acknowledges (92), "les additions de la seconde version renchérissent sur l'adhésion de la première à la nouvelle culture et consistent à renforcer les thèmes philologiques chers à Budé."

Bontems (77–139) offers a transcription of MS 5103, with some modernization. There is a partial modern edition (*Le livre de l'Institution du Prince* [*Kap. I–XX*], ed. Maxim Marin [Frankfurt am Main: Peter Lang, 1983]), but it is based on the printed editions and surprisingly declines to consider the manuscript (p. 22).

163. For an evaluation of the degree and kind of François 1er's absolutism, see Knecht, *Francis I*, 344 ff.

164. Bontems, "*L'Institution du Prince*," 38–39. ("Budé appears . . . a fierce partisan of absolute power. . . . Every means is deployed to assure the Prince of a limitless power; even God is pushed into the background, left without much influence. . . . Nothing is spared to provide France with an unquestioned sovereign; no one will resist him, no one can disagree with him, nor put his power in question. . . . No writer up to this point had dared to go so far on the road to absolutism, and one wonders if any one else dared subsequently.")

165. *De transitu*, 133; *L'Institution du Prince*, 2r. The same distich also adorns the illumination of another manuscript of *L'Institution* (Lausanne, Bibliothèque Publique et Cantonale, MS E. 497, p. 15), reproduced as the frontispiece of Donald R. Kelley, *Foundations of Modern Historical Scholarship*: *Language, Law, and History in the French Renaissance* (New York: Columbia University Press, 1970).

166. Juvenal, *Satires* 11. 27. Cf. Erasmus, *Adagia*, Prolegomena (v) and no. 595. The identical formula also occurs in Poliziano's *Oratio in expositione Homeri* (*Opera*, 485). "Gnothi seauton" also has a place in *De transitu* (168, 171).

167. Budé hesitates between the Latin translation and the Greek. The Vulgate has "gloria regum investigare sermonem," while the Septuagint has "doxa de basileos tima pragmata." These last two words Budé translates as "en portant honneur aux choses" (that is, "c'est gloire royale que de honnorer les livres et ceulx qui ont le scavoir de composer euvres pour enseigner les ignorans et illustrer les sciences et choses dignes de scavoir, car ce sont les choses par lesquelles la parolle occulte est revelee" [34r]). For the first half of this verse, see above on the letter to Erasmus.

168. See Secret, *Les Kabbalistes Chrétiens*, 191, referring among others to Guillaume Postel, and to Guy Le Fèvre's *Galliade*: "C'est la gloire de Dieu la parole cacher/ C'est la gloire des Rois la parole chercher."

169. See 22v on the interpretation of Mercury, of whom the ancients said "que c'estoit son office que de mener les ames en enfers et aussi de les en retirer. Par Mercure est entendue la force et efficace d'eloquence." And 23r-v on *Hercule gaulois* in some detail.

170. However, elsewhere (13r) the two terms are made equivalent.

171. In all fairness, it should be added that Budé also greatly admires the

republican Pompey (97r-98v), although what he chooses to emphasize is the conqueror's triumphal pomp (89v–91v, 94r–95r).

172. Cf. the reply of Dionysius of Sicily to those advising him to rid his court of the eloquent and learned because of their uselessness: "Je les nourris et entretiens, non pas pource que je les ayme fort a veoir ou que j'en face grant estime, mais je veuil estre estimé d'eulx plus que de nulz autres" (54r). Like Philip, Sulla congratulated himself for having spared Athens (84v).

173. There is a brief but important omission in Bontems's transcription of this passage.

174. Alexander knew "qu'il vauldroit autant ou mieulx que les choses demourassent en oubly que d'estre escriptes par gens a ce faire non suffisans" (17r).

175. Timothy Hampton recognizes that this is an "ideal or utopian moment in Budé's text" (*Writing from History: The Rhetoric of Exemplarity in Renaissance Literature* [Ithaca: Cornell University Press, 1990], 38). For Alexander as *cultor* and *studiosus* of Homer and Pindar, cf. *De Asse,* 34, 76.

176. Cicero himself, although not even of Roman origin, became a kind of prince through eloquence: "on disoit qu'il regnoit a Rome" (20v). When advised by friends to change his lowly name, Cicero replied that in the future his name would be more glorious than all the Catos and Catulluses. (Budé follows Plutarch's *Life of Cicero* here.) "Et ainsi advint-il comme il avoit dit, car en sa vie et apres sa mort son nom fut exaulcé a merveilles, et son eloquence et les livres qu'il a escriptz ont fait sa memoire immortelle de laquelle le monde est tout plein" (104r).

177. "Se depuys le commancement des roys de France il y eust eu gens scavans et eloquens en France, et que les roys eussent fait estime d'eulx, la nation francoyse fust autant estimée que nulle autre apres les romains, car les francoys ont fait de grans choses qui n'ont pas bien esté mises par escript.... Et ainsi est venu en oubliance la gloire de tant de nobles et vaillans roys et princes et chevaliers de ce royaume par faulte de la plume" (24v). Cf. 35r, 8v. With typical inconsistency, Budé also recalls that Juvenal called his country "la Gaule faconde" (22r).

178. "Et ferez poetes et orateurs comme vous faictes contes et ducs en leur inspirant vertu d'eloquence par vostre liberalle benignité." "Ie ne doubte nullement que vostre grace ne soit telle que les poetes anciens ont dit estre la puissance et divinité des Muses, inspirant aux gens de lettres invention prompte, disposition ordonnée, et elocution copieuse" (5v).

179. Cf. the passage from *Proverbs* cited earlier, where the Latin and French ("investigare sermonem," "investigant la parolle") prefigure the hunters' deciphering of deer's *vestigia* in *De Philologia.*

180. "Donum hominis dilabat viam ejus et ante principes spacium ei facit. C'est a dire le don presenté par l'homme luy eslargist son chemin pour soy gecter en avant et luy fait ouverture pour soy presenter devant la face des princes" (2r–v).

181. "Ledit prince ... disoit que la liberalité des grans seigneurs et magnanimes ne consiste pas seulement en donner grands dons et de grosse estimation et valeur, proportionnez et accomodez a la qualité, condition et merite des donataires par hault et magnifique vouloir des donnans, mais aussi en acceptant pour les dictz seigneurs par une prompte humanité et begninité courtoise dons et presens de petite estime faictz par discretion et oportunité par leur subjectz et serviteurs ... " (2v–3r).

182. And yet in the same breath, referring to Alexander's acceptance, Budé denies the gift's intrinsic value: "ce fist il non pour l'offre en soy qui estoit de nulle estime comparée a sa grandeur, mais pour l'affection des offrans, qui luy offroient promptement et reveremment la chose qu'ilz avoient plus chere" (4r). Cf. Hampton, *Writing from History*, 36–37 on this vignette.

183. Cf. 26r–v, with its echo of Horace's "Donarem pateras . . . " (*Carm.* 4.8): Budé compares his florilegium favorably to "ung grant vaisseau d'or ou d'argent, car de telz presens n'avez vous que faire sinon pour les redonner et employer en voz liberalitez."

184. For example: the generosity of Alexander to Anaxarchus and Perillus (36v–37r), of Vespasian to Quintilian (9v), of Augustus (19r) and Octavia (20r) to Virgil, of Pompey to the Roman people (91r–v); not to mention the tribute of Asia to Rome (84r), or the treasures borne in a Roman triumph (90v). Cf. Budé's description of what he achieved in *De Asse* (91v–94r). In the latter passage he remarks the coincidence between his decisive illumination of ancient culture and François Ier's accession to power (both occurring in 1515). He also establishes further parallels: between ancient prosperity and French prosperity, and between his book's longevity and that of the king's name as dedicatee.

185. See Ranum, *Artisans of Glory*, 32.

186. The expression "entrepreneurial spirit about writing history" is Ranum's (12).

187. See Bontems, *"L'Institution du Prince,"* 9.

188. See William Farr Church, *Constitutional Thought in Sixteenth-Century France* (1941; reprint, New York: Octagon Books, 1969), 43–44; Julian H. Franklin, *Jean Bodin and the Rise of Absolutist Theory* (Cambridge: Cambridge University Press, 1973), 6; Perry Anderson, *Lineages of the Absolutist State* (London: NLB, 1974), 25.

189. *Annotationes* (*Opera*, 3:67–68). See Church, *Constitutional Thought*, 61–63.

190. For the role of the gift in Roman law, see Mauss, *Essai sur le don*, 229–38.

191. For other examples of exaltation of the royal image (mostly later than Budé), see Jean Céard, "Les visages de la royauté en France, à la Renaissance," *Les Monarchies*, ed. Emmanuel Le Roy Ladurie (Paris: PUF, 1986), 79–85.

192. Claude de Seyssel, *La Monarchie de France et deux autres fragments politiques*, ed. Jacques Poujol (Paris: Librairie d'Argences, 1961), 113–15.

193. See *L'Institution du Prince*, 82r for a parallel between the French king and the Roman dictator.

194. See Mousnier, *Le Conseil du Roi*, 45–56; Anderson, *Lineages*, 28, 90; J. H. M. Salmon, *Society in Crisis: France in the Sixteenth Century* (New York: St. Martin's Press, 1975), 68.

195. Cited by Ferdinand Brunot, *Histoire de langue française des origines à nos jours*, 13 vols. (Paris: Armand Colin, 1967), 2:30.

196. Cited by Brunot, 2:30.

197. See, for example, Henri Franchet, *Le Poète et son oeuvre d'après Ronsard* (1923; reprint, Geneva: Slatkine, 1969), 115–46; Françoise Joukovsky, *La Gloire dans la poésie française et néolatine du XVIe siècle* (Geneva: Droz, 1969), passim.

EPILOGUE

1. Vv. 279–95. Text: Foscolo, *Opere*, ed. Gavazzeni, vol. 1.

Index

Names in the notes are indexed only where there appears bibliographical information (first occurrence).

Item is due back at the Learning Resource
Center on the latest date appearing below: